The KGB's Poison Factory

The KGB's Poison Factory

From Lenin to Litvinenko

Boris Volodarsky

FRONTLINE
BOOKS

ZENITH PRESS

The KGB's Poison Factory: From Lenin to Litvinenko

This edition published in 2009 by Frontline Books, an imprint of
Pen & Sword Books Ltd, 47 Church Street, Barnsley, S. Yorkshire, S70 2AS
and
First published and distributed in the United States of America and Canada in 2010
by Zenith Press, an imprint of MBI Publishing Company,
400 First Avenue North, Suite 300, Minneapolis, MN 55401 USA

Frontline edition: ISBN 978-1-84832-542-5
Zenith Press edition: ISBN 978-0-7603-3753-0

A CIP data record for this title is available from the British Library.

Library of Congress Cataloging-in-Publication Data

Volodarsky, Boris.
    KGB's Poison Factory : from Lenin to Litvinenko / Boris Volodarsky.
    p. cm.
    ISBN 978-0-7603-3753-0 (hbk. w/jkt)
    1. Soviet Union. Komitet gosudarstvennoi bezopasnosti--History. 2. Russian S.F.S.R.
Chrezvychainaia komissiia po bor'be s kontr-revoliutsiei i sabotazhem--History. 3.
Russia (Federation). Federal'noe agentstvo pravitel'stvennoi sviazi i informatsii--History.
4. Poisoning--Political aspects--Soviet Union--History. 5. Poisoning--Political aspects--
Russia (Federation)--History. 6. Assassination--Case studies. 7. Political crimes and
offenses--Case studies. 8. Murder victims--Biography. 9. Soviet Union--Politics and
government. 10. Russia (Federation)--Politics and government. I. Title.
JN6529.I6V64 2010
327.12470092'2--dc22

                    2009042348

For more information on Frontline Books, please visit www.frontline-books.com,
email info@frontline-books.com or write to us at the above address.

To find out more about Zenith Press titles, visit us online at www.zenithpress.com.

Typeset by Palindrome
Printed in the UK by the MPG Books Group

Those, who cannot remember the past, are condemned to repeat it.

George Santayana

To those leaders around the globe who seek to sow conflict, or blame their society's ills on the West – know that your people will judge you on what you can build, not what you destroy. To those who cling to power through corruption and deceit and the silencing of dissent, know that you are on the wrong side of history . . .

US President Barack Obama

To this author: *Leo, stick close to those you know, love and trust today. There's a lot of duplicity around and someone really, really doesn't like you. You don't like them either, but that won't be any comfort if you fall prey to their plans.*

Nikki Harper

For my family

Contents

Acknowledgements

I am deeply grateful to the many people who helped in this project. Some, in fact, were absolutely instrumental in bringing it to life. I am grateful to them all, but first of all, I thank my wife, Valentina. She was as always the first reader and gave daily support and encouragement as well as valuable ideas and comments.

Without William Green, a Washingtonian and an American in the very best sense of this word, this book would never have seen the light of the day.

My British publisher, Michael Leventhal, entrusted me this project and was patient and understanding as it progressed.

As often happens, there are people who, unfortunately, cannot be named, but whose opinion and friendly advice were important for the better understanding of many processes behind the scenes. Thank you, Jim and Richard, for kindly sharing your vast experience.

After Tennent H. ('Pete') Bagley published his *Spy Wars*, he agreed to spend time and effort reading and correcting the text. My gratitude to Pete is profound while any errors that remain are exclusively my fault.

I thank Alex Goldfarb and Marina Litvinenko for the many hours they have spent with me discussing the case.

Two journalists and authors, Steve LeVine and Pete Earley, helped a lot. And the outstanding historians (and good friends) Professor Paul Preston of the London School of Economics and Professor Angel Viñas of the University of Madrid (Complutense) provided great support and help.

Another good friend, Paolo Guzzanti, member of the Italian parliament and former President of the Mitrokhin Commission, helped unlock many doors to better understanding of the Italian part of the Litvinenko story and of the people and events involved. Pal Salamon of the Open Society Archives in Budapest sent me many documents pertinent to the Lapusnyik case. Alexandra Bajka kindly provided footage from the latest documentary filmed by her Polish TVN television channel that threw new light on the life and death of Nikolai Artamonov. Max Fisher of the Windfall Films, London, kindly gave video material covering the Markov case in its modern perspective. And many thanks to Michael Mann, a famous Hollywood film director, screenwriter and producer, and his assistant Maria Norman, for all they did.

I was buoyed up by the interest, encouragement and good humour these men and women showed me throughout the months of research and writing. Without them I could not have done it. Thank you!

Prologue

In February 1997 the then director of the Aeroflot office in Vienna, Konstantin Bushlanov called my wife to ask for a favour. A Very Important Person – Mr Bushlanov gave no name at that stage – was expected to arrive from Moscow and would Valentina be kind enough to use her knowledge and contacts to recommend a discreet luxury hotel in the Austrian Alps in order for the family of the VIP to have a great and so much deserved skiing holiday.

The reason for the call to this particular number was simple. Several months before my wife and I had started publishing a magazine that we called *Business Lunch* that purported to give guidance and advice to the new breed of the Russian millionaires who had started to spend their money abroad without any particular knowledge of what was commonly understood in the West as 'quality': fine wines, excellent food, top-class hotels 'with understatement' and bespoke tailoring. Their usual choice of accommodation was the Ritz in London and Paris (not that I have anything against the Ritz) and typical must-have objects were Versace clothes, leathers and furniture. For jewellery many of the Russian *nouveaux riches* preferred either the Chopard or Chanel brands that proudly called themselves *haut joaillerie*. Such places as Savile Row in London or the Widder Hotel in Zürich were not yet on their map, while the new Ralph Lauren flagship store on Old Bond Street was still under construction. So we thought it might be a good idea to earn a little money from advertisers while at the same time giving good advice to the readers. Our *Business Lunch* became quite popular and, what was more important, Konstantin Bushlanov arranged for its free distribution on board Aeroflot flights going to and from Vienna. Besides, he was a nice, friendly guy, almost certainly not one of those GRU (Russian military intelligence) members who occupied most of the slots in the Aeroflot offices around the world.

Obviously, it was our duty to help: my wife immediately answered that we indeed had contacts in a very suitable venue just outside Salzburg. The offer was quickly accepted and we rushed off to have a discreet talk with Frau Herzog, the owner.

Standing high on the Gaisberg hill, the Vital Hotel Kobenzl is an oasis of tranquillity and relaxation. But what distinguished it from another true luxury hotel, a long-time favourite of ours, the Schloss Fuschl situated only about ten minutes away, was Frau Herzog herself. As a prominent member of the hospitality industry in the Salzburg area, she could 'smell' the right customer, and apart from offering all the appropriate amenities and breathtaking views from most of the rooms and the restaurant, she offered her very personal attention to those who could pay for it – well, but not over the top. With all-understanding Frau Herzog every detail was discussed and agreed upon and several days later we went to the Salzburg airport to pick up the guests.

They were a family of four and they arrived from Moscow by private jet. They introduced themselves as Badri, Olga, Roman and the 3-year-old David. We soon became quite friendly and visited Olga and her sons often, especially because Badri had from time to time to leave for Switzerland to meet a business partner. I sometimes played with David and remember well an odd Russian phrase that he used once when I showed him a simple magic trick. Observing my bare hand that a second ago had held a banknote, he said pensively: 'Hmm, what a naughty child you are, man!'

Olga Safonova and her children enjoyed their skiing amid the tranquillity and splendour of the Austrian Alps tremendously. Badri, a black-haired Georgian in his early forties, was very generous to Frau Herzog and, to her great satisfaction, her wine cellar's stock of great French vintages was regularly required.

At that time we did not know that Badri was actually the chief executive of the ORT, the leading Russian television channel which then belonged to the famed business tycoon Boris Berezovsky. Or that he made his regular shuttles to Lausanne to discuss the Aeroflot privatisation scheme with Berezovsky, who was his closest business associate. Or that his name was in fact Arkady Patarkatsyshvili, and that he would soon become the richest Georgian in the world. In 1997, after eight years away from Russia, there were quite a few things we were not aware of.

The Funeral

7 December 2006 was a lousy day. Only hours before the event a secret message was delivered to a narrow circle of people who were invited to attend the burial ceremony of Alexander 'Sasha' Litvinenko in London's Highgate Cemetery. Oleg Gordievsky, a famous British spy within the KGB's First Chief Directorate (foreign intelligence), his companion Maureen and myself arrived in London from our homes in Surrey and took a tube that brought us most of the way to our destination. Then we walked up the hill into the nearest pub where Oleg ordered three double gin-and-tonics and a cab that arrived promptly. The weather was bad but not rainy yet – a real storm would begin later.

At that time I was working for BBC *Panorama* on a documentary about Sasha's murder. The BBC often does not produce its own programmes directly and in the Litvinenko case the job had been given to a private company named Blakeway/3BM located at a nice house at 32 Woodstock Grove a short walk away from the Shepherd's Bush underground station. John O'Mahony, the company's producer, got hold of my mobile number and called me on 23 November, just hours before Litvinenko passed away, to discuss a business proposal. He had seen my article 'Russian Venom' in the *Wall Street Journal* the day before and invited me to join the team of himself, Fiona Stourton (executive producer), Piers Vellacott (executive manager), Peter Norrey (second producer) and John Sweeney representing *Panorama* itself in an attempt to pitch a programme to the BBC. If the commission were granted, I was to become the film's chief consultant. I immediately agreed and Fiona, John O'Mahony and I met at the cigar bar of the Connaught Hotel in Mayfair to discuss the plot.

All that happened three days after Sasha died in terrible torments in University College London Hospital (UCLH). The world's media had gone crazy trying to learn any tiny detail that could be reported on the front pages or in the prime-time news. So my interlocutors took the bull by the horns at once.

'Who and why?' were their first queries.

Had I then suspected that the whole setup could be a trap carefully organised by the Russian intelligence, I might have acted differently. But the suspicion came later, so during that evening in the Connaught I was perfectly but unprofessionally open and honest and gave them my opinion.

'A politician,' I said, 'an important politician from a NATO country whose road Litvinenko crossed. So they shut him up.'

Both Fiona and John looked disappointed or pretended to be. But now it is clear that this revelation made in November 2006, together with the fact that I was known to be close to Gordievsky, whom the Russian services knew to be in regular contact with British intelligence, secured my position as the consultant to the programme. My contract with Blakeway/3BM was an exclusive one; they had the right to prevent me from producing newspaper articles on the subject without their (or, rather, John O'Mahony's personal) approval. Should I be approached by a major newspaper – a possibility entirely out of my control – the studio would compensate me rather than allow such an article to appear. Indeed, I was paid twice by 3BM when called by some British or American papers.

Exactly one week before the funeral, on 1 December 2006, Sandy Smith, the editor representing *Panorama* signed a letter confirming that Blakeway/3BM was now officially commissioned to produce a documentary on the death of Alexander Litvinenko and that this would air in peak time on BBC One in early 2007. Everyone involved was required to give the studio all assistance in bringing this important project to the screen. The time was short and the challenge great.

* * *

Oleg, Maureen and I got out of the cab at the designated gate at the cemetery, which was surrounded by hundreds of television cameras and photographers who were being kept at a distance by the police. We moved forward, crossed the courtyard and were greeted by a solemn and rather small group of mourners gathered under a wooden overhang, anticipating rain. The group included Boris Berezovsky, whom, together with Akhmed Zakayev, an exiled Chechen leader and close friend of the Litvinenkos, I saw for the first time; Alex Goldfarb, Berezovsky's associate whom I had first met together with Litvinenko at the Connaught almost two years before; Marina Litvinenko, Sasha's widow, and Boris's beautiful third wife, Elena; Walter and Maxim Litvinenko, Sasha's father who had come from Russia, and younger half-brother who had just arrived from Italy; as well as Andrei Nekrasov, a good-looking film producer whom I immediately liked and who would soon become famous for his documentaries about his friend's life and death. I did not notice then that Vladimir Bukovsky, a great Russian dissident and critic of Putin's regime, and Gerard Batten, a UK Independence Party member of the European Parliament, were also there together with Litvinenko's first wife and their two children. Later I learned that there were also two Norwegians – Maria Fuglevaag Warsinski, a documentary filmmaker from Oslo, and Ivar Amundsen, an outstanding man who devoted his life to helping the Chechens in their fight for independence, and who was serving as the Honorary Consul representing the Chechen Republic of Ichkeria in his country. Not surprisingly, given the occasion and the ill-assorted group of people gathered on that tragic day at the London cemetery, a political discussion broke out, and was only interrupted by a signal that the burial was about to start. It was already raining heavily when we entered a muddy road to accompany Sasha Litvinenko to his final resting place.

This is how Alex Goldfarb recalls what happened behind the scenes:

It took two weeks before the authorities gave the clearance for Sasha's funeral. His body presented a major environmental hazard; immediately after he died, it was removed to some secret facility and the hospital space was decontaminated. Pathologists attending his post-mortem wore radioactive protection gear. Finally we were told that the body would be released to us in a special sealed casket, provided by the HPA [Health Protection Agency]. Should the family wish to cremate him, they would have to wait for twenty-eight years, until the radioactivity decays to safe levels – nearly eighty half-lives of Polonium-210.

Before the funeral, our closely knit circle was nearly torn apart by another controversy, Sasha's last surprise. As we were discussing the arrangements, Akhmed Zakayev declared that Sasha should be buried in a Muslim ceremony because he had converted to Islam the day before he died. It turned out that on 22 November, just before Sasha lost consciousness, Akhmed brought a mullah to the hospital and he said an appropriate prayer. As far as Akhmed was concerned, Sasha died a Muslim.

I did not know about the mullah, and I was furious with Akhmed. Sasha had never been in any way religious; in fact, he told me that he did not understand those who were. His only passion was to win his battles and to make his point. True, he often said, 'I am a Chechen,' but I said that too. That did not make me a Muslim. That was a statement of solidarity, not at all an expression of faith. Not to mention that on the last day he surely was not thinking clearly.

'I know why he did it, Akhmed,' I said. 'He felt guilty for what Russia had done to the Chechens and wanted to make a gesture. Like a German would want to become a Jew after the Holocaust. But it was a mistake. This will not help your cause. With what's going on in the world, let's face it, Russian propaganda will do everything to shift focus from the murder to the conversion. You are playing into their hands.'

'I am not playing,' said Akhmed. 'Everything was done properly, so he is a Muslim.'

Akhmed was a stubborn man. That stubbornness is why the Russians will not win the Chechen war unless they kill off the entire stubborn population.

'I am not an expert in conversions,' I said, 'but I am an expert in biochemistry. With the amount of sedation he got on that day, I can't be sure he was rational.'

'Acts of faith are not rational.'

The matter was deferred to Marina.

'Let everyone believe about Sasha whatever he wants,' said Marina wisely. 'You can have your service in a mosque and we will have ours in a chapel.' Marina ruled that Sasha would be buried in non-denominational grounds.

On December 8 [*sic*], Sasha was laid to rest in Highgate Cemetery in London, his grave surrounded by the tombs of famous Victorians and a few atheists, including Karl Marx and the physicist Michael Faraday.[1]

After the funeral we were all given small white security passes that no one ever checked and transported to Lauderdale House in Highgate where the memorial service had been arranged.

As soon as the choir finished the first song ('There is a green hill far away' by Pitts), Boris Berezovsky made the first address. Boris is very articulate and is an excellent speaker. He was aware of his authority and strength, especially in this company and situation. Bukovsky, Zakayev, Amundsen, Goldfarb and Sasha's good friend, David Kudykov, all spoke, but none as well or with as much feeling as Berezovsky.

After the ceremony we were all seated in waiting buses and brought to the Italian restaurant Santini in Ebury Street, SW1, where a dinner was served and everyone remembered Sasha. Though it was both the wrong place and the wrong time, I used the opportunity to speak to Boris and Marina and got their agreement to be interviewed for the BBC programme. From Marina I also learned an extremely important detail that remained unnoticed by anybody, including the police, and managed to discuss the matter with David, who appeared to be very garrulous and who gave me his business card with private numbers.

Later Lord Rea appeared at the party and apologised that he had not been able to attend the funeral. We all ate, drank and talked a lot and I had a strange feeling that this evening symbolised rather the beginning than the end of something.

* * *

Almost immediately after the funeral, our group started filming. I called Goldfarb and we agreed to meet at the Frontline Club near the Paddington Station where Sasha had spoken in October during an event held in connection with the recent shooting and murder in Moscow of Anna Politkovskaya, a renowned journalist whom Sasha considered to be a friend. As expected, Litvinenko's speech attacked President Putin and the FSB (the Russian security service), where he himself had served in a department that conducted operations that might be termed 'unlawful settlements' – actions against people when his chiefs decided that legal measures could not or should not be applied. Officially that department was known in the FSB under the acronym URPO, and was in charge of investigating (and fighting) organised crime. In practice, its officers often took the law into their own hands. So when Litvinenko took the floor during the Politkovskaya event in the Frontline

Club, he spoke as an expert knowing exactly what he was talking about. He may not have killed anybody himself, but he was well aware of how it was done in Russia.

As usual, Goldfarb gave a brilliant interview that was duly filmed and we both hurried away into the busy city.

On Saturday, 9 December, John O'Mahony asked me to call Akhmed Zakayev and invite him to be interviewed for the programme. Akhmed, an extremely pleasant and intelligent man, agreed and promised to bring Walter and Maxim Litvinenko along with him so that we could interview them as well. John chose the venue. It turned out to be the University Women's Club at 2 South Audley Square in Mayfair. Again, as everything took place rather quickly, I did not suspect anything at the time. Only later did I recall that this particular address could be found in the MI5 registry as a signal site for an important KGB operation.

An instruction from the Centre (KGB foreign intelligence headquarters in Yasenevo, near Moscow), attachment to No. 7180/KR, 29th April 1985. Signals:

There are two suitable places for placing signals: one of these is on *South Audley Street*, and the other in the part just behind the street. They are not far from the south section of the American embassy if you go down *South Audley Street* in the direction of *Curzon Street*.

1. Go down *South Audley Street* and about five–six blocks below *Grosvenor Square* you will reach *Tilney Street*. Stop on the west side of *South Audley Street*, facing the east side. You will see a small square called *Audley Square* with a garage for major vehicles. On the right-hand (south) side of this little square there is a prominent lamp-post. A white figure '8' is painted at the base of the lamp-post on the roadside, a metre above the pavement. The lamp-post is easily seen from a car passing slowly by (and judging from the usual traffic in this street, it is impossible to drive fast there). I would put a light blue chalk mark below the figure '8', which would mean that I was filling the DLB ('dead letter box') the same day at a certain time (let us say 16:00). I will place signals only on certain days selected in advance (say, every Thursday up to 12:00). Having placed the signal on the lamp-post, I shall then have to make sure that the signal has been read before going to the DLB in *Brompton Oratory* (a little more than 1 km from the spot).

Attachment: Packet containing 8 photographs, Secret, DM, No. 365/KR. Please return.[2]

The above was a part of a so-called 'illegal' operation. KGB 'illegals', officers or agents who operate under a false identity, fell into three groups. Those in the first group live in the West as 'sleepers', typically running a small business and having irregular though long-planned contacts with the Centre but doing little or no operational work. They are activated only in times of war. In the second group are active spies living in the West who recruit and run agents, act as cut-outs when a KGB case officer from the embassy cannot meet an agent, and themselves try to gather intelligence. The third group of illegals consists of officers of the first or eighth department of the Illegals Directorate who are usually based in Moscow. They make short trips abroad normally either to do a 'false flag' recruitment, i.e. to recruit a person without revealing that he or she will work for the Russians or the KGB; or to 'liquidate' (murder) someone. After an operation, such an illegal returns to Moscow sometimes promptly, sometimes after weeks or months.

As I stood by that very same lamp-post in December 2006 waiting for Akhmed and his friends, I did not know that the photographs from that KGB operation more than twenty years ago would or could be used again.

Akhmed arrived perfectly in time at 3:30 p.m. together with his assistant, known to everybody as Yasha. With them came Sasha's father and brother who were both leaving England soon. All three were interviewed, filmed, thanked and condoled. We finished working well after 7:00 p.m.

Soon Gordievsky, whom I was accustomed to meeting every day, announced that the police would be coming to talk to us. Indeed, one afternoon two pleasant-looking young officers, who introduced themselves as Michael and Lisa, arrived at his house. As they were most of all interested in the operational methods of the KGB, Oleg spoke first. When he finished, I took his place. We told them clearly that Sasha's death was a well-planned joint clandestine SVR (Russia's foreign intelligence service)/FSB operation that only went wrong because polonium-210 was quite by chance found in Sasha's body.

We exchanged telephone numbers and I continued to consult the police while the investigation was going on. There is no doubt that the combined team of Special Branch and the anti-terrorist force of the Metropolitan police that became known internally as SO15 did an excellent job investigating Litvinenko's murder. They came to the most definite conclusions about who committed this crime, and how and when.

The Norwegian newspaper *Dagbladet* grabbed me on Wednesday, 20 December, in the evening at the Connaught Hotel that became my interview headquarters until it was closed for refurbishing. Morten Øverbye, the editor, did a series of long interviews that later became front-page articles.

The next day was going to be hard. First, my own interview with the BBC was scheduled at midday; second, I had to bring in Mario Scaramella.

It was not at all by chance that Scaramella appeared in this story. This rather young and adventurous Italian loved the spying game and had been trying to involve himself in it since the age of nineteen. He managed to become an adviser to the Mitrokhin Commission of the Italian parliament that in 2002–06 did its best to investigate a weird and extraordinary situation that had arisen. Unusually, the Italian government had banned the Italian security service from dealing with certain documents provided by the British government in 1995. These were copies of secret KGB files identifying more than 250 Soviet agents among the Italian political, business and financial elite, including the press, magistrates and courts. The papers had been meticulously copied and later brought to London by the KGB archivist defector, Vasili Mitrokhin. Only part of this treasure-trove was published in the form of books written by the British intelligence historian Professor Christopher Andrew. The secret part of this 'Mitrokhin Archive' was given to the appropriate governments and their security services for consideration. In Italy, under the premiership of Romano Prodi, nothing was done about those potentially scandalous papers. When Prodi became the president of the European Commission in May 1999, he was asked how this material could be kept from prosecutors or the press for so long. The former Italian prime minister responded that he never heard about such documents. And indeed, no investigation was ever carried out. It was clearly no coincidence that for his finals at the Catholic University of Milan in 1961 Prodi had opted to write a thesis on the role of protectionism in Italy.

Scaramella was recommended to Paolo Guzzanti, then a senator and the president of the Mitrokhin Commission, in 2003 and received a mandate to collect documents for the Commission. He rushed to London, where many KGB and GRU defectors lived, and quickly established contacts first with Vladimir Rezun formerly of the GRU (the foreign intelligence agency of the Russian armed forces), now a historian and author writing under the pseudonym 'Victor Suvorov', and through him with Litvinenko. The latter introduced Scaramella to Gordievsky and then to Evgeny Limarev, a self-styled Russian intelligence expert who by that time had moved from Geneva to a small town of Cluses in the départment de Haute-Savoie on the French-Swiss border. Litvinenko also recommended Mario to Oleg Kalugin and Yuri Shvets, both former KGB now living in the USA. By his own initiative, Mario established contacts with several former and even acting CIA officers.

I know Paolo Guzzanti as a very decent man and a shrewd politician. And I am sure that he would never have given orders to Scaramella to collect compromising material on the former prime minister of Italy or to concoct evidence that Prodi had been involved with the KGB. Mario surely did it on his own initiative, spurred on by his aspiration to be engaged in high-level international investigations. Caught up in the situation, Mario made some quick decisions and serious mistakes.

Thanks to his activities in the Russian defector community, his links with representatives of the Western intelligence services, his discovery – in 2005, when the Litvinenko operation was already in progress – of an alleged cargo of twenty nuclear torpedoes buried in the bed of the Bay of Naples by a Soviet submarine in 1978 that caused an international scandal, and, finally, his work for the Mitrokhin

Commission, Scaramella became a great irritant to Moscow. First the KGB decided to discredit him in the Italian press – 'character assassination' is a favourite KGB trick. Then they frightened him using various channels including Limarev, who told Mario that 'Russian intelligence sources in Moscow' had informed him about an imminent attack on Scaramella and Senator Guzzanti, and warned Mario to be extremely careful. Finally – and this is very typical of the KGB's operational mentality – they decided to kill two birds with one stone and push the Mitrokhin Commission adviser into the Litvinenko operation in order to incriminate him and thus destroy the whole work of the commission. It has to be said, the plan worked without a hitch.

Limarev lured Mario into meeting Litvinenko on 1 November – the day Sasha was poisoned. Then after Litvinenko himself and Gordievsky (in an interview with *La Repubblica* in late 2006) accused Scaramella of a foul play, he came into the focus of the international press and all the dirty linen was washed in public. It was quickly found out that he was not an academic (he never pretended to be) or a professor and that the Naples-based organisation Environmental Crime Prevention Programme (ECPP), of which he was a president between 2000 and 2002, was in essence a 'shell' organisation. In late November – early December 2006 the situation was worsened by the fact that the British doctors apparently found (it was a mistake) a deadly level of polonium-210 in Scaramella's body.

Poor Mario was urgently hospitalised, adding fuel to the media hysteria. In Italy, the papers first accused him of poisoning Litvinenko and then, after the British police had dropped and rebuffed all accusations against Mario, accused him of inventing his own polonium contamination. At the time of this writing, Marina and Alex Goldfarb were speaking about Mario with suspicion and distrust, and Alexander Stille, a New York-based author, called Scaramella '*a millantatore di credito* – someone who claims to know a lot more and to have done a lot more than he really does'. Whether Stille knows Mario well enough to make such a claim is hard to say, but immediately after his release from house arrest in Naples Mario Scaramella came to see me in London and complained bitterly that he was still being investigated by the Russian security service as a suspect. The FSB had obviously decided to go with their absurd plan to the very end and nothing – perhaps only a war – could stop them from accusing Scaramella of poisoning his friend and accusing Berezovsky of ordering this crime in conjunction with the British Secret Intelligence Service (SIS).

This is what the Department of Haematology of UCLH (where Litvinenko was treated for a week until his tragic death) stated in the Discharge Summary dated 4 December 2006:

Mr Scaramella was admitted . . . on 1 December 2006. He was referred to the unit by the Health Protection Agency after he was found to have significant levels of polonium-210 in his urine. Initial results suggested a potential dose to bone marrow of 2.0 Gy, to kidneys 9.5 Gy, liver 4.9 Gy, and colon 1.2 Gy [a lethal dose – BV]. The aim of his admission was to assess his clinical state and to monitor for any evidence of polonium toxicity. However, recounting and recalculating on the original urine specimen suggested a considerably lower dose and a further 24-hour urine specimen was completed on 2 December. This showed levels of polonium that may be found in many members of the normal population. Mr Scaramella has been well during his admission and all his investigations – blood tests and chest X ray – have been within normal limits.

We have currently discharged Mr Scaramella from the ward. We do not believe that he will suffer any immediate or long-term effects of polonium exposure. There is no risk to his contacts. He has remained clinically well and his blood tests have remained normal.[3]

On 21 December 2006 I faced the task of bringing Mario Scaramella to the location – a site that was chosen by the crew – to be interviewed by a very experienced BBC reporter, John Sweeney. The venue was an old and nice-looking building called the Cedar House Hotel in Cobham, Surrey, which boasts its Riverside Grill restaurant.

But before Mario arrived, I had to be interviewed first myself. Almost certainly I greatly disappointed both Johns (O'Mahony and Sweeney) by refusing to show my face and only agreeing to sit in front of the camera 'in obscurity'. However, after a short debate they had to accept this, as these were necessary security precautions. I still believe it was a very wise decision.

I was filmed and interviewed for two-and-a-half hours (later having found that what remained was about forty-five seconds). Mario was picked up at the railway station at 3:00 p.m. and brought to Cedar House. After his interview, at about seven, we both went to visit Gordievsky who lived in a small town nearby.

Oleg decided to play detective and started a hostile interrogation of Mario. Terribly tired and depressed by all the previous events, Mario took Oleg quite seriously at first. Then, when a bottle of red wine was opened and everybody had a sip, the atmosphere changed and it was agreed that Mario was a good guy who had got into this mess by chance. After the second bottle Scaramella gave a package of documents to Gordievsky that proved that he was innocent, and soon left.

Christmas and New Year 2007 came and went but I don't think any of us in the 'tightly knit circle' was in a mood to celebrate.

The filming continued until Monday, 15 January, during which time John O'Mahony visited Moscow for a week. John is married to a Russian girl and loves to go to Russia, where he had spent time before. When everything was ready it was announced that I would be invited to the final viewing and that the documentary, now entitled 'How to Poison a Spy', was the BBC *Panorama* programme scheduled for 22 January in a prime-time slot: 8:30 p.m.

I was never invited to the preview. Together with Oleg and Maureen we watched it in Gordievsky's house. What I saw exceeded my worst expectations. The efforts of two months were deeply buried in the Russian snow.

Georgi Markov, London, September 1978

Assassinations like the one carried out in London on 1 November 2006 demand long and meticulous preparation. Usually, after the operation is initiated – by the service itself or from above[1] – the officer in charge is given the task of devising an operational plan that among other things includes a proposed cast of characters and their travel documents, the weapon, the location, the exact timing and the post-operational cover-up. There is also an auxiliary, reserve scenario in case something unexpected happens. The plan is then reported to the chief of the department – in the Litvinenko case it was surely Department 8 of Directorate S (Illegals)[2] of the SVR, responsible for assassinations and subversion on foreign soil, from there to the head of the directorate or his deputy, then to the chief of the service, and then to the president (after Putin left the Kremlin the prime minister would be included and the president might not be told).

According to Russian law, the latest amendments to which were approved by the State Duma (Russian parliament) in July 2006, the president is the sole authority responsible for approving such a plan. To ask whether Putin was informed about a planned assassination in London is the same as asking whether President Bush was informed about plans to invade Iraq. The commander-in-chief *must* be informed. After that the operational plan is returned with any corrections or amendments to the senior officer in charge of the operation and preparations begin.

Here is what KGB General Oleg Danilovich Kalugin, the former head of Directorate K (foreign counter-intelligence), said about one such assassination:

> In all my years in the KGB I have only once been involved in what we call in the business a 'wet job' – an assassination. It occurred in 1978, and though I didn't have a pivotal role in the killing, I nevertheless did not try to talk my superiors out of the plot to kill the Bulgarian dissident Georgi Markov.
>
> The case first came to my attention in early 1978. [Vladimir] Kryuchkov, our intelligence chief, had just received an urgent cable from General Stoyanov, the Bulgarian minister of the interior. The Bulgarian had a blunt

request: he wanted the KGB's help in carrying out President Zhivkov's express order to liquidate Markov. Unquestionably, the KGB chairman, Yuri Andropov, had to approve the plan.

I had heard about Markov from my colleagues in Bulgarian intelligence. He was a former close associate of Zhivkov's who had turned against Communists, fled to England, and was beaming back strong criticism of the regime to Bulgaria through his position with the Bulgarian radio service of the BBC. During my most recent visit to Bulgaria, my colleagues there had several times mentioned what a nuisance Markov had become.

'He lives in London and slanders Comrade Zhivkov,' one Bulgarian intelligence officer told me. 'Our people are very unhappy about him.'

Over the next half a year, using the 'talents' of KGB scientists schooled in the art of poisoning and other methods of murder, we and the Bulgarians stumbled toward the assassination of Markov. It was a wrenching trial-and-error process, right out of the pages of the blackest comedy. But in the end, even the Soviets and the Bulgarians couldn't screw it up: we got our man.[3]

Kalugin went on to describe the steps taken. His directorate, on orders from KGB Chairman Kryuchkov, turned to the KGB's Operational and Technical Directorate (OTU), which had a laboratory designated as Laboratory 12. Its job was to invent new ways of killing people without leaving a trace of the real cause of death. 'The more it looked like a heart attack the better.'

Kalugin's deputy responsible for 'special actions' abroad, Sergei Golubev, accompanied by his assistant Yuri Surov flew to Sofia with the lab's recommendations. They proposed to General Vasil Kotsev, chief of Bulgarian intelligence, three possibilities: poisoned jelly that could be applied to the victim's skin, poisoning his food or drink, or shooting him with a poisoned pellet. The latter course was selected.

In Markov's case, according to the experts from the British Chemical and Microbiological Establishment at Porton Down in Wilshire assisted by their CIA colleagues (and confirmed by Kalugin thirteen years later), the poison was ricin, an exceedingly lethal derivative of the castor oil plant.

Ricin had never before been used for murder in Britain and the toxicologists did not know exactly what its effects would be on a human being. After experimenting the Porton Down specialists concluded that just an ounce of ricin could kill 90,000 people. Furthermore, because the symptoms take a long time to develop, the murderer could be far away before suspicions would be aroused.[4]

Golubev took the ricin pellets to Sofia. One was shot into a horse, which died. The Bulgarians then decided to try it out on a human being. The unfortunate victim was a Bulgarian prisoner who had been sentenced to death. An officer from the Bulgarian Interior Ministry approached the prisoner with an umbrella, the tip of which skilled KGB craftsmen had converted into a gun that would silently shoot the ricin pellet into its victim. The officer shot the poor prisoner with the umbrella, and the fellow yelped as if stung by a bee. Realising that his death sentence had just been carried out in a most unusual manner, the prisoner became hysterical – but the poison failed to release from the pellet, and the prisoner remained alive.

Golubev returned to Moscow with this disconcerting news and the KGB's poison factory went back to experimenting, finally assuring Golubev and the Bulgarians that the pellets would work.[5] (Seven years later, in 1985, Golubev was to supervise the alleged drugging of Gordievsky almost certainly with a psychotropic drug known in the trade as SP-17 from the same secret laboratory in an unsuccessful attempt to get him to confess.)

Since his defection in 1969, Markov had been declared an enemy of the state. They removed his books from libraries, even scratched his name from films. Markov retaliated by writing scripts for Radio Free Europe and running pro-grammes on the BBC denouncing the authoritarian regime. He publicly mocked Zhivkov, calling him a minor dictator with a second-rate sense of humour.

Soon he began to receive ominous calls from Bulgaria threatening that he would be punished for treachery. A very serious warning came from Munich: the caller told Markov that a hit was already prepared.

On 28 August 1978, ten days before the attempt on Georgi Markov's life, the Bulgarians tested the weapon on another victim. Vladimir Kostov was a former colonel of the KDS (the Bulgarian equivalent of the KGB) who had operated in Paris under the guise of a journalist, defected and settled in France. One clear sunny day Kostov was standing on an escalator slowly moving him up from the Paris Métro just below the Arc de Triomphe, when he felt a sting in his back and noticed a man with an umbrella running away. Fortunately, Kostov did not feel anything further and carried on his way.

Copying the operational methods of their big brothers in the KGB, Bulgarian intelligence had at least two aims in murdering Kostov: to get rid of a defector from their own ranks who was under a death sentence and to test the gun and the poison in a real-life situation. The attempt failed for the simple reason that Kostov was wearing such a heavy sweater that the pellet did not penetrate deep enough into his body. He was saved because the poison did not reach his blood stream. Almost miraculously, after forty-eight hours of suffering, Kostov recovered. But he did not forget the episode.

Thursday, 7 September 1978 (the fifty-seventh birthday of the Bulgarian communist dictator Todor Zhivkov, who had so often been the target of Georgi Markov's criticism), 1:30 p.m. At the south end of Waterloo Bridge, Georgi Markov was approaching a bus stop. Crowds of office workers jostled him as they streamed past, and he gazed absent-mindedly across the River Thames. Suddenly he felt a sharp pain on the back of his right thigh. Turning quickly he saw a man bending down to pick up a dropped umbrella. 'I'm sorry,' the man said in a strong foreign accent. A second later, a taxi pulled up, the man jumped inside and disappeared.[6]

As he was dying in St George's Hospital in Balham on 11 September, Markov told Bernard Riley, the doctor on duty who admitted him there three days earlier, about the incident but – exactly as in the Litvinenko case – the doctors did not suspect an assassination and so failed to determine the cause of Markov's deteriorating condition.

'He was complaining of nausea and vomiting,' said Dr Riley in an interview with a Windfall Films team producing a TV documentary on the case, 'and was running a high temperature but it all looked like an ordinary fever.'

Within hours, however, his condition deteriorated. At 10:40 a.m. on 11 September 1978 Markov was pronounced dead.

It was shocking news for the whole Bulgarian exile community in London. Very few believed that he died of 'natural causes' as officially announced, and when the police discovered that Markov was a Soviet bloc defector, they opened an investigation.

The Markov story hit the front pages of every newspaper in Britain and all over Europe, but not in Bulgaria where the media maintained an unyielding silence. His portraits appeared on all major television channels. Titles like 'Death of a Dissident', 'Bulgarian Labyrinth' and 'Poison Brolly Riddle' covered many news-stands.

But the police did not have much to work with: no apparent motive, no weapon and only a corpse with no signs of a violent death. The autopsy at Wandsworth Public Mortuary revealed nothing sinister, so a fragment of tissue at the puncture mark was transported to the special laboratory at Porton Down. Christopher Green, a CIA chemical weapons specialist, joined the British team. They found a tiny pellet made of platinum-iridium alloy with two holes that could only be detected with the help of an electronic microscope. Alas, the holes were empty. But this already offered an answer to the riddle, because it was obvious that such highly sophisticated weapon could have only been manufactured in the USSR.

Then there was a stroke of luck.

When he heard about the death of his friend, Vladimir Kostov alerted the French authorities and they in turn Scotland Yard. French doctors cut out a piece of tissue from Kostov's back and police officers brought it to London. Here Porton Down specialists found and extracted a similar still-intact ricin pellet. As in the Markov case, the ricin had decomposed but it took only a matter of days to find the correct answer, because very few poisons in such miniscule quantities produce such deadly effects.

In 1992 General Vladimir Todorov, a former Bulgarian intelligence chief and a graduate of the KGB Andropov Institute (who had succeeded General Vasil Kotsev after the latter's mysterious death in 1986) fled to Moscow allegedly taking with him all the files on Markov. When he returned to Sofia he was arrested and sentenced to sixteen months in jail for destroying ten volumes of material relating to the Markov assassination. He spent only six months in a privileged Darzhavna Sigurnost (state security) prison and after his release became a member of the powerful organisation of veterans of the DS. When the Litvinenko operation was unfolding in London, he was still alive.

General Stoyan Savov, the deputy interior minister who ordered the murder, killed himself before facing trial over the cover-up of the assassination.

After the fall of Zhivkov's regime in 1989 a stack of the special umbrellas was found in the interior ministry, according to *The Times*. After the collapse of the Soviet Union two years later, H. Keith Melton, an intelligence historian and specialist in clandestine devices and equipment, managed to obtain a replica of the murder umbrella from KGB veterans who, at that time, were pretending friendship with their former enemies. According to Melton the umbrella had been purchased in Washington, DC by the KGB and modified in Moscow at the secret facility of its technical directorate.

Almost thirty years after Georgi Markov's death, in April 2007, I received an email from Max Fisher of Windfall Films and on Friday, 27 April, we met at Claridge's to discuss the Litvinenko case and possible future collaboration. By this time I was aware that the studio had made a documentary entitled 'Revealed: The Umbrella Assassin' that was originally broadcast in London on 17 May 2006, less than five months before Sasha was poisoned. I was anxious to get a copy and Max was kind enough to bring me one.

It is a good film. Jack Hamilton, the investigative journalist and the studio team had pursued all possible leads to find a suspect. They were assisted by two published accounts: one by Vladimir Bereanu and Kalin Todorov entitled *The Umbrella Murder* (1994), and another by Hristo Hristov that came out in Sofia in 2005 under the title *Ubiite 'Skitnik'* ('To Kill a TRAMP'). TRAMP was Markov's codename in the KDS.

The researchers discovered that the suspect's name was Francesco Gullino, a Dane of Italian origin. After his recruitment in Bulgaria Gullino had been set up in Copenhagen under cover as an antique dealer. It is known that he travelled to Europe in an Austrian-registered caravan, which showed (not for the first or last time) that the KGB station in Vienna was in the murder game. Allegedly, Gullino came to Britain to 'neutralise' – Moscow's term would be to 'liquidate' – Markov on the orders of the Bulgarian secret service.

Working under the codename PICCADILLY, he flew to Britain three times in 1977 and 1978. On 7 September he was certainly in London, and left the British capital for Rome the day after Markov was jabbed by the umbrella-cum-pneumatic weapon. On 9 September in Rome Gullino met his Bulgarian handler.

The Bulgarian files say that he was their only agent in London at the time, but it was impossible that Gullino was operating alone. First of all, using only a photo of Markov provided by the DS he could easily have made a mistake and killed the wrong person, so somebody was needed who knew Markov well and could 'point a finger' at him. Second, even if an assassin acts alone there is always a watcher from the service secretly present on the scene to observe and register every movement and later to write a detailed report. There are rules in the KGB that are never broken. Finally, somebody has to remove the killer from the crime scene. It was no coincidence that a taxi appeared at that spot at that moment.

Indeed, according to the British security service, there was surely someone planted in the BBC to watch Markov and other dissident exiles. The best candidate for this role was another Bulgarian broadcaster, Vladimir Simeonov.

Simeonov, or rather Vladimir Bobchev, as was his real name, appeared in Britain in 1971. He was not much liked by his BBC staff colleagues, who suspected him of reporting on them. In the early hours of 1 October 1978, twenty days after Markov's death, Simeonov took a cab from the Bush House to his home after a night shift. The driver later revealed that his passenger had been very upset and even told him his life story while they crossed the city. Several hours later Simeonov was found dead.

As this was the second death of a Bulgarian in the UK within a month, the Scotland Yard Anti-Terrorist Branch under the leadership of Commander Jim Neville was immediately involved. But after extensive research, the Queen's Road Coroner's Court pronounced Simeonov's death accidental. He had fallen down the stairs and suffocated in his own blood, they said.

This was an unlikely explanation for the sudden death of a healthy 30-year-old man under these particular circumstances. Bulgarian investigative reporters discovered that two glasses were found in the sink without any fingerprints. Traces of a bottle were identified on the table – Simeonov was a teetotaller. And he was found dead just two days after having been questioned by Scotland Yard detectives.

Theo Lirkov, another broadcaster who worked with Markov and whom the latter had asked to examine the spot where he had been stung on the way to the BBC, claimed that a week before Markov's murder Simeonov had been noticeably nervous. When he found out that Markov had been assassinated, he was visibly shocked and began to tremble.[7] Although forensic experts found no poison in Simeonov's body, their effort was useless because they had no idea what they should have been looking for. Had it not been for pure chance, neither Markov's nor Litvinenko's murders would ever have been investigated. Both cases are still open.

As for the 'watcher' who must have been near the scene of the crime, the two Bulgarian reporters probably spotted the right person. They called him 'Woodpecker' and erroneously suspected he was the assassin. Their suspicion stemmed from the fact that MI5 had routinely photographed a Bulgarian diplomat at Heathrow on the day of Markov's murder but the name in his passport appeared to be different from the name in the Registry. The journalists went to meet the diplomat, whose initials were T.S., in Sofia and confronted him with several inquisitive questions, after which they stopped challenging him. Only later did they learn that T.S. had been quickly promoted from Third Secretary to Ambassador in a European country just a year after the London operation. That was quite unprecedented and could only be an award for some special services rendered. Whatever his function, any Bulgarian diplomat in London at the time was certainly either a staff officer or a co-optee of Bulgarian foreign intelligence.

As far as I know, the cabbie who conveniently picked up the killer right after the hit has never been found. As for his identity the police came up with an absolute blank.

An interesting episode in the Markov saga took place in Denmark in 1993. On 5 February Francesco Gullino was briefly detained in Copenhagen where British and Danish detectives questioned and fingerprinted him. Christopher Bird and David Kemp representing Scotland Yard together with Bogdan Karayotov, the Bulgarian investigator, acting in concert with their colleagues from the Danish Security and Intelligence Service known as PET produced documents incriminating Gullino as a Bulgarian spy. He admitted signing a declaration of allegiance to DS in 1972, but said he had no connection with the Markov killing. In Copenhagen several false passports were produced as well as receipts for cash paid by the Bulgarian authorities to agent PICCADILLY. It was shown that around the time of the Markov murder, Gullino was in London and had received a payment of £2,000. In fact, Gullino had continued to receive payments from his spymasters until 1990, that is, after the collapse of the Communist regime in Bulgaria. This should have roused the suspicion of his interrogators but as it was Scotland Yard who investigated the case, and not MI5, the possible Russian connection was not pursued. Gullino was later released because Denmark had no case against him. According to Anthony Georgieff, who conducted a brilliant journalistic investigation, a few days after the interrogation Gullino left his house in a Copenhagen suburb and the country altogether. He left a forwarding address in Budapest with the Public Registration Office. His home later went into receivership.

It was eventually learned that Gullino actually lived in Karlovy Vary and only used the Hungarian address as a mail drop. In 2006 he was seen in Denmark and, according to witnesses, visited Copenhagen quite regularly.

Gullino's possible Russian ties have never been investigated.

It is quite possible that Gullino continues to 'do business' for his Moscow bosses and business is now the name of the Russian spy game, taking the place of politically motivated Soviet espionage. In the twenty-first century it is called private banking, stock market operations, terrorism, international drug trafficking and illegal arms sales using countries like Belarus. General Vladilen Fyodorov, former KGB station chief in Bulgaria, explained to a curious reporter that Russian foreign intelligence agents and executives have successfully gone into private business throughout Eastern Europe. The general himself headed the Association of Foreign Intelligence Veterans in Russia that ran its own bank to 'protect the deposits of colleagues working abroad from inflation'.

During his research Anthony Georgieff came into the possession of two Bulgarian State Orders bestowing high awards upon fifteen individuals, fourteen Bulgarian senior security officers and a Soviet. The orders, marked 'confidential', were signed personally by Todor Zhivkov, and were given for 'alacrity, professionalism and the interception of the activities of persons serving a foreign intelligence and of stopping the anti-state activities of Bulgarian citizens'. The originals have disappeared from the Bulgarian State Archives.

Incidentally, by 1995 the Scotland Yard had compiled a list of fifteen people whom they wanted to investigate in connection with the Markov murder. According to Baroness Linda Chalker, Minister of State for Foreign and Commonwealth Affairs at the time, all of these people were KGB agents.

Ten years later a Scotland Yard spokeswoman said on 5 June 2005 that the 'particularly long and complex investigation' into the murder remained open and they were keen to bring the killer to justice, although she declined to comment on the apparent identification of one of their most elusive targets.

On 19 December 2006 Dr Julian Lewis, Conservative MP for New Forest East, raised the Markov problem in the House of Commons and asked questions about Gullino. Unfortunately, the answer given by Tony McNulty, Labour MP and Minister of State at the Home Office, was vague and inconclusive.

Returning to Bulgaria shortly after the Markov affair, Kalugin met Minister for Internal Affairs Dimitar Stoyanov, who gave him an expensive Browning hunting rifle with a brass plaque on the stock that read: 'From Minister Stoyanov to General Kalugin.' Though Stoyanov did not say why he had given the gun to him, Kalugin understood that it was a sign of appreciation for the help KGB rendered his agency in 'physically removing' Markov. Every time Kalugin looked at the rifle he was reminded of the Markov affair, and eventually he stuck it in a closet. Several years later he pulled the plaque off the stock and, with great relief, sold the gun. He is now a US citizen, and he still has the plaque.

In the autumn of 1993 Kalugin was invited to London to participate in a BBC *Panorama* programme about British Intelligence. Upon his arrival on 30 October, Scotland Yard Anti-Terrorist Branch officers arrested the former KGB general at Heathrow on charges of conspiracy to commit murder. In the interrogation room Kalugin met Christopher Bird. The superintendent produced a copy of the *Mail on Sunday* with Kalugin's interview under the title I ORGANIZED THE ASSASSINATION OF GEORGI MARKOV. Several days later after some panic and the personal intervention of the Russian Ambassador, Kalugin was released and told that he was free to leave the UK. For him, the Markov case was closed.

Markov's grave can be found in a small churchyard at Whitchurch Canonicorum in Dorset. His wife, Annabelle Dilk, and their daughter Alexandra survived him. Bulgarian authorities, according to several press reports, have decided to bypass the thirty-year statute of limitation on the Markov murder case, allowing the investigation to remain open.

The KGB's Poison Factory

The attempt took place on 30 August 1918. Fanya Kaplan, the unsuccessful assassin, fired three shots with bullets allegedly poisoned with curare at Lenin who was on his way back from a meeting. Lenin was wounded but survived and Kaplan was shot without trial four days later. The attempt upon Lenin's life provoked the beginning of the Red Terror as a formal response to 'counter-revolutionary activity'. The terror was unleashed that same year after two more Bolsheviks were assassinated: the commissar for press and propaganda and member of the Petrograd committee V. Volodarsky (real name Moisey Goldstein and no relation to this author) on 20 June and Moisey Uritsky, chairman of the Petrograd Cheka (the equivalent at the time of the KGB), on 30 August. Following these events, the Cheka shot approximately 6,000 prisoners and hostages, imprisoned about 15,000, threw into concentration camps another 6,500 and detained over 4,000 people. However, it is still unclear whether an extremely short-sighted Kaplan had shot at all or whether it had been somebody else. In 1992 Boris Petrovsky, a member of the Russian Academy of Medical Sciences, evaluated the description of Lenin's illness after he had been shot. 'There was no poisoning allegedly caused by "poisoned" bullets,' wrote Dr. Petrovsky. 'One should not talk about poisoned bullets.'[1]

After the leader of the world communist revolution and the first head of the Soviet state, whom many serious Russian researchers suspect to have been a German agent, recovered from his wounds, the Cheka provided him with a full report on the incident and the poison. Lenin learned that curare is a dark resinous extract obtained from several tropical American woody plants, especially *Chondro-dendron tomentosum* or certain species of *Strychnos,* and that the actual name, *curare,* is a corruption of two Tupi Indian terms meaning 'bird' and 'to kill'. The curare vine is used by some South American Indians for poisoning arrowheads.

The Bolshevik leader was fascinated. Three years later, in 1921, the first poison laboratory was established – right in Lenin's own secretariat, at that time called the 'Special Room' – under the leadership of Professor Ignaty Kazakov. From the very beginning its 'products' were to be used against the 'enemies of the people'. That, of course, was a euphemism; what the Russian kingpins always meant was enemies of the Kremlin. To be more precise, enemies of the National Leader himself, whatever his name.

Such an establishment naturally became top secret. But during the near-chaos of the early 1990s, several researchers[2] managed to obtain secret documents and testimonies that throw historical light on the KGB's poison factory.

Professor Kazakov was apparently in charge of the special laboratory from its opening in 1921 until about 1938. Boris Zbarsky, then a 36-year old scientist at the Department of Biochemistry and Analytical Chemistry at the First Moscow Medical Institute, served the 'lab of death' as a consultant on narcotics and their administration. He later became a professor and headed the department. His son, also a professor, recalled that in the 1920s his father had a close relationship with Felix Dzierżyński and then, after Dzierżyński's death in 1926, maintained excellent relationships with his deputy, future State Security chief Genrikh Yagoda. Several scientists from the Institute of Biochemistry, then headed by Academician Alexey Nikolayevich Bach and now known as the Bach Institute of Biochemistry, were actively collaborating in the lab's research programme.

Both Kazakov and Yagoda perished as defendants in the so-called third Moscow show trial in March 1938 organised by Stalin to get rid of his opponents and their potential helpers. Ironically, Yagoda, then the chairman of the much feared NKVD (the forerunner of the KGB), was accused of establishing a poison laboratory and of attempting to poison his successor, Nikolai Yezhov, which was not true though Yagoda had indeed been in overall charge of the laboratory.

After the execution of Professor Kazakov, Grigory Mairanovsky, better known as 'Doctor Death', was appointed the head of the facility. Mairanovsky was a Muscovite, a biochemist whose sadism by far surpassed that of his Nazi counterparts.

The State Security department that included the poisons lab was reorganised in the summer of 1938, its designation changed from 12th Department to 2nd Special Department (operational equipment) with Mikhail Alyokhin appointed as its acting head.[3] Within weeks, however, he was arrested, condemned as a 'German spy' and replaced by Yevgeny Lapshin and Arkady Osinkin as his deputy. The same month (September 1938), Valentin Kravchenko, who was to supervise Mairanovsky's laboratory during the second half of the war, joined the department as 'engineer'. In February 1939 it was divided into two special departments, adding to Lapshin's 2nd Special Department (with its staff of 621) another department designated 4th Special Department, ten times smaller and headed by Mikhail Filimonov, of which the toxicological laboratory itself became a part. It was now known as Laboratory No. 1 or the *Kamera*, a word with a sinister meaning in Russian, associated either with a prison cell or a torture chamber. It consisted itself of two divisions – a chemical laboratory supervised by Mairanovsky and a bacteriological laboratory under Sergey Muromtsev.[4]

From this time and until mid-1946, the special department that included both laboratories was masked inside the NKVD clinic in an attractive-looking building on the corner of Bolshaya Lubyanka Street at No. 11 Varsanofyevsky Lane, just behind the NKVD headquarters in the Lubyanka. The previous location of the 'poison factory' had been in two different buildings, one in Kuchino near Moscow and the other on 4th Meschanskaya Street near Butyrka prison.

Vasily Blokhin, who was both the commandant of Lubyanka prison and the chief NKVD executioner, became a close collaborator of Mairanovsky. He was in charge of providing prisoners for experiments.[5]

In January 1942 the department was upgraded into the 4th Directorate of the NKVD and Pavel Sudoplatov, who had successfully 'liquidated' a Ukrainian nationalist exile in the Netherlands four years earlier, was made its chief, with a rank equivalent to that of a general. His friend, Naum Eitingon, whose claim to fame within the NKVD was organising the assassination of Lev Trotsky in Mexico in August 1940, became Sudoplatov's deputy.

Lavrenty Beria, who by November 1938 succeeded Yezhov as the NKVD chief, personally supervised the work of the poison laboratories until – as unceremoniously as his two predecessors – he was arrested and shot in 1953.

In the early stages of experiments, mustard gas derivatives were used. Mustard gas (Yperite), possibly developed as early as 1822, was first used as chemical weapon in World War I by the German army against British soldiers near Ypres, Belgium, in July 1917 shortly before the Bolshevik revolt in Russia. Mairanovsky's experiments were disappointing as the chemicals were immediately detected during autopsies. This contradicted the main goal – to find a poison devoid of any taste or smell that could not be detected in the victim's body after death. Later Mairanovsky experimented with ricin, digitoxin and curare. Finally, a preparation with all the desired properties, called K-2 (carbylamine choline chloride), was created and successfully tested on prisoners. According to Vladimir Bobrenyov, an investigator at the Russian general prosecutor's office who has made a lengthy study of the case, unearthing Mairanovsky's original reports, K-2 killed the victims in fifteen minutes.

* * *

In February 1954, one year before the Soviet occupation of Vienna was over, a man in a shabby civil suit but carrying the powerful credentials of the MGB (another earlier name of the KGB) in his pocket walked into the American barracks on Stiftgasse opposite the large Herzmansky department store. He introduced himself to the duty officer as Major Peter Sergeyevich Deriabin, a member of the Vienna MGB station and a former officer of the elite Kremlin Guard Directorate. Soon a Russian-speaking CIA official was called in and the new defector was driven to a safe house. Here the initial debriefing started.

Tennent H. ('Pete') Bagley, a young CIA officer later to rise to deputy chief of the Soviet Bloc division, conducted the debriefing. Fifty years later we met in

Brussels. Pete still had a wonderfully clear memory and a phenomenal private archive covering half a century of the Soviet espionage in Europe and the USA.

This is what Deriabin told the CIA during his debriefing:

As late as 1953, the interrogators were backed by terror devices which would have done credit to the worst of the Gestapo professionals. From 1946 until that year, the state security maintained at its Moscow headquarters a quietly notorious laboratory called the 'Chamber' (*Kamera*). Its staff consisted of a medical director and several assistants, who performed experiments on living people – prisoners and persons about to be executed – to determine the effectiveness of various poisons and injections as well as the use of hypnotism and drugs in interrogation techniques. Only the Minister of State Security and four other high officers were allowed to enter.

The laboratory prospered. The 'doctor' in charge was given a special degree of Doctor of Medical Science by Moscow University and nominated for a Stalin Prize for his 'researches'. The Soviet regime announced the Chamber's closing to a select group of State Security officials in October 1953, after blaming its existence on the Beria excesses. It has probably not been reactivated; but its researches continue to be exploited by selected personnel of the State Security.[6]

Mairanovsky was arrested in 1951 and spent ten years in prison. During his case investigation in 1954, his former boss Mikhail Filimonov testified about the experiments:

Sudoplatov and Eitingon approved special equipment [poisons] only if it had been tested on humans . . . I witnessed some of the poisoning tests, but I tried not to be present at the experiments because I could not watch the action of poisons the psyche and body of humans. Some poisons caused extreme suffering. To conceal shouts we even bought a radio set which we turned on [during the experiments].

Mairanovsky's assistant, Alexander Grigorovich, testified that he 'and a chemist named Shchegolev were in charge of weighing doses of poison. However, Mairanovsky himself mixed poisons with food. If poison did not cause death, Mairanovsky injected it using a syringe.'[7]

Peter Deriabin was not right about the laboratory *not* being reactivated. What happened is typically described in the professional jargon as double compartmenting, i.e. spoofing the original group who held the information into believing the operation has ended while it was simply moved to a new compartment. Indeed, the deadly experiments continued after the laboratory was officially 'closed down' as part of the Department of Operational Equipment (OOT). After

Mairanovsky's arrest, it resurfaced as Laboratory No. 12 of the 5th Special Department. Now Vladimir Naumov directed the research and poisons were successfully used for executions outside Russia.

In March 1953, days after Stalin's death, Minister of State Security Semyon Ignatyev reported to the new collective Soviet leadership of Malenkov, Molotov, Bulganin and Khrushchev:

> The execution of [Wolfgang] Salus – Trotsky's secretary in 1930 – was conducted with the help of an MGB agent, who gave him a special substance on 13 February 1953. The substance causes the death of a person in 10–12 days. After this Salus got sick and died on 4 March in one of Munich's hospitals. Using different sources it was ascertained that the poisoning of Salus did not cause any suspicion of the adversary. Doctors came to the conclusion that his death was a result of pneumonia.[8]

When I mentioned this episode in an article published in the *Wall Street Journal,*[9] a valuable tip-off came from a reader: the MGB agent who poisoned Salus in Munich was Otto Freitag. Indeed, according to well-documented research published by the German author Hermann Bubke, the East German intelligence service sent Freitag on a secret mission to Munich in 1949. In 1951 he successfully infiltrated the Trotskyite movement that was considered 'very dangerous' – long after the murder of Trotsky himself – by the paranoid Stalinist clique. In 1953 through his East Berlin masters, Freitag received Moscow's orders to 'liquidate' Trotsky's former secretary by poisoning him with a substance provided by the special lab. As can be seen from Minister Ignatyev's report, the operation went as planned.

A year later, in 1954, Freitag was assigned to prepare the kidnapping of General Reinhard Gehlen, then head of the Gehlen Organization, the 'Org' that became the West German Intelligence Service, BND (*Bundesnachrichtendienst*). The MGB had a top-ranking mole inside the Org, Heinz Felfe, who in 1953 moved up to the Org's Pullach Headquarters to oversee, first as deputy and from early 1957 as chief, the BND's whole counter-intelligence effort against the Soviets.[10]

Perhaps to avoid exposing Felfe's activities, the kidnap operation was called off.

After ten years on his undercover mission, Freitag returned to East Berlin to take part in the propaganda campaign against the West and further served as an 'officer in the special employment' (ObE) at the Stasi headquarters.

In the 1950s and 1960s the 'products' of the Special Laboratory, now under Naumov and called Lab X in internal documents, were used against 'enemies of the people' who lived in Europe in exile. In February 1954 Nikolai Khokhlov was sent to Frankfurt am Main to organise the assassination of a prominent anti-Soviet activist by shooting him with a poisoned bullet from a gun concealed in a packet of cigarettes. In September 1957 Khokhlov, who had turned himself in and begun working for the CIA, was poisoned while attending a conference in

Frankfurt. A month later Lev Rebet, a Ukrainian immigrant was poisoned by a Russian operative named Bogdan Stashinsky. In October 1959 one of the leaders of the Ukrainian anti-communist opposition, Stepan Bandera, was poisoned entering his house in Munich. Stashinky subsequently defected to tell the West German authorities all about the Rebet and Bandera assassinations that he had carried out, and the German Supreme Court officially recognised that in both murders the Soviet government was the guilty party.

In 1963 'direct actions', a euphemism used by the KGB to describe such questionable activities as shooting, poisoning, blowing up and subversion, were handed over to the newly formed Department T, and two years later to Department V (as for 'victory') of the First Chief Directorate (FCD) of the KGB with a capability to plan and mount special operations of a quasi-military nature.

In October 1964 a West German anti-bugging specialist, engineer Horst Schwinkmann, was sent to Moscow to discover and remove KGB bugging and recording devices planted in the West German embassy. His techniques caused aural pain to those listening in, and this irritated the KGB. When Schwinkmann was admiring religious relics at the Troitse-Sergeyeva Lavra in Zagorsky Monastery outside Moscow, he was shot in the buttocks with a nitrogen-based mustard gas capsule. The attack, though excruciatingly painful, was apparently not meant to kill but to punish Schwinkmann, so he survived – although, according to some accounts, he almost lost his leg.

In 1978 Laboratory No. 12, which had hugely expanded, became the Central Scientific Research Institute for Special Technology attached to the Operational Technical Directorate (OTU) of the KGB. It was here in the OTU that the notorious assassination umbrella was produced and tested.

However, five years before the tragic events in London and a year *after* the Soviet Union signed the Biological and Toxin Weapons Convention, a quasi-civil entity was established under the Main Microbiological Industry Agency (Glavmikrobioprom). It became known as Biopreparat. Under the cover of a civilian pharmaceutical and vaccine company, Biopreparat was in fact in charge of biological weapons research and production, consisting of some forty facilities that included a dozen major complexes. The staff was more or less evenly divided between development of new weapons and work on cures and antidotes. Both the KGB and GRU (Russian military intelligence) were using the Biopreparat 'product' and contributing to its requirements. Directorate 15 of the General Staff of the Soviet Army directed the military part of the operation.

According to Western sources, at one time the Soviet Union had the world's largest biological warfare program with somewhere between 25,000 and 32,000 people employed in a network of twenty to thirty military and civilian laboratories and research institutions. An additional 10,000 or so worked in defence ministry bioweapons laboratories. Some commentators give a figure of at least forty-seven labs and test facilities scattered across Russia, employing more than 40,000 workers, 9,000 of whom were scientists. Between 1,000 to 2,000 of those scientists were experts on deadly pathogens.

In 1989, the first defector to emerge from Biopreparat, Vladimir Pasechnik, revealed that the Soviet biological warfare effort was ten times larger than estimated by US or British intelligence. And in 1992 Dr Kanatjan Alibekov (Ken Alibek) defected, providing new details of Moscow's extensive biological and toxicological weapons development programme. Dr Alibek, who at the time of writing works as a biodefence consultant and entrepreneur, wrote a highly classified study of the Soviet biological weapons programme for the United States government. Other defectors have provided additional information to Western intelligence agencies.

In September 1992 an article entitled 'Poisoned Policy' written by Dr Vil Mirzayanov and another chemist, Lev Fyodorov, appeared in the *Moscow News*. Mirzaynov wrote:

> I decided to make another attempt to expose before the public eye the hypocrisy of the military-industrial complex, which, on the eve of the signing of a Government convention to ban chemical weapons, developed a new type of chemical weapon five to eight times stronger than all known weapons.

Eighteen months later he was arrested and placed in Lefortovo prison. Referring to the Mirzayanov trial, US Ambassador Thomas Pickering said in Moscow that it seemed 'strange to us . . . that someone could either be prosecuted or persecuted for telling the truth about an activity which is contrary to a treaty obligation of a foreign government'. On 11 March 1994 Russia's Prosecutor General dropped all charges against the scientist.

In February, after Mirzayanov's release from prison, General Nikolai Golushko, director of the Federal Counterintelligence Service, a 75,000-person agency that replaced the Second Chief Directorate (SCD) of the KGB and was to become the FSB, answered a question about organisational changes in the Operational and Technology Directorate (formerly in charge of Lab X). He told the journalist Yevgenia Albats:

> We now have two such directorates. The scientific-technical directorate includes institutes for the design of special technology and intelligence equipment. The scientific-technological directorate, along with the designers and the institutes, numbers about ten thousand people. We also work for intelligence and help the Ministry of Internal Affairs. Through the second of these directorates, Operations and Technology, we carry out operational and technical activity with the sanctions of the procurator – and, today, in compliance with the new Constitution and the courts.[11]

These words should be remembered in connection with the Litvinenko case and the new law approved by the Russian parliament in July 2006 that allows the president to sanction operations, including murder on foreign soil, against the enemies of the regime. The question is, who decides that one is 'the enemy'? That must be the president himself.

Poisons never stopped fascinating Soviet and Russian leaders from Lenin to Putin. Pavel Sudoplatov recalled what KGB Major General Vasili Shadrin had told him in 1988 about Mikhail Gorbachev's interest in the special laboratory. The last Soviet president and the father of *perestroika* read an article by former KGB chairman Vladimir Semichasny in the popular *Ogonyok* magazine. In it, Semichastny reported that then Soviet leader Leonid Brezhnev had hinted to him in the 1960s that it would perhaps be easier to poison Khrushchev than oust him from power. Gorbachev's KGB chief, Victor Chebrikov, summoned Semichasny to his office and ordered him to report in writing on experiments with poisons and on Brezhnev's alleged remarks. Semichasny, however, refused to provide any written statement.[12]

Valery Butuzov was a career intelligence officer and a KGB colonel who in the early 1990s worked in Department 12 of Directorate S ('Illegals') at the Soviet (later Russian) intelligence headquarters in Yasenevo and was temporarily assigned to Bio-preparat. Colonel Kanatjan Alibekov (Ken Alibek), who just succeeded General Anatoly Vorobyov as the deputy director of the establishment, recalled how in the spring of 1990 Butuzov walked into his office seeking professional advice.

'I'm looking for something that will work with a gadget I've designed,' said the KGB colonel. 'Let's say we put this assembly into a tiny box, maybe an empty pack of Marlboro, and then find a way to put the pack under someone's desk, or in his trash basket. If we were then to set it in motion, the aerosol should do the job right away, wouldn't it?'[13]

When Alibekov said that would depend on the substance used, Butuzov asked what would be best in order to kill. Butuzov was thinking of 'something like Ebola'. (Ebola is the common term for a group of viruses and for the disease that they cause, Ebola hemorrhagic fever. Because Ebola is lethal and since no approved vaccine or treatment is available, Ebola is classified as a Category A bioterrorism agent.) Alibekov mused, 'That would work. But you'd have a high probability of killing not just this person, but everyone around him.'

'That wouldn't matter' was Butuzov's reply, upon which Alibekov asked if this was merely theoretical or if Butuzov had someone in mind.

'No one in particular,' he said. 'Well, maybe there is one person – Gamsakhurdia, for example.'[14] Zviad Gamsakhurdia was the new president of Georgia and had long opposed Moscow's policies toward his country, had pushed for independence and led a demonstration against the bloody Soviet repression in 1989 of a demonstration in Tbilisi that left nineteen people dead.

Several months later, Alibekov asked Butuzov, 'What happened to that idea of yours, you know, the one about the watch battery and Gamsakhurdia?'

'Oh, that,' Butuzov chuckled, 'well, to tell you the truth, it never really got anywhere. We had a plan prepared but the bosses finally turned it down. They said it wasn't the right time.'

Soon thereafter Gamsakhurdia was replaced as president of Georgia by Eduard Shevardnadze, and on 31 December 1993 died in mysterious circumstances while trying to get back into power. Though it was said to be a suicide, some claimed agents from Moscow had murdered him.[15]

It is perhaps pertinent that according to Alexander Kouzminov, who had served for almost ten years with Butuzov in the same department, the colonel had been awarded the Order of the Red Banner for a 'clandestine combat operation'.

I recalled this episode when answering a question from the Georgian newspaper *Sakartvelos Respublika* in late August 2008, in the middle of the Russian-Georgian crisis. Do you think that the same thing might happen to President Mikhail Saakashvili as happened to the Ukrainian President Victor Yushchenko and Alexander Litvinenko? (My interviewer, Iya Merkviladze, had in mind an assassination attempt on the life of the then Ukrainian presidential candidate in 2004 that left him disfigured from dioxin poisoning and the murder of the former KGB/FSB officer Alexander Litvinenko with polonium-laced tea in London in 2006.) I answered, certainly, these are Moscow's methods and advised President Saakashvili to apply to the British SAS and the French SPHP (*Service de Protection des Hautes Personnalités*) for assistance. The interview was published in Tbilisi on 3 September.

For almost a year, between 2004 and 2005, I tried to squeeze from Markus 'Misha' Wolf, the legendary former chief of East German intelligence, some drops of information about former East German spies in Austria and the UK and about East German-Russian intelligence collaboration in general. 'Iron Misha' leisurely but very politely responded in decent English, but never provided any information. When I asked about the Jenapharm company that allegedly produced special and highly sophisticated pharmaceutical preparations not only for the needs of Wolf's directorate but also for Russia, this true-born spymaster briefly remarked: 'Read my book.' I followed his advice. Wolf wrote:

> I knew . . . that even after Stalin's death, the Soviets still had a department
> that developed bizarre ways of killing enemies. Even within the KGB the
> existence of this department was a closely guarded secret. In addition to
> murdering Bandera with a poisoned bullet [*sic*, it was a lethal gas], the KGB
> assassinated the defector Truchnovich [*sic*, Dr Alexander Trushnovich, and he
> was *not* a defector], the head of the Russian emigrant organization the
> National Workers Union [*sic*, it should be People's Labour Union], in Berlin,
> while attempting to kidnap him. One KGB man was dispatched to buyers
> throughout the Eastern bloc bearing wares such as untraceable nerve toxins

and skin contact poisons to smear on doorknobs. The only thing I ever accepted from him was a sachet of 'truth drugs', which he touted as 'unbeatable' with the enthusiasm of a door-to-door salesman. For years they lay in my personal safe. One day, in a fit of curiosity, I asked our carefully vetted doctor to have them analysed for me. He came back shaking his head in horror. 'Use them without constant medical supervision and there is every chance that the fellow from whom you want the truth will be dead as a dodo in seconds,' he said. We never did use the 'truth drugs'.[16]

One needed to know General Wolf, who had a fascinating 33-year-long career (1953–86) in the intelligence service, on a personal level to understand that the above is a mixture of rumour, fantasy and exaggeration. The old spymaster had a wonderful sense of humour that, I guess, never left him. In reality, seen from the multiple documentary sources, defectors' testimonies and explanations of those who were directly involved in the programme, Russia's murder poisons have always been considered as an extremely dangerous and efficient weapon by Western experts. Suffice it to say that in 2006, when Litvinenko was dying on his hospital bed, no one in Britain had a slightest idea of what was killing him. It must be said, though, that not a single special operations professional or, to that matter, a chemical, biological or radiological weapons (CBRW) specialist was ever invited to examine Litvinenko while he was still alive.

Obviously, there are conventional poisons like cyanide and many others that could easily be identified during an autopsy or even at a glance by a trained eye, whereas special poisons like ricin or abrin produced specifically for military or intelligence use are very difficult or impossible to diagnose or detect.

The Russian intelligence service's choice of a particular type of substance always depends on the precise effect that is to be reached. Putting aside a strict scientific classification of the 'operational means' produced by the Russian secret laboratories, I propose for the sake of clarity to group them in two categories: 'soft' chemicals and deadly poisons.

'Soft' chemicals are not designed to kill. To this category belongs the serum that Markus Wolf described. It was SP-17, a psychotropic drug that induces a person to share his most deeply hidden secrets with his interlocutor. It loosens the tongue and has no smell, taste or colour and no known side effects. And, according to Alexander Kouzminov, a KGB/SVR officer who worked with the drug, a person exposed to it has no recollection of ever having had a 'heart-to-heart' talk. It is sometimes used during covert interrogations, like that of Gordievsky or of the double defector Vitaly Yurchenko, but more often to test illegals, especially when they return from the first overseas familiarisation trip. SP-17 may also be administered to field agents when they come home for furlough or a briefing. Kouzminov claims that he found evidence of the use of the 'truth drug' in almost all the operational files of illegals and special agents of his department (chemical and biological espionage and subversion) to which he had access in a period of eight years.[17] This former officer of the Directorate S testifies:

> These operations were always held in conditions where there were no distractions. Department 12 carried them out in operational conspiracy apartments [*sic*, safe-houses] usually in Moscow or East Berlin. Officers of the department invited the Illegal or other agent for a friendly dinner 'among our own people' and a grandiose drinking of spirits. At a suitable moment, SP-17 was administered, mixed into the contents of one of the bottles. In order to avoid an accidental overdose, and to control the condition of the 'drunkard' (i.e. the secretly interrogated person), there was always – either in the adjacent room or among the actual 'warm, friendly company' – a medical doctor to neutralize the 'medicine' quickly. If, later on, the interrogated person still tried to recall why he so quickly became drunk, he was shown 'evidence' of the 'wild party' – empty bottles in profusion, sufficient to prove they were drunk all night. We found and used a few other situations in which we could secretly apply the drug – in the sauna, while picnicking, etc. – and, in those circumstances, the episode of 'sleepiness' could be explained as sun stroke, intoxication from the fumes, hot weather, fatigue, etc.[18]

In a way, SP-17 is the legacy of Mairanovsky. For Mairanovsky had not simply worked out how to kill people quickly and without trace, he had also noticed that when he administered the chemical mix he called 'Injection C', victims displayed a tendency to talk and answer questions during the twenty-four hours before they died. He wrote:

> This led me to think that perhaps the mix could be used on suspects during the course of an investigation, to obtain what we call greater openness from suspects during interrogations. It could have been extremely useful . . . with those prisoners who too energetically refused to admit their guilt.'[19]

Mairanovsky was denied the chance to test these theories fully; other 'doctors' carried on the experiments.

'Soft' remedies are also used to frighten the victim, or to incapacitate him or her temporarily to prevent a particular activity. They may also be used as sleep-inducing agents, or in specific operational circumstances to simulate death. Kouzminov recalls an episode of using a malodorous preparation against an agent who was not willing to continue collaboration with his Moscow handlers after being deployed in the West.

And I remember a 'frightening' chemical used against me in Vienna in the spring of 2006.

Fortunately on that day I did not eat or drink anything at all before meeting in a prearranged place – the café Tirolerhof on Führichgasse near the State Opera – an Austrian businessman whom I had long suspected to be a KGB agent or collaborator. Following KGB practice, he pretended to have made this Kaffeehaus his usual meeting place. Indeed, we met with him there at least twice and I was stupid enough to break an important rule that I had learned during my own intelligence training: never become a regular in any particular place. We discussed trivial matters, drank coffee (I also had a glass of tap water) and parted. I went home. Three hours later I felt terrible: vomiting, diarrhoea, weakness and body temperature jumping from 35 degrees to almost 40. I could not sleep that night and my caring wife did her very best to make me feel better. I did not take any medicine and never called a physician, knowing that a civilian doctor would not be able to help. In the morning I felt relieved and by midday was as healthy as before. There was no trace of any disease left. Later I consulted a specialist professor who confirmed that this was a typical case of poisoning by a purpose-made chemical.

A Stapo (Austrian security police) officer visited my house at the end of November while I was away, perhaps to make sure that I knew what had really happened (the story of the Austrian police collaboration with the KGB is legendary), and openly warned my family that the police would not welcome a case of polonium poisoning in their area. My son asked, is this a warning or a threat? In reply, the police officer left a card with his name and telephone number and left. I never called him.

In 2004 Anna Politkovskaya, a crusading Moscow journalist, was poisoned on her way to North Ossetia. At the time of writing, many aspects of the Beslan school hostage crises are still in dispute but this tragedy is well documented. Armed Chechen rebels had kept 1,128 people including 777 children hostages for three days demanding from President Putin to put an end to the Second Chechen War. On the third day the Russian Special Forces stormed the building using tanks, 'Bumblebee' rocket launchers with thermobaric and incendiary warheads, and other heavy weapons, leaving 186 children and 148 adults dead and 728 civilians wounded. Twelve men from the special troops also perished during the storm. Chechen separatist warlord Shamil Basayev, who took responsibility for the hostage taking, blamed the outcome on the Russian president. Politkovskaya was hurrying to Beslan to stop the bloodshed:

It is the morning of September 1. Reports from North Ossetia are hard to believe: a school in Beslan has been seized. Half an hour to pack my things as my mind works furiously on how to get to the Caucasus. And another thought: to look for the Chechen separatist leader, Aslan Maskhadov, let him come out of hiding, let him go to the hostage takers, and then ask them to free the children.

Then followed a long evening at Vnukovo airport. Crowds of journalists were trying to get on a plane south, just as flights were being postponed. Obviously, there are some people who would like to delay our departure. I use my mobile and speak openly about the purpose of my flight: 'Look for Maskhadov', 'persuade Maskhadov'.

We have long stopped talking over our phones openly, assuming they are tapped. But this is an emergency. Eventually a man introduces himself as an airport executive: 'I'll put you on a flight to Rostov.' In the minibus, the driver tells me that the Russian security service, the FSB, told him to put me on the Rostov flight. As I board, my eyes meet those of three passengers sitting in a group: malicious eyes, looking at an enemy. But I don't pay attention. This is the way most FSB people look at me.

The plane takes off. I ask for a tea. It is many hours by road from Rostov to Beslan and war has taught me that it's better not to eat. At 21:50 I drink it. At 22:00 I realise that I have to call the air stewardess as I am rapidly losing consciousness. My other memories are scrappy: the stewardess weeps and shouts: 'We're landing, hold on!'

'Welcome back,' said a woman bending over me in Rostov regional hospital. The nurse tells me that when they brought me in I was 'almost hopeless'. Then she whispers: 'My dear, they tried to poison you.' All the tests taken at the airport have been destroyed – on orders 'from on high', say the doctors.'[20]

Anna was finally shot and murdered in her apartment block in Moscow in October 2006. As expected, at the time of writing the investigation has not moved forward since then. At least they established that the day of the assassination was very special. Somebody had given Putin a birthday present.

On 24 November 2006, less than twenty-four hours after Litvinenko was pronounced dead, Yegor Gaidar, a former Russian prime minister, was poisoned during his visit to Dublin.

'Doctors don't see a natural reason for the poisoning and they have not been able to detect any natural substance known to them in Mr Gaidar's body,' said his spokesman. 'So obviously we're talking about poisoning [and] it was not natural poisoning.'

There is little doubt that Gaidar was used as a pawn just to divert initial attention from Litvinenko. Among the illegals it is known as *imitatsiya*. Obviously, no one was going to kill him but I well remember the *Evening Standard* with a banner-headline on the front page NEW RUSSIAN POISON VICTIM bringing additional mystery to the case. As predicted, it did not last long as the former prime minister was not poisoned to die, just as Anna Politkovskaya was almost certainly not poisoned to die in 2004. In her case, she was incapacitated so as not to reach Beslan.[21] Gaidar was poisoned to mislead the media and the public. As simple as that.

* * *

The second big group are deadly poisons with different toxicity ratings (almost always as high as 5 or 6 – the top marks) that fall under three categories: chemical agents, biological agents and radiological weapons. This arsenal has been constantly refined over the years as advancing science opens new possibilities and as Kremlin leaders develop new requirements. Whenever a new type of poison is used, like the dioxin 2,3,7,8-TCDD-based preparation in the Yushchenko case or polonium-210-based jelly in the Litvinenko case, it is being catalogued and studied by Western experts.

Whenever police investigate crimes where Moscow's hand can be traced or suspected, several 'signature indications' invariably bear the hallmark 'Made in Russia' at the crime scene. First of all, the substance used must make the victim's death or illness appear natural or at least produce symptoms that will baffle doctors and forensic investigators. To this end the *Kamera* developed its defining speciality: combining known poisons into original and untraceable forms.

Second, the poisonous agent is always 'tailor-made' like a bespoke suit from London's famous Savile Row. Those agents are also 'bespoke' as they are first discussed in every detail and then tailored for the specific target in a well-planned and oft-rehearsed environment.

Finally, the operation will always be carried out in such a way that the victim's self-defence instincts or vigilance will be minimised, so that he will not be expecting treachery and may even not see or remember the poisoner. All the cases described in this book follow this pattern.

Because of all the publicity and speculation about the Litvinenko case, I must emphasise that assassination by poisoning is a covert operation. It has to be carried out clandestinely, without any public knowledge or reaction. It is never designed to *demonstrate* anything, only to kill the victim, quietly and unobtrusively. In all cases of the Russian poisonings that I have studied during many years, this was an unbreakable principle.

As a rule, chance plays an important role in uncovering a crime and its perpetrator. Seventy years ago a box of candies found in an abandoned hotel room helped to reconstruct the murder of a Russian dissident.

In the summer of 1937 the NKVD mounted a wide-scale operation in Europe to find and liquidate Ignatz Reiss, an important *illegal rezident* (a station chief residing in a target country and operating without the protection of diplomatic immunity) who had defected to the Trotskyites in Paris. As usual, several groups were involved. One of them, headed by Sergei Efron, the husband of a famous Russian poet, Marina Tsvetayeva, handed a box of strychnine-poisoned chocolates to a Swiss NKVD agent named Renate Steiner with the instruction to bring them to Switzerland where the Reiss family was hiding. On 4 September, Gertrude Schildbach, a family friend and an NKVD German agent, was to hand over these poisoned chocolates to Reiss's wife and their little child, but her nerve failed. She had enough courage, however, to invite her old friend, Ignatz, for a dinner in a restaurant near Lausanne. It was a trap. When they went out late in the evening, Reiss was pushed into the car, shot and killed and his bullet-ridden body dumped on the side of a road in Chamblandes. The police found the poisoned chocolates and were able to retrace the whole operation and identify most of its participants. Unfortunately, they had flown to Russia before they could be arrested.

* * *

In modern chemical weapons there are five classes: nerve agents, blistering agents (vesicants), cyanide, pulmonary agents and riot-control agents.

Most nerve agents are initially in a liquid form that subsequently evaporates and becomes gas and vapour. They can be inhaled, ingested or placed on skin. The LD_{50} (median lethal dose, or dose of a poison that will kill 50 per cent of those exposed) is given in milligrams (mg) for a person weighing 140 pounds.

G-type nerve agents are clear, colourless liquids that are volatile at ambient temperature. They mix in water and most organic solvents, and evaporate at the same rate as water. The odour, when there is one, does not provide adequate warning time. Effects and symptoms are much the same for all the agents. The severity depends on which gas was used, density of the vapour or liquid, and length of exposure. Muscle spasms followed by flaccid muscle paralysis are classic symptoms.

Nerve agents are generally absorbed by eye contact and inhalation, and produce rapid, systemic effects. The liquid is absorbed through the skin, but it may take several minutes for effects to appear.

In severe attacks, the central nervous system collapses, causing violent seizures, confusion, and coma.[22]

Moscow, February 8, 2003 No. 1 Dubrovskaya Street, now known to the whole world as Dubrovka. In a packed theatre . . . there is an exuberant gala atmosphere. Black tie, evening dress, the whole of the political *beau monde* has assembled here. Sighs and gasps, kisses and hugs, members of the government, members of the Duma, leaders of the parliamentary factions and parties, a sumptuous buffet . . .

[Several dozen terrorists from Chechnya] hoped to force President Putin to put an end to the Second Chechen War and withdraw his troops from their republic.

They didn't succeed. Nobody withdrew from anywhere. The war continues as before, with no time for doubts about the legitimacy of its methods. All that changed was that in the early morning of October 26 [2002] a gas attack was mounted against all those present in the [theatre] building, some 800 people, both terrorists and hostages. The secret military gas was chosen by the President personally. The gas attack was followed by the storming of the building by special anti-terrorist units in the course of which every one of the hostage-takers was killed, along with almost 200 hostages. Many people died without medical attention, and the identity of the gas was kept secret even from the doctors charged with the saving of lives.[23]

Vesicants or blistering agents produce skin and mucous membrane irritation, blistering, and then necrosis. In the arsenal of the Russian services, however, there are substances probably based on the venom of some jellyfish that cause severe chest and abdominal pain, difficulty swallowing, skin necrosis, and respiratory and cardiac depression leading to death. According to Kalugin, in the early 1970s a KGB agent rubbed a jelly on Alexander Solzhenitsyn in a store in Russia making him violently ill. In that case, the author of *The Gulag Archipelago* survived.

Agatha Christie frequently killed off her victims with poisons, and cyanide was one of her favourites. In Russia, potassium cyanide is, perhaps, one of the best-known poisons. However, KGB assassins in the early 1920s and 1930s preferred to use prussic acid as it mimics heart attacks.

Pulmonary agents are used in military operations.

Riot-control agents also come under the heading of chemical warfare and include several types of tear gas.

* * *

Biological weapons use toxins from microorganisms, such as viruses or bacteria, to injure or incapacitate people. Odourless, tasteless and invisible to the naked eye, biological agents can be disseminated easily. There is also potential for a greater toxicity than with chemical weapons. This group includes anthrax that became widely known in recent times after the terrorist attacks in the United States in 2001. In April 1979 in Sverdlovsk weapons-grade anthrax was accidentally released into the air from a Soviet biological warfare facility. At least 94 people were infected, of whom at least 68 died. One victim died four days after the release, ten over an eight-day period at the peak of the deaths, and the last six weeks later. Immediately the KGB was engaged in extensive cover-ups and destruction of records that continued for almost fifteen years until Russian President Boris Yeltsin admitted this accident and let a combined US-Russian team investigate what happened.

Other biological agents that can be used as weapons are – just to mention a few – ricin, smallpox, tularaemia and Ebola.

* * *

A radiological, or nuclear, weapon is defined as any weapon using a radioactive or radiation-emitting source as the primary source of destruction. Walter Litvinenko, Sasha's father, was absolutely right when he said that a miniscule nuclear bomb had killed his son – a product of Russian nanotechnology. Besides polonium-210, that gained worldwide infamy after the London poisoning in 2006, other radiological poisons may be built from harmful amounts of thallium-201, cesium-137 as well as radioactive forms of plutonium, americium and curium. The death of Roman Tsepov in St Petersburg on 24 September 2004 was without doubt a result of radiological poisoning. No autopsy records have ever been released.

Symptoms of radiological poisoning depend, among other factors, on how much radiation is received and how one is exposed. Symptoms include: nausea and vomiting; diarrhoea; extensive weakness and fatigue; loss of appetite; fainting; dehydration; inflammation of tissues; bleeding from the nose, mouth, gums or rectum; low red blood cell count (anaemia); and hair loss. Large doses of radiation can cause extensive damage to the cells and result in cell death.

Evidently the physicians in Barnet Hospital and University College London Hospital hadn't read the right books. Until after his death the cause of Alexander Litvinenko's illness was never diagnosed.

Vladimir Bobrenyov, a former investigator at the Russian general prosecutor's office, who had access to many secret documents and had made a lengthy study of the Mairanovsky case, said that not one of the people who worked in the poison laboratory died of natural causes. According to Bobrenyov, 'They hanged themselves, shot themselves, drank themselves to death, or ended up dying in mental institutions.'

Those were the days

Bingo! Weeded and pillaged Austrian archives finally produced several important documents. The archives themselves are spread around the Austrian capital's numbered districts and are as clean and well taken care of as Vienna's proud and self-assured first district, the heart of the city. After the war and during the Soviet occupation, Russian spies like former Major Hans Nielke, who worked in the State Archive, and their collaborators virtually rid the depositories of all valuable documents that were stocked in boxed labelled 'Russian Espionage' in what looked like a well-coordinated mopping-up operation.

But they missed something. Among other papers there was a police report about the defection of the secretary of the Soviet Legation in Vienna, Mieczyslaw Jaroslawski.

His real name was Vladimir Stepanovich Nesterovich and he was a highly decorated Soviet officer, as a matter of fact, the chief of the Vienna station of the Russian military intelligence (GRU). After a career first in the Tsarist and then in the Red Army where he was last commanding the 9th Cavalry Division, Nesterovich graduated from the Military Academy and in 1923 was sent to Austria where he was in charge of organising espionage and subversion in the Balkans.

The turning point of his life happened in June 1924 when he absconded from his post and disappeared. Andrew Cook, a very well informed author,[1] claims in his book *On His Majesty's Secret Service* that Nesterovich (Jaroslawski) actually defected with a considerable sum of legation funds but that seems to be an influence of the Russian deception aimed at attributing larceny to and heaping dirt on every genuine defector. I am aware of only one case when Lev Nikolsky (better known as Alexander Orlov) indeed disappeared from his post in Spain during the civil war with an impressive bunch of money stolen from his station's safe. Ironically, the KGB, represented by Colonel Oleg Tsarev and assisted by the British journalist John Costello, decided to make Nikolsky a hero. And while Costello did it for fame and money, Tsarev was simply fulfilling the statutory job obligations.

Further evidence that Cook's supposition is wrong may be found in a letter allegedly written by Mikhail Trilisser, the then head of the Cheka foreign department (INO), dated 1 October 1925, and quoted by several Russian historians. The letter ties Jaroslawski to a famous British spy, Sidney Reilly. Amazingly, Cook also refers to an English translation of this letter that he obviously saw in the SIS archives (*Reilly Papers: CX 2616*):

Top secret
No number/PL
1 October 1925
Dear comrade
On 29 September [1925] while crossing the boarder we arrested the Englishman, Sidney Georgiyevich Reilly, who sneaked into Leningrad from Finland with a forged passport in the name of Nikolai Mikhailovich [Cook's version *Nikolas Nikolaivich*] Steinberg; two of his companions were killed during shootout. Reilly was heavily wounded.

As a result of investigation it transpired that Jaroslawski had maintained long-term secret relations with Reilly, and that he had asked Reilly to retrieve valuables of his located in Leningrad. Reilly was captured in possession of these valuables.

It is necessary to establish:
1. When the relations between Jaroslawski and Reilly began.
2. How and through whom they liaised.
3. What Jaroslawski could communicate to the British and Americans via Reilly in Vienna, Berlin or Moscow.
4. Who the companions of Reilly were and what they had to do with Jaroslawski.
5. To investigate and find out plans of the wife of Sidney Reilly.
You are obliged to accept this assignment as the top priority.
With communist greetings, *M. Trilisser*[2]

Apart from obvious discrepancies and evident lies, even Alexander Kolpakidi and Dmitry Prokhorov, whose books are packed with factual errors, quickly recognised the letter as a forgery. Actually nothing in this 'top secret message' is true, not even the details of the arrest of Reilly but it is demonstrative that a fake found its way to the British, as it was intended to.

This document was produced and distributed, without doubt sold to Frank Foley, the SIS officer in Berlin, by its real author who introduced himself as Mikhail Georgiyevich Sumarokov, a former Cheka operative from Ukraine.

Sumarokov, whose real name was Pyotr Mikhailovich Karpov, worked in the Soviet Legation in Berlin until 1 August 1924 when he decided to stay in the West. Soon he joined Vladimir Grigoriyevich Orlov, the former chief of intelligence of General Wrangel's army, who set up the whole forgery workshop. It was a profitable business in the 1920s and 1930s and a mass of faked documents landed in the intelligence headquarters of Berlin, London, Paris and Tokyo. Sumarokov brought out with him what became perhaps the most valuable of Orlov's treasures: a genuine register of the Kharkov Cheka for 1922. As a Russian mole inside the Orlov organisation reported to Moscow, when Orlov wanted to register newly created correspondence, he simply inserted an additional page between the real ones.

Nigel West, a British intelligence historian who collaborated with Tsarev on a book project and was given some selected snippets from the KGB Orlov's file (*The Orlov Archives*, File No. 30633), writes that

> admittedly some of the material supplied by Orlov and his friends was of quite high quality and, according to A-3 [the Soviet mole], Orlov possessed the signatures of Bustrem, Trilisser, Yevdokimov, Ausern, Rakovsky, Proskurov and Smirnov. 'The forgeries look very real,' wrote A-3. 'The signatures are extremely well imitated by Orlov's assistant, the former public prosecutor, [Alexander] Kolberg. Their authenticity was enhanced by the fact that Orlov, an experienced specialist, managed to convey the very essence of the style of Soviet correspondence.' Doubtless Orlov and his friends were also responsible for the notorious Trilisser letters . . .[3]

Nesterovich said that he left the GRU because of political differences with the regime. Very soon it became clear that a person who was in charge of all Soviet covert operations in the Balkans had every reason to do that. On 16 April 1925 the Bulgarian communists under the leadership of the Comintern, which was nothing else but the Cheka-GRU branch of the Soviet secret service, planted a bomb in the Sveta Nedelya cathedral in Sofia aiming to finish off the entire political leadership of Bulgaria under the Premier Alexander Tsankov in one blow.

Miraculously, with 123 dead and several hundred wounded, not a single government official appeared to have been hurt and Tsankov started merciless purges of the members of the Peasants' and Communist parties. That was quite a surprise for Moscow where it was expected that immediately after the explosion the communists would start an uprising and eventually seize the power. The miscalculation led to very tense relations with Bulgaria who only established diplomatic relations with the USSR in 1934.

Having left Vienna, Nesterovich moved to Berlin where he visited the French consul to ask for political asylum in exchange for information. He was taken seriously and the consul sent Nesterovich to the French occupation headquarters in Mainz under the command of Generals Mangin and Fayolle. He was quartered in military barracks until the final decision came from Paris.

Some Russian sources assert that Nesterovich also contacted the British intelligence but I have all reasons to doubt it. Soon Trilisser sent out orders to find the defector and dispose of him.

On 6 August 1925, Nesterovich left his secure shelter and went to a nearby café. He had spent enough time in the city to notice a peculiar feature of the place. Some of the street signs were painted blue while others were red. French officers explained to him that it was done especially to help the garrison men find their way back to the barracks as they knew that the red signs led to the Rhine and the blue ones ran parallel to the river.

The Russian was not afraid of getting lost. Most certainly, exactly like Litvinenko, he felt quite secure but was a little depressed being in a foreign town on his own. So he was glad when he met two Germans who were very friendly and joined him for a beer. One of them, Gustav Golke, was a Comintern official and an assassin. Nesterovich was poisoned and died.

It may be a coincidence but in Moscow Golke lived on 3rd Meschanskaya Street quite near one of the laboratories that was working to produce new poisons for the predecessor of the KGB. In 1921 he married Ruth Fischer, a famous German communist and a sister of Hans and Gerhart Eisler. Both these brothers worked for Soviet intelligence and for some time Gerhart headed its illegal network in the United States. In February 1948 *Newsweek* described him as 'Number One Red Agent' in the USA.

In March 2008 MI5 released information about Gerhart Eisler to the National Archives. The file summary states:

> Eisler, who was supposed by many to be the covert leader and director of the Communist Party in America during and after the Second World War, became the centre of a diplomatic incident in 1949 when, having stowed away on a Polish ship out of New York, he was forcibly removed and arrested in Southampton. This file documents the Security Service's involvement in the case. The earliest traces of Eisler in the file (KV 2/2773, 1936-1949) date from 1936, when Comintern efforts to secure a false American passport in the name of Edwards were reported. In 1947 information obtained from Eisler's former wife, Hedwiga [Hede] Massing, suggested that Eisler had used this cover name in New York in 1934.

Massing was herself a Russian spy and courier who later left her NKVD employ and moved to the USA.

In the early hours of 30 April 1937 a police van nicknamed 'Voronok' (small raven) in Russia (like the 'Black Maria' in Britain) stopped near the house no. 58/60 at 3rd Meschanskaya. A former OMS (the acronym stood for 'International Liaison Department', used as the Comintern's intelligence service) official, Golke knew better not to ask why he was being arrested. He received the usual verdict and was shot as a German spy and member of a terrorist organisation (this time Stalin's henchmen were right) on 30 November of the same year.

***

A lot of murderers and murders were spattering the European landscape, largely unseen and unrecognised by the public that was under assault.

Like Golke, Ignati Gintowt-Dzewaltowski worked for the OMS, which was an intelligence service only lightly disguised, with foreign communists as most of its employees. Many party members and fellow travellers (Communist sympathisers) in the West were much more likely to respond to an appeal for help from the Communist International than to a direct approach from the Soviet intelligence. Some of the best OGPU and NKVD foreign agents in the 1930s believed initially that they were working for the Comintern.[4] In 1932 Trilisser, whose letters were so expertly forged by Orlov and his con artists, was transferred to the OMS as assistant to its chief. He was executed as an 'enemy of the people' in 1938.

Dzewaltowski was born into a noble Polish-Lithuanian family and like many representatives of intelligentsia of the period was captivated by the theories of Marx and Engels. According to one Russian source[5] whose authenticity I was not able to corroborate by cross-checking, Dzewaltowski actively participated in the Bolshevik rising in Petrograd (St Petersburg) and the storming of the Winter Palace in November 1917.

An anonymous eyewitness, who managed to escape, described those events to the *Guardian* in the following way:

> The Palace was pillaged and devastated from top to bottom by the Bolshevik armed mob, as though by a horde of barbarians. All the State papers were destroyed. Priceless pictures were ripped from their frames by bayonets. Several hundred carefully packed boxes of rare plate and china, which Kerensky had exerted himself to preserve, were broken open and the contents smashed or carried off. The library of Alexander III, the doors of which we had locked and sealed, and which we never entered, was forced open and ransacked, books and manuscripts burnt and destroyed. My study, formerly the Tsaritsa's salon, like all other rooms, was thrown into chaos. The colossal crystal lustre, with its artfully concealed music, was smashed to atoms. Desks, pictures, ornaments – everything was destroyed. I will refrain from describing the hideous scenes which took place in the wine-cellars, and the fate to which some of the captured women soldiers were submitted.[6]

At 10:00 a.m. on 25 October 1917 (Old Style) the Petrograd Military Revolutionary Committee proclaimed:

> To the citizens of Russia. The Provisional Government has been deposed. State power has passed into the hands of the organ of the Petrograd Soviet of Workers' and Soldiers' Deputies – the Revolutionary Military Committee, which heads the Petrograd proletariat and the garrison. The cause for which the people have fought, namely, the immediate offer of a democratic peace,

the abolition of landed proprietorship, workers' control over production, and the establishment of Soviet power – this cause has been secured. Long live the revolution of workers, soldiers and peasants![7]

With such a backdrop Dzewaltowski moved higher and higher in the new workers and peasants bureaucracy until he became – according to the same Russian source – the war minister of the Far Eastern Republic (DVR). This nominally independent state, established in Blagoveshchensk in April 1920 and headed by a communist, covered the former Russian Far East and Siberia east of Lake Baikal. The idea of the DVR was to create a buffer zone between Russia and the territories occupied by Japan. Soon Dzewaltowski became the foreign minister of the republic but after it appealed and was accepted by Russia to become its part in November 1922, he was sent to Rostov as the federal government's representative.

In May 1924 the former nobleman became one of the Comintern functionaries. That was no surprise, as they needed people with good pedigree and command of foreign languages. Almost immediately Dzewalkowski was sent to Vienna where he had studied before the revolution. It is possible that in Austria he replaced Nesterovich as, according to Kolpakidi and Prokhorov, he was put in charge of the Balkan operation. Russian authors state that Dzewaltowski reported to the OMS from Bulgaria signing his messages with the codename MARIAN.

However, at the end of 1924, shortly before the infamous explosion in the Sofia cathedral Dzewaltowski disappeared exactly like his predecessor.

It is interesting that the only informed party who understood what had happened to the Russian agent was Vladimir Orlov again. He immediately cooked up another forgery, also allegedly signed by Trilisser, where it was stated that Dzewalkowski defected to the Poles.

Almost certainly Orlov was right in his assumption and it was not until much later that the Russians learned exactly how he gained his quite unprecedented access to sensitive information. It turned out that Orlov's main preoccupation, apart from a workshop that brought him a modest return, was his active engagement in intelligence-gathering by secretly running a White Guard network of agents in Europe.

It is amazing that despite the number of 'confidential sources' in Orlov's organisation, the KGB only learned about his intelligence activities in 1945, when new information made it possible for them to build an accurate retrospective assessment of what Orlov had been up to twenty years earlier. Just as the Red Army started surrounding Berlin, slowly tightening its stranglehold on the remaining Nazi defenders, the head of the 9th Department of the NKGB's First Directorate, Grand Gukasov, reported in a note dated 23 April 1945 and addressed to the chief of Soviet foreign intelligence that in Belgium his officers had managed to seize the archives of the former chief of 'intelligence unit of the

Russian General Staff' and that they were sending those documents to Moscow.[8]

In November 1925, a year after Dzewalkowski fled to the West, émigré newspapers started to publish reports that he had indeed applied for political asylum to the Polish authorities.

No definite details emerged about exactly how the KGB managed to organise Dewaltowski's assassination, but in the collection of Vladimir Lvovich Burtsev in the State Archive of the Russian Federation (GARF) researchers found a note about Dzewaltowski. Burtsev wrote that a Soviet female agent poisoned him on orders from Moscow.

* * *

I learned a true story of the life of Baron Peter Nikolayevich Wrangel from his own memoirs first published in English in 1929, a year after his tragic death. The book is a wonderful expression of his love of Mother Russia and hatred of her autocratic leaders who came to power in November 1917.

In contrast to some modern-day Russian Army commanders, General Wrangel did not tolerate lawlessness or looting by his troops. He became commanding general of the entire Volunteer Army in December 1919. When a year later he was elected commander-in-chief of the White Guard forces in the Crimea, he instituted sweeping reforms together with a coalition government, and as a result the Crimea became the most economically prosperous of all Russian regions. He also recognised and established relations with the new anti-Bolshevik independent republics of Ukraine and Georgia.

The last commander-in-chief of the Russian National Army wrote in his memoirs:

> The Polish Army which has been fighting side by side with us against the common enemy of liberty and order has just laid down its arms and signed a preliminary peace with the oppressors and traitors who designate themselves the Soviet Government of Russia. We are now alone in the struggle, which will decide the fate not only of our country but also of the whole of humanity. Let us strive to free our native land from the yoke of this Red scum who recognize neither God nor country, who bring confusion and shame in their wake. By delivering Russia over to pillage and ruin, these infidels hope to start a world-wide conflagration.[9]

The general's penultimate act of epic heroism was to evacuate almost 150,000 civilians and troops from Sevastopol, Yevpatoria, Yalta, Sudak and Kerch in the Crimea. Though very much limited in funds, he brought together 126 vessels and was the last one to come on board the last cruiser. Nobody, not a single person was left behind, even the wounded. When the ships left the anchorage, the mooring was virtually empty.

The French, who had helped to supply the vessels and were overwhelmed by

Wrangel's act, sent him a telegram that read: 'The Admiral, officers and sailors of the French Navy deeply bow their heads to General Wrangel, saluting his valour!'

They left Russia on 17 November 1920 and settled for a time on the Gallipoli peninsula in the Dardanelles Straits. Here Wrangel organised the Russian Council as a kind of a provisional government of non-Bolshevik Russia, though Western powers were reluctant to support his efforts.

I can imagine the broken morale and sadness of the exiled soldiers. Nevertheless, as one Russian diarist wrote, they preserved their discipline and élan. A veritable tent city grew up on the peninsula. Baron Wrangel, in particular, was a shining example of composure and devotion to duty.

It was in Gallipoli that the Soviets attempted their first assassination of Baron Wrangel. Seven years after the event, when both founders of the *Time* magazine, Briton Hadden and Henry Luce, were still alive and managing what they considered 'something important but also fun', it was recorded in *Time* that:

> [General Wrangel's] misfortune was made complete when Fate snatched from him his wife, her immensely valuable jewels, and his personal fortune which he had converted into cash. These three most valued possessions were lost when the yacht *Lucullus* sank in collision with the British steamer *Adria* off Constantinople harbor. After that triple misfortune Baron Wrangel gradually became little more than a lanky, itinerant White Hope.[10]

The real name of 'Fate' was the Cheka. Fortunately, nothing happened either to Peter Wrangel or to his darling wife and the steamer *Adria* was not British, but Italian. She was also not 'off Constantinople harbour' but was speeding from Batum (now Batumi) off the Georgian coast. In order to ram the yacht *Adria* had to change her route considerably and on the way between the Sea of Marmara and the Aegean Sea make a sharp turn right to make the hit.

On 15 October 1921 the steamer broke into the starboard side of the yacht *Lucullus* exactly where the Wrangels' bedroom and his study were, and then quietly retreated backwards as if nothing happened. As reported, the baron, his wife and his aide-de-camp just left the yacht, leaving all their possessions behind. Astoundingly, this included all of the army's cash locked in a safe and Baroness Wrangel's jewels that she was hiding in her young child's rag doll. She had been selling them when it was necessary to support her husband, now it was all gone.

In the course of investigation, the *Adria*'s captain, Simic, and pilot Samursky tried to blame the collision on a strong current but this could not explain her sharp turn off the route and the cold-blooded retreat after the crash. Further, some passengers recalled that a week before the ship left Batum, a Moscow train had brought a whole new staff of officers to the local Cheka. It was established that the captain had attempted to delay his departure so that the steamer would be opposite the yacht at night.

The shipping company quickly agreed to pay a life-long pension to the widow of the warrant officer who died in the accident. The case was written off as a misfortune.

About a year later the émigrés moved to the Kingdom of Serbs, Croats and Slovenes and settled in the town of Sremski Karlovci where Wrangel set up his headquarters. Almost immediately the Cheka started their usual game of infiltrating moles into his closest circle.

Vasili Mitrokhin, a former KGB archivist who defected to the British soon after the collapse of the Soviet Union, brought with him copies of secret documents showing that in 1922 the Berlin residency (a permanent Cheka, later NKVD and then KGB, now SVR, station in the country under the legal diplomatic cover of the embassy) recruited the former Tsarist General Zelenin as a penetration agent within the émigré community. A later OGPU report claimed, possibly with some exaggeration, that Zelenin had engineered 'a huge schism within the ranks of the Whites' and had caused a large number of officers to break away from Baron Peter Wrangel. Other OGPU moles praised for their work in disrupting the White Guards included General Zaitsev, former chief of staff to the Cossack Ataman A. I. Dutov, and the ex-Tsarist General Yakhontov, who emigrated to the United States.[11]

By 1924 Moscow had become greatly alarmed by the fact that Wrangel founded the Russian All-Military Union (ROVS), which united all veterans of the White Guard movement in order to coordinate and actually carry out operations inside the USSR for the purpose of starting a national anti-communist uprising.

When in May 2008 heirs and offsprings of the former Wrangel's officers and soldiers gathered in Gallipoli (now Gelibolu) to open the memorial to the White Guards, Grigory Cherepennikov, a son of those who arrived there with the Russian National Army eighty-eight years ago, recalled what his parents told him about the Bolshevik revolution:

> Thanks God, a lot of Russian officers escaped. When the revolution began, they [the revolutionaries] immediately came to us. At that time we had a house on Fontanka [the Fontanka river embankment, residential area of the Russian nobility]. They wanted money. My grandfather said: 'Take as much as you want.' Then they started shooting at him, wounded his ankle. A bullet brushed my mother's head burning her hair. One of my uncles was killed. And several of my nephews – two or three – were also murdered. Five or six people perished there.[12]

The ROVS consisted of four geographical departments: 1 – France and Belgium; 2 – Germany, Austria, Hungary and the Baltic states; 3 – Bulgaria and Turkey; 4 – Serbia, Greece and Romania. Later branches were opened in all European countries where there were Russian communities and former military men.

During that period the Russian secret police was engaged in what would later become known as Operation TREST ('Trust'). The basic idea of the counter-intelligence chief, Artur Artuzov, was to create a fake underground, that is, an allegedly pro-monarchist organisation in Russia in order to lure most prominent members of the ROVS and other similar formations to the USSR, where they could be arrested, under the pretext of meeting (false) conspirators. Among the victims of this plot were Boris Savinkov, the leader of the Society for Defence of Motherland and Freedom, Sidney Reilly, a one-time British intelligence officer, and General Alexander Kutepov, who was in charge of all clandestine operations on behalf of the ROVS.

From the very beginning General Wrangel advised his deputy, General Kutepov, not to trust the TREST. He was especially suspicious after meeting General Potapov who was indeed an OGPU agent and who was sent to Warsaw, Paris and Sremski Karlovci to pose as the chief of staff of the fake Soviet underground. When it became clear that all the time there had been a deception game against the White Guards, Wrangel personally took over all special operations. Nevertheless, less than two years after his untimely death, on 26 January 1930, General Kutepov, who became the head of the organisation, was kidnapped in Paris by the Russian agents and secretly transported to the Soviet Union. According to the Russian sources, he died on the way from asphyxiation.

In 1925 Baron Wrangel sent his mother, wife and their children on leave in Brussels while he remained in Serbia working at his memoirs on the bank of the Danube. In February 1928 he summoned A. von Lampe from Berlin and gave him the manuscript for publication in the annals of the White movement.

In early March the general's batman, Yakov Yudikhin, asked his permission to house his brother, also a soldier, for just a few days. The permission was granted though neither the general nor other members of his family heard about Yudikhin's relative before.

Peter Wrangel was alone with the assassin and his accomplice and quite certainly talked with them and drank tea served by the butler. When they both disappeared he was not exceedingly suspicious but when on 18 March he suddenly fell ill and the doctor diagnosed the flu (erroneously), he called for his family. As his mother, Baroness Maria Dmitriyevna Wrangel recalled, 'those were 38 days and nights of excruciating torment'.[13]

The general suffered from a very high fever, chills and fatigue and was losing weight. After some time breathing disorders started. His bone marrow was affected and that resulted in severe anaemia and other blood problems. His central nervous system and lymphatic system were also attacked.

Later, Belgian physicians and a Russian doctor from Paris diagnosed tuberculosis.

The disease was progressing very rapidly. Baron Wrangel died on 25 April 1928 in Brussels at the age of 49. *Mycobacteria* were found in the autopsy – which shows that the general was almost certainly poisoned with strains of Koch's bacilli, a biological agent that can easily be used as a weapon.

General Wrangel's daughter, Yelena Meindorf, had all the time insisted that her father was deliberately poisoned. Several years ago the St Petersburg historian Vladimir Bortnevsky working with some declassified new documents on the Russian immigration of the 1920s also concluded that Baron Wrangel was poisoned by the OGPU. In October 1929 General Wrangel was finally laid to rest in the Trinity Church in Belgrade.

In early summer 2005, the *New York Times* published a short obituary:

WRANGEL—Baron Alexis, 83, of Tara, County Meath, Ireland, died peacefully on May 27, 2005 after a lengthy illness. He is survived by his wife Diana and his sister Nathalie Basilevsky as well as an extended family. Baron Wrangel was a diplomat, author, equestrian and former U.S. Air Force Officer who was a son of General Baron Peter N. Wrangel, the last Commander in Chief of the White Russian Army during the Russian Civil War.

A funeral service was held on Friday, 3 June 2005 at St Colman of Oughaval Russian Orthodox Church in Stradbally, County Laois, Ireland. Father Peter Baulk conducted the service assisted by members of the Russian Orthodox Church in Dublin. It was in strict accordance with the rites of the Russian Orthodox Church and was attended by a large congregation, more than a hundred people.

The hearse was escorted along the route from St Colman to Celbridge under the watchful eye of the Guard who took it turns to ensure a trouble free journey. Baron Wrangel was laid to rest in the Conolly-Carew family burial plot in Celbridge Church, which is the parish church of Baroness Wrangel's family home, Castletown House. A bugle was not sounded on that day and no salvo echoed over the grave. The family and close friends enjoyed a pleasant lunch for the wake afterwards in the Setanta Hotel, which was built as a charity school for girls by the Lord Conolly-Carew in the nineteenth century. The party toasted the memory of Baron Wrangel with his favourite drink, champagne.

Some time later the family received a message from Russia, a faraway country that all the men and women of the Wrangel family loved so much. Their reply read in part:

I thank you for your letter from January 29, 2007, and the offer for the re-burial of the ashes of General Baron Pyotr Nikolayevich Wrangel in the Donskoy Monastery in Moscow. Our family was deeply touched by your letter and we understand that thousands of other Russian people stand behind it. Your proposal made us deeply consider the meaning and purpose of such a step and to weigh all the arguments for and against, so that we may provide a serious, reasoned answer and explanation.

It is well known that the main feature of General Wrangel's character was his principled nature. He fought against Bolshevism and the system it created not because of feelings of class hatred, but from a deep conviction that Bolshevism is an absolute evil for Russia and for mankind in general.

In the past two decades, a huge change has occurred in the understanding of Russians of the meaning of Bolshevism and the Soviet regime. Unfortunately, the most important thing has not occurred, the condemnation of this evil on the governmental level. Subsequently, the confusion in people's minds leads to such a state of affair that in recent years polling of the populace resulted in almost half the population of Russia considering Stalin to be a positive figure.

General Wrangel passed away in Brussels in 1928. A little more than a year later, at his own behest as expressed while still alive, he was interred in a tomb in a Russian church in Belgrade. There he lies in peace to this day, and at a cemetery nearby, lie thousands of his compatriots, members of his army, devoted to him eternally and to whom he gave every last ounce of his strength. This mutual trust between a commanding officer and his troops knows no limits. It is not bound by his death or the passage of time. As in life and as in death, he is in formation together with his officers, soldiers, and Cossacks. To remove him now – only him – to bury again in Moscow, to take him away from the ranks of those devoted subordinates (and their descendants who are devoted to his memory) can be possible only for a very good reason. If he were alive today, it is unlikely that he would agree to forsake his army for the privilege of traveling to Moscow alone, knowing that Lenin and Stalin lie in a place of honor near the Kremlin to this day.

The final words of General Wrangel on Russian soil in 1920 were of fulfilling one's duty to the end. Just as the memory of General Wrangel lives on within us, his descendants, so does the memory of his compatriots endures, before whom the duty and pledge of the Commanding Officer of the Russian Army will not be fulfilled while the mausoleum still stands on the Red Square and the Red murderers remain buried at the walls of the Kremlin. The words of Archpriest Vasiliy Vinogradov at the funeral come to mind, said at the gravesite in Belgium in 1928: 'Paying our respects to his remains, which are sacred for us, let us avow before them to keep an eternal love burning within us for our unfortunate homeland and the sacred flame of resistance to the satanic, atheistic regime, and to not give in to any compromises or agreements from whomever they may arise. As Saint Theodosius said, 'One must live with one's enemies in the world, but not with the enemies of God.'

Though we appreciate your sincere offer, we must admit with a heavy heart, that the time for the re-burial of General Wrangel in the homeland has not arrived yet. General Wrangel was and still is a symbol for many of implacable and principled resistance. The troops and even enemies never felt the same way about Denikin and Kappel, though they were important historically, as they did for General Wrangel. The émigré community honors his memory to this day, along with the ideals for which he fought. His struggle is not over and his premature re-burial will only diminish the meaning of the effort and sacrifice of not only Wrangel himself, but also of all those White warriors, who gave their lives for the good of Russia.

Pyotr A. Basilevsky'

General Wrangel himself could not have put it better.

Operation VLADIMIR, Part I

As you sow, so shall you reap. The chief of the largest secret service in the world knew that rule. He was a career intelligence officer and before coming to the FOREST, as the Russian intelligence headquarters was known among its dwellers, to take over what was left from the crazy restructuring under *perestroika* and the Yeltsin period of confusion and disorder. Before this, Sergei Nikolaevich Lebedev had been spending his time in Washington, DC. There he had been liaising with the Central Intelligence Agency on unimportant issues, while on the side running the most extensive network of spies his service ever had. Now back in Moscow, he had just been told to concentrate on a different geographical area. Britain was not as important as America and housed fewer Russian spies, though 'our people' sat in the House of Lords, in Parliament, major newspapers, the BBC, the biggest banks and even in the London Stock Exchange. He surely smiled when he thought how quickly his service could trigger a mini-crisis on the ISLAND (i.e. Britain in Soviet intelligence reports) – but that wouldn't help now. Those agents would be almost useless in this new task, and he couldn't refuse it – the order had come in person from the man closest to Vladimir Putin. Lebedev pressed a button and asked the head of Directorate S to come to his office at once.

At about that time in April 2005 I was sitting in the cigar room of the Connaught Hotel drinking my second espresso. I had flown in from Vienna to meet Alexander 'Sasha' Litvinenko and Alex Goldfarb to discuss a business project. Waiting with me was an elderly Englishman who often served as Sasha's interpreter during public events, who had offered to introduce us. Our visitors were late.

Goldfarb was getting ready to take off for Kiev as Boris Berezovsky's envoy to deliver some very hot material. It was secret recordings from the office of Leonid Kuchma, who until only a few weeks earlier had been president of the Ukraine. These tapes would become known to Ukrainian prosecutors as the 'Melnichenko tapes' and would inflame a scandal that had broken out in 2002 which would be remembered in the Ukraine and beyond, as 'Kuchmagate'.

While waiting for Alex Goldfarb and Sasha Litvinenko, my companion and I went through some details of this scandal, because it was related to the business that I intended to discuss with them.

In about 1998 Major Mykola Melnichenko, who served as one of the bodyguards of President Leonid Kuchma, was ordered to start secretly recording all conversations that took place in the presidential office. Litvinenko later told me the orders came from Yevhen Marchuk.

Marchuk, formerly a high-ranking Ukrainian KGB official, had occupied important Ukrainian government posts after the collapse of the Soviet Union: minister of national security and defence, prime minister, presidential candidate and, after Kuchma won, secretary of the National Security and Defence Council, the position he held when the bugging operation unrolled. Later he was reappointed minister of defence. He had earlier served in the 9th Directorate of the KGB (the government protection service) in Moscow and Kiev from where he was transferred to the newly formed State Protection Directorate (UDO) responsible for the security of the president and other important persons.

In November 2000, when news about tapping of the presidential offices began to circulate in Kiev, Melnichenko fled the country with his tapes. First he went to the Czech Republic and then, the following April, was granted political asylum in the USA. This unusual (for the time) decision of the US authorities to accept a low-profile defector was prompted by Melnichenko's claims that his files contained crucially important information. First of all, the recordings allegedly proved that President Kuchma was involved in the plot to murder the independent Ukrainian journalist Georgy Gongadze, who had been kidnapped by local police and whose beheaded body was later found not far away from Kiev. Also the tapes would show that the Ukrainian president authorised the sale of several sophisticated *Kolchuga* passive sensors[1] to Iraq in violation of the international agreements prohibiting such exports to a rogue regime. This information greatly troubled the United States – the lives of American and British pilots tasked with flying sorties over Baghdad were at stake.

After Melnichenko's testimony and the subsequent investigation by the combined US/UK expert team, the incriminating secret recordings were declared to be authentic by the US State Department. 'Foggy Bottom', as the Department is known, had then suspended $54 million of government-to-government aid to Ukraine, the fourth-largest recipient of US foreign aid. In the autumn of 2001 NATO withdrew its invitation for Kuchma to attend the planned NATO Prague Summit. In December the Italian prosecutor's office also accused Marchuk of violating the UN embargo on supplying arms to various parts of the world. As far as I know, the accusations were never investigated or prosecuted. In August 2008 former president Kuchma happily and luxuriously celebrated his seventieth birthday in Sardinia among friends and visiting dignitaries.

Quite unbeknownst to me, I came to London on 11 April 2005 in the middle of yet another scandal relating to the former bodyguard.

When he arrived in Washington DC in early 2001, Melnichenko was a lost soul. The CIA did not need him, his command of English was almost zero and he had no money. His only hope was that through the support of his friend and fellow exile, former parliamentary deputy Alexander Elyashkevich, he would gain fame in his public campaign against the president and leading members of his team. He hoped that would secure him a triumphant return to Kiev, a place in the parliament and further favours from the opposition. It appeared that he wanted to become a sort of a celebrity, as he knew this status brought not only recognition but also quick money.

Melnichenko and his family had to find some way to make a living and (like everyone who followed political developments in the former USSR) he was aware of Boris Berezovsky's special interest in Ukraine and support of the opposition there. So exactly a year after his escape to the USA, in April 2002, as Alex Goldfarb told me, Melnichenko turned to Berezovsky for financial help. Through the mediation of Yuri Felshtinsky, author, historian and US citizen who, like Goldfarb himself, was a close political adviser to the former oligarch, Melnichenko received a $50,000 grant from the Foundation for Civil Liberties founded and financed by Berezovsky and managed by Goldfarb. In addition, according to Goldfarb and Felshtinsky, Melnichenko demanded $10,000 as a monthly fee for his work on decrypting the tapes he had brought with him.

An operation was set up under the command of Yuri Shvets, a former KGB intelligence officer who once spied in the USA and later went to live there, becoming a professor at the Centre for Counterintelligence and Security Studies in the Washington area. Berezovsky's foundation financed the decoding of the records by a leading US forensic laboratory, Bek Tek, and their posting on the website *5th Element* set up especially for this purpose. To this job, Melnichenko contributed all or at least a large part of his recordings (or, as Litvinenko suspected, their clones). Strangely, though, Bek Tek had already analysed these or similar files and equipment long before Melnichenko joined the operation, in fact as early as 30 August 2001 and 23 January 2002, and had reported on it to the 'Provisionary Commission of the Supreme Council of Ukraine on the Investigation of the Criminal Case on the Disappearance of Journalist Gongadze and Other Cases'.

Goldfarb had a good explanation. Even before Melnichenko appeared in the Berezovsky circle, Shvets had already received one Toshiba memory recorder DMR-SX1, one 80-minute CD-R compact disc, one black plastic 16 MB SmartMedia card and some other material. Knowing Alex, I have no doubt that the evidence was legally obtained from a representative of the Supreme Council commission. Hence I believe that the $50,000 that Berezovsky's foundation paid to Melnichenko would have seemed like more than an adequate remuneration for recordings and equipment which by that time he could not sell anyway.

While the Ukrainian scandal was gaining force, Litvinenko and Vladimir

Bukovsky, one of the most prominent Soviet dissidents who had spent twelve years in prison camps and psychiatric hospitals and whom Litvinenko had befriended in London, actively supported Melnichenko.

I well remember the meeting at the National Union of Journalists Freelance London Club at the end of February 2003 where Mykola introduced Litvinenko to the audience as 'a close friend'. Bukovsky told the meeting that the Melnichenko tapes provided a 'unique opportunity to look into the structure of the post-Soviet states and the catalogue of crimes committed from presidential offices'. Russia, Ukraine and other post-Soviet states, Bukovsky said, are ruled by 'a criminal clique, a merger of the underworld, security services and so-called business', which had become 'completely uncontrollable'. The former dissident said that whereas in Soviet times dissidents could rely on support from the West, 'in post-Soviet times the West has decided that democracy has prevailed, and no such support need be given'.

For his part Litvinenko provided as much support as he could to the former major from Kiev. Mykola Melnichenko was a regular at the Litvinenkos' house and they spent plenty of time together. At the end, as Sasha complained to me during our meeting, Melnichenko began to tap their conversations and those in Berezovsky's office.

It seems that in this whole operation Melnichenko was acting an agent of Russian intelligence, the SVR. Most likely, the SVR started his recruitment in late 2002 after Melnichenko wrote a personal letter to Putin.[2] The Russian aim was evidently twofold: to get the original recordings so they could know what really was happening in the Ukrainian top echelons in 1998–2000, and to infiltrate another of their men into the entourage of Berezovsky. By this time, I should say, Berezovsky's office had already been well penetrated by Russian agents. The SVR had almost certainly pitched Melnichenko in the United States and formalised his recruitment during one of his visits to London. The actual recruiter could have been Sergey Gennadyevich Federyakov, a high-ranking diplomat at the Russian Embassy who worked under the guise of an arms control specialist. In reality Federyakov, codenamed (Comrade) ALLEN, was an experienced recruiter and the London SVR deputy station chief. He had previously served in New York posing as Second Secretary of the Permanent Mission of the Russian Federation to the UN. General Federyakov is now masquerading as a counsellor of the Department for Security & Disarmament Affairs at the Ministry of Foreign Affairs in Moscow and is a member of the Security Committee of the Russian Duma. There is multiple and well-documented evidence of Melnichenko's meeting Ukrainian intelligence (SBU) officials in May 2002 in Ostrava, then in Strasbourg and in the South Tyrol, then in February 2004 in Vienna, and later in August he was spotted with the SVR/FSB representatives in Moscow. Finally, it was arranged that a Ukrainian millionaire hiding from his country's prosecutors in Moscow would purchase all the master records.[3]

On 4 March 2005, one day before his birthday, former Ukrainian Minister of Interior Yuri Kravchenko was found dead in his dacha near Kiev. Suspected as one of the important players in the Gongadze killing, Kravchenko chose a highly original way to leave this world: he shot two bullets, one after another, into his own head.

Almost immediately Melnichenko called Berezovsky in London, insisting that his life was in danger and begged Boris to promptly send a jet and bodyguards for him. Whatever else may be said about Boris, he is a generous person especially to those he needs. Soon Mykola was in London and checking into a hotel. The idyll, however, did not last long as Melnichenko started to make public claims seriously undermining Berezovsky's standing with the future Ukrainian leadership and pouring mud on what he called 'an international criminal gang' with the tycoon as its leader. The 'gang' members, in Mykola's version, were Goldfarb, Felshtinsky, Litvinenko and Shvets. Perhaps that was exactly the role SVR/FSB spymasters scripted for Melnichenko to play. Otherwise, it is hard to explain why the fugitive's statements were officially passed to the chief of the Ukrainian security service (SBU) through diplomatic channels and were widely circulated by the Russian media. Melnichenko also announced his 'plans' to meet President Yushchenko during his official visit to the USA. The Ukrainian leader, however, had a different agenda.

The Kremlin was clearly irritated. In late February 2005 Berezovsky, 'Enemy Number One', came to Latvia with a British-issued refugee document that allowed foreign travel in spite of the Interpol arrest warrant secured by Russia. Just weeks before, the former oligarch had taken a short trip to Tbilisi, and now was planning a visit to Kiev. The Russian Foreign Ministry, using popular phraseology of the time, declared:

> Once they did nothing to arrest Berezovsky, official Riga ignored its responsibilities as an Interpol member and showed its unreliability as a partner in the struggle with organized crime. Latvia should realize that such actions couldn't stand.[4]

In October Prime Minister Aigars Kalvitis confirmed this view, adding Berezovsky to the list of persons unwelcome in Latvia.

When Goldfarb and Litvinenko finally arrived at the Connaught and we settled around a small corner table in the bar, our talk quickly turned to recent events and the upcoming flight of Goldfarb and Felshtinsky to Kiev. Indeed, two days after our meeting, Alex said to PRIMA-News:

> We have brought the evidence in the cases of Gongadze, Elyashkevich and the sale of the weapons system Kolchuga to Kiev for consideration by the prosecutor's office. These materials include the masters in digital audio file format analysed by experts in the USA, the equipment that Melnichenko

admitted that he used, and the original expert reports confirming the authenticity of the audio recordings. The evidence (recordings and equipment) is contained in bags sealed by the experts in 2001–2002 in the state of Virginia immediately after the analysis.

Goldfarb and Felshtinsky explained that Bek Tek had carried out the analysis and that the reports produced by this laboratory were widely used in legal proceedings in the USA. 'These materials are presented in a format required of the evidence by American courts,' Goldfarb said. 'Our legal experts believe that these materials are sufficient to include "Kuchma's conversations" in the criminal case file and use them as evidence.'

During that visit to Kiev both Goldfarb and Felshtinsky testified as witnesses in the Gongadze case. Several weeks later Litvinenko made his own statement to a Ukrainian prosecutor who came especially to London to interview him.

***

It was a nice spring day, no rain or drizzle, and everybody felt easy and relaxed. Sasha asked me whether I knew Oleg Gordievsky, a former KGB intelligence officer who had famously escaped from Russia and was living in Britain, and also about Oleg Kalugin, another KGB legend, albeit of a different nature and calibre, with whom Litvinenko communicated regularly. But his main interest was in my book about Nikolai Khokhlov and his poisoning that was about to be published in Vienna. Sasha had little knowledge of Soviet intelligence history; during his years in the KGB and then the FSB he had been operating in the field and never outside Russia, and hardly had or needed to have access to classified histories of the Soviet espionage. The Khokhlov story was important for him in assisting his friends in *Novaya Gazeta* in Moscow in their investigation of the alleged poisoning of the famous reporter and a Duma member Yuri Shchekochikhin. Tons of papers have been written about Shchekochikhin's weird end but his medical records and the autopsy report remain classified by the Russian government to this day.

I promised to send the book as soon as it came out but it would help little in the Shchekochikhin case. I do not think now that Sasha picked up on the the fact that Khokhlov had been poisoned with *radioactive* thallium, that is, a radiological weapon similar to the one that would be used later on Litvinenko himself.

We chatted and laughed, beautifully trained and groomed waiters and waitresses did their job perfectly never forgetting to take away empty glasses and cups and to offer new drinks. I enjoyed my favourite tomato juice (plain) and Sasha, not yet accustomed to such places, asked Goldfarb to get him hot chocolate. Alex, who had the great advantage over Litvinenko of speaking and reading English fluently, told a story about his relative who had worked for the NKVD in Europe and the United States in the 1930s.

The relative's name was Grigory Kheifetz (also transliterated as 'Kheifits'), widely known in professional literature as a rather successful Soviet spy handler at the time of the atomic bomb. I remembered the colourful events surrounding J. Robert Oppenheimer, the father of the atomic bomb, and other leading scientists involved in the famous Manhattan Project, their wives, mistresses and their former husbands and lovers mixing with each other and with famous Communists and, of course, Kheifetz and other NKVD officers and illegals seeking American nuclear secrets.

From Alex Goldfarb I learned some new details about the case of Nicholas Daniloff, a *US News and World Report* correspondent reporting on the Soviet Union. On 2 September 1986 Daniloff was, in his own words, sandbagged by eight strong men on a Moscow street and bundled into a van, his hands tightly handcuffed behind his back. The KGB did it in retaliation for the arrest three days earlier of Gennady Zakharov, a Soviet employee of the UN secretariat. The FBI charged him with conspiracy to commit espionage. The Soviets charged Daniloff with receiving classified information from his Russian contact. The Reagan administration took a particularly strong position over this event because the evidence of Zakharov's involvement in espionage was indisputable while Daniloff had not worked for the CIA in any capacity.

After intense discussions between the two presidents and their top aides, Daniloff was handed over to the US Embassy in Moscow and allowed to leave the USSR without charges while Zakharov was released to the Soviet embassy in Washington after pleading *nolo contendere*, a plea where the defendant neither admits nor disputes a charge, and left America for good.

However, the diplomatic crisis did not end there. The situation escalated to the point when by the end of October 1986 eighty KGB and GRU intelligence officers, assigned under diplomatic cover in New York, San Francisco and Washington, were declared *persona non grata* (PNG) and ordered to leave the United States.

These expulsions had a devastating impact on the Soviet espionage capabilities in the US. The Soviets expelled ten US diplomats and withdrew all 260 of the Russian support staff working for the US embassy in Moscow.

Daniloff later contended in his autobiography that he had never held classified documents.

The journalist did not know that he had been the object of the KGB interest for two years before the botched arrest. According to Goldfarb, officers were trying to persuade his father who was Daniloff's friend, Professor David Moiseyevich Goldfarb, to hand him incriminating documents prepared by the secret police with the suggestion that Daniloff would take them to the West.

There was nothing new or unusual in such a scheme.

In the mid-1970s, Edward N. Trifonov, at the time of writing a professor of molecular biophysics at the Weizman Institute of Science in Tel Aviv, decided to emigrate to Israel. The Kurchatov Institute of Atomic Energy (now just

'Kurchatov Institute'), Russia's leading nuclear energy and nuclear weapons research facility, where he was then teaching, had to call a party meeting. After a lot of debates Trifonov was refused an exit visa. However, in two weeks the *Los Angeles Times* published the minutes of this meeting. That led to a huge scandal, as the Kurchatov Institute was one of the most secret if not the most secret scientific establishment in Russia.

It turned out that the head of one of the laboratories of the Radiobiological Department managed to copy the protocol and bring it to Goldfarb Snr who passed it to Alex. He, in turn, handed the document over to his close friend, a famous Russian dissident and refusenik Anatoly Shcharansky (now a leading Israeli politician Natan Sharansky), who gave it for publication to Robert C. Toth. Toth served as the *Los Angeles Times* Moscow correspondent from 1974 to 1977. Finally, Trifonov was permitted to leave. Shcharansky was arrested and Toth, barred from leaving the Soviet Union, was questioned by the KGB in June 1977. Soviet prosecutors accused him at Anatoly Shcharansky's treason trial of having acted as an agent for the CIA by collecting information with the dissident's help.

Alex Goldfarb immigrated to Israel in 1975. Thirty years later I asked him in London: what did your father respond to the KGB when they asked him to compromise Daniloff?

'My father rejected the proposal out of hand.'

'And what happened then?'

'By the time the Daniloff story broke off, he had been interrogated for a year and was still in the Soviet Union.'

In September 2007 I went to the funeral ceremony of Lord Nicholas Bethell, not far from the Russian Embassy in London; dissident Vladimir Bukovsky was also there. After the ceremony James Bethell, who inherited the title, gave me a copy of his father's book, *Spies and Other Secrets: Memoirs From the Second Cold War*. In relation to the Daniloff story, Lord Bethell wrote: 'If this was to be Soviet policy in the future, *glasnost* and *perestroika* were without meaning, and East–West summit meetings were without purpose.'

The purpose of my visit to London, however, was not to spin old histories of Soviet spying. Since September 2004 I had been privately investigating the poisoning of Victor Yushchenko, who had been treated in Vienna. By April Yushchenko's personal doctor, Professor Nikolai Korpan had collected enough evidence that his patient was deliberately poisoned and there was no doubt about who was the perpetrator. Korpan wanted to publish his findings in the form of a book and needed a grant to do the job as he was very busy and would have to cancel several engagements to start working on the material. I asked Goldfarb whether his foundation could help. Litvinenko was very enthusiastic and immediately supported the idea. We agreed that they would have a word with Boris and let me know.

My English companion and I saw the duo to Mount Street from where they unhurriedly proceeded in the direction of the Berezovsky's office. The response never came.

* * *

It was on one extremely dark night in January 2004, as the midnight hour was fast approaching, when three figures met at a shabby bistro in a small French village named Cluses for a secret conference. The two visitors were Mario Scaramella and Alexander Litvinenko and the host was Evgeny Limarev, a self-styled consultant who had registered his business in France. The aim of the meeting was to discuss the infamous Italian Red Brigades and their secret links to the Soviet KGB.

Though it was Litvinenko who was a seasoned KGB/FSB operative and the one who had set up the meeting by a telephone call from Naples (the conversation was recorded) where he was visiting his friend Mario, Limarev decided to play the tough professional. First of all, he demanded that Scaramella should arrange for his personal protection by engaging the Italian security service, and then he made it clear that his collaboration would come at a price.

Who is Limarev, the second KGB man after Mykola-the-tape-recorder, whom Litvinenko recklessly vouched for as someone trustworthy in spite of his insider knowledge of the KGB and the tricks of its trade?

Evgeny Lvovich Limarev was born on 19 July 1965 in the town of Frunze (now Bishkek), the capital of Kyrgyzstan, in the family of the KGB officer Lev Limarev and Maria Limareva.

In 1974 in Morocco he met and quickly befriended Misha, a fellow schoolboy and like himself the son of the KGB officer Vitaly Margelov. Both fathers worked under the cover of the Soviet embassy in Rabat, one handling agents and assignments in the line known as Line PR (political intelligence) while the other, Limarev, was taking care of illegals in what was called Line N.

It is not surprising that when they were back in Moscow and the time came, both boys entered the Institute of Asian and African Countries affiliated to Moscow University. There Limarev studied Farsi while Mikhail sweated over Arabic. As was required, both learned English and yet another language. This excellent institution was under the patronage of the International Department of the Central Party Committee, formerly called the OMS, the intelligence service of the Comintern. As before, the International Department controlled friendly Communist parties around the globe and decided how much to sponsor their work. And the institute was a known recruitment pool for future KGB and GRU officers.

I myself graduated from a similar university. During my time, the KGB officer in charge of the Moscow Institute of Asian and African Countries was Nikolai Sakalin. When Limarev graduated in 1987 there was certainly a different talent-spotter, but the rules remained the same.

In those days Limarev, the son of a foreign intelligence officer, had three career opportunities: he could either enter a one-year course at the KGB Andropov Institute to become an operative, or opt for post-graduate academic studies, or get a job as teacher or interpreter at one of the KGB institutions. Both Mikhail and Evgeny decided not to become staff officers. The former joined the International Department as interpreter and the latter tried to make a career in Balashikha, sixteen miles east of Moscow. It was actually not Balashikha itself, but the famous Balashikha-2 where the much-feared Centre of Special Operations of the FSB is headquartered now.

From 1969 until the early 1990s Balashikha-2 was a training base for Advanced Officers Courses (*Kursy Usovershenstvovaniya Ofitserskogo Sostava* – KUOS) of the KGB Special Forces. During a seven-month course the students were taught the use of firearms, parachuting, mountain climbing, handling of explosives, topography, guerrilla warfare and other energetic subjects. Annually the course prepared about sixty special force commanders of the KGB to operate deep in the enemy's rear. It is likely that the instructors of Balashikha-2 trained the Republican guards of Syria, Iraq and Iran and other special forces units across the world. And a lot of terrorists.[5] Limarev says that he was a language instructor there.

According to his own words, in 1990 Limarev successfully passed exams to enter the KGB Andropov Red Banner Institute (KI) but for whatever reason was advised not to start the course. This statement doesn't look plausible. Students for the KI are previously selected and admitted without formal exams.

In 1991 a new foreign intelligence service, SVRR, was founded in Russia headed by Yevgeny Primakov and Lev Limarev, Evgeny's father, was transferred to this new service together with other officers of the former KGB's First Chief Directorate including Vitaly Margelov and those who would later be planning, supporting and carrying out the Litvinenko operation in London.

In 1991–2 Limarev spent about a year learning how to do international business. According to his written biography in the files of the Mitrokhin Commission of the Italian Parliament, during this time he had regular contacts with his KGB handlers.

From 1992 until 1994 he worked as an interpreter at the Volokonovsk sugar refinery in Belgorod (now a public joint-stock company, Nika). According to at least two Russian newspapers, during his work he was involved in some shady deals that led to criminal prosecution, but the case never came to court. Whatever the truth, in 1995 he suddenly moved with his family to Geneva, Switzerland. That same year his father retired from the service. According to all available sources, his father had never been a general as Limarev asserted in a written, signed and notarised statement at the police station of Avellino in Italy in November 2004 (see Document 1). However, it has not been possible to prove this from records.

In Geneva Limarev was busy setting up SVR-backed trading and finance businesses pursuant to a secret order issued by Chairman Kryuchkov in 1991.[6] In 1998 he became a vice-president of the National Fund of the Stable Development of Russia (NFURR) registered in Geneva. This was almost certainly an SVR front.

TO WHOM IT MAY CONCERN

My name is Evgueni Limarev. I was born in July 19, 1965 in Frunze city of the ex-USSR. Now I live in France in the city of Cluses. I work as independent consultant.

I was requested by Mr Mario Scaramella from the Italian's parliament "Mitrokhin commission" to consult and brief about KGB and it's inheritors' activities, in particular to assist him in searching information and data on this topic. In the USSR times and some time later I worked in the "Special Training Centre" of KGB's intelligence (Balashiha-2 city nearby Moscow), which is now known as "Antiterrorist Centre" of the FSB. Till 1999 I have collaborated with a group of highly positioned officers of SVR and for many years was adviser to the Chairman of the Russian Parliament. My farther was general-major of SVR, specializing on illegal and anti-NATO activities.

Before coming to Italy and meeting Mr Mario Scaramella, I asked him to provide me with the names of persons whom I could face in the frames of my cooperation with him, especially those of ex-USSR origin in the frames of normal security procedures. Among the names given by professor Scaramella to me was Vladimir Kobyk as one of his translators. I have checked this name through my personal contacts among the acting SVR officers in Moscow, and I discovered that among Ukrainian intelligence officers or enlisted agents in Italy they a certain Taras Kobyk is known to my SVR contacts. All the data and information I have received on this Mr Taras Kobyk, makes me believe that he can be this Ukrainian / Russian intelligence officer / agent and brother of Vladimir Kobyk. Mr Scaramella confirmed me that Vladimir Kobyk has a brother named Taras. That's why I have interrupted this week's work session with Mr Scaramella, because I considered to be risky and unsafe to enter in contact to a such person.

Mr Scaramella also told me that he was receiving some strange phone calls from another Ukrainian named Evgueni Totsky known as intelligence officer of the Ukrainian embassy in Rome. The same SVR sources of mine from Moscow confirmed that they know perfectly well this person in the Russian / Ukrainian intelligence activities. Moreover, I was told by my contacts that this Evgueni Totsky was a known specialist in military counter-espionage and espionage anti-NATO activities in the field of nuclear submarines, mines, torpedoes, etc. issues. I clearly understood that this Totsky has never interrupted to work in this nuclear sphere till nowadays.

Taking into account all I was told by Mr Scaramella about his nuclear investigations in Italy and especially in Russia and what I have heard from my various Russian intelligence friendly sources, I have serious grounds to suspect that due to all that Mr Scaramella became an object of special interests of the Russian (and their Ukrainian colleagues) intelligence. Analyzing all what is happening to Mr Scaramella lately, I come to a conclusion that he is in the centre of a special intelligence operation of the official and mafia-like structures of Russia and Ukraine.

That's why I have informed Mr Scaramella that I consider him to be in high danger, and the same can concern me and anybody close to him.

Regione Carabinieri "Campania"
- Stazione di Avellino –

Visto presentare alle ore 10.15 del 13.11.2004 da Evgueni Limarev, nato il 19 luglio 1965 in Frunze city of the ex-USSR, domiciliato in Francia CLUSESS alla via Noiret nr.1146, identificato a mezzo carta d'identità nr. F743018374 rilasciata il 08.11.1999 autorità Francesi, Governo Alta Savoia, a cui, a sua richiesta, viene consegnata copia.-

IL COMANDANTE

Document 1

Two years earlier, probably to enhance his profile and surely not without the SVR/FSB help, Limarev became 'a public adviser' to the communist Duma deputy Gennady Seleznev, the editor-in-chief of *Pravda* at the time when the communist hardliners attempted to rebel against the Gorbachev reforms in the failed coup of August 1991.

Later, when he was introduced to Mario Scaramella in an Alpine French hamlet and started collaborating with him actively, Limarev wrote in his *curriculum vitae*:

> My relations with the SVR developed from its initial phase of information exchange. It became more active. My companies enjoyed the protection and support of the special services and my commercial activity was considerably integrated with SVR operations in Western Europe. I provided them with funding and carried out a large number of operative [*sic*] missions. The bulk of my activity for them concerned financial operations and gathering of economic and financial information regarding, mainly, Russian and CIS citizens.

This looks like a confession and is a direct proof that he was informing on the Russian community in Geneva (so-called Line EM of the SVR station).

As Limarev was quite proud to admit (the documents are filed in the Mitrokhin Commission collection, see, for example, Document 2), during his sojourn in Switzerland he was personally run by Vitaly Vasilyevich Margelov, the SVR chief in Geneva under the guise of First Deputy Head of the Russian Mission to the UN. It is, however, doubtful that the *rezident* and general would spend his time on such a small fish. More likely his handler was Colonel Vladimir Sergeyevich Kozlov, another Asian and African specialist, who was Margelov's deputy in charge of Line N ('illegals'), or his colleague from Line EM. Before this posting Kozlov was one of the commanding officers of Vympel, the most elite KGB special forces unit whose tasks included overt and covert operations behind the enemy lines, sabotage and subversion, as well as 'direct action' (assassinations). After Vympel Kozlov served in Alfa, a similar unit. Ironically, as soon as his spy mission abroad was accomplished, Kozlov was invited to the Anti Terrorist Centre of the FSB. While it was more likely a more junior officer who handled Limarev, the latter may have met Margelov senior on several occasions, as he knew his son. (In the meantime, Margelov junior moved from the International Department to the KGB High School also becoming Putin's foreign press liaison during presidential elections in 2000. Appropriately, since 2002 he has been a member of the European Democrat Group in the Parliamentary Assembly of the Council of Europe (PACE) and in January 2008 was preparing to be elected its president. It did not happen then but there would be another chance.)

Either Limarev was 'burned', or the financial activities of his fund caused suspicion among the Swiss authorities (according to Limarev, his companies

CONFIDENTIAL

0113 AC Italian Green Party - 1\2\2004

Statement by Evgheniy Limarev, born in Frunze City – Bishkek, Kirgizstan URSS, 19\6\65, (son of Lev Limarev - General Major KGB-SVR and Maria Limareva), previously employed at SVR and member of "Sistema" Patriotic Organization at SVR, Advisor to the Chairman of the Russian Parliament, at present resident in France in the city of Cluses.

Mr. Alfonso Pecoraro Scanio

In the year 1998 at the United Nations H.Q. in Geneva, during a meeting organized by the Russian Mission to UN and (or) by the Club Diplomatique, the SVR (former KGB) Resident in Geneva Marguelov Vitaliy Vassilievitc*, I was linked with, introduced me Mr. Pecoraro Scanio. He was joint with the President of the Club Diplomatique de Geneva, the SVR agent (Swiss citizen) Schneider André**, I identify Mr. Alfonso Pecoraro Scanio in the enclosed photo n. 1. The SVR Resident presented me Mr. Pecoraro Scanio as an influent person available for operations in Italy: He also specified that Mr. Pecoraro Scanio was a contact of Mr. Schneider, and that they were members of a gay network linked with the club diplomatique, very useful for our activities. There are no chances of error, I am sure about the identification. I have meet one more time him but without speaking with him.

(* Marguelov, was in charge in the PGU KGB (after SVR) for illicit financing of political parties in Italy well before 1992, he was also appointed head of all the European activities and after he was appointed the Deputy Head of the SVR. Now he is also a member of the Parliament and a member of Sistema. Telephone numbers are Michael (the son, head of a special team at SVR in Strasbourg and Moscow in charge for Italian operations) XXXXX ; direct in Moscow XXXXX, SVR Dacia , and office SVR .
(** Schnaider tel. Office in Ginevra XXXXX \ XXXXX, cellular XXXXX , direct XXXXX).

Document 2

reached an annual turnover of US$60 million), or it was decided to send him on another mission – by August 2000 he suddenly moved to a small village of Cluses in France, just across the Swiss border between Geneva and Chamonix at the foot of Mont Blanc.

Having established himself in France, Limarev managed to contact Litvinenko and in 2001 finally succeeded in meeting him and Alex Goldfarb. It is quite possible that after Litvinenko's successful defection from Russia in 2000, Limarev was instructed to get in contact with him and penetrate the Berezovsky circle. He was quite successful in this task and soon Berezovsky's Foundation for Civil Liberties gave him a grant of US$20,000 to build and run a website named *RusGlobus*. The site was launched in 2002 with the help of Limarev's brother-in-law.

In the spring of 2002, what now looks like a double-target operation was probably mounted by the resourceful Moscow planners. They sent a former police officer, Oleg Sultanov, now an investigative journalist writing for an FSB newspaper, *Shield and Sword*, to join Limarev in France and allegedly to work on an anti-Putin book. But when after six months Sultanov was invited to visit London, he was immediately recalled back to Moscow. There he published several anti-Berezovsky interviews portraying Limarev as the latter's chief adviser 'in charge of the propaganda operations in Western Europe'. All this seriously enhanced Limarev's status with Litvinenko and Goldfarb and even Berezovsky whom he met several times.

In 2003 Limarev met Litvinenko in Turin, Italy, and Sasha advised him to start collaborating with Scaramella in the latter's efforts to gather evidence for the Mitrokhin Commission about KGB operations in Italy. That meeting and a telephone call the following January preceded the midnight supper in the Alps and later determined Limarev's role in the Litvinenko operation.

Limarev offered Scaramella his (unnamed) 'reliable sources within the SVR/FSB' and volunteered to write a book about Soviet submarine operations in the Mediterranean. Scaramella agreed to pay him and his two 'assistants' – a former submarine officer and a nuclear scientist – €3,000 a month for six months. The book was never written but Limarev occasionally supplied Scaramella with some disinformation, without doubt concocted by the SVR in the form of intelligence reports, that Mario accepted at face value and continued to pay the informer. The reports looked useful and truthful to the Italian who was naïve and inexperienced in intelligence matters but since early teens had fallen for espionage games. At that stage Limarev's primary assignment became to learn all he could about the work of the Commission and as much as possible about who of Scaramella's multiple intelligence and near contacts in Britain and the USA provided what. And, importantly, Limarev continued to develop relations with Berezovsky and Litvinenko who was calling him Zhenia, a friendly diminutive for Evgeny. By 2006 Zhenia was moving into the home stretch.

***

In 2002 two more agents moved into the sphere of Berezovsky. One was Vladimir Chekulin and another simply 'Slava'.

I first thought that perhaps Chekulin was not sent by the SVR or FSB from the very beginning. Berezovsky found him himself, I reckoned, and the Russian services used the opportunity later when Melnichenko casually pitched him in London in January 2003.

But then I thought better of it: the pattern, the bloody pattern. As in many other cases, it was Shchekochikhin who incidentally brought Chekulin into Berezovsky's sight. In the autumn of 2001 Chekulin gave to the Duma deputy who was also a member of the Committee for Combating Corruption all documentary evidence of his institute's allegedly illegal activities.

The arrival of Chekulin on 2 March was not accidental. For some time Boris, Sasha and Yuri Felshtinsky had been preparing a major press conference where the accent would be put on the FSB's role in the series of apartment-house bombings that took place in September 1999 in Moscow, Buinaksk and Volgodonsk and cost more than 300 lives. The press conference was about presenting a new French documentary 'Assassination of Russia', based in part on the findings from the book by Felshtinsky and Litvinenko, *FSB Blows Up Russia*,[7] recently published in New York. It aimed to provide an expert insight of why Putin, then the newly appointed prime minister, and the FSB should be accused of these horrific bombings, rather than Chechen terrorists.

'The question of "who", is very significant,' writes David Satter, a senior fellow of the Hudson Institute and a visiting scholar at the Johns Hopkins University Nitze School of Advanced International Studies. 'If, as the available evidence indicates, the bombings were carried out by the FSB, it means the present government of Russia is illegitimate. It also means that a tradition has been established in Russia that can only lead to the country's degeneration.'[8]

This is exactly what Berezovsky and the people around him intended to prove. But a ten-minute version of the original 52-minute-long TV documentary would not be explosive enough. They needed something else as well. So when Chekulin approached Pavel Voloshin, a reporter for *Novaya Gazeta* in Moscow, with his story and his documents that gave an unusual angle to the conspiracy, word reached London at once and Chekulin was summoned to produce his evidence.

Straight from Heathrow he was chauffeured to Berezovsky. As a starter, Chekulin declared that he was a secret FSB agent recruited by Department T (see Document 3). In May 2000 he was appointed acting director of the Russian Explosives Conversion Centre, a scientific research institute under the Ministry of Education. Chekulin explained and proved with documents that he brought with him, that in 1999–2000, a large quantity of hexogen, the explosive believed to have been used in the apartment bombings, was purchased by the institute from various military units and then, under the guise of gunpowder or dynamite, shipped all over the country to unknown destinations. That was not yet a definite fingerprint, no 'gotcha, bastards', but everybody decided it was a 'go' and Berezovsky was sure he could persuade the audience of the same.

As it turned out, the press conference did not offer much that was new. Nonetheless, it was significant because it renewed discussion of an issue that had never really gone away. At the same time a pamphlet novel by Alexander Prokhanov, a Russian nationalist leader, entitled *Mr Hexogen*, was enjoying a wide

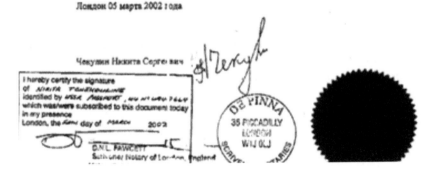

ЗАЯВЛЕНИЕ

Я, Чекулин Никита Сергеевич, бывший и.о. Директора НИИ «Росконверсвзрывцентр» в 2000 году был завербован ФСБ в качестве секретного агента департамента Т (борьба с терроризмом).

В моем распоряжении имеются документальные доказательства тайной схемы хищения взрывчатых веществ с военных складов и участия высших чиновников российского правительства в сокрытии фактов и предотвращении расследования по этому поводу.

Согласно имеющимся у меня накладным, платежным поручениям, доверенностям и иным документам НИИ Росконверсвзрывцентр Министерства образования России, располагавшийся по адресу Большая Лубянка, дом 18, строение 3, в 1999 – 2000 г.г.закупал значительные количества гексогена. Источником взрывчатки были в частности В/Ч No 68586 и No 92919. Тонны этого материала с фальшивой маркировкой (порох и тротил) по доверенности этого института направлялись различным подставным учреждениям в регионах.

Внутреннее расследование этой цепи в Министерстве Образования привело к обращению министра Владимира Филипова к высшим должностным лицам России с просьбой о расследовании с привлечением ФСБ. Среди лиц, поставленных в известность о возможной террористической деятельности были Вице-премьеры Валентина Матвиенко и Илья Клебанов, Директор ФСБ Николай Патрушев, Министр Внутренних Дел Владимир Рушайло и Секретарь СБ Сергей Иванов.

Однако господин Патрушев запретил расследование, о чем его заместитель Юрий Заостровцев официально уведомил Министерство Образования.

Лондон 05 марта 2002 года

Чекулин Никита Сергеевич

I hereby certify the signature of *NIKITA TCHEKOULINE* identified by *VISA PASSPORT*, no *NT UU.U 7644* which was/were subscribed to this document today in my presence
London, the *5th* day of *March* 2002

D.N.L. FAWCETT
Sub Under Notary of London, England

Document 3

circulation in Russia. The novel, based on information from sources in the intelligence agencies, described a conspiracy to unleash the Second Chechen War.[9]

Chekulin, who arrived in London with his 12-year-old son, was quickly accepted into Berezovsky's company of friends and confederates and became a regular guest at Litvinenko's house. He was taken good care of and Berezovsky provided the newcomer with a traditional monthly allowance of £5,000. His son went to a good English school. Chekulin was helped with accommodation and everyday chores. Sasha and Marina trusted him completely and Sasha often used

Chekulin as interpreter during meetings that he and those people whom he met did not consider confidential. And those meetings had absolutely nothing to do with Her Majesty's secret or security services, contrary to what Chekulin later claimed.

In his book *Bloody Oligarch and Russian Justice* published in Moscow after Chekulin's flight from London in April 2004, the author names Martin Flint and calls him 'a representative of the British security service MI5'. In reality, Flint is one of four directors of the company Risk Analysis, a private entity, one of many in London, providing a discreet service 'of comprehensive business intelligence, investigation and security risk management services to its financial, legal and corporate clients around the world' as stated in the company brochure. At one time Berezovsky used the good services of Risk Analysis. When Litvinenko was granted political asylum in May 2001, George Menzies, the solicitor, introduced Sasha to Flint with the hope that Litvinenko's knowledge of Russia and Sasha's contacts in Moscow and elsewhere could help him (Litvinenko) to get consultancy commissions.

I know the trade. Indeed, on the staff of such companies are often former officers of intelligence or security services, Scotland Yard, the British or US Army, and many from banks. They also employ a considerable number of journalists and even academics. People of very different backgrounds are invited to join such businesses for obvious reasons but there is one thing these private companies *never* do. They never spy. Martin Flint, for example, one of the directors of Risk Analysis – and the company name speaks for itself – has 'extensive experience as a security consultant in the fields of corporate fraud investigation, asset tracing and recovery, investigation and litigation support and due diligence enquiries'. He indeed spent twenty years working for the MI5 (Security Service) but that was long ago following ten years in the petrochemicals industry.

Unfortunately, Sasha could provide only limited help to such companies because he lacked the excellent command of English and other special skills and knowledge that such work demands. So for a year and a half his services had not been called for.

On 18 June 2002 a British banker named Peter Shaw, leaving his home in Tbilisi, Georgia, was bundled away from his car by a gang posing as police. The British government applied great pressure but after two months Shaw was still not found. The Georgian authorities said seven men had been held in connection with the abduction but no charges had been laid and the banker remained in custody of the bandits. On 21 August Martin Flint asked Berezovsky whether he could help in Shaw's case and Boris promised to use his contacts in Tbilisi to do whatever was possible. Without doubt Badri Patarkatsyshvili, who by the time moved to Georgia and was one of the richest and most influential people in this former Soviet Republic with a small army as his private security service, could do a lot.

A week later Martin Flint and George Menzies met Litvinenko and Chekulin who acted as interpreter to discuss the situation. This was Litvinenko's turf. He was very familiar with the area, and investigating such crimes on the territory of what was formerly the Soviet Union was exactly the job that he loved and could do very well. Of course, from overseas, without seeing the crime scene and all the evidence, it was impossible to carry out the investigation properly, but Sasha offered his best advice.

It was considered valuable enough for Litvinenko to be put in touch after some time with David Douglas of the Scotland Yard who was in charge of negotiating the release of Britons abducted on foreign soil. Sasha tried to be as useful as he could.

By October Peter Shaw had still not been found and many people came to be involved in the rescue operation including Peter Hain, then the Foreign Office minister, who was undertaking diplomatic moves to secure the businessman's release.

During that month Litvinenko, again taking Chekulin along as a helping hand, met Flint in the lobby of the Sheraton Park Lane hotel on Piccadilly to discuss all possible leads and suggest measures including his own trip to Georgia as by the time it was suspected (correctly) that the 57-year-old banker was kept captive in the remote Pankisi Gorge area.

However, on 6 November Georgian television beamed the news that the Georgian Special Forces had successfully released Shaw after a dramatic operation. Next day the happy banker was already in London tired and gaunt and dishevelled after 141 days in captivity. He told a news conference at the airport how he had feared that his kidnappers – who had demanded a ransom of $2m – were taking him out to be shot. He said he dived into a bush to escape and one of the kidnappers was shot by mistake instead. Shaw described his escape as a miracle and said he could not wait to get home to Wales, the BBC reported.

Martin Flint invited Litvinenko and Chekulin for lunch and was happy to hand over a letter addressed to Berezovsky expressing gratitude for whatever help he had provided to secure a successful outcome. Later, the Kremlin propaganda machine would use this episode as one of the proofs that Berezovsky and Litvinenko were 'British agents'.

In early summer, at the outset of those stressful events, a person appeared in London who had been known to Berezovsky and Goldfarb as 'Agent Slava' or simply Slava Petrov. His real name was Vyacheslav Zharko and he said he was unemployed and needed money. This was, of course, almost a universal refrain used by people seeking Boris's help.

But a man from the street would not be able to approach the tycoon and Zharko was no ordinary beggar. He was a former GRU Spetsnaz officer who later worked in the tax police directorate of St Petersburg. This is what Yuri Shcheko-chikhin, a Duma member and Politkovskaya's boss as deputy editor-in-chief of *Novaya Gazeta*, wrote to President Vladimir Putin exactly one month before Zharko suddenly appeared in London:

Several years ago [1999][10] a young inspector of the tax police of St Petersburg, Vyacheslav Zharko, passed over to me some documents that proved that the harbours of the Russian Navy, Lebyazhy and Lomonosovo, were regularly visited by vessels that passed in without any border control or customs clearance. The documents that legitimised this financial affair had several signatures, among them one of the then vice-premier Soskovets[11] and one of yourself, Vladimir Vladimirovich . . .

I do not want to bother you with the details of this criminal case though I believe you know them. I want to discuss a different matter. Zharko, who by this time had been transferred to the GRU Moscow Headquarters, was detained in December 2001 at the Sheremetyevo-1 [Moscow] airport on false accusations of possessing a forged passport and illegal crossing of the state border. He was arrested and put in Lefortovo prison on the orders of the Deputy General Prosecutor of Russia. Such a high level order for such a minor crime with a maximum punishment of two years and an actual release by the decision of the General Prosecutor Ustinov, would seem strange if not for one detail. During his time in Lefortovo the FSB interrogators did their best to find out whether Zharko still had documents with your signature pertaining to that old 'Naval' case. What especially astonished me was the fact that those very FSB people were seeking his confession that he, Zharko, and myself had connections with Berezovsky.[12]

In July 2007, days after the British police foiled another assassination attempt on Berezovsky's life (the first was in Moscow in 1994), I met Alex Goldfarb for a late breakfast in the Hilton Hotel on Park Lane. It was the same Hilton, located conveniently round the corner from Boris's office, where the Russian suspect was arrested. (He was later deported to Moscow where he was abducted in January and no one ever heard of him again.) I asked Alex about Zharko. Goldfarb said he had seen Slava in Berezovsky's jet when they were visiting Karachay-Cherkessia, a republic and an electoral district in the north Caucasus that elected Berezovsky as their independent State Duma deputy in 1999. Slava was a good guy, women liked him, Alex said, and he liked the former Spetsnaz man. At that time people like Zharko and a former bodyguard, Andrei Lugovoy, as well as Litvinenko himself were part of the oligarch's protection and security team often moonlighting for him while still employed by the government.

Both Zharko and Lugovoy were arrested in 2001 but soon released. Russian gaols are places where no person in his right mind would think of spending even an hour, so they are generally considered to be ideal venues for KGB recruitment, especially regarding those who themselves were part of the system. They do not actually need to be recruited as they are in the reserve anyway. What is asked for first of all is repentance for keeping up a company with such 'enemies' as the former oligarch who had left Russia. Then agreement that they will provide information on other enemies of the state like Shchekochikhin or Patarkatsyshvili. And indeed, Zharko was close to the journalist up to the latter's tragic death in Moscow in 2003 and Lugovoy remained among those few whom the Georgian billionaire trusted even after the Litvinenko operation until Badri's last day in London in February 2008. Unfortunately, all three (Berezovsky, Patarkatsyshvili and Shchekochikhin) had at least one dangerous feature in common: their assessment of people close to them was often wrong. So two of them are no longer among the living and Boris's life is certainly in danger.

A month before Zharko arrived in London to meet Berezovsky, Limarev started collaborating with Shchekochikhin who came to visit him in France. For the State Duma deputy it was the project called 'Patriots of the GeBe' (mocking the name of the state security), which he hoped to develop with Limarev's help. Limarev, using his critical website and his good contacts with the Berezovsky people as demonstration of his trustworthiness, surely did not miss this opportunity to learn as much as possible about Shchekochikhin's attempts to reveal financial crimes of high-ranking FSB officials. As further developments proved, it was extremely important for Moscow generals to keep a constant watchful eye on the reporter.

It is known that Limarev passed Yuri over to 'friendly hands' when the lawmaker proceeded to Italy to study ways of fighting organised crime. Shchekochikhin's hosts in Palermo were journalists Carlo Bonini and Giuseppe D'Avanzo of *La Repubblica*. Limarev had collaborated with *La Repubblica* since 2000. It was this Italian newspaper that later published his 'revelations' directed against Litvinenko and Scaramella that were so beneficial to the Kremlin.

In London, Berezovsky introduced Zharko to Litvinenko and Sasha's vigilance failed again. He was happy to have a service veteran, like himself or Melnichenko, as a friend and coworker and immediately decided to do him a favour by introducing him to Martin Flint. The Risk Analysis director did not forget Sasha's help in the liberation of Peter Shaw and gave Zharko a simple and routine assignment to collect some background information on a Russian telecoms company.

Such requests are common, because foreign investors are extremely careful when entering the Russian market, especially in the sensitive telecommunications industry, which has been beset by scandals connected with major Russian telecoms ventures.

One example is the MegaFon scandal involving a major mobile services provider that broke as a result of the court hearings in the USA. It produced a lot of market stress when the Russian corporation Alfa Group Consortium and its US entity, Alfa Capital Markets, Inc., were named 'a criminal enterprise that has used US banks and stock exchanges as an integral part of their theft schemes, costing American taxpayers and stockholders hundreds of millions of dollars'.[13] Then, only the professionals noted that the Swiss lawyer Hans Bodmer was among the defendants. Bodmer pleaded guilty in an earlier case accepting his role in organising a complex money-laundering scheme, trailing back to 1997 but still in court in the time of writing, when international investors were stripped of almost $200,000,000. After such cases a British corporate investor would be interested to know as much as possible to plan his strategy in the Russian market.

Among other things, he or she would wish to be informed that Yuri Pavlenko, a former first deputy Telecoms minister appointed as MegaFon CEO in July 2002, was the first managing director of the British–Soviet joint venture Comstar that virtually disappeared to be replaced by Comstar United TeleSystems. This public company, whose shares are being traded at the London Stock Exchange, belongs largely to AFK Sistema and certainly this financial corporation's business record would be of great importance to big market players. As much as the fact that before he started his work in telecoms in 1989 as the boss of Comstar, Pavlenko had already pursued an interesting career in the Russian military intelligence, as he told me during our several meetings in his spacious office on Tverskaya-Yamskaya Street in Moscow.

Further useful information that a professional risk assessment firm would be able to provide to a client is the fact that in 2006–7 Russian government officials actively canvassed investors to take part in the so-called 'people's IPO', or initial public offering, where such companies as Rosneft, Sberbank and the Foreign Trade Bank (Vneshtorgbank) offered their shares to members of the public seeking additional capital. Although most IPOs are of companies going through a transitory growth period, and they are therefore subject to additional uncertainty regarding their future value, it was declared that in the fast-growing Russian economy it would be wise to invest. In the first half of 2008, however, when the shares were at attractive prices, such strategic investors as Yelena Baturina, the wife of the Moscow Mayor Yuri Luzhkov, and Suleyman Kerimov, a member of the Federation Council and a billionaire known as 'the richest civil servant of Russia', sold their stock in the Sberbank getting maximum value for their investment, and left. Since mid-2007 the Russian equity market was cooling as major foreign investment funds were packing off. 'People's investors' of Russia could not know that, of course, but the Economic Department of the FSB as well as the Kremlin were forewarned about the tendency.[14] An experienced analyst from a professional company advising a British investor would know preciously enough not to let his client down in a situation like that.

Zharko did not deliver anything useful to Risk Analysis as, according to his own words, he collected all his information from the internet. But, he said, the report was accepted and he was paid well. The Russian provocateur could not know that a similar assignment is usually given to several contacts and that the company itself makes a meticulous research from all public sources in many languages so they knew perfectly well what his report was worth. This could explain why Zharko did not stay in London but returned to Russia and thereafter was used by Litvinenko only for minor errands from time to time.

After allegedly surrendering himself to the Russian authorities in June 2007,

Zharko spun a tale for the media. He claimed that during his next visit to the British capital, in April 2002, Litvinenko had introduced him to men calling themselves Paul and John 'who spoke good Russian' and did not conceal the fact that they represented Her Majesty's Secret Service. Because Litvinenko had introduced Zharko to them as a Russian military intelligence officer, they quickly recruited him and paid him cash, explained Zharko to a Moscow interviewer.[15] Again, the SVR mole betrayed his ignorance. He was evidently unaware that the Intelligence Services Act 1994 directs SIS to operate *overseas* and that his true identity, affiliation and intelligence-gathering capabilities would be many times cross-checked before any approach would be made.

To make Zharko's story seem more convincing, the FSB gave him several names of former and serving MI6 officers who worked in Russia or with Russian assets for his interviews. However, as usual, their version is inconsistent. Zharko says, he 'categorically refused to share any information on military subjects'. An SIS case officer would need only a few minutes to establish that he was not for real – a dangle, to use a professional term, meaning an operation in which an enticing intelligence target is dangled in front of an opposition service in hopes they might think him or her a bona fide recruit. So the whole of Zharko's story was concocted for the Russian media market with only several English names inserted for gullible Westerners to pick up.

Right up to his death Litvinenko never learned the true role of his 'trusted friend Slava'.

In January 2003 Mykola Melnichenko was flying back to Washington and Chekulin was seeing him off to the airport. On the way, the former KGB officer explained to Chekulin, the self-declared FSB agent, that the latter's future with Berezovsky might be at risk because sooner or later the Russians would find a way to silence the tycoon. Mykola-the-tape-recorder suggested a simple way for Chekulin to bargain immunity from prosecution in Russia – buy a recording device and record all conversations and anything that could be of any use for the Russian services. Of special value would be all Litvinenko's contacts with Western authorities and virtually anything to do with Berezovsky: his circle of friends and business associates, his tastes, his women, his system of security, anything and everything. Chekulin thought it over and soon acquired a light and compact digital voice recorder (using funds from Berezovsky's Foundation for Civil Liberties) with which he made, as he later claimed, a hundred hours of secret recordings.

Chekulin even used a sophisticated disguise in order not to be caught with a device switched on in his trouser pocket. During conferences and outings with Berezovsky and his friends, Chekulin asked his son to bring him a small innocent looking bag where he placed the working recorder so in case it were to be found by Berezovsky's security detail, he could always deny knowledge.

Spring 2003 was quite stressful for the tycoon. Several months before, the Office of the Prosecutor General of Russia sent another request to London demanding the extradition of Boris Berezovsky and Yuli Dubov, his old and close business associate. Boris was almost certain that the British were not going to extradite him but on 23 March he and Dubov were arrested and transported to the police station. It was, of course, a formal act and they were soon released, but the episode left an unpleasant feeling for quite a while.

On 2 April the pair was giving a press conference in Le Meridien Hotel in Piccadilly after preliminary hearings at Bow Street Magistrates' Court, when a tall man approached Chekulin and started a conversation.

The choice of target was correct for Chekulin had already been working for Russian intelligence. The stranger's name was Vladimir Teplyuk.

Teplyuk was strange. According to some sources, he was born in Karaganda, Kazakhstan, on 8 April 1951, but even ubiquitous Russian journalists in the country where virtually any information could be bought for a dime were unable to dig up anything on him until May 2000. Then he applied for foreign travel permission, received a Kazakh passport and a year later left for Germany.

This total lack of information on Teplyuk's fifty years spent in the former Soviet Union, this inability of researchers to get more than his official passport data present reasonable grounds for suspicion and speculation.

I do not see Teplyuk as an illegal SVR operative. He simply doesn't fit the pattern. He is tall, attracts attention in the crowd, lets himself be photographed, and obviously does not speak good English. I met Teplyuk at a seminar in the London University of Westminster in February 2007 where it was seemingly not his business to attend and he uttered no sound as he towered in a front row as a silent and indifferent observer. On that spring day on 2 April 2003 he had already been noticed stalking Berezovsky at the London Economic Forum where his presence could also not be explained.

So when spotted again talking to Chekulin, a call was immediately placed to find out who he was. Teplyuk had introduced himself as 'Vladimir Ivanovich' (later the Kazakh immigration authorities would state that his patronymic is 'Afanasyevich') and said that he had been living in England for four years, whereas in reality he had come quite recently. He claimed his only reason for seeking Berezovsky's company was to do business with the tycoon. Litvinenko immediately suspected Teplyuk of being a Russian agent – dressing, speaking and behaving like one.

This actually did not sound too far-fetched. There is something in the tradecraft called a 'passive probe' when someone, not necessarily a full-fledged agent, is sent on an intelligence mission just to observe passively and record details about the target location or organisation. I heard that Teplyuk had been recruited in the late 1970s when he worked in the special garage belonging to the 9th Directorate of the KGB. Credit should be given to Berezovsky's security for spotting him. Amazingly, even after he had been quickly uncovered, he continued to consort with Berezovsky's people including Goldfarb, Litvinenko, Litvinenko's English friend and interpreter, and even Julia Svetlichnaya, a post-graduate student of the University of Westminster who met Litvinenko for a series of interviews in May 2006. Teplyuk attended all magistrates' court hearings in 2003 until Boris was granted political asylum in Britain. He was omnipresent. No wonder in May the security officials at Bow Street asked Teplyuk to identify himself and made notes of his passport data.

Chekulin returned to Russia in April 2004 and after an obligatory repentance period started actively collaborating with the FSB and the prosecutors. He then began accusing Berezovsky and all those who helped him in London of every sin. These included a cynical accusation that Marina Litvinenko was involved in her husband's death and probably poisoned him herself. Chekulin also started to write books that were promptly published and widely advertised. Interviews were arranged with the author who was placed on the 'protected witness programme' in Russia.

In his writings and public statements Chekulin maintained that Berezovsky had offered Teplyuk millions in cash for a false testimony and that Litvinenko had drugged the poor Kazakh and then video-recorded him 'confessing that he was dispatched by the FSB to kill Berezovsky' – a video that influenced the Home Office decision on Berezovsky, he claimed.

These statements, directed not only to Russia but also for export, had their effect.

London, House of Commons:

Boris Berezovsky

Dr Julian Lewis [Conservative MP for New Forest East]: To ask the Secretary of State for the Home Department if he will make a statement on the outcome of police investigations into the claims made during the hearing of the extradition case against Boris Berezovsky that an assassin had been sent from Russia to attack him.

Ms Hazel Anne Blears, MP [then a Home Office Minister]: The Commissioner of Police of the Metropolis informs me that the Metropolitan Police Service was made aware of an alleged threat to Boris Berezovsky. Inquiries made were unable to either substantiate this information or find evidence of any criminal offences having been committed. Investigations into this matter have been concluded.[16]

Thus, Boris Berezovsky was not granted political asylum in Britain because of Teplyuk's supposed 'confessions', as the above statement shows they could not be substantiated. The Russian scriptwriters had evidently failed to understand the dominance of Justice in this country.

The chief of Russia's Foreign Intelligence Service now saw something behind that top-secret order he had been handed by the Kremlin. In front of General Lebedev was the highest-precedence cable (known as FLASH in the CIA) from the London SVR station that read:

Today Scotland Yard arrested Major Andrei Ponkin of the FSB and [codename for Aleksey Alyokhin]. Our source [codename] reports that on 9 October they met [codename for Litvinenko] on a bench near the Wagamama restaurant on Leicester Square near Piccadilly Circus. Ponkin and Alyokhin allegedly told [codename for Litvinenko]: 'There is growing discontent with [codename] within the FSB. People think that as soon as [codename] has dealt with the oligarchs, it will be their turn to be in the shoes of the "werewolves in uniform". So there is a plan to use Chechen separatists to assassinate [codename] with a sniper rifle during one of his foreign trips.' We are closely following the developments and will report asap. [Codename for London Rezident].

Lebedev chuckled. 'Let the idiots spend some days behind the bars,' he thought. These were obviously the dirty games of his opposite number, General Nikolai Platonovich Patrushev, director of the FSB. The chief knew that Patrushev had long been very keen to place his own operatives on the lucrative turf formerly given exclusively to the foreign intelligence directorate, the elite FCD or *Pervyi Glavk*. Such clumsy and stupid provocations could spoil everything. But before making a direct call on a hotline to the Kremlin, Lebedev decided to wait how the events in London would unveil.

On 17 October Boris Berezovsky, accompanied by lawyers, visited Scotland Yard. He was told that on 13 October the police had informed the Russian Embassy of the arrest of two Russians suspected of planning the assassination of President Putin. Berezovsky reported this to the press: 'The police were very surprised that there was no reaction to this from the Russian diplomats,' he said.

As usual, the police issued a laconic statement. Scotland Yard Press Secretary Paul Clark told a correspondent of the Moscow's *Kommersant* the following:

We can confirm only that two men of Russian origin aged 36 and 40 were arrested on the morning of 12 October on suspicion of breaking the 2000 Terrorism Act and were released without charge on 17 October. They returned to Russia at their own will. We are not entitled to confirm or deny any other information.

After the news reached Yasenevo, Lebedev picked up the phone and had a short discussion with a man who had just returned from St Petersburg where an Orthodox bishop baptised his baby son. He didn't bother to dial – in fact, the telephone did not have any dial or a keypad, for it was a direct and highly protected line.

In late October 2005 Andrei Lugovoy, a former major in the Federal Protection Service (FSO), who, unlike Zharko, had earlier been acquainted with Litvinenko, made a telephone call from Moscow to Sasha's mobile number in London suggesting a meeting.

That December the Berezovsky's Foundation for Civil Liberties quit the 'tape scandal'. Goldfarb made a statement that the fund 'from today is not going to pursue the public debate on the so-called "Melnichenko tapes" '. He told the press,

> We have done everything in our power. At this moment all records are at the Ukrainian prosecution disposal, and Melnichenko himself is being guarded on Ukrainian territory. We believe that our efforts played a major part in making this possible, but there is nothing more we can do. Right from the day when three years ago Melnichenko had submitted the evidence, our only intention was to lend a helping hand for the investigation to be fair.[17]

If there was an investigation, no charges followed.

On 23 January 2006 Lugovoy was among the numerous guests whom Boris had invited to celebrate his sixtieth birthday, an extravagant and very formal black tie event. Together with the others coming from Russia, he arrived in a specially rented private jet. During the reception Lugovoy sat at the same table as Sasha and Marina. The preparations for stage two of what I call Operation VLADIMIR started on that very night. All agents were in place.

Victor Yushchenko, the Ukrainian Patient, Kiev, September 2004

In 2005 the Orthodox New Year, or the Old New Year as it is called in Russia and Ukraine, fell on the night of 13 to 14 January. Therefore, when I arrived at the Rudolfinerhaus clinic in Vienna and took a lift to the fourth floor to interview Nikolai Nikolayevich Korpan in his new office, I found him in festive mood. Dr Korpan, whom I had known quite well for several years, started by telling me that he had been invited to attend the Russian Embassy that evening to take part in the celebration. He did not plan to go but an embassy official called early in the morning asking him to reconfirm and adding that Nikolai Nikolayevich was considered a very important guest and His Excellency the ambassador himself was eager to see him. Korpan was proud and agreed to be there.

This talented physician, quite used to dealing with microscope and bacilli, could not know that during that reception he would himself become an object of a close, almost anatomical, study.

On the morning of 13 January University Professor Dr Korpan was a happy and confident man, well respected as one of the leading surgeons of a very prestigious private clinic in Vienna – the consultant-in-charge and in fact personal doctor to Victor Andreyevich Yushchenko, the president-elect of his native Ukraine. It was only weeks before this that Nikolai felt he had personally saved the future president's life and helped in his own way to win the election.

Four months earlier, on 5 September 2004, Alexander Tretyakov, a Ukrainian politician who used to be his patient some time ago, called Korpan's mobile number in Vienna. Now a top aide of Victor Yushchenko, an opposition candidate running for the presidency, Tretyakov asked if Nikolai Nikolayevich could arrange a place in Rudolfinerhaus for a patient who would be coming that same day by a regular commercial flight from Kiev. Dr Korpan said he could.

There was no patient when Korpan arrived at Schwechat Vienna international airport that afternoon. Apparently Nikolai then got another call assuring him that his future patient – still unnamed at that stage – would be coming shortly. In his cosy office on Billrothstrasse in the upmarket 19th District, Korpan gave instructions for a reinforced night shift of emergency specialists and informed his boss, the Rudolfinerhaus president Dr Michael Zimpfer, a leading Austrian anaesthesiologist and critical care specialist, that they were waiting for a VIP, a very important patient.

Late that night another call came and Dr Korpan drove his small BMW to Schwechat again. Among the group of compatriots that arrived after midnight from Borispol in Ukraine were a woman, a child, three strong men and a very sick but rather handsome gentleman who introduced himself as Yushchenko. Dr Korpan knew very well who he was.

'Doctor, I have a terrible pain in the back,' he said after they shook hands. 'Please, could you relieve me of it?'

Of course, but first they had to go to the hospital. They drove to the Rudolfinerhaus with Yushchenko lying on the back seat of Nikolai's car and the others packed in Mercedes of Walter Komarek, an Austrian who had also come to meet them.

The ward was ready; a team of doctors got straight to work. It was 1:17 a.m.

They were not forensic experts but it was perhaps the best emergency team that Austria could provide. The laboratory tests had shown toxic effects in the body, so they immediately started detoxication procedures. The Ukrainian patient was given an endoscopy (but not biopsy) and was tested for *Helicobacter pilori*, with negative results. They found mucosal inflammation of the alimentary canal. Yushchenko's liver and large intestine were affected as well as his skin and nervous system. But the doctors found to their amazement that all those symptoms seemed to show remarkable resistance to therapy.

More than a year before, in March 2003 with the presidential election campaign looming, the Kuchma government in Ukraine had shut down Radio Continent, a private station that re-transmitted programmes about the country and its current politics that were being broadcast by the BBC, Voice of America, Deutsche Welle and other Western outlets. The Ukrainian Service of Radio Free Europe/Radio Liberty (RFE/RL), by giving the population news from the opposition camp, was becoming an important factor in the election campaign. The president of RFE/RL, Thomas A. Dine, told me in Prague that they were seeking collaboration with local stations in the former Soviet republics to reach listeners on easily accessible short waves (HM), and the Ukrainian authorities were not happy about it.

HM transmission required a government license, so Sergey Sholokh, Radio Continent chief executive, was called on the carpet and advised to review his policy. 'The first thing they told me,' he said later, 'was that if I put RFE/RL on air, it would be the end for me and my station. But if I secretly collaborated with them, all claims against Radio Continent would end and I would have free rein with all the funds and support I needed. I agreed to their demands – to win time to escape.' After Sholokh left the country, security forces raided the station, arrested three of his staff and took away broadcast equipment. 'It was an act of revenge,' Sholokh said, 'because they understood they could not get at me physically. They wanted to destroy Radio Continent. This was simply an attack by bandits.'[1]

Later that year 2003 the authorities took other harsh steps to weaken the opposition. In October they thwarted Yushchenko's attempt to chair his party congress in Donetsk, the stronghold of the pro-Kremlin Ukrainian politician Victor Yanukovich. A mob armed with bats and crowbars physically prevented Yushchenko from entering the town.

The opposition leader then decided it was time to add security of his own to the two bodyguards the government had provided him. In early 2004 he appointed Evgeny Chervonenko, a former motor racing professional who had been an aide to President Kuchma until he joined the opposition, as coordinator of a special security detail to guard the candidate full time. Chervonenko had previously had nothing to do with security but he was devoted and reliable, second only to the candidate's wife in the closest circle of Yushchenko's friends and supporters, a man he could trust with his life. Chervonenko quickly added a team of more than fifty professionals to the State Protection Service (SPS) men attached to Yushchenko, Pavel Alyoshin and Peter Plyuta.

Chervonenko and his people were guarding Yushchenko and his family during their holidays in Crimea in the summer of 2004 when they spotted the police surveillance teams watching and even filming them. In the government dacha Chervonenko took upon himself the tasting of the food that was offered to Yushchenko.

While Yushchenko was vacationing in the Crimea, Russian President Vladimir Putin was also there attending a one-day business forum in Yalta where together with the Ukrainian President Kuchma and his Prime Minister Yanukovich, Putin was trying to promote the so-called Common Economic Space, a loose alliance encompassing Russia, Ukraine, Belarus and Kazakhstan.

Speaking at this forum on 26 July 2004, Putin accused the secret services of Western countries of interfering with the Russia's plans to integrate economically with Ukraine. '[Western] agents, in our countries and outside them,' he said, 'are trying to discredit the integration of Russia and Ukraine.' The former Chekist used the word *agentura*, the KGB term for networks of secret agents that penetrated foreign countries during the Cold War on behalf of the Kremlin. That was a Freudian slip: speaking about a Western threat, the President of Russia was contemplating his own operations.

Yushchenko and his people returned from the Crimea on 19 August to prepare for the final stage of the presidential race.

On 28 August Vladimir Satsyuk, first deputy director of the Ukrainian Security Service (SBU) was spotted in Moscow meeting his Russian colleagues. During the same month Mykola Melnichenko was also in the Russian capital negotiating a deal with the SVR/FSB representatives. Upon his return to Kiev, Satsyuk arranged a meeting with the opposition leader Yushchenko at his dacha without delay.

It was David Zhvaniya, a Georgian member of and heavy donator to Our Ukraine (Yushchenko's party) who had been approached to organise this secret meeting between the SBU leadership and the opposition candidate. Zhvaniya was a trusted person and one of two contact men in Kiev for Boris Berezovsky who was supporting and funding the Orange Revolution from his London exile.

Without seeing the files it is impossible, of course, to accuse Zhvaniya of working for the FSB. I have never seen any evidence that shows any involvement by Zhvaniya. This was suggested much later, in September 2007 after the poisoning of Yushchenko, when Boris Berezovsky sued Tretyakov and Zhvaniya, who had in the meantime became the emergency minister of Ukraine, for misusing nearly $23 million that the tycoon had allocated for Yushchenko's campaign. And more importantly, Zhvaniya took a pro-Kremlin position and joined an FSB-orchestrated propaganda operation designed to prove that there had never been any attempt on the candidate's life and all that happened in September 2004 was nothing but Yushchenko's subterfuge aimed at bringing himself to power.

At the end of August, Yushchenko accompanied by Zhvania visited Satsyuk's dacha to discuss the security measures during the final days before the elections. He was greeted by Satsyuk and served a friendly and substantial dinner of Uzbek pilaf and plenty of good wine. Serving the dear guest this way was without doubt a final test-run of Moscow's operation to assassinate him.

By that time a team of assassins had already infiltrated Ukraine and established themselves in the dacha and around it. Yushchenko was accompanied at all times by one of the SPS bodyguards and by Chervonenko, who claimed that he never left his friend and boss alone – except for one notable day in September. Thus at that stage the assassination team's task was only to establish the target's profile: the pattern of his movements, his reaction to persuasion, his protection and its weaknesses. Much of this information had already been available to intelligence sources in Moscow and Kiev including photographs of the target, plans of the dacha, maps of the surrounding areas and the escape routes.

The means by which the target would be assassinated had also been determined and a specialist delivered a sophisticated poison produced by a special laboratory to the scene.

A support team consisting of the 'cleaners' should also have been available, this time not to dispose of the body, but to professionally clean up the place so that the future investigation would not be able to find traces. Certainly also, a back-up team was ready for a hit should something go wrong during the planned operation.

As all professionals learn during their training, assassination is all about getting the target into a position where the deed can be done. That late-August dinner with Satsyuk at his country house was of paramount importance for the operation's success. It worked well and Yushchenko behaved according to the expected pattern.

In the assessment that followed, the assassination team evidently decided that Chervonenko, with his zeal and vigilance, would be an unwanted presence in the final phase, so a simple plan was designed to deal with the problem.

On 5 September the Our Ukraine presidential nominee accompanied by his security detail under the watchful eye of Evgeny Chervonenko arrived in Chernigov where Yushchenko would speak to a rally of his supporters.

It was a good day and the candidate felt well. He delivered a strong speech and the voters were impressed and excited. Much of Yushchenko's speech focused on the issues he had been pushing throughout the week – corruption in the government and errors in carrying out economic changes. Yushchenko also touched on key issues like joining NATO and integrating with Europe.

At the end of the meeting, a listener came forward to present Yushchenko a cross and thank him for all he did for the Ukraine. It was an acquaintance of Yushchenko's whom the locals called Shur-the-antiquary. Shur asked Yushchenko and his team to his home to perform a wake for his dear wife who had passed away. They agreed and Shur toasted them with some home-made alcohol distilled from bark. (It was later tested and found to be perfectly all right.)

Then the team drove to a cottage in the country that belonged to Oleg Golovin, one of the founders of the group of companies known as Foxtrot, an important Ukrainian retailer. Knowing that Yushchenko, like every Ukrainian, loved good company and long feasts around a groaning board, Golovin had organised a big party in his honour. Present were Alexei Ivchenko, one of the Our Ukraine party leaders and a one-time CEO of Naftogaz Ukraine, a leading oil and gas company; Vladimir Shulga, another founder of Foxtrot who arranged this visit; Vitaly Hrisko, the company's executive director, and David Zhvaniya who accompanied the candidate on that trip. Yushchenko recalled that as soon as he left the podium in Chernigov, Zhvaniya came up to remind him that after Golovin's lunch party, Yushchenko was expected in the evening at a dacha in the country for an important meeting with the SBU, which they should attend by all means. Yushchenko later said he had not wanted to go.

As the late lunch slowly progressed from sushi to warmed trout fillet, Yushchenko's security chief Chervonenko noticed another Georgian, Thomas Tsyntsabadze, the owner of a car dealership, talking to Zhvaniya, after which Zhvaniya went out to make one of his frequent telephone calls. Returning, he firmly said to Yushchenko: 'They are waiting for us at the dacha.'

Again, precisely according to his established psychological pattern, the future president let himself be persuaded. Chervonenko boarded his car. Yushchenko and Plyuta, one of his SPS bodyguards, went in the Audi. Zhvaniya behind them in his own black SUV with the Kiev number plate 555-55, driven by Tsyntsabadze, while the rest of the security detail followed in a caravan.

When they reached Nika Motors car showroom in Podol, an old district of Kiev, they stopped. In his headset Chervonenko heard a soft click and the words

'All right, you may go.' It was the voice of Plyuta, communicating his boss's order via a two-way radio. When Satsyuk's black 4WD SUV came up, Chervonenko was ordered to call off his team of guards. He started communicating with his 'eagles': Orlan-1, Orlan-2, and the rest. His own call sign was Orlan-10.

Slowly the group left, led by Satsyuk in his car followed by Zhvaniya and then by the Audi with Yushchenko and his government bodyguard, this time with Tsyntsabadze driving.

Though he felt uncomfortable about this strange setup, the conscientious Chervonenko duly followed until, near one of the bridges over the Dnepr, he again heard Plyuta's voice on his headset, telling him that Yushchenko insisted all the security should be removed.

Chervonenko was not a professional guard and his indecisive reaction at this moment was the weakness his opponents were counting on: he obeyed the command and dropped out of the motorcade. 'This is a pain I have to live with,' he said in an interview years later. Though he probably saved Yushchenko's life, this loyal friend nevertheless still blames himself for failing to protect him.[2]

At the dacha Yushchenko and Satsyuk were greeted by Igor Smeshko, chief of the SBU, Ukraine's KGB. (There is no suggestion that Smeshko was involved in the operation.) With his high authority Smeshko announced that this was to be a top-level secret meeting, not to be attended or even known by anybody else. Why Zhvaniya might be more trustworthy than Chervonenko would remain a mystery, but the fact is that those in charge of the operation did their best to rid the company of Yushchenko's devoted security adviser. Still, it seems likely that the only man who was informed of the unfolding plot, and even he only in very general terms, was Satsyuk, the host.

Satsyuk could have been in the dark and simply instructed in Moscow to arrange a meeting between his SBU boss and the opposition candidate, perhaps ostensibly to find out what Yushchenko planned in the way of security if he appeared to be winning the elections. That information would be useful for the Moscow planners in case Plan A – 'The Last Supper' poisoning – did not work as planned.

The meal that night, as recalled by Yushchenko and Zhvaniya, consisted of boiled crayfish, a salad of tomatoes, cucumbers and corn, followed by cold meats and washed down by beer and vodka. There were only four of them and whatever bodyguards were present were moved to the garden summerhouse. The supper was served by two waiters and prepared by a cook. An ideal setup.[3]

After the meal brandy was drunk, followed by large chunks of watermelon, plums, grapes and other fruit, and coffee. Before Yushchenko left at or about 2:00 a.m., Zhvaniya took a photo of the two SBU chiefs in the company of the presidential candidate, with Satsyuk's friendly hand on his right shoulder.

It was indeed Yushchenko's last supper with the SBU men. In just a few hours he felt a strong headache coming on.

***

One year later, in October 2005, I advised President Yushchenko to clean up his security service.

I reminded the Ukrainian leader how in February 2004 an outraged SBU general walked into the Berlin studio of the German radio station Deutsche Welle to accuse his own president and chiefs of misusing the service. Major General Valery Kravchenko, a declared officer of the SBU in the Ukrainian Embassy in Germany proclaimed to the listening public that the then President Kuchma, with the willing support of the SBU chief Smeshko and the full knowledge of the military intelligence chief Oleg Sinyavsky, was using the SBU for his own political advantage to spy on opposition members.

The SBU dates from Ukrainian independence in 1991. But that was not so much a date of birth as a simple renaming. It used to be the Committee for State Security (KGB) of the Ukrainian Soviet Republic, the largest and most powerful of all the republican security organisations in the USSR outside of Russia. Its leadership remained intact through the transition to independence, retaining its chief who had served since 1987, Nikolai Golushko. On independence he made his loyalties clear by transferring to Moscow the SBU archives, including the files of its agents and informants. This made it easy for the FSB to carry out the Yushchenko operation and other actions in the Ukraine, because they were playing with open cards in the former Soviet republic.

The Kremlin rewarded Golushko by calling him to Moscow to lead the Russian Security Ministry, the largest KGB directorate and one of the two components most directly responsible for internal repression during the Soviet time. When this ministry became the Russian Federal Counterintelligence Service, the FSK, Golushko was appointed its director. It was in Moscow that Yevgenia Albats met him for an interview. For just one year Golushko was Litvinenko's boss in Moscow until President Yeltsin fired him in 1994.

His successor in Kiev, Yevgeny Marchuk, had headed the Soviet-era 5th Directorate, the one that combated dissidents. In independent Ukraine his SBU tenure was marked by his failure to stem the tide of corruption or to solve high-profile killings. He admitted to 'losing' the videotape on which one of his officers had told of the murder of a political activist by a special police squad.

After the short stint of his successor, Valery Malikov, yet another career Soviet KGB officer rose to the top: Vladimir Radchenko, known as one of President Kuchma's men. In 2002, the slant of Mr Radchenko's SBU was exposed when he expelled a US diplomat and reportedly bugged the embassies of Turkey and Spain.

Leonid Derkach, the head of technical spying and communications operations who also had close links to President Kuchma and Moscow, took over in 1998. Radchenko was the chief before (1995–8) and after Derkach. He was removed in 2003 for overwhelming corruption in the service.

It was this besmirched organisation that Lt General Igor Smeshko came to head in September 2003. He was its first chief who did not start his career in the

Soviet KGB (though his was in military intelligence).

President Yushchenko sacked Smeshko in February 2005 and Alexander Turchinov, the SBU's first post-Orange Revolution director, who had never worked for the intelligence service, was imposed on Yushchenko by his prime minister. Turchinov was an apparatchik of the Communist Party and then a member of parliament and lecturer. On the desk of his office in the SBU building there was a pistol with the engraving: 'I believe! I know! We can!' Back in the autumn of 2005 it was clear that Turchinov knew little to nothing about intelligence. His 'I can' rang hollow, as he exercised no apparent influence on the SBU. The source of his confidence only became clear when he announced that he had managed to collect a lot of dirt on his president while in office.

When I called to talk to Turchinov, Marina Ostapenko, the SBU press officer, told me that her boss was busy meeting Mykola Melnichenko and arranging for his giving evidence regarding the Kuchmagate scandal. I realised that the man had been successfully played by the experienced FSB. Turchinov was dismissed from his post in September 2005.[4]

Igor Drizhchany, who succeeded him, was an equally unlucky choice. Even in the Prosecutor's Office of Ukraine, where he served before coming to the SBU, Drizhchany became notorious for his inability to collaborate with the American and European authorities in investigating major crime cases such as the murder of Georgy Gongadze and the financial fraud of Pavel Lazarenko, a former Ukrainian prime minister arrested in the USA for allegedly stealing hundreds of millions of dollars. In the SBU Drizhchany was in charge of monitoring the activity of the opposition, i.e. first of all, Yushchenko, Timoshenko and others. It would be unthinkable to appoint such a man to the top security post but Yushchenko had little choice in the political turmoil of September when he made the government and the prime minister step down. Following the advice of his old supporter Oleg Rybachuk who, after the scandalous resignation of the State Secretary Alexander Zinchenko got his place and promoted Drizhchany to the post of the chief, Yushchenko approved this appointment. Fortunately, he only served until December 2006.

A totally new man and a former ambassador, Valentin Nalivaichenko, became the new SBU chief on Christmas Eve. He finally announced a completely new ideology for his service to follow – the de-KGB-isation of the Ukrainian security service and active collaboration with Western partners. Finally, President Yushchenko followed good advice.

* * *

The day after the 'Last Supper' it was the turn of Pavel Alyoshin, another government bodyguard, who had arrived to find Yushchenko's American-born wife Katherine worried about her husband's health. Yushchenko's headache was followed by nausea and vomiting and severe abdominal pain. He also felt his back was not in order and went to a sauna for relief.

On Tuesday, 7 September, Chervonenko left to prepare a rally in Cherkasy, a city in central Ukraine about 200 km from Kiev, that Yushchenko planned to attend. Alyoshin called him asking that he come back urgently, as the boss was starting to feel really bad. Chervonenko rushed back to the capital and parked his car in front of Yushchenko's house on Malaya Zhitomirskaya Street.

On Wednesday morning a council of doctors gathered to decide what could or should be done about Yushchenko's problem. They were nonplussed by the variety of symptoms but finally decided it was gastroenteritis, an inflammation of the gastrointestinal tract involving both the stomach and the small intestine. As this is a dangerous and potentially lethal disease, they wanted their patient to check in to the government Feofania hospital for closer examination. Chervonenko did not let them. 'I knew that in communist times some intelligence officers and politicians were leaving this place feet-first,' he said to the *Ukrayinska Pravda* in August 2008.

On the same day Katherine Yushchenko and Chervonenko started to discuss a medivac – medical evacuation – to a foreign medical facility. Zhvaniya, who was also there, advised against it. 'Are you going to make a mess of the election campaign by flying him to a foreign hospital with this diarrhoea?' he asked.

While he was musing about the subject, Yushchenko continued discussing with his wife what to do as his pain in the back was becoming unbearable. On the street outside, on the steps of the nearby church, members of the radical Fraternity party were burning effigies of Yushchenko and Timoshenko, the future 'Princess Julia' of the Orange Revolution. That party was headed by Dmitry Korchinsky who had made a striking entry into the presidential race by presenting himself at the central election commission in Kiev aboard an armoured personnel carrier, with another one as a backup and accompanied by followers and bodyguards. (With all this extravagance, he managed to collect about 50,000 votes in the first round.)

On Thursday, 9 September, the Feofania hospital physician Shishkina continued to insist on the Yushchenko's hospitalisation as the tests showed that his lipase level was three times the upper limit of normal. That pointed to possible acute pancreatitis (for which alcohol is the second most common cause).

Chervonenko and Yushchenko's top aide Tretyakov realised it was high time to fly away as quickly and as secretly as possible. They went to Vadim Rabinovich, a Ukrainian media tycoon, and luckily got a private jet ready to be airborne at once. Now the question was where to fly.

They first decided to go to Switzerland, a quiet and secretive place not only for money sharks. There was a good private clinic in Geneva but after they called they were given twenty-four hours waiting time before the final confirmation so they decided to try elsewhere. In Israel, next in the line, they were told, unsurprisingly, it would take at least three days to make a decision. So Tretyakov called Korpan who appeared to be in Vienna and ready.

Just before take-off Chevonenko asked a doctor to give Yushchenko an anaesthetic injection that could reduce his pain. He also called his Austrian friend Komarek asking to meet him at Schwechat as he needed an extra car. He never said who else was coming.

In the aircraft there were Yushchenko, his wife Katherine and their eight-month-old son Taras, the government bodyguard Alyoshin, as well as Tretyakov and Chervonenko. The jet landed in Vienna after midnight.

In the morning after a sleepless night the aide and the security adviser grabbed a short nap. But sleep ended on the next day, Saturday 11 September, when doctors became alarmed at the malfunction of five of Yushchenko's internal organs. They were as unable as their Ukrainian colleagues to diagnose any specific disease. They observed what is known in medicine as the scissors effect, when negative symptoms increase with therapy. Chervonenko started to pray.

One day Yushchenko was suddenly feeling better and together with his wife made a short pilgrimage to one of the famous Viennese *Heurigen* accompanied by Chervonenko, Tretyakov, a couple of recently hired Austrian bodyguards, and Walter Komarek acting as a guide. The Austrian explained to his new friends that *Heuriger* is a young wine from the last harvest that becomes 'old' on 11 November, St Martin's Day. According to an old Viennese tradition people go to city suburbs where there are gardens and taverns serving the young wines and local food with live music and a relaxed mood. Yuschchenko enjoyed the evening, but did not eat or drink anything.

On Sunday, however, the Ukrainian patient started to feel worse again. The doctors noticed his face was becoming disfigured. Some health care specialists suspected a heart attack. He was still being treated for acute pancreatitis.

On 16 September Dr Korpan made a first draft medical conclusion, diagnosing his patient as suffering from acute pancreatitis with interstitial swelling, second degree; acute eruption of stomach ulcers; reflux gastritis in the second degree; acute proctolitis on the left side, atypical poly-segmental skin disease; peripheral paresis; and ottis on the left side. He stressed that the earlier diagnosis given to his patient in Ukraine was inadequate, and if the suggested treatment of anaesthetisation and blood transfusion had been applied, the patient's condition would have deteriorated with an 80 per cent chance of death within the following 24 to 72 hours. Next day Alexander Zinchenko, Yushchenko's chief-of-staff, later to become Secretary of State, arrived from Kiev, took Korpan's (unauthorised) medical conclusion and after a short private conference with the party leader returned to Ukraine. It was the hottest time of the election contest.

In April 2005 Goldfarb and Litvinenko told me that at that decisive moment Boris Berezovsky called Yushchenko in Vienna and urged him to return to Kiev to continue the election marathon. According to Goldfarb, they talked for about an hour and the former oligarch managed to persuade the future president that he had to go on with the election until the very end. Whether that call really happened would not be as important as the fact that one day later, on 18

September, Yushchenko was released from hospital and returned to Kiev.

First of all the candidate made important changes in his staff, replacing Zhvaniya and Roman Bessmertny, his campaign manager, and putting Zinchenko in charge. Then he addressed a rally of his supporters and on 21 September spoke to the parliament.

Among other things, Yushchenko made these comments to the deputies:

I am fortunate to be in this chamber today and will not take too much time, but let me comment on some matters concerning each of you.

During the last two weeks a number of Ukrainian politicians and journalists have been talking about what to eat and drink in this country in order to stay alive, and not die.

What I have to say may sound inappropriate, as the remarks concern me, but it will help to establish the facts.

Look at my face.

Listen to the way I speak.

This is a small fraction of what I have suffered.

Take a good hard look . . . so that the same thing does not happen to you.

This was not caused by cuisine, by my diet, as some have indicated.

I am not a gourmand, or a fan of Asian or Western cooking. I eat the same borscht and potatoes with lard that you and 47 million other Ukrainians do.

What happened to me was not caused by food or my diet, but by the political regime in this country.

Friends, we are not talking today about food literally, but about the Ukrainian political 'kitchen' where murders are on the menu.

Speaking about murder, I would love to name the assassin . . .

Do not ask me who is next. Each one of you will be next! When you ask why I avoided the same fate [as other Ukrainian politicians who were assassinated in the past few years], the answer is it was the wrong dose [of poison] at the wrong time . . . and my angels weren't sleeping. This helped me to return to this world.

Don't forget this lesson because you could be next.[5]

However, Yushchenko did not stay long in Ukraine. On 25 September Dr Korpan arrived in Kiev, took his patient's blood sample and flew back to Vienna. During the night of 29 September Chervonenko received a telephone call from Austria. The results of the laboratory tests were so bad, he was informed, that the patient had to return to the hospital at once. It was the matter of life and death, most probably the latter.

Next day Yushchenko checked into the Rudolfinerhaus clinic again.

It is called anamnesis. The patient is asked for his recollections pertaining to his case history. During Yushchenko's anamnesis Dr Korpan kept asking him what might be the cause of his disease, and the idea of poisoning never came to his patient's mind. Austrian forensic experts were unable to determine what was wrong with Victor Yushchenko, and their colleagues from the Institute of Toxicology did no better. The crisis that started on 5 October reached its peak on the seventh when the pain in his back was so acute that Yushchenko nearly fainted. Dr Zimpfer had no choice but to inject opiate intravenously, and had to repeat it again and again. When that did not work, the physician resorted to epidural anaesthesia, inserting a catheter into Yushchenko's spine. Just in case, he was transferred to the resuscitation room. Chervonenko accompanied him everywhere.

It was the first and the last time this big, grey-haired man prayed on his knees. He asked God to help his dying friend. And to save Ukraine.

Those sudden changes in the patient's condition and his absolute resistance to massive treatment – indeed it looked as if he had survived an extremely hard surgical operation or a bad car accident – was a very atypical syndrome. Even Lothar Wicke, an old x-ray specialist and – during Yushchenko's sojourn in Vienna – director-administrator of the Rudolfinerhaus, should have realised it. He should have also figured out that the doctors were going to lose their patient.

While Victor Yushchenko and the health care specialists were struggling for his life, President Kuchma's son-in-law, the Ukrainian oligarch and billionaire Victor Pinchuk, travelled to Vienna to meet with the Rudolfinerhaus physicians. But his interest was not the state of health of his fellow countryman. Soon after Yushchenko's speech to parliament claiming he had been poisoned, a PR team from the Paris office of Euro RSCG, part of Havas Group, headed by Yffic Nouvellon, followed Pinchuk to Vienna.

As the *Financial Times* later found out, Nouvellon's team had been especially selected because they had worked before for Pinchuk and his wife in Kiev.

In Austria there is a well-established company's branch, Euro RSCG Vienna, which for long time had an office at 26 Argentinienstrasse just vis-à-vis the Russian Trade Delegation. After the Yushchenko events, they quietly changed the address and moved to 123 Hasnerstrasse, in Vienna's remote 16th District.

On 28 September the Nouvellon team distributed a press release that was sent to the news agencies and international media, including the *Financial Times*, offering evidence that Mr Yushchenko had not been poisoned. Reuters later disseminated this information with a reference to the alleged 28 September press release of Rudolfinerhaus saying that doctors at the Vienna hospital had ruled out the possibility that Yushchenko was deliberately poisoned.

That reeked of old-style KGB provocation. The false press release sent to Reuters in London was picked up by many of the world's largest and most prestigious newspapers. (A few days later Reuters officially admitted their error and managed to find out that the fake came from a fax machine in Germany that was registered to an individual named Markus Reugamer). In their turn, Yushchenko's staff had traced the distribution of the falsified press release to TriMedia,[6] a public relations firm with an office in Moscow.

The Euro RSCG visitors from Paris had not only got access to the clinic's letterhead. Almost certainly Pinchuk actually met Dr Zimpfer, the Rudolfinerhaus president, and offered his help in selecting and financing an appropriate international PR company that the hospital would need to handle the complex problem of dealing with the international press after Yushchenko's sensational statement in Kiev. Dr Zimpfer, unaware of the consequences, agreed and the hospital officially hired the Paris team. That later allowed Owen Dougherty, Euro RSCG's New York-based chief communications officer, to state that 'We worked for the clinic in Vienna where Mr Yushchenko had his exam[ination]s and organised a press conference for the clinic, [but] the content of the press conference was controlled by the client.'[7] Dougherty never specified who was the *real* client.

The *Financial Times* also conducted their own investigation pointing out that Yffic Nouvellon 'did not reveal his connection to Mr Pinchuk, and when confronted about it insisted he did not know Mr Pinchuk and that he had never been to Kiev'.[8] Such toughness would do credit to any spy caught red-handed. Michael Zimpfer told the *Financial Times* that he had cut the clinic's contact with the French after Yushchenko had informed him of Euro RSCG's ties to the Kuchma family. 'It was a big mistake,' the Rudolfinerhaus's president said, 'to involve a company that was clearly biased to one side.'

Apart from carrying out this international disinformation operation, Nouvellon's team also arranged a press conference on Wednesday, 29 September, in which Lothar Wicke, the Rudolfinerhaus 'Medical and Managing Director' contradicted Yushchenko's allegations of poisoning. From that day on Wicke became a cause célèbre in the anti-Yushchenko propaganda war.

However, on 3 October Wicke had to sign an official statement issued by the hospital's president. It said:

> At present we are investigating the possibility of an external cause of poisoning. It is impossible at the moment either to confirm or deny whether it was intentional or unintentional. The press release of 28 September 2004, according to which poisoning could be excluded is wrong and is refuted by this report.

The document emphasised that only Dr Zimpfer or Dr Korpan, Yushchenko's attending physician, were authorised to talk about the state of Yushchenko's health and his treatment, and only with the patient's permission.[9]

Wicke's extraordinary statements started a battle. Speaking to the press on 4 October, Dr Korpan revealed that in the previous week his Kiev apartment had been searched and his neighbours questioned by Ukrainian law enforcement officials. On Thursday, 7 October, a criminal police squad arrived at

Rudolfinerhaus in all their gear including cars with beacons and sirens blaring. The aim of the operation was the seizure of Yushchenko's medical records.

The next day, Friday the 8th, the second international press conference was held at the clinic with a crowd of journalists from many countries waiting in a long queue to get admission. Lothar Wicke repeated his allegations that a 'medically forged diagnosis' had been circulated by someone 'not permanently employed in this clinic,' referring to Dr Korpan. Wicke appeared especially irritated by one of Dr Korpan's phrases in his draft of the medical conclusion stating (correctly, as it was established later) that 'the patient's condition may be caused by the administration of toxic agents that are not usually included in food products'.

After his press conference of 29 September, Wicke received a written request from the Rudolfinerhaus president to retract his remarks. He said he refused to do it and had signed the memo with the word 'Acknowledged', meaning that he had seen it. It was after that, Wicke claimed, that he received a telephone call. According to his version, the caller introduced himself as 'a friend from Ukraine' and allegedly warned the old radiologist, who had nothing whatsoever to do with the treatment of Yushchenko, to 'take care as your life is in danger'. Wicke was immediately put under 24-hour police protection.

When I observed him in early spring 2005 going to a meeting with his contact in the Hotel Bristol, a guard looking very much like a Russian embassy employee was still accompanying the old man. He later said to the Austrian *Profil*, 'I was not ready to be used as an instrument in the Ukrainian elections manipulations'.[10] In reality, that was exactly the role he wittingly or unwittingly accepted and continued to play long after several independent expert commissions concluded without any doubt that the Ukrainian patient was deliberately poisoned. This, however, had not happened until Victor Yushchenko came to Rudolfinerhaus for the third time.

At seven o'clock in the morning of 7 October, after a catheter was inserted into Yushchenko's spine following a very complex surgical operation performed by a visiting leading light of anaesthesiology who had been brought in by helicopter, Dr Zimpfer summoned Chervonenko to his office. As the latter later recalled, the physician said: 'I do not know what has happened to the patient. It could be anything, including some form of a biological weapon. You are a Jew, call your Jewish friends and let them access the best secret laboratories in the world to help us. Otherwise, we shall lose him.'[11]

According to Evgeny Chervonenko, he called the USA, Israel, Switzerland, France and Britain and in every country his contacts agreed to help. Yushchenko was extremely lucky. (In the case of Sasha Litvinenko the situation was almost completely the opposite.)

After the operation, Yushchenko started feeling better and together with Dr Zimpfer his small group began discussing his return to Ukraine to continue the marathon. The scenario had been worked out in Vienna: two injections of strong medicines allowed Yushchenko to address the audience for about 20–25 minutes without the special device that weighed 10 kg which was to be permanently connected to his back.

The candidate was released from the clinic on 10 October to take part in the campaign. On his way to Lviv, Yushchenko was accompanied by Dr Zimpfer and another anaesthesiologist, while a catheter in his spine reduced his pain.

During political rallies when he felt really bad Yushchenko would make a signal and Chervonenko would come to help him retreat backstage for a quick injection that would let him continue speaking for a while. Afterwards Yushchenko would be taken away and reconnected to the machine.

There were very successful rallies in Lviv and Odessa though hardly anybody in the public could recognise Yushchenko's face, so much it had changed. But he continued to joke. 'They know my voice,' he used to say. Otherwise Yushchenko spent all his time confined to bed.

Ukrainian physicians who could do something for him were practically barred by the government from attending the sick man. Should they still attempt to help, they were either threatened or fired from their jobs. Only one doctor, according to Chervonenko, was with them all the time. His name is still unknown.

One day it became obvious that catheters could not remain in Yushchenko's spine any longer – his body started to reject them. The politician had to be operated on again. They brought him secretly to the Tretyakov's holiday cottage outside Kiev where both Tretyakov and Chervonenko assisted. A suitable space was transformed into an improvised operating theatre. So as not to affect the patient's alertness, only local anaesthesia was possible. Chervonenko later said his boss was gritting his teeth in pain but survived and the operation went well.

While Yushchenko was shuttling between rallies and his hospital bed, Victor Yanukovich, Putin's favourite, the prime minister and the only candidate of the regime, a man who had twice, in 1968 and 1970, been convicted and imprisoned for robbery and assault, decided to visit the city of Ivano-Frankivsk in western Ukraine. The area only became part of the USSR as a result of the Stalin-Hitler Pact of 1939, so many people did not very much like Russian imperialism, not to mention Communism.

The Russians were no more sympathetic to Ukrainian nationalists (as they were known) than the Soviets had been. Most of the 'nationalists' came from the territories of the former Austro-Hungarian Empire like Galicia and Transcarpathia that had been forcibly brought under Stalin's rule. And Moscow used its murder weapons to eliminate their leaders. On orders from Moscow Simon Petlyura, a leader of Ukraine's fight for independence and briefly head of state, was shot and murdered in Paris in May 1926. In October 1947 the young and popular bishop Theodore Romzha, who had called his parishioners to resist the Soviet occupiers and was hated by Khrushchev, the Ukrainian leader at the time, became Moscow's murder target. Initially, the Ukrainian NKVD under Sergey Savchenko mounted the operation, using their favoured technique of a road 'accident,' but the bishop survived and was hospitalised. In panic, Khrushchev called Stalin for help. A special group from the Pavel Sudoplatov's Bureau No. 1 flew from Moscow and on the night of 31 October a new relief nurse was assigned to care for Bishop Romzha. Soon after midnight she used the syringe provided by Mairanovsky to poison the priest with curare. In the morning he was found dead. The nurse disappeared.[12]

It was to this area and to these people that the pro-Moscow candidate Yanukovich came to reintroduce himself as a future president at a raucous rally:

> The bus drew up in front of a crowd shouting anti-government slogans, the doors opened and Yanukovich stepped out. A few seconds later something flew through the air, Yanukovich clutched at his right side, then fell to the ground where he remained. Security men swarmed around the prone figure and dragged him to an accompanying van that sped the stricken prime minister to the emergency ward of a local hospital. Later the nation was relieved to see, on its television screens, that Yanukovich had survived, although, as he spoke haltingly from his hospital bed, he appeared extremely weary and there was a near-death-experience look in the eyes staring at the camera. In a grave voice Yanukovich bemoaned the wickedness that had landed him in hospital. He said he now understood that 'nationalism is a disease', sighed that he did not hold the perpetrators responsible but blamed Yushchenko and the maleficent opposition that had twisted his assailant's mind.[13]

What was it that rattled the former convict and Moscow's only hopeful? The slow-motion video showed an egg splattering into Yanukovich and his collapsing in fear. His nervous breakdown would bring an end to any political campaign in the civilised world, but not in the Ukraine.

On 14 October a biopsy was conducted in Kiev and a skin sample removed from Yushchenko and delivered to Vienna for examination. Experienced pathologists examined it under a microscope and analysed the tissue chemically. They realised that their patient's disease was almost certainly linked to toxic exposure to chloracnegens, most probably dioxins, and that their knowledge and experience in this area were close to nil. Telegrams, email messages and plenty of telephone calls followed. Some were answered in Porton Down, Britain's germ warfare laboratory that had found ricin in a pellet that killed Georgi Markov.

Three days before the elections on 28 October a Soviet-style military parade shut down the streets of Kiev as Ukraine entered the final stretch of a tense campaign marred by dirty tricks and intimidation tactics. Thousands of uniformed soldiers flooded the capital.

Alongside the Prime Minister and presidential hopeful Viktor Yanukovich watching them parade was Vladimir Putin. The Russian leader used this show of force as an occasion for some high profile campaigning on behalf of the pro-Moscow candidate. The parade itself – to commemorate the sixtieth anniversary of Ukraine's liberation from the Nazis – was brought forward by a week, without explanation, to make it as close as possible to the election day. Quite typically of Putin's regime, the bitter political campaign had been conducted against a backdrop of bomb explosions and beatings and detaining of opposition supporters. The latest scandal in Kiev had arisen after the opposition's claim that police masquerading as skinheads at a rally had attacked some of its members. The assailants were found to have police identification cards and pistols.[14]

The military parade, a show of force much favoured by Putin, was a culmination of his three-day visit that was a flagrant attempt to boost the chances of Yushchenko's competitor. During all three days Putin was shamelessly campaigning for Yanukovich, praising his economic policies and promising the Ukrainians free non-visa travel to Russia – a step seen as winning many votes for his favourite.

Yurko Pavlenko, an opposition MP, said: 'It's disgusting that the Ukrainian government, knowing its candidate will lose in any fair contest, needs to enlist the help of the Russian President.'[15]

The initial vote of the Ukrainian presidential election was held on 31 October 2004. The results were a near draw according to the central election commission: official figures gave Yanukovich 39.32 per cent while Yushchenko was leading with 39.87 per cent. As no candidate reached the required 50 per cent for an outright victory, a runoff election was set up on 21 November. President Kuchma and his chief of staff Victor Medvedchuk, another former convict who, according to General Derkach of the SBU, had been recruited by the KGB as agent 'Sokolovsky' and trained as a lawyer to persecute dissidents, were blatantly warned by the West that if any attempt were made to rig the election, they would face a revolution.

Nevertheless, President Putin noisily supported Yanukovich and there was no way out for the Moscow's puppets to act contrary to the Kremlin's orders. As a result, the Ukrainian authorities got involved in a colossal election fraud that almost ended in bloodshed when General Sergey Popkov ordered his interior storm troops to march on Kiev in full gear.

As predicted, what followed would forever be remembered as the Orange Revolution. But some commentators are wrong when they say that it was the generals who had changed the nation's fate.[16] It was Victor Yushchenko, together with Yulia Timoshenko, who managed to bring their country on the road toward Europe. The generals, including Smeshko, were hedging their bets.

Timoshenko, a petite and good-looking female politician, was styled and directed by unknown but gifted image makers and PR professionals and became one of the biggest draws at election rallies. People were fascinated by her powerful speeches where impassioned diatribes were often leavened with good humour. She told those who came to listen, and they came in hundreds of thousands, that the oligarchic clans aimed to use Yanukovich to hang on to their power, their money and their domination of Ukraine. Timoshenko warned: 'And if we don't oppose this, Yanukovich will come not just for five years but forever and will rule Ukraine always, because in five years they will eradicate from Ukrainian territory any different views.'[17]

In November the FSB played another of its dirty tricks. A Ukrainian claiming to work for one of the secret services was dangled in front of the US intelligence officials saying he knew who was behind the Yushchenko assassination attempt. The man was promptly spirited out of Ukraine to neighbouring Romania and then transported to Hungary. A London journalist of Ukrainian descent, Askold Krushelnycky, was offered the opportunity to meet the defector and interview him before he was flown to Washington, DC. But just before Askold went to Budapest, he was told that the defector appeared to be a double agent claiming that Yulia Timoshenko had masterminded the poisoning. When the 'defector' realised he was not believed, he returned to Ukraine and dropped out of sight.[18] This Moscow attempt to split the opposition had failed, but it was to succeed some time later.

During the November runoff, Plan B – bombing Yushchenko's election headquarters – was averted when two men were arrested and their car, parked just outside packed with Russian plastic explosives, was seized. Had it detonated it would have blown up the entire three-storey building wiping away all anti-government opposition. The arrested twosome had forged Russian passports and their car bore Russian license plates. They claimed, in what was obviously a clumsily designed story, that they were part of an attempt to fake a terrorist attack that would boost Yushchenko's rating. However, the SBU investigation team found out that the explosive had been pre-tested as part of routine practice. On 21 November Yanukovich was declared a winner in what Senator Richard Lugar, senior US observer, called a 'concerted and forceful programme of election day fraud's.' It brought out hundreds of thousands of people to protest on the streets and to camp day and night on Independence Square. As a result, the election was re-run on 26 December and brought Yushchenko a clear victory with 52 per cent for him and democracy and 44 per cent for Yanukovich and Moscow.

On Christmas Eve, a courier arrived at the Channel 5 popular television programme in Kiev bringing an anonymous letter and a CD with some recordings of intercepted telephone conversations between two men, one in Moscow and another in Kiev. Here was a new FSB provocation aiming at diverting attention from the Kremlin and directing it at some 'rogue elements' in the FSB allegedly opposed to Putin.

Tom Mangold was covering the story for the *Mail on Sunday* and managed to listen to the CD and obtain a copy of the transcript. He spoke to Vladimir Ariev, a young Channel 5 journalist (whom Nikolai Korpan wanted to make our co-author for the book about the medical evidence behind the Yushchenko poisoning). Ariev told him, 'I now know the identity of both men on the intercept. The man in Kiev has admitted to me that the conversation is real and that Moscow was indeed involved in the poisoning, but it doesn't follow that Putin knew or ordered it.'

I told Nikolai to think it over because Ariev would be a liability rather than an asset in our future team. The deception technique used here is well known as 'substitution.' In this ploy to mislead the investigators, the real player is substituted by a figure who might have played the role ascribed to him, but could not and did not take any part in the operation. (The same technique was to be used in the Litvinenko operation when one of Limarev's email messages pointed to 'Honour and Dignity' – an organisation of the KGB veterans – as possible perpetrators of the crime while real assassins: the united SVR/FSB/FSO team remained in the shadows.) Normally, this technique has only a short-lived effect, but produces an impression on the public and media.

Weeks before Victor Yushchenko got a chance to celebrate his victory, he was in the Rudolfinerhaus hospital again.

An editor of the London *Independent* knew Dr John A. Henry, professor of accident and emergency medicine at St Mary's Hospital and former head of Britain's National Poisons Service. The journalist decided to try his luck and send to the toxicology expert some recent photos of Yushchenko together with scraps of information. On 24 October the *Independent* quoted Dr Henry as saying: 'This looks very like chloracne to me. There are many types of dioxins that could have caused it. The effects would be seen all over the body. Although it looks nasty it gets better, but there are long-term effects.' According to the expert, the dioxins might have been put in food or drink.

That short publication would bring world fame to Dr Henry, although the Rudolfinerhaus specialists had already suspected the dioxin poisoning. After seeing the deformed face of the Ukrainian presidential candidate on the evening news, the Dutch toxicologist Professor Abraham ('Bram') Brouwer contacted the Rudolfinerhaus to test their patient's blood for dioxin. According to Dr Zimpfer, these tests provided conclusive evidence that Yushchenko's condition resulted from 'high concentrations of dioxin'.

In February 2005 Bram Brouwer, then CEO of BioDetection Systems in Amsterdam, confirmed to me that indeed their laboratory had first discovered the dioxin exposure in the Yushchenko case and that the toxin was reliably identified as 2,3,7,8-TCDD, that is, Tetrachlordibenzo-*p*-dioxin. The toxicologist stated that indeed the solubility of this substance was extremely low in water, but it could be easily dissolved in oils and fats like corn or fish oil or butterfat. Therefore it is not difficult to administer 2,3,7,8-TCDD via food.

Professor Brouwer further commented:

With respect to the onset of its toxic action, there is quite limited information in humans regarding such high dose exposure. However, there is a good database on health effects in humans exposed accidentally to 2,3,7,8-TCDD mixed with 2,4,5-T in the Seveso explosion that occurred in 1976 [in Italy]. The onset of abdominal pains and ulceration of stomach, etc. is described as the early onset effects in, for example, monkeys exposed to these compounds. This occurs within the first week after exposure. The onset of chloracne comes later . . . The earliest I have heard of is 3-4 weeks or even more after the exposure took place. Whether or not the onset of abdominal pains in Mr. Yushchenko's case the next day after the dinner has been caused by 2,3,7,8-TCDD is still not completely clear, because it is an effect which has not previously been reported so early. Alternatively there was something else in the material containing the 2,3,7,8-TCDD, which may have caused the early onset effect . . . But the sequence of symptoms, i.e. starting with abdominal pain first and chloracne later fits well with what we know of 2,3,7,8-TCDD's toxicity.[19]

Modifying the effect of a known toxin was a signature feature of the Russian secret laboratory. For a time this misled even honest and serious researchers – but never world-class specialists whose job is to know.

Victor Andreyevich Yushchenko was terribly lucky but then he was only one step from becoming the president of the country that had been the second most important part of the Soviet Union after Russia herself for almost a hundred years. Against Russia's will, Ukraine would finally turn its face towards Europe after his election. Yushchenko had millions of his countrymen and women supporting him. The old adage is right: God is on the side of the big battalions.

In October a member of the Ukrainian parliament, the American-born Roman Zvarych, travelled to Washington to meet a lawyer named Robert A. McConnell and his Ukrainian wife, Nadya, who ran the US-Ukraine Foundation and had good contacts in the capital. He carried with him professionally packed samples of his president's hair, nail and blood for further analysis in the USA. For this purpose Mr McConnell retained Dr Gregory Saathoff, the lead doctor and executive director of University of Virginia's Critical Incident Analysis Group (CIAG) in Charlottesville. As soon as the samples arrived, they were taken to the laboratory.

Dr Saathoff organised a remarkable team of six US experts in various specialities including dermatology, neurology, toxicology and neuroradiology. One of the specialists was Dr Christopher P. Holstege, Associate Professor of Emergency Medicine and Paediatrics and Director of Blue Ridge Poison Centre as well as member of the Department of Emergency Medicine, Division of Medical Toxicology, University of Virginia. On 31 October Dr Holstege sent an email to the executive director of the CIAG in which he said dioxin was at the top of his list of culprits. 'It's not every day you're asked to evaluate someone of this stature,' he said to the *Washington Post* in March 2005. 'It's probably the poisoning of the century.' Christopher Holstege was right about the toxin used against Yushchenko, but wrong about the century.

Again the Ukrainian patient was back in his Rudolfinerhaus ward under the watchful guard of Chervonenko and those whom he hired in Vienna. Jeremy Page of the *The Times* called Nikolai Korpan from Kiev and reported on 8 December:

> Medical experts have confirmed that Victor Yushchenko was poisoned in an attempt on his life during election campaigning . . . This is no longer a question for discussion, Dr Korpan said. 'We are now sure that we can confirm which substance caused this illness. He [Yushchenko] received this substance from other people who had a specific aim.' Asked if the aim had been to kill him, Dr Korpan said: 'Yes, of course.' Proof that Yushchenko was deliberately poisoned would be a devastating blow for his rival Victor Yanukovich, the prime minister, as the two candidates prepare for a repeat on of a presidential run-off on December 26.[20]

On the same page and written by the same author *The Times* published an account of the Kremlin's reaction under the title 'Russia accuses West of meddling in Kiev'.

In mid-December Dr Gregory Saathoff and Dr Christopher Holstege flew secretly to Vienna to see the patient in person. They were warned by the State Department that the US government could not become involved in this situation because that would be interference in the election of another country.[21]

Doctors Saathoff and Holstege were almost certainly also warned to be careful because Vienna was the capital of Russian espionage, saturated with SVR and GRU agents.

But all went well and together with Dr Zimpfer and Dr Korpan they visited Yushchenko in hospital, examined him and studied his medical records. They saw that the substance found in his body was similar to highly concentrated dioxin that had been produced by a Russian laboratory earlier in the decade.

Their trip ended with an amusing cloak-and-dagger coda reported by Glenn Kessler and Rob Stein. On 12 December, as the doctors stood outside their hotel to head to Schwechat airport, an unmarked car arrived and the driver announced in somewhat accented English, 'Dr Saathoff, this is your car.' The Americans started to put their luggage in the trunk but suddenly recalled that they had never ordered any limousine. Both quickly withdrew their bags, flagged a cab and sped off to the airport. It was later found out that the US Embassy had indeed sent the car for them.[22]

Neither of the American doctors still in Vienna on that day attended an international press conference held on 11 December at the Rudolfinerhaus, nor was their famous patient there. Among the many journalists who packed the conference hall, however, was Bojan Pancevski writing for the *Daily Telegraph* and *Sunday Telegraph* in Austria. On the next day he published an article 'Yushchenko poisoned by "Agent Orange" ' in which, among other things, Pancevski wrote: 'Dioxin is a component of Agent Orange, the herbicide used by the Americans in

Vietnam and blamed for causing birth defects and cancer.' Though I did not have any illusions about the newspaper, this reflection of Soviet-style disinformation caused me to keep my eye on their Vienna correspondent.

On 12 December Yushchenko attended a press conference at the Rudolfiner-haus and made a short statement but refused to answer questions. He simply said that he was quite sure of his victory in the upcoming elections that should be free and fair.

In mid-December Yushchenko looked terrible but felt much better. He, his wife and their baby boy Taras had time to enjoy a visit to the Christkindlmarkt, a central attraction of Vienna at Christmas. Very few people recognised the Ukrainian wearing a dark coat with a warm beaver-lamb collar and an orange scarf, a symbol and colour of his election campaign and of the Orange Revolution. I noticed only one Ukrainian government bodyguard behind the couple but obviously there were more from a private security firm and certainly from the Vienna police that traditionally worked for both East and West. Karl Wendl of the Austrian *News* magazine approached Yushchenko:

'On 26 December the elections will be repeated. What result do you expect?'
   'After these elections the world will see a different Ukraine. An open, optimistic country, free from corruption and criminality. You shall see a country that will quickly integrate itself into the European community. Ukraine is part of Europe, there can be no more doubt about it.'

However, there would be a long way to Europe and NATO and Moscow would make it incredibly difficult for Yushchenko to realise the programme he described in Vienna in December 2004.

Just a week before the elections he briefly skipped to Geneva to see Jean Saurat, the dermatologist.

In the meantime, Matthew Chance, CNN international correspondent, approached Oleg Gordievsky in London.

Chance (on camera): So what do you believe happened in the Ukraine case? How would this have played out? If the idea would have been conceived by somebody in Ukraine and they'd have gone to Russia, how do you think it would have played out?
Gordievsky: Very simple. Head of the Ukrainian KGB, or somebody important, went to Moscow and said, 'We need an effective and easy-to-use poison and some instruction how to use it because we have something on our agenda, something of national importance. Did they tell Moscow against whom or not, it is difficult to tell . . . The best thing is actually to put it in the gravy or in the soup. The Ukrainian borscht is very red, very aromatic, full of garlic and other vegetables with spices. So a poison can easily be hidden in the soup.

Oleg had just read in a newspaper how Dr Zimpfer suggested that the poison could be put in the soup and coined all the rest. Exactly as two years later in the Litvinenko case, Gordievsky liked to entertain himself by making a comment to the media and seeing what the newsmakers were going to do with it.

In a long analytical article published by the *Financial Times* just one day before Yushchenko was finally declared the winner on 10 January 2005 after the failure of a legal action brought by Yanukovich, Chrystia Freeland, the newspaper's deputy editor, discussed the situation. She argued:

> For the Kremlin, a Yanukovich victory was important for philosophical, political and geopolitical reasons. Philosophically, a triumph for 'managed democracy' and state capitalism in Ukraine would have been a validation of Russia's own renunciation of open democracy in favour of President Vladimir Putin's increasingly overt neo-authoritarianism. Politically, installing the Kremlin's man in Kiev would have been a victory for the neo-imperialist vision that Putin and his supporters have been propagating to shore up domestic support. Geopolitically, the Kremlin made its traditional calculation that vassals make better neighbours than independent states.[23]

Russia backed the Kremlin candidate with tremendous zeal. Putin visited Kiev twice to appear for Yushchenko's opponent. Moscow's best image makers, PR specialists and political technologists flooded Kiev trying all modern psy-ops techniques to influence the audience's value systems, beliefs, emotions, motives, reasoning and behaviour in favour of Putin's protégé.

Even some of Kuchma's cohort were enraged. Vasyl Baziv, his deputy chief of staff, told Chrystia Freeman: 'It hugely angered me when I walked through the presidential administration and saw how citizens of another state were lying on the divans and brutally forcing themselves into the state life of Ukraine.'[24] Anders Åslund, a Swedish economist and expert on economic transition from centrally planned to market economy who served as an economic adviser to both the governments of Russia and Ukraine, estimated that Moscow spent $300 million on the Ukrainian elections.

Those were lost funds but somebody in Moscow learned a lesson. For the following years the catchword behind the Kremlin walls would be 'Ketchum'.

***

The official ceremonies took place on Sunday, 23 January 2005 at about noon. Yushchenko was sworn in as President of Ukraine. The President appointed Yulia Timoshenko, the Orange Revolution princess, as his prime minister. At that time she was a subject of an international arrest warrant issued on trumped-up charges put forward by Russia. I watched the CNN news broadcast but failed to notice Nikolai Korpan in the overcrowded hall of the parliament, though I knew he had been there as one of the honoured guests of the president. The astrologers commenting on the inauguration ceremony noticed that Jupiter was the main planet in presidential inauguration charts so they concentrated on Jupiter, advising the newly elected president:

> You may feel that you have been wronged or something has been taken from you. At the moment there is, however, no way of finding who or what is the cause. You could spend your time searching for perpetrators, but a much better solution is to just get on with your life. Things will most probably come to light at a later time.

In spring 2005, Nikolai Korpan was very much content with life. Interesting offers came from every side. He was the centre of media attention, gave many interviews and his photos regularly appeared in the Austrian and international press.

As the media was so much interested in his person, Korpan took it for granted when three Moscow correspondents officially accredited by the Russian Embassy at the Austrian Foreign Ministry's International Press Department suddenly became his close friends. Igor Anatolyevich Belov, former APN,[25] then representing the *Russian News* ('Rossiiskie vesti') but mostly writing for the *Russian Courier* published in Budapest – part of the ever growing net of pro-Russian and pro-Kremlin émigré media actively sponsored and supported by Moscow; Yuri Alexandrovich Kovalenko, correspondent of the *Young Communist of Moscow* ('Moskovsky komsomolets') and Moscow's *Tribune*; and Leonid Nikolaevich Sumarokov, from *Science & Business* ('Nauka i biznes') and *Investments in Russia* ('Investitsyi v Rossii') – publications that had no reason to keep their own correspondents in Austria and certainly no funds to pay for them. The trio started to see the now famous doctor regularly.

As soon as I came back from London after meeting Goldfarb and Litvinenko and presenting them with Dr Korpan's book project, we met at the Landtmann, a famous Viennese café on the Ring.

His first question was: 'Did you see Berezovsky?'

I had no plans to see Boris, neither had I informed Nikolai that I would be meeting Litvinenko, so I simply said: 'No, why?' To which he made no comment. But it alarmed me that Korpan suddenly appeared to be so well informed. Obviously, he was meeting people who had good sources in London. Nikolai could not know at that moment that the Russians were playing not against me but against him.

On 27 March the *Sunday Telegraph* published another article by Pancevski entitled 'I received death threats, says doctor who denied that Ukrainian leader was poisoned.' It was, in effect, an exclusive interview with the old radiologist Lothar Wicke who had refused to meet the press since his September press conference. Evidently, Wicke was now repeating all his previous allegations, even months *after* dioxin had been recognised by international experts as the murderous component of the poison administered to the Ukrainian leader. Dr Wicke told the *Sunday Telegraph* that, as the crime writer Agatha Christie liked to point out, there was 'no murder without a corpse, and no poisoning without poison'. 'Speculation that the politician was the victim of a dirty tricks campaign,' wrote Pancevski in the article, 'helped him to victory in the elections on December 26.'

The *Telegraph* interviewer repeated Wicke's accusations that in September a 'medically forged diagnosis' had been circulated by Korpan and pointed out that Wicke was now suing the Rudolfinerhaus for substantial damages, claiming that he had been forced out of his job for refusing to go along with the poisoning diagnosis.[26]

Not realising how sensitive his situation had become since he had got involved in the case frowned upon by Moscow and especially since he was preparing to publish his evidence in the form of a book, Korpan explained to Pancevski that he would have more to say on the poisoning at another time.

I sent an email to Pancevski to which he quickly responded. I suggested meeting at any convenient place in Vienna to discuss the Yushchenko case, but he never agreed to meet me.

In 1992 the scientist and chemical weapons specialist Vil Mirzayanov published an article in *Moscow News* criticising the Russian military-industrial complex for violating the Paris Convention on the Prohibition of Chemical Weapons. As a result, he was accused of high treason and put into Lefortovo prison. Upon release, Dr Mirzayanov quit his job at one of the secret Russian research institutes and emigrated to the USA.

There he echoed the words of Prof. Brouwer, saying that there was only limited information regarding high-dose dioxin exposure on humans and that in Russia, only a very narrow circle of specialists with high security clearance would be informed on dioxin research. According to Dr Mirzayanov, in the Soviet Union and later in Russia there were two specialised facilities that worked with traditional and non-traditional chemical weapons like dioxins, namely the State Research Institute of Organic Chemistry and Technology and the Moscow All-Union Scientific Research Institute of Chemical Means of Plant Protection. Under orders from the Communist Party leadership and the Russian Ministry of Defence, according to the expert, they were engaged in two classified research programmes codenamed FOLIANT and FOLIANT-T. The requirement was to find an analogue to Agent Orange, a highly toxic defoliant used for tactical purposes. Obviously, said Dr Mirzayanov, while studying the reaction of plants to dioxins, it was also necessary to evaluate the effects of the exposure of humans to toxic agents. Therefore some Russian army units took part in the exercises. The scientist recalled that in Kiev there was also the Institute of Toxicology and Professional Pathology, but that it had never worked with dioxins, so it was quite clear that the

Russian services were involved in the Yushchenko's poisoning.[27]

An informed specialist could not miss the article written by a group of Russian scientists that was published in the *FEBS Letters* on 30 April 1999, a publication dealing with new achievements in highly specific research. A. I. Sotnichenko and his colleagues from the Moscow Research Institute of Medical Ecology had experimented with dioxin and fetal proteins, in particular with a- or alpha-fetoprotein (AFP), a molecule produced in the developing embryo. AFP levels decrease gradually after birth and it has no known function in normal adults. Except as material for quickly developing scientific research.

As a result of Russian experiments, a stable complex had been formed between 2,3,7,8-TCDD and AFP. It was observed that the solubility of this particular dioxin in water increased 105-fold while its toxicity was similar to that of free TCDD administered in oil solutions. The death of experimental animals (mice) was followed up to day 45 after the injection, and the cytotoxicity of the TCDD:AFP complex, i.e. its toxicity to cells appeared to be much higher than that of free dioxin.

The fact that Yushchenko was obviously poisoned not just by 2,3,7,8-TCDD but by a much more complex agent, a product of a special laboratory, as confirmed by the British Defence Science and Technology Laboratory in Porton Down, clearly demonstrated that the murder attempt was a Russian operation. Additionally, in March 2005 Dr Korpan at the Rudolfinerhaus received a report from a research centre in Munster, Germany, confirming the dioxin poisoning. Korpan said to the *Ukrayinska Pravda* that 'there is no doubt that Mr Yushchenko has been poisoned deliberately' and added that the amount of dioxin in his patient's body exceeded the norm by 5,000 times. This does not mean that the Ukrainian had eaten five buckets of dioxin. The dosage would have been measured in milligrams but the concentration and toxicity was so very high because it was a tailor-made poison specifically designed for Victor Yushchenko, taking into account his age, weight, nationality and, most important, his medical record.

On 7 April the *Wall Street Journal* published my article describing the Yushchenko poisoning case and comparing it to other historic cases when assassinations were planned and carried out by agents of the Kremlin against political targets. In the article I mentioned the so-called 'active measures', steps taken in such cases to create disinformation campaigns to confuse the issue. I recalled that officials in the government of Victor Yanukovich and close to President Kuchma had been saying that Yushchenko ate bad sushi, or maybe caught a virus, or even disfigured himself on purpose to win electoral points. Former KGB Colonel Victor Cherkasov, distinguished in deception operations through his handling of two notorious American traitors, Aldrich Ames and Robert Hanssen but no toxicologist or health-care specialist, chimed in to say, 'I have my doubts whether Yushchenko was poisoned at all. It looks more like a dermatological problem.'

The conclusions of the international experts, however, differ from the opinion of the KGB colonel. They unanimously confirmed Dr Korpan's initial statement that Yushchenko had been poisoned with the aim of disfiguring him and weakening him – in fact, murdering him – before the elections.

It was Nikolai Korpan who first spoke about poisoning, it was Korpan who managed to prove that he was right, and it was Korpan who stood at the side of Yushchenko while he was a patient of the Rudolfinerhaus hospital. As a result, this good doctor had to respond to tough questioning.

On 27 April 2005 Manfred Lackner, a Socialist (now Social-Democratic) member of the Austrian Parliament (Nationalrat), officially filed a parliamentary enquiry[29] directed against Dr Korpan in connection with the latter's role in the Yushchenko case. In the document containing sixteen detailed questions the deputy wondered when and why Korpan was invited to Austria, what were his scientific and medical achievements, and whether a validation of Dr Korpan's academic degrees and titles had been done by appropriate Austrian institutions. He asked also that the Austrian parliament check the legality of Korpan's Austrian citizenship, his qualifications and his right to treat patients.

That same day deputy Lackner filed a second parliamentary enquiry,[30] this time consisting of twenty-nine detailed questions and devoted entirely to Dr Korpan's medical practice. Here Lackner, a two-year student of political science at Salzburg University and a one-time chief of the financial department of the hospital in Bludenz questioned whether it corresponded to legal principles and practices for surgeons to diagnose poisoning, i.e. engage in internal toxicological issues, and whether it was not punishable that in the telephone book Dr Korpan was registered as 'University Professor,' a title that he, deputy Lackner, was not sure had been properly validated. The Austrian politician also referred to various passages from Dr Korpan's medical books and scientific publications, raising questions about the Ukrainian doctor's methods in various complex cases.

In May, more than half a year *after* the events, a Vienna newspaper published a full-page article about how Dr Lothar Wicke refused to take part in the 'poison affair' and how he claimed before the TV cameras that there was no proof whatsoever of Yushchenko's poisoning. The paper also noted that the radiologist was suing the Rudolfinerhaus hospital for sacking him.

In June the same paper (and the same author) reported that the Vienna Prosecutor's Office (VPO) received an anonymous letter presenting the 'facts' of the Yushchenko case. The prosecutors, according to the newspaper, took the letter seriously as, quoting the VPO's speaker, Hofrat Dr Erwin Kloiber, 'the anonymous author must have a certain legal as well as medical background'.[31]

The *Russian Courier* published a series of articles about the case throughout the year most of them written by Igor Belov who was still pretending to be Korpan's friend. Just before the final round of presidential elections he warned that the 'inevitable' division of Ukraine into east and west by Yushchenko's presidency would be fatal for the country. His next article, entitled 'More questions than answers', mocked the four press conferences that were held at the Rudolfinerhaus and gave the impression that Lothar Wicke had been directly involved in the medical treatment of the Ukrainian patient. (In the meantime, the Rudolfinerhaus president Dr Michael Zimpfer made an official statement making it clear that 'Dr Wicke had [only] once met with Yushchenko on administrative issues' and 'Mr. Wicke is a radiologist, and as a specialist he can neither approve nor disprove Yushchenko's diagnosis'.) Other issues reprinted Russian translations of the Wicke interview published in the *Sunday Telegraph* and the anonymous author's ungrounded claims from *Heute*.

In September a long interview with me was published in the *Ukrayinska Pravda* fully explaining the case. I predicted that it could hardly be brought to the court, because inexperienced (and unreliable) Ukrainian prosecutors were dealing with a crime committed by the Russian state and its secret service well versed in covering its trails.[32] In October my article 'Getting the Reds Out of the Orange Revolution' appeared in the *Wall Street Journal* and a week later one of the Reds – another Socialist turned Social Democrat and member of the lower chamber of the Austrian parliament, Ruth Becher, filed another enquiry[33] directed against Dr Korpan demanding a response from his ministry (the Federal Ministry for Education, Science and Culture).

Ms Becher, whose speciality is German studies and history, had turned her intellectual efforts to medicine, to deal with cryosurgery, one of its most sophisticated and modern disciplines.

Cryosurgery is the application of extreme cold to destroy diseased tissue that may be recommended in the treatment of some benign and malignant skin conditions. It is a minimally invasive procedure, often preferred to more traditional kinds of surgery especially when it heals lesions with minimal pain, scarring and cost.

Becher placed thirty-five highly sophisticated and detailed questions to the ministry regarding the professional activities of Dr Korpan as a cryosurgeon, in many cases repeating two previous enquiries filed by MP Lackner that had already been answered in detail by the Federal Minister.

I last visited the Rudolfinerhaus hospital in October 2008. It was no great surprise to learn that neither Dr Michael Zimpfer nor Dr Lothar Wicke were there any more. Shortly before Wicke's contract expired in August 2008, Michael Zimpfer was 'not elected' to the house's presidentship, having been previously removed as the General Hospital's chief anaesthesiologist.

Also not surprisingly, Dr Nikolai Korpan was still there. My former friend had lost his 'University Professor' title but retained his job and his Austrian citizenship. He will probably never write anything and will never tell anybody about the events surrounding Yushchenko's poisoning.

As this book goes to press five years on, the investigation is still not finished. In

March 2008 one of the key witnesses, a Ukrainian businessman Vladimir Shulga, 51, died in Kiev of heart failure during interrogation. Vladimir Satsyuk, the former deputy chief of the Ukrainian security service was granted Russian citizenship to the great surprise of the Ukrainian authorities. When Ukraine asked for his extradition, Moscow announced that it does not extradite its citizens.

Ukraine's next presidential elections are expected to take place on Sunday, 17 January 2010. Moscow is evidently preparing revenge for its December 2004 humiliation. Zhvaniya has joined Timoshenko, now portrayed as the most popular candidate with some lead over Yanukovich.

The polls place Yushchenko in third place supported by slightly over 10 per cent of those surveyed. In the Russia of Vladimir Putin the country's media have brainwashed any memory of Yushchenko's deliberate poisoning, and portray him as a sick man. In early August 2008 *Izvestia* published a long interview with Dr Igor Gundalov, described as a medical doctor and philosopher, member of the Russian Academy of Natural Sciences and head of the scientific research laboratory of public health of the I. M. Sechenov Moscow Medical Academy. The article embodied Moscow's disinformation line about the Yushchenko case. What Yushchenko was really suffering from, goes this tale, was multibacillary Hansen's disease, otherwise known as lepromatous leprosy, and that there were no grounds for suggesting that Yushchenko had been poisoned. Gundalov quoted the chairman of the parliamentary commission Vladimir Sivkovich to this effect, failing to mention Sivkovich's long service in the Soviet KGB before moving to its Ukrainian equivalent, the SBU, as well as Dr Wicke whom he called the chief physician of the Rudolfinerhaus 'who had been attending the [Ukrainian] patient from the moment of his arrival in Vienna'. The radiologist's expert opinion, according to the author, was extremely important because he demonstrated honour and dignity contrary to his colleagues who had signed a false diagnosis, and because he had been supported by the Austrian court. Gundalov further asserted that Dr Zimpfer had added a 1,000-fold amount of dioxin before sending Yushchenko's blood sample to the laboratory, while Korpan put in a 5,000-fold portion just to be sure in the result. According to Gundalov the American specialists who had come to help their Austrian accomplices had carried with them Agent Orange, which is why that substance appeared in Yushchenko's blood.

Those in Moscow who created Dr Gundalov's disinformation as much as his academic colleagues who were labouring on the design of the special poison for the Ukrainian leader must have a vicious sense of humour or suffered from primitive ignorance when they inserted in his tale the claim that Agent Orange was involved in the poisoning of the Ukrainian presidential candidate. They must have thought that Agent Orange had something to do with the Orange Revolution.

Béla Lapusnyik, the victim,
Vienna, May 1962

I love Austria and especially its beautiful capital on the Danube that writer Kid Möchel calls *Spionagedrehscheibe Wien* (Vienna, an espionage turntable). Kim Philby lived here and was first approached in an agent probe by his own Communist wife Litzi. It actually ended by lovemaking in the snow but later, some time after June 1934, he was fully recruited in London by another talented Austrian, Dr Arnold Deutsch, with the help of Deutsch's former contact back in Vienna's OMS named Edith Suschitzki. Known in Britain as Edith Tudor Hart with some of her photographic works proudly displayed in the National Gallery in London to this very day, Edith later helped to handle Anthony Blunt and Robert 'Bob' Stewart not to mention Philby himself who until the war was a rather hopeless little spook. Almost all successful pre-war Soviet spy runners in London, several agents and their couriers came there from Vienna. Since April 1945, when the Soviets launched their Vienna Offensive and their troops finally liberated the city – to occupy it for another ten years, longer than the Nazis – the Austrian capital has become the most important place for Russian spies and their spymasters from all over the globe, from the phantom Emerald Island off New Zealand's coast to Grant Land in the Arctic Ocean to the cold, wet and windy Coronation Island in the South Orkneys near the Falkland archipelago. Here to this wonderful city they have come to meet, dine, get recruited, paid, and sometimes killed. No wonder *The Third Man*[1] is still being shown in Vienna's cinemas.

On the night of 8–9 May 1962, a 24-year-old Hungarian AVH[2] Lieutenant Béla Lapusnyik defected to Austria by riding a motorcycle to a Hungarian border checkpoint near Nickelsdorf. He fired warning shots at two Hungarian border guards, forcing them to seek cover, before leaping over the barrier amid a hail of automatic fire from Hungarian guards.

While the Hungarian was making his dramatic escape, Yuri Ivanovich Nosenko, an officer of the Second Chief Directorate of the KGB (internal security) on a three-month assignment to a Soviet conference delegation in Geneva, was drinking whisky and ogling girls in a downtown nightclub together with a friend named Yuri Guk from the local KGB *rezidentura*. Several days later, in the marble halls of

Geneva's Palace of Nations, he made his move during a break in the proceedings of an arms-control conference. Nosenko eased himself to the side of an American delegate he knew to have served in Moscow, shook hands, and, after a glance around to be sure he was out of range of fellow Soviet delegates, asked urgently for contact with CIA. Two days later Tennent H. Bagley, known to all his friends as 'Pete', greeted Nosenko in a small safe apartment in the Old Town.[3]

Four decades after the events, Pete told me in Brussels:

> Our service learned about Béla Lapusnyik soon after his escape from Hungary and it was agreed that this important defector would be transferred to the USA in June. In the meantime, the Austrian Stapo (state security police) had been interviewing him. I must say that since I served in Vienna in the early 1950s we were well informed that the Austrian police, controlled by the Socialists and previously Communists, was thoroughly penetrated by the Soviet agents. I heard that Lapusnyik brought with him secret documents sewed up in the lining of his leather overcoat in addition to notes and observations that allowed us to identify Hungarian agents and their clandestine operations in Austria. He also threw light on Hungarian security police operations against Western diplomats and businessmen in Budapest. One doesn't need to say that the Hungarian intelligence and security services worked for their Soviet spymasters.

After the initial questioning by the Burgenland police, Lapusnyik was immediately taken to Vienna where Dr Hejkrlik, the Hungarian affairs specialist of the Stapo, started to interview him.

The young lieutenant appeared to be a very valuable source indeed. He delivered high-grade intelligence about espionage activities, foreign currency smuggling, and rosters of agents in Austria straight from the Hungarian Interior Ministry files. Lapusnyik presented documents about the methods employed by the Hungarian secret service in Austria and revealed obscure channels through which information was smuggled from Austria to Hungary. He told the police about secret 'loopholes' in the Iron Curtain, and named agents in Austria and their meeting places.

During the questioning Béla Lapusnyik was held in protective custody in the top-security police prison known as 'Liesl' on Vienna's Rossauerlände. Every day before noon he was taken to Vienna city police headquarters for debriefing and was usually brought back in the evening. Therefore he took his meals at the police building and when it was noticed that he and the police inspector both loved pastry, cakes and other treats, they were often delivered from a nearby bakery.

Before noon on Saturday, 2 June, Lapusnyik in his isolated cell complained that he did not feel well and asked for a doctor. The police physician's diagnosis suggested tonsillitis. On Sunday he was transferred to the Vienna General

Hospital (AKH, Erste Chirurgische Klinik) where he was kept in room 125 under the constant guard of the two members of the state police. After repeatedly losing consciousness during the day, Lapusnyik died of a brain haemorrhage on the Monday morning, 4 June 1962, at 5:45 a.m. Shortly before his death, he tried to say something but no one could understand his Hungarian. By the time an interpreter was sent for, Lapusnyik could no longer speak, but managed to scribble a note: 'Pump my stomach out', meaning that he considered himself to be poisoned. But then he lost conscience and soon passed away.

Not surprisingly, Austrian medical experts concluded that this young and strong Hungarian defector had died of natural causes – despite the amazing diagnoses that during the hours of his agony Lapusnyik had gradually suffered not only from tonsillitis but also from an inflammation of the narrow intestine, the beginning of pneumonia, and finally paralysis of the brain. Based upon the conclusions of the Vienna court's forensic experts, Professor Dr Holczabek and Professor Dr Wölkart, the Austrian socialist Minister of the Interior Josef Afritsch reported to the parliament on 14 June:

> The medical, chemical, and bacteriological test results so far provide no basis for the assumption that death could have been caused by outside action. The police investigations also have not revealed any circumstance, which could lead to the conclusion that Lapusnyik was exposed to health-harming influences from any direction. Before the final determination of the cause of death the pending results of the biochemical tests will have to be awaited.

It is hardly surprising that the Austrian Federal Minister for the Interior decided to turn a blind eye on this evident poisoning. Starting with his post-war predecessor, Communist Franz Honner, who was a Russian agent, Austrian state security has always been well penetrated by the KGB and its satellite services. The files noted by Mitrokhin record the recruitment of a series of major agents in the police: EDUARD in 1945, VENTSEYEV in 1946, PETER in 1952, two further recruits in 1955, ZAK in 1974 and NADEZHDIN in 1978.[4] In the 1990s it was established that the chief of the Vienna Stapo, Gustav Hohenbichler, was himself a Soviet agent who previously worked for the East German Stasi.

The usual reaction followed this evident murder of the defector. After his death was officially pronounced 'non-violent', the Austrian Communist paper *Volksstimme* came out with an article entitled 'Has the US Secret Service Murdered Lapusnyik?' Their logic was simple: 'If it indeed a fact that he had become the victim of a murder, then the culprits are to be sought only in the American secret services, nowhere else.'[5] Period.

However, this is what Laszlo Szabo, another Hungarian AVH defector, who served under cover as First Secretary of the Hungarian Embassy in London, testified under oath:

I recall after Lapusnyik's death there was a formal statement or order on Lapusnyik circulated by the chief of the AVH. This order was read to AVH personnel at departmental or section meetings. In the order from the AVH Chief, Lapusnyik was represented as having been an immoral, corrupt person who hung out in bars and brought loose women to the apartment where he lived. He was also accused of misusing official money and not taking an interest in the Communist Party affairs. The facts of his case were outlined briefly: he had escaped from Hungary by misusing his AVH status and in so doing had shot down a border guard [this was a deliberate lie]. Throughout the document he was referred to as 'the traitor, Bela Lapusnyik'. The report also noted that he died in jail. According to this statement, Lapusnyik had caused very serious damage to the AVH because he had revealed AVH secret locations, identities and surveillance methods . . .

Then I asked why I hadn't been shown the whole file. I was told that this was understandable since the case was top secret. I had not been permitted to see the whole file because Lapusnyik had been poisoned by the Czech intelligence service in the Vienna jail.[6]

On 30 January 1967 Allen Welsh Dulles (AWD), the first civilian and the longest-serving director of the CIA, met the editors to discuss his book *Great True Spy Stories* (1968) that was soon to be published. Regarding the Lapusnyik case, AWD stressed:

Bela Lapusnyik. Again, defection, which ends in elimination of defector, should probably not be used. Press accounts [illegible], but Szabo's testimony itself should be used. The introduction should say that the Sovs and Sats are the only services which have components working full time on planning, executing, and concealing murders.[7]

Several hours before the funeral, set for 11:15 a.m. on 26 June 1962, Austrian policemen in civilian suits arrived at the Zentral Friedhof (central cemetery) and 'inconspicuously' placed themselves at their posts. Four of them stood at Chapel III, a fifth at the open gravesite. The time of the funeral was not made public. Almost unnoticed the funeral procession moved to a recently dug grave. In the lead the cross-bearer, then the clergyman, four undertaker's employees who pushed the burial cart, and then four men of the police. No wreaths, no flowers.

Several years after lieutenant Lapusnyik's mysterious death, rumours about a top secret Czech (read Soviet) agent in the Austrian police only known as 'Mister 7' started to circulate among counter-intelligence professionals. When Ladislav Bittman, a press attaché at the Czech Embassy in Vienna woke up early in the morning on 21 August 1968, he could hardly get over the shock of the previous night. Soviet tanks were in Prague shooting at his countrymen, women and children, and he was sitting in Vienna unable to do anything. Moreover, as a senior officer of the Czech StB, the country's state security service monitoring and cutting short any activity that could possibly be considered anti-communist, that is, anti-Soviet, he was expected to be on the side of executioners.

But Bittman was born a painter, not a soldier, and he decided it was time to start a new life. He walked out and in several days was calling the American Embassy in Bonn. After some time he was 'cleared' and left Bavaria, where he was in hiding, for Washington. Before he left Munich, he asked his contact at the US Consulate to take care of his dog, a charming poodle named Tommy, and find somebody who could adopt him. On 23 November Bittman was sitting in a comfortable safe house in Virginia briefing the CIA officers of the SB (Soviet Bloc) division about the activities of his service.

Among other things, Bittman revealed that the StB had a highly placed agent in the Austrian police whose name he did not know. He could only recall the codename – 'Agent 7' or 'Mister Seven'. The information was not too valuable at the time, as the Americans knew anyway that the Austrian police was well penetrated.

Bittman's knowledge about his own agents was much more precise. In 1958 he was transferred to the German-Austrian desk and became the case officer of several assets recruited among the German politicians. Among them were some very prominent individuals like Alfred Frenzel, a member of the German parliament who supplied the Czech intelligence with the most sensitive reports about the West German army and the US contingent stationed in Germany. Frenzel, according to Bittman, was a member of the parliamentary Defence Committee so he was able to provide his communist masters with thousands and thousands of documents to which he had access.[8]

At that time the Czech service had three or four members of the German parliament working for them as agents with more than ten other deputies recruited by Markus Wolf's operatives.[9] Both Warsaw Pact services reported directly to Moscow so the Kremlin's influence on West German legislature was considerable. Apart from providing sensitive information, they could, if necessary, exert influence upon political decisions.

When Bittman's debriefing session was over on that evening, the officer in charge told the defector that there was something waiting for him in the next room. And there was Tommy, the poodle, who survived not only a flight across the ocean, but another fourteen years making Bittman's adjustment to a new life much easier.[10] His dream finally came true when after an academic career he became a popular and a very successful painter.

The case of the 24-year-old Second Lieutenant Lapusnyik remains closed and is still considered 'death from natural causes'. Hence a possible culprit has never been officially identified in Austria. No one in the Alpine republic will dare to reopen it. A small country that gets about 60 per cent of its gas from Russia, it is not only a convenient hub for the Kremlin's financial affairs, but also for Russian espionage, its most important operational centre. The entire force of Russian intelligence officers based in Vienna and Salzburg outnumbers the US and UK stations combined.

My personal estimate is that a highly toxic and volatile DMS (dimethyl sulphate) was used to murder the defector. First discovered in the early 1800s, it could have easily been turned into a chemical weapon in the 1960s by the Soviet special laboratory. Exposure to DMS, a colourless, odourless, oily liquid that can also be vaporised, produces no immediate effect. There is a latent period of up to ten hours before the onset of symptoms. Exposure to the vapour immediately produces tears, runny nose, swelling of the mouth and throat tissues, sore throat, difficulty breathing, cyanosis and death that may occur within three days.

In spite of the overwhelming evidence, the body was never re-examined. In 1996 a representative of the Vienna Police Directorate, Oberrat Dr Schwabl, in an official letter to a journalist who was researching a book on the case, stated that 'The Lapusnyik File' does not exist.

Many years after those events I was walking our intelligent (my mother believes that he understands Russian, German and English equally well) family dog, a kind, friendly, eager-to-please and patient golden retriever named Philby, around 'Liesl', the Vienna police fortress quite near our house. It was a wonderful summer morning but my mind was thinking back fifty years to that dark Saturday when the Hungarian lieutenant woke up in his locked cell here preparing to die.

I was thinking that both my favourite writer Frederick Forsyth and the American spy chief Allen Dulles were right. There's a thing called *maskirovka* and it is Russian: it is the art of building phoney airfields, hangars, bridges, entire tank divisions out of tinplate and plywood so as to fool the Americans with their satellites and their electronic intelligence. And only the Russians have components working full time on planning, executing, and covering up murders. So, sometimes, you have to go in on the ground, put a mole deep inside the FOREST, recruit a malcontent, employ an agent-in-place. If you do not have good field men, the KGB will have your balls for cocktail olives in two weeks flat.[11]

Things were changing, all right, but in the first decade of the twenty-first century the world was going their way.

Nikolai Artamonov, the triple agent, Vienna, December 1975

Lieutenant Commander Nikolai Artamonov, a tall and handsome Soviet destroyer captain on a navy mission to the port of Gdynia in June 1959, fell in love with a young Polish beauty, Ewa Blanca Gora, and they defected to Sweden. Their Swedish hosts knew from the very beginning that they could not guarantee security of the fugitives, so their alternative was to go either to Britain or to the United States. The pair chose America.

In Washington DC, after an exhaustive debriefing, Artamonov, who had shown himself to be an experienced and knowledgeable navy officer, became an intelligence expert and lecturer. The young family settled in Virginia, documented under the new identities of Nicholas and Ewa Shadrin. Asked fifty years later about where this name came from, Ewa recalled that there was a Captain Shadrin in Pushkin's famous *The Captain's Daughter*.

Until June 1965 the Washington KGB station had had its troubles, in part due to the increased professionalism of the FBI's efforts to curtail Soviet espionage in the US capital. But that summer of 1965 a new *rezident* arrived from Moscow bringing along a young and enthusiastic team. Boris Solomatin, a heavy-drinking but efficient operative, worked under the guise of a counsellor at the Soviet Embassy and commanded a station of forty KGB officers out of about a hundred embassy staff. There was also a smaller GRU station. Oleg Kalugin, officially listed as second secretary and press attaché, was Solomatin's deputy in charge of Line PR (political intelligence). Three other deputies were chiefs of Line KR (counter-intelligence and security), Line X (scientific and technological intelligence) and Line N (illegal support). There were also officers responsible for Line EM (émigrés) plus technical and support staff. General Kalugin later wrote: 'Our activities in Washington were hardly confined to cultivating and handling spies such as John Walker. In my five years there, we also were deeply involved in 'active measures' (dirty tricks), efforts to locate and re-recruit – or even assassinate – Soviet defectors, and attempts to expand electronic surveillance of US institutions.'[1] Indeed, Line KR officers headed by Nikolai Popov worked quite aggressively.

While Solomatin and Kalugin were enjoying their new responsibilities in the USA, a telephone call one Sunday morning in March 1966 was the beginning of one of the most bizarre stories of the Cold War.

The telephone rang at the house of Richard Helms, who was soon to become Director of Central Intelligence. The voice on the other end identified himself as an operative of Soviet Foreign Intelligence, and asked for contact. After Helms had conferred with two of his top officers and with the FBI, Bruce Solie of CIA's Office of Security and Elbert ('Bert') Turner from the FBI were assigned to meet the caller, beginning the operation that received ill fame under the codename KITTY HAWK.

Though the details of this operation have not been declassified to date, there are several published accounts that allow better understanding of what really happened.

The caller identified himself as Igor Kochnov, and told his interlocutors that he was the son-in-law of Ekaterina Alekseyevna Furtseva, the Soviet minister of culture at the time. Solie and Turner apparently thought such a high-level contact augured well for his prospects of promotion within the KGB. In fact, while Furtseva had once been perhaps the most influential woman in Soviet politics – since 1957 the first and only female member of the all-powerful Politburo – she had been overheard by the KGB in 1960 denouncing Khrushchev's policies over the telephone. She had been promptly ousted from the Politburo and tried to commit suicide by cutting her veins. This dramatic sign of repentance, and the fact that the Soviet leader still sympathised with her, gained her pardon and appointment to the honourable but powerless position of minister of culture.

Such was the backdrop of a meeting between two Americans and the Russian in spring 1966. But that was not all.

Exactly six years before, in September 1960, Captain Artamonov was summoned to testify before a subcommittee of the House Un-American Activities Committee (HUAC). He said:

> The Russian people have no use for [the system]. The Russian people are
> gifted and industrious, mighty and strong. They are not interested in wasting
> their energies and talents by solemnizing the dictators of the Kremlin, or
> enslaving other nationalities for the sake of the very same dictators. They are
> not interested in surrounding themselves with bereavement and tribulation
> for a concept that is profoundly antidemocratic and which is bringing misery
> to them and to others; the concept in which no one, especially the leaders of
> the party themselves, believes . . .[2]

News agencies, radio and television stations all over the world carried the story of Artamonov's verbal assault on the Kremlin and both Vice Admiral Leonid Bekrenev, naval attaché at the Soviet Embassy on Belmont Road, and his assistant,

Lieutenant Commander Lev Vtorygin, were closely following what Artamonov had to say. Vtorygin felt unsettled, as Artamonov was his friend – they had studied together at the Frunze Naval Academy, then served on the same warship, roomed together on their first assignments and spent time together on leave. But during his vetting for the job in Washington, Vtorygin had, logically, seen no reason to inform either his superiors in the GRU or the KGB about his colleague and friend.

On their side, the FBI, CIA and Office of Naval Intelligence (ONI) were afraid that Vtorygin might have been assigned to Washington to assassinate the defector. They need not have worried: Russian naval officers were a proud folk and would not play such dirty KGB games. Commander Vtorygin left the United States in August 1965 after his tour of duty was over.

Kochnov explained to Solie and Turner that he had been sent to find defectors Golitsyn, Nosenko and Artamonov[3] in order either to assassinate them or lure to the Soviet territory. If the Agency would assist him in these tasks, he could expect rapid promotion to the chief of the American section of his directorate where he would agree to work as an American agent-in-place.

So juicy were Kochnov's future prospects that the Americans decided to play along and use the KGB favourite tactic of killing two birds with one stone. They even intended to surpass the Russians. The plan was to get Artamonov to pretend to cooperate with the Soviets and in this way feed a bit of disinformation to the KGB while tracking their case officers and possibly illegals who often act as cutouts, while at the same time boosting Kochnov's career. Artamonov was selected for the job not due to his intellectual brilliance or other outstanding qualities but because Golitsyn could not be a candidate for such a job (nor would he have ever accepted it) and Nosenko was confined in a CIA cell, suspected of having been sent by the KGB to misinform the Agency.

Artamonov loyally accepted the role of double agent despite the danger and the unpleasantness of a double life.

Happy Kochnov returned to Moscow after 'recruiting' Artamonov and turning over the controlling contact to Alexander Alexandrovich Sokolov, a Line KR officer operating under the alias 'Oleg Kozlov' and posing as vice-consul in the Washington embassy. The CIA never met their KGB colonel again.

Kalugin maintains that when he became the head of Directorate K and Kochnov's boss, 'we strongly suspected Kochnov of being a CIA agent and put him under surveillance. But we were never able to prove it.'[4] Kochnov conveniently died of an acute myocardial infarction before his relations with Langley were disclosed in *Time* magazine on 22 May 1978.

James P. Wooten, the last FBI handler of Artamonov/Shadrin, left out the Kochnov aspect when he talked to the Shadrins' friends one evening in January 1976, at a time when Nikolai's fate was still unknown. Wooten told the gathering that during the summer of 1966 a Soviet intelligence agent approached Shadrin in downtown Washington. The agent, according to Wooten, proposed that Shadrin start working as a spy for the Soviet Union. Instead of rejecting the overture at once, the FBI man said, Shadrin stalled the agent and then reported the approach to the FBI, which had its Washington field office in the building where Shadrin's office was located.

At that point, Wooten stated, Shadrin refused. According to the five people at the meeting that night, Wooten said that for 'close to a year' Shadrin refused the FBI's request that he play a double role. Finally, Shadrin's friend and mentor Admiral Rufus Taylor persuaded him to cooperate with the FBI.[5] Four weeks later, Wooten bluntly denied that he ever pronounced those words.

There was perhaps a more powerful factor that made Artamonov agree to take part in the risky and tricky game. He was working at ONI under a five-year contract that expired at the end of 1965 and for some reason had not been renewed. Now he was offered a job with the Defence Intelligence Agency (DIA). 'Already becoming despondent over his situation,' wrote Henry Hurt who made a long and painstaking research on the case working closely with Artamonov's wife, 'Shadrin was profoundly depressed at the prospect of losing his ONI job. There was nowhere else acceptable that he could go.'[6] At the DIA his talents could not be used and all he was offered was a translation job in a department staffed by defectors. But the pay cheques had stopped so after three months walking with his dog and brooding over the situation, he joined the DIA.

On 20 November at 9:00 p.m. in Alexandria he secretly met Kozlov/Sokolov, his resident Soviet controller, for the first time. Artamonov was given the codename LARK.

The year 1967 saw several important events in the Soviet-US spy war. In June two army code clerks were arrested as they began to collaborate with Soviet Intelligence. Accordingly, Nikolai F. Popov, head of Line KR in Washington, and Anatoly T. Kireyev, head of Line PR in New York, were PNGed from the United States. Kozlov/Sokolov, who was handling LARK, was put in charge of counter-intelligence and promoted to second secretary In December, John Anthony Walker Jr, a former warrant officer and communications specialist for the US Navy, walked into the Soviet Embassy and asked to talk to the security officer. Kozlov/Sokolov was on duty and he promptly called in Yakov Bukashev, an elderly serviceman who was responsible for the embassy's security and whose job was to initially debrief visitors. Very soon he reported to Popov and the latter to the *rezident* that Walker had with him important secret documents and looked and sounded quite much like the real thing. That was the beginning of Walker's very successful espionage against his own country that continued for seventeen years. He was mainly met in Vienna under the KGB's set of rules that later became known as the 'Vienna Procedure'.

As LARK continued to meet his Russian handler, the KGB worked out a plan to watch him more carefully. He had done nothing wrong but had on occasion failed to deliver material that had been asked of him, like the classified ONI telephone directory and a bugging device that he was given to secretly install in a CIA safe house which failed to transmit. In the spring of 1971, when Kozlov/Sokolov was preparing to return home after his tour of duty, it was decided to test LARK by sending him to Montreal, where the KGB had a reliable penetration agent, a mole deep inside the Royal Canadian Mounted Police (RCMP), whom the Americans would presumably notify if LARK were coming onto Canadian territory under American control.

Gilles Brunet, the KGB's mole, was a native-born Canadian, the son of a Mountie, J. J. Brunet, who had been the first head of the Security and Intelligence Directorate when it was established as a separate division in 1956, and who had finished his career as deputy commissioner. Born to the manor, as it were, Brunet was marked for a meteoric career in the force. He joined the Security Service in the early 1960s. At the Russian desk, he won promotion in 1966 for investigative work that led to the conviction of an Ottawa civil servant for espionage. The following year Brunet was enrolled by the service in a Russian language course and scored top marks.[7]

The KGB told Artamonov that in Canada he would meet an important representative from the Centre, the KGB headquarters.

Artamonov arrived in Montreal in April and after checking into the hotel went straight to see his Russian contact. This time it was Boris Kopeiko, a deputy of Vitaly Boyarov, the head of the counter-intelligence directorate (Directorate K) of the FCD (foreign intelligence). (In 1972 Kalugin would be promoted to this job and personally direct the LARK operation.) The meeting was short and of no importance for Artamonov – in fact, not really justifying the trip. From Montreal the Shadrins travelled north and spent several days at Mont Tremblant; from there they went on to Quebec. Ewa, according to Henry Hurt, remembered the trip as exhilarating.

It was, however, no fun for the KGB. By the time LARK returned from his trip, the KGB had learned through Brunet that Artamonov was in fact under American control. When Kozlov/Sokolov met him in Washington in May, for the last time as his control, he knew the truth – and was already planning an elaborate ruse to lure him to 'neutral grounds' where a final act could be staged.

Like every good intelligence service, the KGB have patience. They also see it necessary to set up a pattern to create a feeling of familiarity and comfort, to rehearse everything in real circumstances to see how the target will react, and create a situation offering the target little choice.

So they called Shadrin to a meeting in Vienna. In August 1972, the Shadrins flew there and checked into the Hotel Bristol on Vienna's Ringstrasse. Nick told Ewa that he would have to leave the next morning to meet his Russian friend. Just as he had done for the Montreal meeting, Nick gave Ewa a piece of paper with telephone numbers on it to call if he did not return on time. She paid little attention to the paper, simply stashing it in a place where she could find it if needed. What was different for the Vienna meeting was that Nick was going to be away overnight and she was not to expect him back at the hotel until the next evening, around eight o'clock.[8] It was played by the KGB book, and he was let out some time earlier.

The pretext for an all-night meeting was an alleged need for LARK to study and practice working on a new radio transmitter. That offered good enough reason for a drive out of Vienna to suburban Purkersdorf where the Russian embassy maintains a comfortable villa. A decade earlier, in May 1961, Nikita Khrushchev had stayed there briefly before meeting President Kennedy. No doubt Shadrin felt flattered when told about the historic event and that he was now considered so important. The following day he and Ewa flew to Athens to spend five days swimming, sunbathing and enjoying the sea views. After they came back to Washington the transmitter was duly delivered and collected by Shadrin from a dead drop. He never had any chance or necessity to use it.

In December 1975 two groups of officers left Moscow for Austria. Colonel Mikhail Ivanovich Kuryshev, Kalugin's deputy in Directorate K, headed one group that included himself, Alexander Alexandrovich Sokolov (whom the FBI, CIA and Artamonov/Shadrin knew as 'Oleg Alekseyevich Kozlov'), and another officer about whom little information is available apart from the fact that after the operation he went on to serve in the Russian Foreign Ministry. Another group was directed by General Kalugin personally and included himself, two other officers and a KGB nurse. They settled in a forest on the Czech side of the Czech-Austrian border. Still another KGB general was in Prague coordinating the operation with the Czech authorities.

Bruce Solie, from the CIA Office of Security, who had first met Igor Kochnov in Washington and then played a major role in clearing the defector Yuri Nosenko of CIA suspicions, was the first to arrive from the USA. 'Solie was a taciturn, cigar-smoking man whose lean features gave him an air of the American farm-lands,' recalls Pete Bagley. 'He sat in on some of our interrogations of Nosenko prior to Kochnov's advent, not contributing but maintaining a generally approving if reserved demeanour. With Nosenko's earlier interrogators removed from the scene and being himself convinced by Kochnov of Nosenko's genuineness, Solie set out to prove that we had been wrong.'[9] When Nosenko decided to marry soon after he left Camp Perry, Solie acted as his best man.

Cynthia Hausmann was the next escort to come. Tall, thin, angular Miss Hausmann had won good marks for her performance in the Soviet Division, primarily as a researcher in the counter-intelligence branch. After a flight delay she reported in at 9:30 a.m. on Wednesday, 17 December.[10]

The chief of the CIA Vienna station asked if surveillance would be required for the Shadrin meeting. Hausmann replied that it was thought in Washington not to be necessary, and would only risk exposing the whole operation.[11]

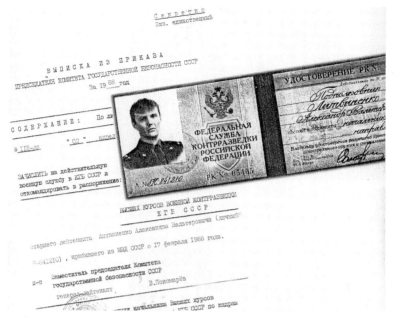

25 April 1988: Lieutenant Colonel Litvinenko is accepted by the FSK (successor to the KGB) after an enhanced positive vetting. *Courtesy of Alexander ('Sasha') Litvinenko.*

14 October 1994: The wedding of Sasha and Marina Litvinenko.
Courtesy of Marina Litvinenko.

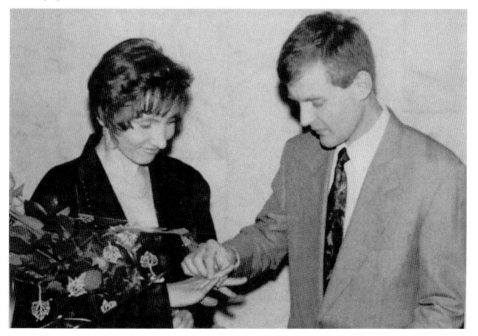

Three good friends:
Sasha, Akhmed and
Vladimir Bukovsky,
2006. *Courtesy of
Marina Litvinenko.*

From left to right: Akhmed
Zakayev, Anna Politkovskaya and
Alexander Litvinenko, 2006.
Courtesy of Akhmed Zakayev.

Sasha and David
Kudykov, 2006.
*Courtesy of David
Kudykov.*

7 December 2006, the funeral of Alexander Litvinenko. From left to right: Yaragi ("Yasha") Abdullayev, Akhmed's personal assistant at the time; Walter Litvinenko, Sasha's father; Akhmed Zakayev. Behind: Ivar Amundsen, the Honorary Consul of the Chechen Republic of Ichkeria to Norway; Maxim Litvinenko.

The Highgate cemetery: Boris Berezovsky, Vladimir Bukovsky, Andrei Nekrasov, Akhmed Zakayev, the mourners.

22 April 1954: Nikolai Khokhlov gives a press conference in Bonn, the year after he defected to the United States. He survived an assassination by poisoning by the KGB in 1957.
Courtesy of Nikolai E. Khokhlov.

Bela Lapusnyik, 1962.
Courtesy of the Open Society Archives, Budapest.

Tennent H. ("Pete") Bagley, 1973, then a
high-ranking CIA officer.
Courtesy of Pete Bagley.

Nikolai Artamonov, 1972.
Courtesy of Ewa Shadrin.

The Bristol Hotel in Vienna where Nikolai
Artamonov and Ewa stayed in December
1975, when Nikolai was abducted and killed
by the KGB.

Mikhail Gorbachev
and his bodyguard
General Medvedev,
1989. *Official photo,
collection of Vladimir
Medvedev.*

18 August 1991: Putsch in
Moscow. Boris Yeltsin and his
bodyguard General Korzhakov on
the tank. *Photo Associated Press.*

Vladimir Putin accompanied by his bodyguards General Murov and General Zolotov, May 2006. Photo *Komsomolskaya Pravda*.

London, April 2003: Boris Berezovsky leaves court hearings about his extradition to Russia wearing a mask of Putin. *Photo Associated Press*.

The dedication to the author from Alex Goldfarb and Marina Litvinenko on their book. Alex wrote: 'To the only one [among the former intelligence officers] with whom it is certainly safe to drink tea.' The author as a young Spetsnaz officer in 1983 (below).

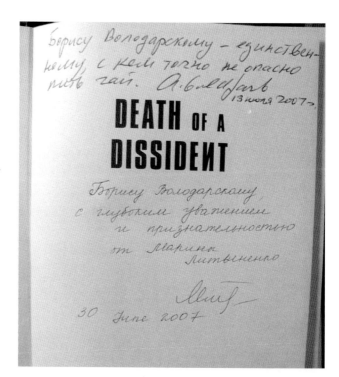

Dmitry Péskov during the G8 session in Japan, 2006. Peskov has acted as Putin's press attach since 2000. *Official photo/Voice of Russia.*

Vyacheslav Zharko during his television interview in Moscow, June 2007. *Screenshot of the Russian NTV broadcast.*

The KGB (FSB)
poison laboratory
today.

The espionage paraphernalia
collector H. Keith Melton
(USA) at the KGB Lubyanka
building with a replica of the
poison-tip umbrella that had
been used to assassinate Georgi
Markov. *Courtesy of Windfall
Films.*

Stalin and his bodyguard,
General Vlasik, 1945.
The U.S. Library of Congress.

Though some American commentators give a different interpretation of the role of Solie suggesting that he was in Vienna exclusively for a chance to meet Kochnov, who was allegedly expected to appear, I see his primary duties, given his job status, as providing security for Artamonov/Shadrin. Cynthia Hausmann was there to brief the double agent after his every meeting with the Russians and to send SITREPS (situation reports) to headquarters. Both botched their assignments terribly.

When Mr and Mrs Shadrin checked into the Hotel Bristol at about 3:00 p.m. on 18 December 1975, they were accompanied to room 341 on the third floor. Nick told his wife that he would have to leave at five for his meeting that was scheduled on the steps of the magnificent Votivkirche in the 9th District about five minutes' walk from the American Embassy.

The Russians had chosen the location with great care. First of all, the neighbourhood of the embassy gave a feeling of security, and second, the church was surrounded by a park with many roads and convenient parking places around that not only meant it could be watched from every angle but also allowed easy movement in and out. The KGB would later use the same place to meet the CIA traitor Aldrich Ames.

Nick returned from the meeting at about 10:30 that evening and was not surprised to see Miss Hausmann in his hotel room together with his wife. They conferred secretly in the bathroom where the CIA operative debriefed the agent for about a quarter of an hour and left to write her report.

According to Nick, the meeting went very well. He met Kuryshev and Sokolov ('Kozlov') in front of the church exactly as planned. They then proceeded to the parked car and drove away. Artamonov knew Kuryshev from their last meeting in Vienna three years before when the Russian was the chief of Line KR at the Vienna station. Since then he had moved to Moscow but explained to LARK that he was well known in the city so he'd better leave them alone. Soon Kuryshev left and the two went to a fish restaurant rather far away from the centre for a friendly chat, a carp and a few vodkas. The former Lieutenant Commander was informed that he had been promoted to the rank of colonel in the KGB. Amazingly, Artamonov believed this obvious lie and was happy and proud to tell his wife about his success. It never occurred to him that he had just taken part in the final full-dress practice run.

The next day, Friday, was all theirs and they spent it at leisure getting up late and then shopping and going to the theatre. The Shadrins finished the day in the very cosy Bristol Bar with live music and a wide choice of hugely overpriced drinks. It is still one of the most expensive places in Vienna.

On Saturday, at about 6:00 p.m. Artamonov put on his gold-buttoned blazer and pocketed the envelope with about a thousand dollars received from the Russians during their last meeting. As usual, he handed Ewa a card with two telephone numbers, one for the day and another for the night alarm, just in case. The card also had a notation in Nick's handwriting: 'Ann stay with Grimm' meaning that Cynthia Hausmann who operated under the alias of 'Ann Martin' was staying with the family of her old friends one of whom was a member of the CIA Vienna station.

Thirty minutes later Artamonov kissed his wife, looked into her eyes and smiled. He said that as before his friend would be waiting for him at the entrance of the Votivkirche and that he expected to return early enough to meet Ewa in front of the Opera House, where she intended to go that night, conveniently opposite the Bristol on the same side of the Opernring. Then he left.

Gustav Hohenbichler, a high-ranking officer of the Vienna security police, was sitting in his undistinguished office just around the corner from the square in the middle of which towered the Votivkirche. Hohenbichler was recruited by the Stasi as agent BAU in the early 1970s, but was also working for the KGB under the codename ZAK. In the personal dead letter box (DLB) that he had fitted out for himself in the basement of his apartment house in Helfersdorferstrasse, just yards from his office, he found a note from his handler suggesting a meeting. During a lunch in a far less luxurious place than the Bristol, the policeman was told that the CIA planned a clandestine operation in his city and must be carefully watched day and night. He was also asked to provide additional security to the area surrounding the Votivkrche so as to be able to intervene in case something might happen. The assignment was not a problem for Hohenbichler as this type of thing was actually part of his service duties.

The eye – the person who has the target under visual observation at any given moment – was focused on both Solie and Hausmann backed by appropriate surveillance teams. Plain-clothed agents reinforced the usually active police presence in the Freud Park and in the direction of the American Embassy and consulate that at that time was near the City Hall. Several hours before the meeting Kuryshev, Sokolov and Vladimir Dzerzhakovsky left for a long and boring surveillance detection run (SDR) in order to erode or flush out any possible surveillance. Kalugin later reported: 'Our people did not spot any tails, and our informers in the Austrian police also told us that the Americans – probably from the CIA – were rarely venturing out of their hotel.'[12]

When Ewa left the opera her husband was not there to meet her. He was not in the hotel at eleven, or twelve, or one o'clock. At 1:35 a.m. she dialled the number Nick had given her. There was no one on the other side to answer her call and the line went dead. Ewa Shadrin started weeping.

She only reached 'Ann Martin' later that night and they spent three days together still hoping that Nick might return, while the CIA station was flashing urgent telegrams to headquarters. On Christmas Eve, accompanied by Bruce Solie, Ewa Shadrin left Vienna for Washington, DC. Miss Hausmann asked her to be patient as the United States government was working for a resolution.

And – contrary to the fierce criticism of Ewa and her many supporters – the government did act and quite promptly.

On 30 December the US Embassy in Moscow contacted the Soviet Ministry of Foreign Affairs, which stated that no Soviet official was in contact with Shadrin on 20 December. However, the Soviets expressed a desire to 'cooperate' and deal with the matter 'constructively', according to an FBI report.

In early January, Secretary of State Henry Kissinger met privately with the Soviet Ambassador Anatoly Dobrynin in Washington to plead for Shadrin's return. On 5 February, Brent Scowcroft, President Ford's assistant for national security, telephoned Mrs Shadrin to say that he had just reviewed Shadrin's file and would be in touch soon to advise her of the administration's plan of action. Later that day General Vernon Walters, Deputy Director of the CIA, called one of Ewa's friends to report that Scowcroft had arrived at CIA headquarters late in the afternoon and was meeting at that hour with CIA Director George Bush to reach an agreement on how to pursue the Shadrin matter. After the meeting Bush appointed George Kalaris, CIA counter-intelligence chief, as the contact for Ewa and her lawyer, Richard Copaken, instructing him to assist them wherever possible. Finally, on 1 December 1976 President Ford sent a letter to Leonid Brezhnev asking the Soviet leader about what had happened to Shadrin.[13]

It took Kalugin and his colleagues in Service A ('active measures') about a year to work out a complex disinformation strategy.

On Christmas Eve, one year from that miserable day when Ewa Shadrin had flown home without her husband accompanied by the enigmatic Bruce Solie, the White House received Brezhnev's response. Yuli Vorontsov, then the second highest official at the Soviet Embassy in Washington, conveyed it orally to William G. Hyland, an intelligence veteran then serving as assistant to the President on national security affairs. Hyland informed President Ford. He also called Ewa and Copaken to the White House to read them his notes. According to Hyland, the Soviet leader stated that records had been consulted in Moscow and that he could report to the US President that Shadrin had never arrived for his second meeting with the Soviets.[14]

Everybody present was stunned. How could Brezhnev speak with such confidence, people asked. How could he know that there was no surveillance by the CIA of the meeting? Whatever was behind the message, it was compelling evidence for many that indeed, Shadrin had never reached the meeting site.

Still, the new administration of President Carter gave Mrs Shadrin and her lawyer, whose mounting invoices were paid by the government, a new set of officials upon whom they could try their skills. As early as February 1977 Copaken succeeded in getting Secretary of State Cyrus Vance to raise the Shadrin issue with Ambassador Dobrynin, who stated, as he had so many times before, that the Soviets knew nothing of Shadrin's whereabouts.

What had really happened that evening of 20 December 1975 only became known much later. Kozlov/Sokolov picked up Artamonov on the Roosevelt Platz in front of the Votivkirche just between the headquarters of the Vienna state police and the American embassy. He accompanied agent LARK to the car where Kuryshev and Dzerzhakovsky were waiting. A new face with a tough, hulking figure should have put Artamonov on guard but after warm greetings the KGB thugs explained that he would be introduced to an illegal with whom he would later be in contact in the USA and that the man in the car was a case officer from Directorate S (which he almost certainly was).

To get even a lead to an illegal would be a great prize for the FBI and CIA who were hunting for them everywhere and seldom spotted any. Actually, that was what the FBI's whole operation was about – to get in contact, through Artamonov, with some prized Soviet agent operating 'in black' under the cover of an innocent American businessman, trader or a technician.

Several minutes after Artamonov sat down in the back seat of the embassy car, the husky KGB man slapped a chloroform-soaked cloth over his face. LARK himself weighed about 220 pounds and began struggling, and one of the men pulled out a syringe filled with a powerful sedative and jabbed in the needle. Artamonov lost consciousness. In fact, the Vienna KGB team, concerned about their victim's size, had administered twice the normal dose needed to knock out a man. The KGB car sped out of Vienna heading for the Czech border crossing.

Reinvestigating the case in Vienna thirty years later when plenty of new tiny details came into my hands, I found out that the KGB carefully planned the operation. For example, a disguise technique known as *podmena* (substitution) was used to confuse the police and future researchers, which it did. One of the officers, as mentioned, was M. I. Kuryshev, colonel in Directorate K working under cover as first secretary and consul at the Soviet Embassy. Shortly before M. I. Kuryshev finished his term and left Vienna (to come back later with a diplomatic passport to snatch Artamonov), a double named 'V. G. Kuryshev' was accredited in the same consular section as second secretary. The 'substitute' was in Vienna when the original Colonel Kuryshev returned in December to prepare and carry out the operation; Kuryshev 1 then disappeared with his victim behind the Czech border while Kuryshev 2 continued to serve in Vienna until the dust settled. Austrian journalists, who tried to reconstruct the case in articles and books, were as confused as the Austrian police.[15]

According to Kalugin, the night of the rendezvous at the Czech border was cold and moonless. Though it was below freezing, there was no snow on the ground. In front of them were the woods and a field. It was pitch black, and the only sound was the faint whispering of the wind through the dry leaves that had remained on the trees from autumn.

The KGB officers had been there for two days, scouting out locations where their Vienna colleagues could cross with their valuable cargo without delay. The Czech border police, informed that there was an important KGB operation going on, had given the general and his small group free rein. Pretending to be hunting and wearing camouflage fatigues, they found a seldom-used old asphalt road running through a wooded area with no Austrian border checkpoints. The road ran through a no-man's-land directly into the barbed wire fences and lookout towers manned by armed Czech guards.[16]

As Kalugin described the moment,

We waited in some bushes, my stomach churning in anticipation. Our plan was to get Artamonov back to Moscow, where he would be informed he had two choices: either tell us everything he knew, or face a firing squad. We were certain he would tell all, at which point KGB would parade Shadrin before the press in Moscow, where he would describe his many years of working as a loyal Soviet mole inside the dastardly US intelligence community.

Suddenly, we saw the headlights of a fast-moving car heading down the road on the Austrian side. The lights illuminated the Austrian border markers, about 20 yards in front of them. The car roared up the road, then came to a halt a few yards from the agreed position. Car doors slammed, and we heard the excited whispers and curses of our three KGB colleagues.

When I walked up to the car, our colleagues from Vienna were huffing and puffing as they dragged Artamonov out of the vehicle and plopped him on the road. He was breathing heavily and occasionally letting out a moan.

'A stretcher!' someone called out. 'There is no other way we can carry this boar!'

Fortunately, someone had brought a large canvas poncho, and we slid it under the unconscious Artamonov. Four of us began the arduous task of hauling LARK back to the Czech border and our car. We made it halfway there when we decided to take a break. We laid him on the ground, and someone pulled out a pocket flashlight to see how our prisoner was doing. Illuminating his face, we saw that he wasn't breathing. We massaged his chest, then forced open his clenched jaws and poured brandy down his throat. Nothing worked.[17]

The KGB nurse was helpless in the situation. LARK was dead.

At about 11:00 a.m. on 5 August 1977, three weeks after the Shadrin story broke out in the American press (but eight years before anyone knew what happened in Vienna), Richard Copaken answered his telephone at the Washington offices of Covington & Burling. A bright, cocky voice, laced with an apparent British accent, said airily, 'I understand you are looking for Nicky Artamonov.'[18]

Identifying himself as Benson, the caller described himself as a former British agent interested in assisting in the search for Shadrin. He told of 'a mercenary character' named Agnew who had supplied Shadrin with false documents in Zurich six days after he had vanished in Austria. 'Benson' told Copaken that he believed that for money Agnew might lead him to Shadrin.[19] The caller hinted that Agnew could be contacted by placing an ad in the *International Herald Tribune* with a coded message that he dictated. However, after a meeting with the CIA it was decided to wait.

On 17 August Moscow's *Literaturnaya Gazeta* ('Literary Gazette') published an article by Genrikh Borovik, a famous Soviet journalist (and a known KGB collaborator). The article was entitled 'Broken-Winded Horses Are Shot, Aren't They?'

Kalugin later recalled:

Borovik was one of our 'pet' journalist who always did our bidding. The article, purportedly relying on documents and inside information, described how the CIA had actually killed Artamonov when it realized he was playing a double [triple] game and working for the Soviets. When I was feeding Borovik our account of what had occurred, he asked me several times, 'Now, Oleg, are you sure that this is the way it really happened? Artamonov was really working for us?'

'Absolutely, Genrikh,' I answered. 'It's the truth, I swear.'

In all the years I was in Foreign Counterintelligence, *Literaturnaya Gazeta* was our prime conduit in the Soviet press for propaganda and disinformation.[20]

After the article was published, many, including Ewa Shadrin, believed it. The case proceeded as far as suing the US Government, which much later was to help Ewa and her lawyer finally to learn the truth. But in 1977 it prompted her and Copaken to place the ad in the *IHT*.

They were promptly contacted: the caller said that Shadrin would pay his fee and he would only ask to cover his travel expenses in the amount of $3,000. The sum was to be wire transferred to the National Bank of Paris in Monaco to the account in the name of W. Flynn. Copaken wired the money immediately.[21]

Sooner rather than later it was clear they were facing a fraud. Nevertheless, with the help of the FBI and CIA Copaken managed to establish that in the bank the caller had produced a forged Australian passport in the name of William Joseph Flynn, who was a real person living in Australia but having nothing to do with the affair. For me it is clear that this was the work of the Second Department of Directorate S (Illegals) whose speciality is documentary support of agents and that 'Benson' acted on KGB instruction. It is not at all uncommon to hire criminals for support or cover operations.

Finally, the culprit in the scam turned out to be one Walter James Flynn, also from Australia, who had fled the country the preceding March. Copaken finally got his hands on Flynn in France in December. But the story did not end here. Flynn insisted that there was an Agnew who knew Shadrin's whereabouts and that he would agree to take a lie detector test to prove he was right. Copaken finally got Flynn to London where he promptly failed a polygraph. Nevertheless two weeks later Flynn called Copaken and said that if he would just meet him in Vienna, it would be to his and Mrs Shadrin's advantage.[22]

In late December 1977, the FBI Special Agent Leonard Hulse Ralston from the US Embassy in Bern arrived in Vienna to see Flynn. Again, it was Hohenbichler who was dealing with the FBI man[23] and informing the KGB about all details of the operation. After several attempts to meet 'Agnew' and a few days beating around the bush, Ralston managed to get Flynn on the next flight to London where he was arrested.

For another fourteen months the Flynn case dragged on until finally he was convicted in Knightsbridge Crown Court to eighteen months in jail. Announcing the verdict, the judge, Andrew Phelan, said to Flynn: 'You have preyed most callously upon the desolation of that desperate woman.'[24]

It took the widow (and the American government) exactly ten years to learn the truth. On 1 August 1985 the KGB Colonel Vitaly Yurchenko walked into the US Embassy in Rome and defected to the USA. Among other golden nuggets he described the Artamonov operation.

Being under court obligations, the State Department immediately informed the widow and lodged a protest with the Soviet Foreign Ministry charging that in 1975 the KGB in Vienna had paralysed an American intelligence agent, named Nicholas Shadrin, with drugs, and transported him across international borders to Czechoslovakia,[25] where he died.

In 1992, Ewa Shadrin called Kalugin in America. She told me in May 2007: 'I asked him, 'You took part in the operation. Did my husband die?''

'Yes, he did,' he replied.

'How did he die?'

'I feel sorry for you,' the former KGB man answered, 'but I can't tell you anything over the telephone. I can only confirm that he died.'[26]

Mrs Shadrin finally met Oleg Danilovich Kalugin personally in Washington. A TV group from Poland was shooting a documentary about her husband and the KGB plot and arranged to interview Kalugin in the International Spy Museum. After the interview, Ewa suddenly approached him face to face.

She recalled: 'I asked him, "Did you kill my husband? Why did you do it?" And he started to mumble that it was an operation against the traitor and so on and so forth.'

Shortly after the operation General Kalugin was awarded the prestigious Order of the Red Banner.

As a reward for his successful work, in 1979 Gustav Hohenbichler was placed in charge of Chairman Brezhnev's security during the US–USSR summit in Vienna that became known as SALT II. Before the fall of the Berlin Wall, he was handled by the Stasi officer Hans Ulrich Fritz from the East German Embassy.

According to the Austrian police investigation documents, Hohenbichler personally met Markus 'Misha' Wolf in a safe house in Prenden near Berlin. I tried to discuss the case with Wolf several times but he always refused to go into details or name the names. When interviewed by the police in Vienna, Wolf said that 'the DDR is proud to have won [recruited] high ranking officials of the Vienna *Stapo* (security police)'.

This came at a price. The chief of the Vienna Stapo, Hofrat Magister Gustav Hohenbichler, was a mercenary agent. During his collaboration with the Stasi, he allegedly received about DM 100,000 (€50,000) in addition to his fixed monthly agent's 'salary' of DM 2,000 plus different bonuses.

In 1990, Minister for State Security Colonel General Karl Grossmann personally handed Hohenbichler's Stasi files to the KGB in Moscow together with those of other most important agents.

In early April 1991 the Austrian EBT (*Einsatzgruppe zur Bekämpfung des Terrorismus* – a special unit within the Stapo to counter espionage, organised crime and terrorist activities) represented by Dr Oswald Kessler and Erwin Kemper initiated an investigation against Hohenbichler, which was widely reported in the Austrian press in the spring of 1994. Thus warned, he checked into a hospital and his lawyer, Hermann Gaigg, declined all attempts of the judges to contact him. Hohenbichler died a year later.

Long after Kalugin moved to the USA and became an American citizen, and exactly thirty years after Nick Shadrin was ruthlessly murdered in Vienna, that 'snake pit of Soviet spies' (in the words of one CIA officer), a former member of Kalugin's team, the retired SVR Colonel Alexander Sokolov published a book entitled *The Anatomy of Treachery. Supermole of the CIA in the KGB: General Kalugin's 35 Years of Espionage* (2005). In the book Sokolov promotes a theory that Kalugin had all the time been an American spy in the KGB and murdered LARK with the help of a special poison provided by the CIA to get rid of the triple agent who could become dangerous should he appear in Moscow. The legend lives on.

Operation VLADIMIR, Part II

Most of the people become celebrities because of their extraordinary lives. Sasha Litvinenko became a celebrity because of his extraordinary death.

His first claim to fame was on 17 November 1998 when, together with a group of other FSB officers, he took part in a press conference organised by the Interfax news agency. Andrei Ponkin was among those who testified that several months earlier they had been given clear and unmistakable orders to murder Boris Berezovsky, recently the deputy secretary of the Security Council of Russia and a media mogul.

Goldfarb, who is usually well informed and who worked with Marina Litvinenko on his book, describes what happened:

> An assistant to the general who commanded Sasha's unit called the officers in. 'We are the department of special tasks,' he said. 'Have you read this?' He produced a copy of *Special Tasks*, the recently published memoirs of Pavel Sudoplatov, the head of NKVD special tasks under Stalin. 'This is our role model!' He waved the book. 'Everyone is ordered to read it. We have a new set of objectives ahead of us. There are people, criminals, who cannot be gotten in the normal way. They are tremendously wealthy and can always buy their way out of court. You, Litvinenko, you know Berezovsky, don't you? You will be the one to take him out.'[1]

The conference caused a great scandal. Not only was the FSB publicly accused of organising murders or conspiring to do so but also it was the first time ever that active duty officers had spoken out against the *kontora* ('bureau'), as the security service is mockingly called in Russia.

According to Goldfarb, the event was a sensation, but not in the way the participants hoped. The press focused on only one among the many charges the conference had made: the plot to kill Berezovsky. Boris's notoriety overshadowed their intended message.

By that time Putin had been the FSB director for four months. He was actively flirting with Berezovsky and Yeltsin's group of closest presidential advisers (that had become known as 'The Family'). But now he firmly took the side of the service. The whistle-blowers were quickly given short shrift. All were sacked from the FSB, and their unit was disbanded. In March 1999 lieutenant colonels Alexander Litvinenko and Alexander Gusak, his department chief, were arrested and sentenced for 'exceeding their official powers and causing bodily harm to witnesses' without any mention of the press conference.

Whatever I think of the man, in one thing the director general was right: intelligence officers should not stage public shows.

Litvinenko was put in Lefortovo prison, the same place in which Dr Vil Mirzayanov had spent his term for revealing in a newspaper article that Russia continued experimenting with biological weapons contrary to its international agreements. It was also here that Vyacheslav Zharko, 'Agent Slava', would be locked up two years after Litvinenko.

Sasha wrote in his book *Organized Crime Group from the Lubyanka*:

Initially, I was in shock. The first night I did not sleep, I stared at the ceiling. On the day I was arrested, the weather was lousy, snow mixed with rain, sludge all over. I don't like this time of the year and by the end of March I live in expectation of the sun. The next day they took me out into a small recreation box, five to six steps across. I looked up – and the sky was blue, with the sun somewhere out there. I was pacing like a beast between those walls. Over me – the iron grid with barbed wire and blue-blue skies. I was in a terrible state: spring had arrived, and I can't see it. I am here, in the damp, cold box. I got so upset that I asked them to bring me back to my cell.

Later, during our many meetings, Marina Litvinenko told me that friends never stopped supporting her and her husband while he was in jail.

'Lefortovo crushes you spiritually,' he further wrote. 'There is some negative energy coming from those walls. They say that birds avoid flying over it. Perhaps it's the legacy of the old days when Lefortovo was a place of mass executions and torture.'[2]

What Sasha almost certainly did not tell Marina is that during his seven months in the FSB prison they had been exerting great pressure upon him to turn him against Berezovsky. That Litvinenko stood firm is proved by the fact that as soon as he was let free, they arrested him for a second time.

Alex and Marina recalled that day:

The trial resumed on November 26. Journalists and TV cameras packed the court building. The defence made its final argument for acquittal. The judge left the courtroom to deliberate. It took him four hours to reach a verdict. Marina waited in the hallway, 'all frozen inside, feeling as if all this was not real'.

Finally, the judge returned and announced his decision: 'Not guilty. Free to go.'

As the guard unlocked the dock cage to let Sasha out, there was a sudden commotion at the door. A squad of armed men in camouflage and masks ran past Marina and stormed into the courtroom, pushing the guards aside.[3]

He was rearrested, handcuffed and taken away. The TV cameras recorded Litvinenko being dragged past his wife, an FSB man pushing her away and hitting him with a rifle butt when he moved to protect Marina. The whole country watched the disgraceful scene.

This time they took Litvinenko to Butyrka, the most notorious criminal prison in Moscow.

Berezovsky was still in a position to help. In mid-December the military tribunal released Litvinenko from preventive detention but only on condition that he would not leave Moscow. His internal passport was taken away while his passport valid for international travel (in the name of 'Alexander Volkov,' Sasha's operational alias) was safely locked in the personnel department of the FSB. However, he had another set of identity documents in the same name under which he had operated in Chechnya in 1996. No doubt his second 'Volkov' passport and the FSB warrant card were taken away, but what about the driving licence?

When at large he had to have some sort of identity paper to show to the authorities when asked, and he used one set or the other in August 2000 to travel with Marina to Sochi allegedly for vacation on the Black Sea. In reality, Sasha had already been preparing for his escape.

By September Yuri Felshtinsky was deep in research for his new book about the role of FSB in provoking the Second Chechen War. Most of all he was interested in the apartment bombings in several Russian towns that cost so many lives and gave Premier Putin a perfect *casus belli* and boost for his presidential campaign. But Felshtinsky is a historian and he needed an intelligence professional to give him an inside view. So when he met Berezovsky who was travelling between New York and Washington at the time meeting officials at the Council on Foreign Relations, they agreed that Sasha would have the necessary knowledge. Besides, Boris was seriously worried for Litvinenko's security in Russia. So he took Felshtinsky with him to Nice from where the latter flew to Moscow and met Sasha.

Like every KGB officer Litvinenko was taught that the best places for meeting his contacts were parks and stadiums. The rule is honoured to this day; I have several times observed, in the Rose Garden that is conveniently located between the Burgtheater and Heldenplatz in Vienna, SVR operatives from the Russian Embassy receiving reports from agents and informers from the local Russian community and giving them instructions. A practised eye can easily spot a KGB officer. Among other signs, he will often have a newspaper in his hand. To identify watchers in the crowd is an essential part of intelligence training, and officers in the field don't look much different from their colleagues from the surveillance teams whom I spotted many times in Russia. (Before the general restructuring of the service in the 1990s they were part of the 7th Directorate of the KGB.)

As the autumn leaves crunched under their feet, Sasha gave Yuri his take on the apartment bombings. There was no doubt in his mind that it was a *kontora* job.

'It's the signature,' he said. 'Every crime has a signature. I have worked long enough in the Anti-Terrorist Centre to tell you right away, this was not some fringe Chechens. The sophistication, the coordination, the engineering expertise needed for bomb placement – all point to a highly professional team.'[4]

The next day Felshtinsky boarded an early aircraft to London to have a word with Berezovsky.

It is clear that while on holiday in Sochi Sasha had been carefully planning his escape route out of the country. So it was no surprise that at the end of September, telling Marina that he had to visit his father in Nalchik in the Caucasus region of Southern Russia, he again flew to the Black Sea resort only a short distance away from Georgia. Georgia had regained its independence in 1991 and by this time was gradually stabilising after its early post-Soviet years of civil unrest and economic crisis. It was a free land although still under Eduard Shevard-nadze, a cunning Soviet apparatchik nicknamed *tetri melia* ('white fox'), who rose to the rank of general in the police later becoming Soviet Foreign Minister and finally the President of Georgia. Sasha's only problem was to get into Georgia.

Marina and their son Tolik stayed at home until further notice.

Litvinenko strongly suspected that Ponkin was moonlighting for the FSB so he fed him the Nalchik legend and explained that he was going to come back in a couple of days. Nothing suspicious, wife and son in their Moscow flat, he set off for the south. He had to solve yet another problem – he needed a new passport in a different name that would allow him to go abroad.

Several published accounts suggest that Litvinenko somehow bought a forged Georgian passport. I doubt it. Though he certainly had agents all over Russian territory, several in the law enforcement agencies, it was terribly difficult and risky for him trying to obtain a new 'book', as passports are called in the KGB lingo, in an independent country like Georgia. There he would hardly have anyone trusted enough to do the job and not report him to the security service. Besides, I know for sure that Sasha could neither speak, read nor write Georgian, so if asked a simple question anywhere abroad, he would immediately be 'burned' with a good chance to be expelled to Russia. So professional logic dictates that he would have obtained a Ukrainian passport, for this was the language he could certainly read and pretend to speak. And he looked Ukrainian all right.

The natural port of call would have been Poti where Litvinenko could have arrived from Sochi in six hours using the hydrofoil. On 8 October he called Yuri Felshtinsky in Boston. In the meantime Marina was instructed to buy a family tour and leave the country as soon as possible.

Litvinenko moved to the capital, Tbilisi, where Felshtinsky promptly joined him, coming from London with Berezovsky's instructions and a sufficient amount of dollars to secure an easy escape. Felshtinsky didn't see much of a problem here as Litvinenko was a former FSB officer and for Yuri, inexperienced in such matters, it would be natural for Western authorities to accept his friend. But not in the year 2000.

By that time quotas for defectors were virtually non-existent. Since the collapse of the Soviet Union Russia had been considered a friendly state rapidly moving towards democracy. In less than a year President George W. Bush would meet President Putin in Ljubljana, Slovenia, and describe his Russian counterpart as a straightforward and trustworthy person. 'I looked the man in the eyes,' the US President pronounced in a famous phrase (that made him a laughing stock seven years later when Russia ruthlessly invaded Georgia). 'I was able to get a sense of his soul.' With the advantage of hindsight, Senator John McCain later went on record as saying that he too looked the man in the eyes, but was only able to see three letters: KGB.

In such an amiable atmosphere it was difficult to get accepted as a fully-fledged defector with all the benefits provided by the resettlement programme, though it was not entirely impossible. During that same year an SVR colonel defected in New York and in the following April the US Embassy in Prague accepted Major Mykola Melnichenko. But they both had more to offer than Sasha, though he was not entirely empty-handed. So when Litvinenko insisted that Felshtinsky should go to the American embassy in Tbilisi to give it a try, Yuri complied. Felshtinsky held several meetings with US diplomats, who did not reject the young lieutenant colonel out of hand. But the bureaucrats took their time to sort things out.

In a comfortable lobby of the Baur au Lac hotel in Zurich eight years after the events, I asked a former high-ranking US Government official, who was certainly in a position to decide Litvinenko's fate, how the machinery worked in Washington. My friend explained that the first and immediate reaction would be mistrust. General wisdom would dictate that the man could be anything from an SVR dangle to a violent lunatic and that defections are not done through the doors of the embassy. 'It is the policy of the United States,' he said, 'not to grant asylum at its units or installations within the territorial jurisdiction of a foreign state.' He also recalled that even the KGB archivist Mitrokhin had been turned down in 1992 because the material that he offered – not genuine secret documents but hand-made copies mostly of historic value – were not considered good enough to offer him and his family a government-protected shelter for life. Some defectors were only accepted because they proved they possessed information that was of a paramount importance to the US Government at the time of their changing sides. No doubt, most of them delivered. But many, like Oleg Penkovsky, were not taken seriously for quite some time.

My American friend in the Baur au Lac, wearing a golden-buttoned Ralph

Lauren blazer with a white button-down dress shirt and a striped yellow silk tie, looked more like a kind grandfather entertaining his family in a luxury Swiss hotel than a former intelligence chief. However, when he spoke about his former job, I detected some metal in his voice.

'It is also a matter of responsibility,' he said. 'What do the Russians do if an American who walks in turns out to be an empty shell?'

'Dunno. I think they can always send him back.'

'Here we are. And nothing ever happens to him. But the Agency cannot do that. There are many, many restrictions and obligations. A huge responsibility. And laws. If he were unable to tell us something really important, there was no way we could accept the man.'

Precisely eight years before this discussion of mine in Switzerland, Sasha Litvinenko in Georgia was becoming a petulant, irritable grouch, worrying about his family in Marbella and fearing that Russian agents in Georgia might spot him. One day, not yet having got a final answer from the embassy, he and Felshtinsky boarded a fourteen-passenger luxury charter jet rented by Berezovsky in Paris. They were about to take off for Munich, where Litvinenko wanted to settle, when Berezovsky called and redirected them to Antalya in Turkey. There, Felshtinsky dropped off his friend and flew to Malaga to pick up Marina and Tolik. By now Litvinenko was under considerable stress and the arrival of his family the next day did not ease him much. He started seeing FSB agents everywhere. Felshtinsky was losing confidence. He actually regretted letting Berezovsky entangle him in this affair and wanted to be back home. He even feared that if the Russians really got at them, he might become a target like the former FSB man whom he was helping to escape. So Felshtinsky was genuinely happy when Boris dispatched yet another emigration expert and a US passport holder, Alex Goldfarb, to take over. Yuri hurriedly retreated back to the USA.

Though Goldfarb was of a totally different calibre, he was as inexperienced in defection matters as his predecessor. Alex decided to give it another try and took Litvinenko to Ankara to see an American emigration lawyer who kindly agreed to come for a few hours to consult them. Berezovsky footed the bill.

As might be expected, it didn't work out at the American embassy in Turkey either. Although they set up a videoconference with CIA headquarters, during which a Russia expert with an extensive knowledge of Sasha's service grilled him for several hours, the wizards finally decided not to take him. Goldfarb had to improvise.

On 1 November 2000 a lawyer sent by Boris to take care of legal matters met the Litvinenkos at London Heathrow. While they were enjoying their first moments of freedom, Her Majesty's Government declared Goldfarb *persona non grata* and sent him back to Turkey.

For Litvinenko, the six-year-and-twenty-three day count began.

***

It is clear that Berezovsky saw Sasha as a trusted associate and considered him a friend. The family was put up in an apartment in London's upmarket Kensington and Litvinenko was provided with a £5,000 'English professor's' allowance, a handsome sum by any standard. Boris could have been planning for Sasha to become his counter-intelligence chief – he had always had enough security, he thought, but it was a challenge to learn about Putin's plans against him, to be able to unmask Russia's secret agents inside his close circle, and finally, to monitor discreetly the activities of SVR officers in charge of Line EM (émigrés) in the Russian embassy. Their primary target, he was quite convinced, was himself, Boris Abramovich Berezovsky. Besides, Litvinenko could do plenty of other things.

To get used to life in Britain, Sasha and Marina started to attend English language courses while Sasha was spending the rest of his time labouring with Felshtinsky over a book that later became known as *Blowing Up Russia*. Boris Berezovsky considered the book project an important element of his campaign against President Putin.

Berezovsky disdained the man. Only a short time after the billionaire settled in Britain, he visited Oleg Gordievsky in the small, attractive market town of Godalming, Surrey, where the former double agent was spending his days living on a fat government pension. 'He came here in a limousine, and sat at this table, and told me the story of his life. It was like he felt he had to explain himself to me,' Gordievsky recalled at a lunch with Steve LeVine, an American journalist who was researching his book, *Putin's Labyrinth*, published in 2008.

Steve is a gifted journalist with subtle appreciation of facts and people he is dealing with. He reports that the old spy and the rich man shared a mutual contempt for the Russian president. Gordievsky, who considered himself the ass of espionage, degraded Putin's modest exploits in Dresden to snooping on his own colleagues. And Boris knew that if it had not been for his colossal effort 'Volodya' would never have become Vladimir Vladimirovich. The newly elected President of Russia was his own creature. Ironically, it was this same person who forced Berezovsky to choose between becoming a political prisoner or political émigré. He chose the latter.

Following his boss's example, Litvinenko sought friendship with Vladimir Bukovsky and wanted to meet Gordievsky. But the former spy at first refused to see him. He was not inclined to meet a lieutenant colonel in the FSB who had never worked for the British or American intelligence and was not super rich or famous – just one of Berezovsky's lieutenants. Finally, Bukovsky vouched for his new friend and from then on Litvinenko and his family became regular guests in the small English town. 'But he talked a lot,' Oleg remarked, 'and carried two mobile phones. He was always on them.'

That was not Gordievsky's only problem with Sasha. What irritated him was that Litvinenko did not drink alcohol, was young, fit, well paid, busy and had a loving family. Gordievsky's second wife, Leila, had left him taking their both daughters shortly after a difficult and dramatic reunion when they had finally been allowed to joint him in Britain after both President Ronald Reagan and Prime Minister Margaret Thatcher asked the Soviet leadership to let them go. The reason they left was not because Leila wanted his money and brainwashed the girls that he was a traitor, as Gordievsky told Steve LeVine; they simply realised who he really was. They looked the man in the eyes.

Litvinenko did not have any such complexes and lived a happy live in London. Soon Akhmed Zakayev, the Chechen leader in exile became his best friend and neighbour. Litvinenko actively contributed to the Chechen government commission investigating Russian war crimes during the first and the second Chechen wars. The material was to be passed over to the International Criminal Court in The Hague, a permanent tribunal to prosecute individuals for genocide, crimes against humanity and war crimes, established two years after Litvinenko settled in London. Zakayev was sure that what the Russians did in his country ideally fitted the court's jurisdiction. Litvinenko, who had been on an intelligence assignment in Chechnya during the war, was supplying the commission with names of the Russian generals who committed crimes against the Chechen people and with facts he knew firsthand that tended to establish violations of human rights, mass tortures and killings.

After the first book was written, printed and almost delivered from Riga to Moscow (only to be intercepted by the FSB and confiscated), Sasha started working on a second book project that he called *Organized Crime Group from the Lubyanka* (as the old KGB headquarters are widely known) with a foreword written by Alex Goldfarb. The book was published in New York in 2002 and has never been translated into English. I find it fascinating.

As soon as he was granted political asylum in May 2001, Litvinenko also started travelling. He soon got involved in the work of the Mitrokhin Commission of the Italian parliament that was examining Mitrokhin's documents revealing KGB activities in Italy. He became friends there with Mario Scaramella. Former senator Paolo Guzzanti has recently published the only inside story of the Mitrokhin Commission, of which he was the president, outlining Litvinenko's contribution in the most precise and detailed way. The book, entitled *Il Mio Agente Sasha: la Russia di Putin e l'Italia di Berlusconi al Tempi della Seconda Guerra Fredda* became an instant success in Italy when it came out in May 2009, but I expected that there would be a barrage of questions and attacks on the author because of the sensitivity of his revelations. (Needless to say, it has never been even mentioned in Russia.)

After the Peter Shaw experience when Litvinenko was asked to assist Scotland Yard, Sasha realised that his knowledge of the Russian organised crime world might be very useful to law enforcement agencies of many countries. So in addition to Italy, where he went quite regularly, he began to visit Spain, Estonia, Bulgaria, Georgia and Israel.

He also discovered that he had a penchant for writing and soon became quite a prolific journalist contributing mainly to the Chechenpress website.[5] Litvinenko also gave interviews to the Russian services of the BBC and Radio Free Europe/ Radio Liberty, commenting on important issues mostly related to organised crime and unlawful activities of the FSB. As a former officer of the anti-corruption and anti-organised crime task force, Litvinenko knew better than anyone else about mass corruption in the FSB and about Mafia-style crimes performed by the Russian security officials: abduction of people for ransom, murder of business competitors, money laundering, so-called *kryshevanie* ('sheltering'), when state protection against street gangs is offered in exchange for cash.

By the end of summer the film *The FSB Blows Up Russia* was completed and in March 2002 Boris Berezovsky presided over the world premiere of what the *Kommersant* daily called 'An Assault On Russia' in a packed hall of the Royal United Services Institute for Defence and Security Studies at the heart of Whitehall. The two French producers, Jean-Charles Deniau and Charles Gazelle of the Transparencies Production Company, were present alongside Andrei Babitsky, now with the Radio Free Europe/Radio Liberty, as well as Litvinenko, Felshtinsky and Chekulin. Sasha and Yuri were the film's principal consultants.

It is interesting that in 1994 Jean-Charles Deniau co-authored a book *My Five Cambridge Friends: Burgess, Maclean, Philby, Blunt and Cairncross* written by their last KGB controller, Yuri Modin. It has been suggested that that the book had been part of a wide-reaching disinformation operation conducted by the KGB, which passed seemingly unnoticed and quite well accepted even by the specialists.

Four weeks before Litvinenko was granted political asylum, on 11 April 2001, Berezovsky's long-term business partner Nikolai Glushkov, officially in custody, left his Moscow hospital ward wearing only gown and slippers. Glushkov, a top manager of Aeroflot who had been arrested by Russian authorities on fraud charges, had been hospitalised at Moscow's Scientific Haematological Centre for a blood condition. That evening he was going home as usual for an overnight stay. A former Aeroflot colleague was waiting at the gate. As Glushkov was about to get into the car, a squad of plainclothes FSB officers appeared out of nowhere, arrested both men, and charged them with 'attempted escape from custody'. On the next day, the former head of the ORT security, Andrei Lugovoy, was detained and charged with organising the alleged escape. Two months later Badri Patarkatsyshvili, Berezovsky's closest friend and my former guest in the Vital Hotel Kobenzl on the Gaisberg hill near Salzburg, fled to his native Georgia. The whole group was indicted in the escape plot.[6]

However, when Goldfarb interviewed Glushkov for his book years later in London, the former airline official (who once noticed that 3,000 people out of the total workforce of 14,000 in Aeroflot were Russian intelligence officers on active duty) offered a different version of the events of that evening. 'He believed,' writes Goldfarb, 'that he had been set up and insisted that he had no intent to escape.

He wanted the Aeroflot case to be tried because he knew he was innocent. In fact, he was under the impression that he would be released pending the trial "through a secret high-level deal", as his lawyers had hinted to him. He was walking in his slippers to the hospital gate simply to go home for the night, with his guards' knowledge, as he had done a few days earlier.'[7]

In March 2004 charges of fraud and money laundering were dropped. Instead, Glushkov was found guilty of attempted escape from custody and abuse of authority. He was released from Lefortovo.

When Goldfarb asked him whether his stubbornness was worth three years in gaol, he said, 'Of course, I proved my innocence.'

Lugovoy was found guilty of conspiracy to organise the escape and served a prison term of fourteen months.

I remember Sasha's words: 'Lefortovo crushes you spiritually. There is some negative energy coming from those walls.' Strangely, Lugovoy marched out of prison a businessman and a millionaire and quickly obtained a license to run his own security firm of armed guards. Just as in the case of Roman Tsepov, his company, named Ninth Wave (he served in the KGB's 9th Directorate, the home of government bodyguards), became one of the prime security agencies in Moscow providing services to visiting celebrities, leading businessmen and banks. No wonder Berezovsky used Ninth Wave to guard his daughter in Russia. The tycoon also invited Lugovoy to his pompous birthday party in January 2006.

By this time the assassination operation codenamed VLADIMIR was in full swing. Known only to a handful of people, all pertinent reports of the operation were classified 'Top Secret' and flashed either to Mr Lebedev at the Yasenevo foreign intelligence headquarters or to Mr Patrushev at the Lubyanka – but they finally landed at yet a third secret service, the one that in fact supervised the whole affair.

* * *

2006 was perhaps both the most difficult and the most fruitful year for Alexander Litvinenko. In February he went to Italy where, with the help of Mario Scaramella, he recorded a sensational video testimony openly accusing Romano Prodi, who would soon be prime minister again after defeating charismatic Silvio Berlusconi in the April 2006 elections, of being 'a KGB man'. This was the last help Sasha could provide to the Mitrokhin Commission, because at the end of March its mandate expired.

Litvinenko's articles for the Chechenpress became fierce and crushing, recalling the style of Anna Politkovskaya whom he greatly respected and sympathised with. His work for the Chechen commission, preparing evidence for the International Criminal Court in the Netherlands, became more organised and systematic. He had already visited Georgia using his new British identity in an attempt to find the key witness of the 1999 Russian apartment bombings, and was now actively assisting security services and law enforcement agencies in Europe and Israel to arrest Russian gang bosses many of whom, he knew, were tightly linked to the SVR and FSB.

In June 2005 in a sweeping police operation, codenamed AVISPA, that involved 400 officers from the Costa del Sol and elsewhere in Spain, twenty-eight alleged 'Russian Mafia' members were arrested, many of them high-level *capos* (Mafia bosses), according to the Spanish police. The operation involved the national police forces of six countries. In the weekend raids, carried out mostly in the Costa del Sol, Catalonia and Alicante, police searched 41 homes or premises, froze 800 bank accounts at 42 banks and seized 42 high-end vehicles, according to the *Costa del Sol News*. The authorities said the mobsters, mostly from former Soviet Bloc republics, brought criminally acquired money from their home countries to launder it in Spain via commercial or financial entities created for the purpose. Among the many properties held by the gang were a number of luxury 'chalets', some with high-security 'safe rooms', as well as a 16,621-square-metre property in Benalmádena on which the mobsters planned to build a 38-house development called Los Eucaliptus.[8] This demonstration of unprecedented police competence and expertise in dealing with Russian serious organised crime was only the beginning, the first experience of the Spanish police that would culminate in Operation TROIKA in 2008.

Litvinenko knew and was eager to share much more information than the Spanish authorities could process quickly. He knew, for example, that in November 1996 a group of eight cofounders had signed an agreement to establish a cooperative on the shore of a picturesque lake in the most expensive and fashionable area near St Petersburg. One was a former petty spy who then headed the presidential property management department in the Kremlin. His name was Vladimir Putin. The business was being protected by Rif, a private security firm owned and headed by Vladimir Barsukov-Kumarin, known as 'Kum' in the local underworld. Kumarin was an associate of Roman Tsepov, chief of Putin's bodyguards during his time as an official at St Petersburg City Hall. Russia's police also considered Kumarin to be the founder, leader and brains behind the Tambov gang.[9] Litvinenko, who had investigated Russian organised crime for years, was aware that many members of this gang moved to Spain in the 1990s and were setting up and running businesses using KGB money.

As his relations (but not friendship) with Berezovsky gradually cooled down, Sasha was eager to start earning money independently by getting a permanent job in one of many London private companies providing a discreet service 'of comprehensive business intelligence, investigation and security risk management to its financial, legal and corporate clients around the world' as it was elegantly formulated on the website of the company of his friend Martin Flint. After evident flops with Melnichenko, Chekulin, Sultanov and Teplyuk, Sasha realised that he might be failing to meet Boris's job requirements for counter-intelligence chief. But he knew that on occasion Berezovsky retained the services of Risk

Analysis and others, so he expected to be of use by working in or with one of them. Therefore he had high expectations for his newly formed friendships with Andrei Lugovoy and Vyacheslav Zharko, whom he regarded as possible sources in Russia. He also maintained relations with Evgeny Limarev, a registered consultant in France, though he had a low opinion of Limarev's possibilities.

The previous year Sasha had met Lugovoy in London for the first time after their casual acquaintance in Moscow ten years earlier. It happened after the former ORT[10] security chief called him on an unregistered mobile number and suggested a meeting to discuss some possible business together. Sasha first hesitated but then agreed. He badly needed money because several months earlier Berezovsky had reduced his monthly allowance to £1,500.

In April Lugovoy was again in London – one of a dozen visits over the course of a year. Before he had contacted Sasha the previous autumn he had never been to Britain. Along with an interpreter they went to a meeting arranged at 1 Cavendish Place, at a company called RISC Management. It was probably Yuli Dubov, a long-time business associate and another friend of Berezovsky, who set up a meeting on Boris's behalf. He was acquainted with Keith Hunter – an appropriate name for the chief executive of such a company.

Keith's initial career in the Metropolitan Police Service involved investigating serious and organised crime on a national and international level while based at New Scotland Yard and the then Regional Crime Squad. He subsequently ventured into the private sector and successfully established a company specialising in corporate investigations for law firms, media and medium- to large-size companies. In 2001 he moved to ISC Global UK Ltd as joint CEO, rebranding it in 2005 as RISC Management.

ISC Global's founder and chairman was Stephen Curtis, a lawyer whose contacts in Russia included Boris Berezovsky and Mikhail Khodorkovsky, the CEO of the Yukos Oil Company, one of the world's largest private oil companies. Curtis died in a helicopter crash close to his palatial home in Dorset in March 2004 – a fortnight after he had gone to Scotland Yard saying that he had received death treats and feared that a hit team had been sent from Moscow to assassinate him.[11] 'If anything untoward happens to me, it will not be an accident', were his words.

RISC offered a diverse range of services, including risk management, corporate investigations, litigation support, business intelligence and physical security. Now Lugovoy said he had some first-class material to offer so they took a lift to the fifth floor and were soon escorted to a conference room. According to Alan Cowell, a British journalist and author, the meeting with RISC did not go very well.

The visitors were offering consultancy services, claiming access to first-hand, non-public information about businesses and personalities in Russia – something that is always of great interest and value to such companies as RISC. To demonstrate their capabilities, Lugovoy handed over a document that he claimed was based on information that could not have come from an open source. The RISC official accepted the document and later cross-checked the information. After some time Litvinenko was informed that the product was found satisfactory. He started cherishing hopes for quick and easy profits. Sasha even called Limarev to boast about the success. When he finally received the fee from RISC, he left 20 per cent to himself and gave the rest to Lugovoy.

But there was no reason to celebrate.

In reality, the document had been concocted by the FSB in Moscow, based on two sources: one was an open directory entitled *The System of Moscow Clubs: Elite, Lobbyists, 'Brain Centres'* by E.A. Kozlova and N.V. Melnikova, published early in the year, and another a report (No. 122) reflecting the changes of power balance in the power structures that was distributed to a very limited group of paying subscribers in March 2006. Both were produced by the organisation named Centre for Political Information (CPI) and could be accessed from the CPI Internet site polit-info.ru. (I read both.) Obviously, the FSB forgers knew their job well. The quasi-analytical report was allegedly based on the CPI's sources in the 'power structures' but in fact was nothing more than a non-official estimate of what its writer imagined was going on behind the Kremlin walls. If presented in its original form, any security company in London would reject such a paper at once, so a certain amount of plastering was applied by specialists to make it look at least acceptable.

Sasha did not know that leading security companies normally employ competent experts.

In July Litvinenko accused Putin of being a paedophile. The *Daily Mail* reported: 'Putin was walking in the Kremlin grounds when he stopped to chat some tourists, among them a 5-year-old boy. The president lifted the boy's shirt and kissed his stomach. The incident was covered by the Russian and international media at the time but Litvinenko wrote: 'The world public is shocked. Nobody can understand why the Russian president did such a strange thing as kissing the stomach of an unfamiliar small boy.' President Putin later explained why he had kissed the young boy on the stomach in the Kremlin saying he wanted to 'stroke him like a kitten'. The normally dour former KGB officer insisted that it was a spontaneous decision to approach the 5-year-old, who was in a group of tourists, to lift his shirt and kiss his stomach. 'People came up and I began talking to them, among them this little boy. He seemed to me very independent, sure of himself and at the same time defenceless so to speak, an innocent boy and a very nice little boy,' Putin said. The report ended: 'Some political analysts suggested that the kiss was a clumsy attempt to soften Mr Putin's image in the run-up to the G8 summit in St Petersburg. The Kremlin had launched a huge publicity drive, with the help of Ketchum, an American PR firm, to counter critics of its campaign to curb democracy.'[12]

One day when Marina and Tolik were on holiday at a camp with other children and their parents and Sasha was 'home alone', Lugovoy suddenly arrived in London with his wife saying that he wanted to buy some property in England. Litvinenko invited them to his house being happy to show what a real English house looked like. He felt it natural to help his friend establish himself in the British capital and started looking for an appropriate property. Evidently the Moscow planners were trying to lull any possible suspicions that Sasha, as former FSB operative, might have.

During that summer Litvinenko had been investigating possible wrongdoing by the Russian authorities in connection with the Yukos Oil Company. While the president was softening his image in the Kremlin, the company was bankrupted. Putin strongly defended his government's record in the crisis over Yukos and the arrest of its CEO. In September the company's cofounder, Leonid Nevzlin, who had fled to Israel, met with Litvinenko in the beach resort of Herzliya (named after Theodore Herzl, the father of modern Zionism). Litvinenko said he had uncovered an FSB plan to claw back millions of pounds from the former executives of Yukos who had managed to leave the country and settle in London and other Western capitals. Litvinenko had visited some of the alleged targets to warn them that the Russian intelligence and security services planned to intimidate them and their families to recover the money. Litvinenko came to Israel to warn Nevzlin and handed him the so-called 'Yukos Dossier'.[13] Later *The Times* quoted Nevzlin as saying the Litvinenko investigation 'shed light on most significant aspects of the Yukos affair'. He passed the dossier to Scotland Yard.

On 6 September Sasha met Peter B. Reddaway, professor emeritus of political science at George Washington University and former director of the Kennan Institute for Advanced Russian Studies, for a seven-hour-long interview. They discussed Litvinenko's relations with Berezovsky and his take on other oligarchs, Sasha's life and work after he stopped being a regular employee of Boris, the Teplyuk affair, and an array of other topics including Russian organised crime. In particular, Litvinenko told Reddaway that Sergey Lalakin, nicknamed Luchok, leader of the Podolsk organised crime group, had recently hired Vyacheslav Ivankov, nicknamed Yaponchik, a notorious mobster with convictions in both the former Soviet Union and the United States, to control and orchestrate organised crime groups that were closely associated with Gazprom, the giant Russian gas monopoly.

A week after their meeting, on 13 September, the deputy head of the Central Bank of Russia, Andrei Kozlov was murdered in Moscow. Men wielding pistols walked up to the banker in the parking lot of a soccer stadium and shot him in the head.

Natalia Morar wrote in *The New Times*, a liberal Moscow magazine: 'According to the MVD [the interior ministry], the examination uncovered a unitary scheme for sending abroad the money of officials close to the oil companies controlled by the Kremlin and lieutenant-general Alexander Bortnikov, deputy director and head of the Economic Security Service of the FSB. Bortnikov is known for his close relations with the deputy head of the presidential administration Igor Sechin and with Vladimir Putin's assistant Viktor Ivanov. According to the sources of *The New Times*, Bortnikov supposedly oversaw the outflow of the money of various commercial structures engaged in the sale of electronics in Russia.'[14] During the course of one working day $60 million were wire-transferred from two Russian firms to the accounts of three foreign companies: Ennerdale Investments Ltd, Ideco Engineering Ltd and Fontana Invest Inc. Ltd. These companies were registered in Cyprus and the British Virgin Islands and held accounts at the Raiffeisen Zentralbank (RZB) in Vienna. On that day the books of the Diskont Bank in Moscow, an obscure 'pocket bank' that operated discreetly and without visible customers (and whose licence Kozlov revoked shortly after) showed no turnover. The next morning, Diskont instructed RZB to transfer money from the three companies' accounts to twelve foreign banks. The whole amount believed to be laundered exceeded $1.5 billion.

Two weeks before his murder, Kozlov had been cooperating closely with the Austrian authorities on the money laundering case, a detail made public in a report posted on the website of the Austrian Ministry of Interior. It said the Austrian police could not rule out 'official corruption' in Russia as a motive for murder. I was in Vienna at the time and learned that the state attorney passed important information to his Russian colleagues but it was disregarded and no answer ever received.

Sasha could clear up the puzzle. He would explain that for almost thirty years (1975–2004) Bortnikov, a Brezhnev-era functionary, worked in the Leningrad KGB and before his transfer to Moscow in February 2004, was the chief of the St Petersburg and Leningrad district directorate of its successor organisation. Putin had been his pupil all along. On 12 May 2008 General Bortnikov was appointed director of the FSB.

While Litvinenko was helping *Novaya Gazeta* in their investigation of the poisoning of Yuri Schekochihin, its deputy editor, bad news came from Moscow announcing the murder of Anna Politkovskaya.

Anna wrote:

Why do I so dislike Putin? This is precisely why. I dislike him for matter-of-factness worth than felony, for his cynicism, for his racism, for his lies, for the gas he used in the Nord-Ost siege, for the massacre of the innocents, which went on throughout his term as President . . . His outlook is the narrow, provincial one his rank would suggest; he has the unprepossessing personality of a lieutenant colonel who never made it to colonel, the manner of a Soviet secret policeman who habitually snoops on his own colleagues. And he is vindictive.

In the Frontline Club near the Paddington Station Sasha, speaking through interpreter, addressed the gathering:

The question was asked here who killed Anna Politkovskaya. I can give an answer. It was Vladimir Putin, the President of Russia. After her book *Putin's Russia* was published in the West, Politkovskaya started to receive threats from the Kremlin. Only one person in Russia could kill a journalist of her standing, only one person could sanction her death. And this person is Putin.

As if all those insults were not enough, Sasha continued to be very close to Boris Berezovsky, Putin's 'Enemy No. 1'.

* * *

The executive phase of the Litvinenko operation started in London days after the death of Politkovskaya. As reconstructed later by the Scotland Yard investigators, it began with a puzzle.

For several weeks members of an FSB special surveillance team who arrived from Moscow under various guises followed Sasha in London. They studied, analysed and cross-checked all his movements and regular places of meeting his contacts, and recorded his telephone calls.

But they probably missed one important event: on 13 October Alexander Litvinenko and his family were granted British citizenship.

On 16 October the commercial Transaero flight from Moscow landed on schedule at London Heathrow. Two Russian passengers in economy class proceeded to the immigration hall to join the crowd waiting in the line of passport control officers. Above and to one side a mirrored wall contained a two-way mirror with a room behind it. The Metropolitan Police Detective Inspector in charge of the airport security, whom his friends called simply Matt, stood in that room looking down. I later met him during a reception at Windsor Castle.

The Russians did not cause any suspicion and soon came out through the 'Nothing to Declare Green Channel'. They were followed but noticed nothing.

In about an hour they checked into a four-star Best Western Premier Shaftesbury Hotel in Soho. Just around the corner were Piccadilly Circus where Sasha always arranged his meetings and Leicester Square where he met Ponkin. The KGB had long before marked Leicester Square as a recommended meeting place. The files hold many pictures of secret rendezvous here; a very old one showed agent NORMA (Kitty Harris) waiting for agent LYRIC (Donald Maclean) on 10 April 1938. (And the latest one probably featured Michael Mann, Johnny Depp, Alex Goldfarb, Marina Litvinenko and myself gathering at the very same place on 1 June 2009 to watch the premier of Public Enemies and discuss the Litvinenko movie.)

Though the Shaftesbury venue advertises itself as 'a boutique hotel that embodies a haven where you can be sure of warm traditional hospitality', only one room was available for the guests when they arrived there. So they left their luggage in this room and rushed to the meeting at the entrance to the Nike shop on Oxford Street.

Sasha did not expect to see Lugovoy with anybody else, but was not surprised when Lugovoy introduced his partner as Dmitry Kovtun who had recently joined Ninth Wave. According to Lugovoy, they graduated from the same military school and were friends since childhood. Kovtun had never served in the KGB but was an army officer stationed in Germany before the collapse of the USSR and disappearance of the DDR

Litvinenko was satisfied. After an introductory meeting at Erinys International, a private security company (whose motto is 'Creating a safe and secure environment rather than just security management within an unsafe and insecure environment') he invited his guests to Itsu on Piccadilly, his favourite Japanese eatery.

In the evening the two Russians were left on their own and dined at the Dar Marrakesh, a Moroccan restaurant on Rupert Street just off Shaftesbury Avenue, and then mooched around the attractions of Soho.

The following day, 17 October, Lugovoy and Kovtun checked out of the Shaftesbury Hotel and moved into the upmarket Parkes Hotel, a luxury establishment located in a tree-lined cul-de-sac a hundred yards from Harrods in London's exclusive Knightsbridge. No doubt by pure coincidence their elegant new lodgings were conveniently placed between the unmarked doors of the Special Forces Club and the Berezovsky's favourite Lanesborough Hotel.

According to Alan Cowell, Moscow's emissaries had another meeting this day with RISC Management at Cavendish Place, at which, one source asserted, Lugovoy and Litvinenko were accompanied by a third man [not Kovtun] with striking black hair, possibly Georgian, who pronounced not a word but had a laptop containing what was said to be the product of 'black bag' operations in Moscow[15] – surreptitious entries into structures to obtain information, usually into denied areas like houses and apartments of foreign diplomats or businessmen.

After the meeting they went back to the Parkes Hotel, then dined together in Chinatown. Says Lugovoy:

> On October 17 we met again with Litvinenko in the afternoon. We went to-
> gether for a meeting at another security firm. After the meeting we went back
> to the hotel where I had a meeting with an old acquaintance while Litvinenko
> waited for us downstairs. Then we went for dinner with him in Chinatown.[16]

Litvinenko felt quite at ease. Later in the evening Lugovoy and Kovtun, who had a few drinks in Chinatown, proceeded to the Hey Jo/Abracadabra lap-dancing club on fashionable Jermyn Street that some say is frequented by the 'new Russians'.

On Wednesday, 18 October, they went back to Moscow on Transaero landing at the airport of Domodedovo. They were duly met and reports collected from both at once.

As was learned weeks later, both hotels, Itsu, the Moroccan restaurant and the club were found to be contaminated with polonium-210. Hey Jo and Dar Marrakesh had lower levels while the Best Western and the Japanese eatery gave higher readings, exceeding 10 megabecquerel (MBq).[17] As for the aircraft that had carried Lugovoy and Kovtun to London, Russian authorities refused to provide it for inspection.

Litvinenko had not left any radioactive trail until later in the afternoon of 1 November. And his guests knew nothing about radiation.

How was it possible that the two men left so many traces behind them two weeks *before* they met Litvinenko again on 1 November? While discussing the puzzle with my contacts from the SO15 Metropolitan police team in December, I was able to suggest only one version. Now I think there may be more.

Lugovoy came to London again on 25 October. He checked into the Sheraton Park Lane Hotel where Litvinenko and Chekulin met Martin Flint four years before.

After a full dress rehearsal with Kovtun the week before, it appears that they decided to stage yet another final practice run. To cover his tracks, Lugovoy brought with him a hastily compiled report, part of a due diligence check that Litvinenko had been commissioned to prepare which he had split between Lugovoy, Shvets and himself. The larger portion was given to Shvets, a former Russian intelligence officer living in Washington, who was involved in the Tapegate operation. According to Shvets, the work was for a risk analysis company and included a due diligence report on five Russian figures.

Litvinenko had called him in September and Shvets provided an eight-page document that he emailed to Sasha on 20 September. 'Within the next two weeks Litvinenko gave the report to Lugovoy,' Shvets told Tom Mangold, a British journalist, in a programme for BBC Radio 4. Two Scotland Yard detectives had been promptly despatched to the United States to interview Shvets.

During this customarily brief visit, Lugovoy is reported to have had a meeting at Erinys International. Lugovoy claimed that he also visited Boris Berezovsky, near whose office the Sheraton Park Lane Hotel was conveniently located. He said Boris called him to discuss security measures to protect Elena Tregubova, a former *Kommersant* correspondent accredited in the Kremlin. She showed a certain disdain towards ambitious and politicking Kremlin staffers, labelling them 'mutants' in her best-selling tell-all, *Tales of a Kremlin Digger*, published in October 2003.[18] Though this visit must have taken place before Lugovoy's departure on 28 October, Berezovsky was later strangely adamant, in interviews and in meetings with investigators, that the meeting had taken place on 31 October.

Berezovsky said they drank a bottle of wine *à deux* and that the chairs Lugovoy sat in, both in his private office and in the reception area, contained 'an awful lot' of polonium traces. 'I trusted Lugovoy completely,' Berezovsky stressed. 'And of course the fact that he had been jailed [for an alleged attempt to free Nikolai Glushkov] enhanced my trust, my level of trust to him.'

For two days, 26 and 27 October, Lugovoy had met Litvinenko in the evening in the Sheraton bar, the same place where Sasha had discussed ways of helping the

English banker, Shaw, with Martin Flint of Risk Analysis. Pattern, always establish a pattern.

On Thursday, 28 October, Lugovoy left for Moscow. Later British Airways discovered traces of radiation on its aircraft making flights BA875 Moscow – Heathrow and BA872 Heathrow–Moscow on the same dates as Lugovoy arrived and departed.

Precisely four weeks later the HPA statement for the day noted that 'the key public areas of the Sheraton Park Lane Hotel' had been monitored for radiation. For months later, two rooms on the eighth floor were sealed and a makeshift barrier confronted reporters trying to approach them. Two rooms? Lugovoy was supposed to be travelling alone that time.

In the course of the frenzied preparations, Kovtun flew to Hamburg on 28 October. A good planner must foresee everything and the possibility that his visit was a false trace to mislead the investigation should not be dismissed. Kovtun could have been advised just to visit his former family in Germany with whom he maintained good relations and who were the only people close to him.

His ex-mother-in-law picked him up at the airport and drove him to the Altona district where his former wife shared an apartment with her boyfriend and their children. Kovtun went shopping and spent the night on a sofa.

While Kovtun entertained his former family in Germany, on Monday, 30 October, Scaramella received the first message 'to be continued tonight' from 'Eugenio Lomov'. The subject was MARIO SCARAMELLA (MS) / PAOLO GUZZANTI (PG) – SECURITY-2. It read (quoted verbatim):

1. Names of MS and PG are often mentioned in confidential talks of intelligence officers of Russia who work in SVR, Kremlin, Shebarshin's RNSES[19] and (starting from August 2006) 'SVR veterans association DIGNITY AND HONOR' (Moscow, headed by acting SVR colonel Velichko Valentin).

  1.1. All SVR officers are sure that PG and MS still closely collaborate with 'enemy No. 1 of Russia' – Boris Berezovskiy and his 'companions-in-arms' – first of all A. Litvinenko and V. Bukovsky.

  1.1.1. They suspect that recent rumours initiated by Litvinenko about his receiving of the UK citizenship are false, are designed to mislead Russia's endeavours to obtain his/Berezovskiy extradition to Russia and are (at least partially) inspired by PG/MS, who, in their turn, try to obtain citizenship of Italy for Litvinenko for his 'outstanding services for the 'Mitrokhin commission' investigations', which are in considered in Moscow as purely provocative towards Russia.

  1.2. A.m. [above-mentioned] intelligence officers also think that MS and PG in fact formed 'stable criminal group which serve interests of the most conservative/rightist wings of special services of Italy, USA and UK', falsify investigations and reports on KGB/Russia international affairs and seek to profit from it by any possible mean (including financing from SISMI,[20] FBI and CIA).

1.2.1. In the frames of this general understanding they take all activities of and latest developments connected with MS and PG.

1.2.2. They think that the case of arms traffickers – Ukrainians (now under court hearings in Teramo, Napoli region) and presumable attempt to assassinate PG in November 2005) were trumped up by PG and supported by false evidence of A. Litvinenko, set up by Ukrainian 'unscrupulous' friends of MS from secret services. They say this case is under investigation now in Kiev in SBU and very likely 'plot will be revealed with help of Russia's colleagues'.

1.2.3. Anyhow, possibility that Russian intelligence side could be involved in this attempt seems to be invalid (there is no single indication of it).

2. Meanwhile above mentioned Russian intelligence officers speak more and more about necessity to use force against PG and MS, considering their 'incessant anti-Russian activities' – as well as against Berezovskiy and Litvinenko.

2.1. The most troubling and dangerous development is Velichko's involvement into planning of actions against PG and MS.

(Velichko and his fund are well known in the security community in Russia and Europe, mostly because it was him who 'liberated' MsF's[21] representative in Dagestan Arian Erkel in April 2004, in cooperation with SVR/FSB, for the cash ransom of USD 1 mln, paid by the Netherlands' government, which is still under legal proceedings against MsF (Geneva) on this case. Besides, Velichko's agents are presumably involved in the assassination of Anna Politkovskaya in October 2006 as well as in elaboration of other similar assassination plans in Russia and Baltic states – by order and on behalf of FSB/SVR . . .)

2.1.1. Yesterday an agent who works with Velichko's deputy and closest collaborate Ubilava Anatoliy (intelligence officer) said that Ubilava mentioned that he has an agent who stays in Napoli for over 1 month already, follows up displacements of MS and PG (who visit the Teramo court hearings), has local network of KGB agents as his disposal and prepares 'final act' (could be serious provocation or even assassination attempt – Ubilava at least once mentioned that it's 'decided by our superiors', meaning chiefs of SVR (or FSB)).'[22]

Mario was frightened. He was going to London to attend the next session of the International Maritime Organization (IMO) as he had done for years before and decided to take this alarming two-page message with him to show to his friend Litvinenko. Scaramella knew the warning came from Evgeny Limarev.

When he arrived in London, an even graver message was awaiting him in his mailbox, though he would only see it later.

While Scaramella was driving to the Naples Capodichino International Airport to catch his EasyJet flight to London (as the logbook would soon record 'NAP to STN') on 31 October, Lugovoy arrived at Heathrow accompanied by his wife, two daughters, his 8-year-old son and good old friend and Ninth Wave employee Vycheslav Sokolenko. This time there were many Russians on board, mainly soccer fans coming to 'Londongrad' to watch Moscow TsSK play Arsenal at the newly opened Emirates Stadium. Perfectly mingled with the shuffling column moving through the Green Channel were several FSB watchers who had little interest in sports but were fully concentrated on the 'rabbit' in front of them.

Lugovoy with his wife and children and Sokolenko in tow went directly to the four-star Millennium Hotel near the US Embassy where they took three rooms: one on the first and one on the fourth floor for the Lugovoy family, and one on the third for Sokolenko. The booking for Lugovoy specifically asked for room 441. There was a little confusion at the reception as only a double room was initially allocated for the whole family but that was quickly sorted out.

Kovtun spent his last night in Hamburg drinking and talking with his former family until early hours. At about 05:00 a.m. of 1 November his ex-mother-in-law took him to the airport to be in time for a Germaniawings flight to London.

His presence in the old Hansa town on the River Elbe would have passed unnoticed if one December morning a postman had not put a thick copy of *Der Spiegel* in the post box of the Hamburg police headquarters. The article 'Todesurteil aus Moskau' on page 124 immediately attracted attention. It occupied half of the magazine and mentioned Kovtun by name saying that he came from Hamburg.

Officers who read the article reported to the chiefs and soon a special radiation unit from the German Federal police supported by specialists from the Federal Office of Radiation Protection arrived at the site.

The officer who took over the case was Thomas Menzel, the head of the organised crime branch.

Menzel was tall and slender, a thirty-year veteran of the police force who wore his greying hair swept back and who worked out of an office at the Polizeipräsidium in a pleasant suburb of Hamburg.

He codenamed the Kovtun operation THIRD MAN after the Orson Welles movie, and used the signature tune – the 'Harry Lime Theme' – as a ring tone on his cell phone.[23]

The German police began by searching the apartments where Kovtun had stayed, and followed the trail from there. They did not have to wait long for results: a pale lilac glow of polonium-210 lit up across Hamburg. Suddenly an operation that began with an idle glance at *Der Spiegel* became a major police inquiry. Some 600 officers were drafted on to the case, scouring stores and restaurants. White-suited inspectors with radiation detection equipment appeared outside suburban homes. The apartment building where Kovtun spent the night on his ex-wife's sofa was evacuated and her children hospitalised to be tested for radiation. Detectives tracked Kovtun's movements from the moment he touched down to the moment he left. Polonium traces seemed to be everywhere.[24]

On 1 November Mario Scaramella woke up in the Thistle Victoria Hotel on Buckingham Palace Road at 7:30 a.m. London time. He had a modest breakfast of some melon juice and a bun that he bought a night before at Marks & Spencers at the station. At about nine he called Litvinenko from the hotel. Marina responded and handed over the receiver to Sasha.

Mario suggested a meeting before noon but Sasha explained that he was having a meeting shortly after twelve so they agreed to meet at three at the usual place, Piccadilly Circus, under the statue of Eros.

Scaramella was at the Victoria tube station at 9:25 and had to wait five minutes before buying a day travel card. He then went to his conference at the offices at 22 Berners Street. He was here for the first time as usually the IMO conferences were held in a different building.

Mario was at the conference about ten o'clock. At one a lunch break was announced and he went to a nearby 'all you can eat' joint and had a snack. He was much troubled by the email that he received the day before from Limarev and expected more. So he decided to look for an internet café, a difficult task in those narrow streets of Soho if you don't know them well. He finally found one at Dansey Place in Chinatown, a shabby access road south of Shaftesbury Avenue, where few would care to linger. But there was a computer and he found his message and printed it out.

It was from Limarev again. I have a copy (see Document 4). The Russian was brazenly frightening poor Mario, telling him stories about the stern Spetsnaz instructor Vlasov and a gang of professional killers from St Petersburg, all of whom had already arrived in Naples. Add this to the atmosphere of one of London's back alleys where the young Italian was reading all that, and one can imagine how quickly he left the place and rushed towards sun-lit and noisy Piccadilly.

Arriving there a little early, Mario decided to go charge his mobile phone. He managed to do so in the Pizza Hut at the corner of Regent Street and Piccadilly where he also feasted on a chocolate cake and a Pepsi. Then he looked at his watch that still showed European time, an hour later, and decided it was time to move to the meeting point.

At about eleven Marina was ready to leave. It was agreed that she had a lot to do that day and they were going to celebrate in the evening, so would Sasha take a bus to the centre? He said 'no problem' like a real English gentleman, wished her a good day and Marina left. Litvinenko stayed at home a little longer and then dashed off to town without breakfast. He never took his breakfast alone.

In six years he had come to know London public transport well and caught a bus to Charing Cross. Shortly after noon he was strolling towards the American Embassy.

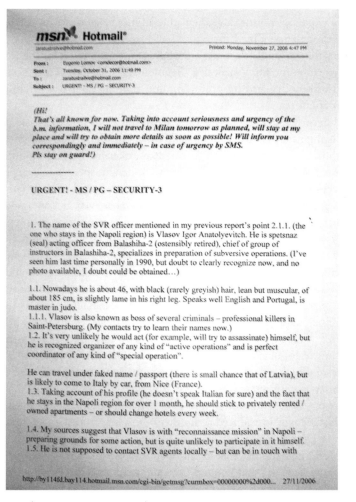

msn Hotmail®

jarabustralive@hotmail.com   Printed: Monday, November 27, 2006 4:47 PM

From :   Eugenio Lomov <corndecor@hotmail.com>
Sent :   Tuesday, October 31, 2006 11:49 PM
To :   jarabustralive@hotmail.com
Subject :   URGENT! – MS / PG – SECURITY-3

(Hi!
That's all known for now. Taking into account seriousness and urgency of the
a.m. information, I will not travel to Milan tomorrow as planned, will stay at my
place and will try to obtain more details as soon as possible! Will inform you
correspondingly and immediately – in case of urgency by SMS.
Pls stay on guard!)

URGENT! - MS / PG – SECURITY-3

1. The name of the SVR officer mentioned in my previous report's point 2.1.1. (the
one who stays in the Napoli region) is Vlasov Igor Anatolyevitch. He is spetsnaz
(seal) acting officer from Balashiha-2 (ostensibly retired), chief of group of
instructors in Balashiha-2, specializes in preparation of subversive operations. (I've
seen him last time personally in 1990, but doubt to clearly recognize now, and no
photo available, I doubt could be obtained...)

1.1. Nowadays he is about 46, with black (rarely greyish) hair, lean but muscular, of
about 185 cm, is slightly lame in his right leg. Speaks well English and Portugal, is
master in judo.
1.1.1. Vlasov is also known as boss of several criminals – professional killers in
Saint-Petersburg. (My contacts try to learn their names now.)
1.2. It's very unlikely he would act (for example, will try to assassinate) himself, but
he is recognized organizer of any kind of "active operations" and is perfect
coordinator of any kind of "special operation".

He can travel under faked name / passport (there is small chance that of Latvia), but
is likely to come to Italy by car, from Nice (France).
1.3. Taking account of his profile (he doesn't speak Italian for sure) and the fact that
he stays in the Napoli region for over 1 month, he should stick to privately rented /
owned apartments – or should change hotels every week.

1.4. My sources suggest that Vlasov is with "reconnaissance mission" in Napoli –
preparing grounds for some action, but is quite unlikely to participate in it himself.
1.5. He is not supposed to contact SVR agents locally – but can be in touch with

http://by114fd.bay114.hotmail.msn.com/cgi-bin/getmsg?curmbox=00000000%2d000... 27/11/2006

Document 4

Dmitry Kovtun arrived at the Millennium Hotel on Grosvenor Square about
nine o'clock but did not check in, as he had no reservation. Instead he went to
Sokolenko's room. He knew him well from their years in the military school. Like
Lugovoy, Sokolenko had been invited and accepted to serve in the KGB's 9th
Directorate (government bodyguards) and later transferred to the newly
established Federal Protection Service (FSO).

After the sleepless night, a lot of booze and an early flight, Kovtun immediately
went to bed and slept until late afternoon.

The taxi that had brought him from the airport was later found to be
contaminated with polonium-210.

Lugovoy woke up as usual and they all took lifts to go down to the breakfast room where Sokolenko joined them.

The plans for the family were to go shopping and sightseeing for the whole day and Slava, a pet name for Vyacheslav (Sokolenko), was prepared to accompany them. He was a bodyguard by profession and training so it was a familiar job. They left at about ten.

Andrei Lugovoy remained in the hotel 'to do some business'.

An undistinguished man dressed like all others in the service staff entered the Millennium from the back door on Adam's Row, casually flashing his hotel ID at the uniformed girl. He knew the building well, having spent a few nights there recently as an American tourist using a forged passport. Somebody, obviously from the same department, had been there even before he arrived in London, and had provided him with a detailed plan that he had memorised during his preparation. The man quietly went up the stairs to the fourth floor emerging from the personnel entrance five yards away from the door to room 441. Exactly as agreed, at 10:30 a.m. a blond man inside the room made a few steps and unlocked the door. The visitor crept in. The CCTV camera on the other side of the corridor close to the guest lifts caught an image of him but only in a blur – too dark and too far away. Bingo! Nobody in the hotel turned a hair. In fact, nobody saw him at all.

Both SAS sergeants on attachment to SO15 and two plainclothes Met detectives in the room nodded and made notes. Should have been exactly like that. A trained illegal. A car to Calais. A sandwich in the shuttle while crossing the Tunnel. Thirty-five minutes to Folkstone. Roger.

Litvinenko was very interested and paid little attention to a new face in the room, whom Lugovoy introduced as another businessman with good connections. The man did not say much. Lugovoy was doing most of the talking, explaining incredible new opportunities that might open up for Sasha and his new friends. It was about liquidised gas and copper. Direct exports to Latin America, fantastic prices. We shall deliver by sea via Latvia, minimal taxes. Do you have anybody there?

Sasha had. He immediately called the mobile phone of David Kudykov, who lived in London but originally came from Latvia. Moreover, David was a partner in a private shipping company.

As usual, David answered his friend's call at once. He was abroad taking care of one of their cargo vessels in the Netherlands and was now on the way to Berlin. He listened to Sasha attentively and then asked several questions. As he later told the police, he didn't like what he heard.

The people in that room were clearly ill prepared for discussing the details of the deal. They didn't know elementary terms, could not specify the conditions, were confused about prices, and could not tell CIF from FOB.

David told Litvinenko that the deal looked unrealistic and advised against it.

But Sasha was overexcited. Millions, man, bloody damn millions! He'll be rich and won't have to bother about stupid and complicated analytical reports for which he was not qualified. Money, money, money! Now he will travel and take Marusya and Tolik around the world.

He stayed for a while longer, then looked at his watch and said he had to go to meet his Italian friend but could see them again at about an hour.

'Give me a call,' said Lugovoy. 'We may be at a conference, but surely there will still be time.'

Litvinenko shook hands, picked up his khaki bag with a long shoulder belt of the kind usually used to carry laptop computers and, smiling, left the room, turning right to reach the lifts.

The man's instructions were brief. Lugovoy must leave the room at once. He'll do the cleaning. They will not see each other again. Bye.

Lugovoy went one floor down to collect Kovtun who had woken up and was waiting as instructed. They proceeded to the familiar address just a short walking distance away at 58 Grosvenor Street.

In the meantime, the undistinguished man in room 441 quickly but very carefully collected an empty cup of tea wearing special gloves and a mask, which he brought with him, and put it all in a small container that was standing near the dustbin. He did his best not to leave a drop but that was hardly possible. 'The assassins . . . dropped the polonium on the floor of a London hotel room,' a senior government source told the *Daily Telegraph* on 1 December. Looking back and checking whether everything was in order, the man quietly closed the door and vacated the premises. By 5:15 p.m. he would be in Harwich ready to board a ferry to Esbjerg, Denmark. An officer from the illegal support unit would take care of his cargo.

According to the *Daily Telegraph*, a senior government source who was aware of the discussions of the Cabinet's emergency committee, Cobra, said: 'Clear traces of the radiation were found on the floor in a room, thought to be in the Millennium hotel in central London, as well as on a light switch in the same room. The traces were so strong that they indicated the actual source of the radiation was present, not a secondary source such as excretions from Mr Litvinenko's contaminated body.'[25]

The room was sealed and guarded by the police for almost half a year.

Sasha was only a few minutes late and as usual arrived unnoticed. They greeted each other in a friendly way and Mario kissed Sasha twice in the Italian fashion saying 'in Italy we give two'. Litvinenko was very relaxed and looked casual. He was wearing blue jeans and a jeans jacket, a khaki T-shirt matching his bag, and was hungry. Sasha said in English: 'Mario, there is a good restaurant; they have very good fish at a very low price.'

So they walked down Piccadilly talking. Litvinenko said that he was interested in starting to deal in natural resources. He explained that in Russia the secret services had complete power over companies that were exporting oil, gas, metals and other commodities and the companies would do what they were told. 'I have a friend in the secret services,' Sasha said, 'who knows a president of one such company and for whom goods will be offered at very special prices.' He told Mario that he was about to make a deal for shipping a cargo of copper. 'Millions, Mario, millions!'

When they finally settled at table on the lower ground floor of the Itsu, it was Mario's turn. He showed Litvinenko the second message from Limarev that the Russian was not able to understand properly as it was in English. Nevertheless, he dismissed all threats as 'bullshit' and told Mario that he would check with his Moscow sources. In about twenty minutes they parted. Litvinenko never saw his Italian friend again.

In the meantime, Sasha hurried to the offices of Berezovsky at Down Street just off Piccadilly. He wanted to show the papers to Boris.

Meanwhile the Russians, having made an appointment from Moscow, were being received in the offices of ECO3 Capital, an independent financial advisory firm acting on behalf of companies for which they did consultancy work.[26]

For Lugovoy and Kovtun the alleged purpose of the meeting was to solicit a new commission. For its part, ECO3's client wanted them to produce the report they had already promised but failed to deliver. During that meeting, Lugovoy's mobile phone jangled as Litvinenko called him suggesting that they all meet up.[27]

'We will be at the Millennium in half an hour,' said Lugovoy. 'Let's meet at one of the bars. Call us when you come.'

Sasha had not managed to see Berezovsky who was busy preparing for a trip abroad, but left copies of the Limarev's messages for him by the secretary. 'Gosh, this is important', he thought, 'Boris should see it.'

At about 4:30 p.m. he was at the hotel calling Lugovoy's number as he moved.

They were already celebrating at a table at the centre of a rather small hotel bar. Kovtun started to feel much better, had six gin and tonics and was now smoking a cigar. Lugovoy also had a few and was quite relaxed. He met Litvinenko at the lobby and they turned to the Pine Bar on the left side. Sasha was generously offered a drink though they knew perfectly well he was a teetotaller and pointed to the cup of green tea that was already cold. Sasha drank a little and asked for a fresh pot. While the elderly headwaiter, Norberto, was preparing it, Lugovoy went upstairs to check his room and found it in perfect order. He would later be exasperated by the fact that his clothes and personal items as well as those of his wife and children appeared to be contaminated with polonium-210.

There was actually nothing to discuss, so after a few minutes of jokes and idle talk Sasha left for the Gents and was soon prepared to leave. At that moment, through the open bar door, he saw Sokolenko and Lugovoy's children entering the lobby. It was five o'clock, the time set for them to return. A good English tradition.

Sasha greeted Sokolenko, whom he saw for the first time but who reminded him of the man he had met earlier that day in the Lugovoy's room, and left.

Everyone started getting ready for the soccer match they had come to see.

The bar was later found to be one of the most contaminated places in London, except, perhaps, the gentlemen's washing room visited by Litvinenko. The Government Decontamination Service took nineteen days in March 2007 to clean it up. The operation ranged from a somewhat domestic wipe-down to the destruction of hotel bathrooms with hammers.

Sasha went straight from the hotel back to Berezovsky's office. This time he managed to meet him and quickly explained that Mario brought a paper that possibly identified the murderers of Politkovskaya.

'Who's the source of this paper?' asked Boris.

'Limarev.'

'Give it to my assistant.'

But Sasha insisted, so Berezovsky agreed to take the four pages with him and read them on the plane if he had time.

From the office Litvinenko called Akhmed Zakayev to ask whether he was in the centre and could perhaps give him a lift home. Zakayev indeed appeared to be on Shaftesbury Avenue where he was having a meeting with a PR agency that was retained by the Chechnya Peace Forum in London. They agreed to meet, Akhmed picked Sasha up and they drove north to Muswell Hill where they were close neighbours.

By 7:30 p.m. Litvinenko was at home checking emails in his computer and preparing for a festive dinner – his favourite, Russian 'chicken-on-a-bottle'. There had been exactly six years since he, Marina and Tolik stepped on British soil once and for all.

At about 11:00 p.m. Sasha Litvinenko began to die.

Nikolai Khokhlov, the illegal,
Germany, 1954–57

Never speak to strangers.

On the evening of the eighteenth day of the winter month of Heshvan a man rang at the door of an apartment on Inheidener Strasse in Frankfurt am Main occupied by Georgy Sergeyevich Okolovich, one of the leaders of the anti-Soviet émigré organisation NTS (People's Labour Union). The business at hand was murder. But things took a very different turn when Okolovich opened the door. The caller came straight out with it on the threshold: 'I'm a captain in the Ministry of State Security (MGB) and I have been sent from Moscow to organise your assassination. I don't want to carry the order out and I need your help.'[1]

Until the ring of a telephone in my Vienna apartment a half-century later, all I knew about that encounter at the door was what anyone could read in the many books and articles that have reported it. But on Monday, 22 September 2003, my caller – the same who had called at Georgy Okolovich's apartment a half-century earlier – identified himself as Nikolai Yevgenyevich Khokhlov, a retired professor of California State University and a former KGB captain in Pavel Sudoplatov's special task force. Khokhlov's voice sounded firm and there was no trace of age in spite of his venerable 81 years. He still remembered many details related to events as far back as 1943 as if it was yesterday, and he spoke clearly and consistently about what happened to him after he was sent on a special mission to Germany in February 1954. And during our many long conversations that followed, it became clear that Khokhlov had not changed much over those many decades.

Born on 7 June 1922 in the town of Nizhny Novgorod, Nikolai Khokhlov became a professional variety performer after moving to the capital. Leonid Finkelstein, formerly of the BBC Russian Service, still recalled the famous duet of whistlers, Khokhlov and Shur, when we discussed the story in 2007. As a young actor, Khokhlov was recruited by the Third Department of the Secret Political Directorate to inform on the Moscow intelligentsia. In the spring of 1941 he became a fully-fledged agent, signing his reports with the pseudonym WHISTLER.

In September, his wartime handler Mikhail Maklyarsky, the section chief and one of Sudoplatov's men, laid before Nikolai his first operational assignment.

From now on his whistling act was to be used as cover for an underground stay-behind role, which would begin for him when and if the Germans took Moscow.

A surprise came when Sudoplatov appeared in the safe house, where the Khokhlov group of two men and two women was quartered, to announce that he had personally selected Nikolai, who was good-looking and blond, for training as an illegal. The service had managed to find among the war prisoners a young German officer looking very much like Nikolai. The task was to go and join that German in the prisoner-of-war camp where he was kept, get in contact, study his life and habits, and then – with that officer's papers – 'secretly' flee to Turkey and from there to Germany, where he would meet his Moscow contact in the Berlin Zoo. An almost impossible mission for those who know.

Fortunately for him, soon after his arrival in Georgia, where the camp was, Khokhlov came down with typhus and this crazy plan was not carried out.

Due to his blond looks, he was anyway destined for future operations in German-speaking countries. Khokhlov started to study German under the supervision of a professional instructor from the department and was sent to several PoW camps to mix with German prisoners. His acting experience proved as useful as his musical talent and his good ear for language and by April 1943 Khokhlov could quite successfully communicate in German. (Sixty years later I tested him; his German sounded perfect.)

Based on an agreement signed in Moscow in September 1941, the British wartime sabotage and subversion organisation, SOE, had pledged to train Russian secret agents in Britain and arrange their dispatch to targets in Western Europe. At least twenty-five such agents were successfully dropped by the RAF between 1942 and late August 1944.[2] Men destined for resistance, sabotage or intelligence-gathering operations consisted mainly of German and Austrian anti-fascists. About thirty Austrians resident in the USSR were trained as parachutists and sent by different Soviet services to target areas in Germany, Austria and the occupied territories. In the summer of 1942, Sudoplatov's department was also given the order to prepare four agents to be dropped in German uniforms. Among the candidates three were native German speakers and the fourth was Nikolai. He decided to share a flat with one of the Germans to have more language practice. The name of his flatmate was Karl Kleinjung.

Nine years earlier, just after the Reichstag fire that signalled Hitler's imminent attack on German communists, Kleinjung like many other party members fled the country. Soon he would start a career as a Soviet illegal in Holland and Belgium and then in November 1936 was among the first volunteers to arrive in Spain to fight on the side of the Republicans. Here he took some training in one of the NKVD special sabotage schools set up on the Republican territory. Among his instructors were Soviet specialists in terror and assassination like Naum Eitingon ('Colonel Kotov') and his assistant during Barcelona's 'May Days' of 1937, a Latin American named José Ocampo, advisor and friend of the future

Spanish communist party chief Santiago Carrillo, as well as the later renowned murderer Stanislav Vaupshasov ('Comrade Alfred' *aka* Soviet 'diplomat' 'Stanislav Alexeyevich Dubovsky.'[3]

Prepared for the job by this extraordinary training, Karl became personal bodyguard for Eitingon who, after the desertion of his chief, Alexander Orlov, was put in charge of all NKVD operations in Spain.

In 1939, as the Republican cause failed, all these Soviet specialists, Kleinjung with them, retreated to Moscow.

When Hitler's troops crossed the Soviet border on 22 June 1941, Karl was summoned from Nizhny Novgorod, where he had been working at an automobile plant, to continue his illegal training. By then he was 29 and well fitted for the special tasks that his Soviet bosses had in mind. His case officer was again Eitingon, who had become first deputy of Sudoplatov.

In February 1943 Karl was assigned a mission that he later described as 'the most complicated, difficult and dangerous' in his whole wartime career: he was to be sent to Minsk to assassinate Gauleiter Kube. The future General Kleinjung often talked about this episode but never mentioned that an accomplice named Nikolai assisted him. He only said that on 23 September the partisans were able to radio to Moscow about the success of the operation.[4]

On 2 September 1944 Kleinjung was the only German to be invited to the Moscow Kremlin to be awarded a high Soviet decoration for the assassination of Kube. The Chairman of the Presidium of the Supreme Soviet of the USSR personally presented him with an enamelled gilded star and shook his hand. Many years later he was awarded the Order of the Red Banner for his achievements in Soviet Security, in addition to five of the highest decorations of the DDR.

If Khokhlov played any role at all in this wartime operation, it was a minor one.

Early in 1945 Maklyarsky summoned his secret agent to his office and gave him a new assignment: Romania. With a forged Polish passport in the name of 'Stanislaw Lewandowski', born in Lwów (now Lviv), Khokhlov was to go to Bucharest to live and get accustomed to life abroad. That was a standard path for every Soviet illegal.

Khokhlov was given enough cash to open a private radio shop at 11 B-dul Decebal, main street in the centre of the city, as a respectable front. Soviet intelligence has always had an understandable preference for 'white goods' as they are known in the trade. The then illegal Lev Nikolsky used the cover of an American refrigerator retailer in London; Rudolf Hermann, a Soviet illegal in the USA, used to sell cameras.

Khokhlov bought a car and established himself comfortably in 'bourgeois-capitalist' society. In 1946 he married Emilia, whom he remembered in his memoirs as 'Valeria', a 22-year-old girl from the household in which he had lived for a year.

In 1949 Nikolai had his first breakdown. He panicked and wrote several letters to the headquarters asking to recall him to the USSR as soon as possible.

Illegals abroad are commonly victims of nervous failures. Under the tension of their lives abroad they may commit irrational acts. So when his controller met him on his return to Moscow in October, he greeted him with a friendly, understanding smile. Nikolai was given back his internal Soviet passport, cash for initial expenses and time to readjust to Soviet life. He was also provided with arrangements to meet his chiefs.[5]

According to Brook-Shepherd:

> Khokhlov wound up his private affairs in brutal fashion. He admitted to the long-suffering Emilia that he had been unfaithful to her on several occasions, that he was trying to get to the West and did not propose to take her with him, and that he therefore suggested a divorce. A fortnight later, he was gone for good. The woman who was still his wife (there was indeed to be no record that the divorce ever took place) was left with the apartment and a pay-off of 100,000 lei from the NKVD's Romanian cash-box.[6]

Back in Moscow, Nikolai, who could never last long without the solace of a woman's arms, and who had an affair with a singer named Taissiya Ignatyeva throughout the war years, was probably unable to rekindle the flame, and in an impulse called at the apartment of Yanina Timashkevich, who had sat next to him for seven years at school. His schoolmate, now 27 and an orphan, happened to be at home and opened the door. That was in November 1949. By Christmas he had moved in with her.[7]

The main legacy of the cumbersome and short-lived intelligence structure in Moscow from the late 1940s to the early 1950s that was called the Committee of Information (KI) was a renewed emphasis on illegals. They were seen as establishing a more secure and better-concealed basis for foreign intelligence operations. In 1949 forty-nine illegals were in training. The chief of the 4th (illegals) Directorate of the KI set up departments specialising in the selection and training of candidates and the fabrication of documentation to support their legends. By 1952 the documentation department had forged or doctored 364 foreign identity documents, including seventy-eight passports.[8] Moscow sent illegal support (Line N) officers to all major outpost stations operating under the cover of Soviet embassies.

But Sudoplatov's service had its own mission for its illegals. Those were either 'sleeping' or active saboteurs, assassins and demolition men.

By the time the Allies had settled into post-war Austria, drinking coffee in the Vienna cafés and giving American cigarettes to their local girlfriends, the multiple Russian espionage agencies were busy filling the Austrian police and security service with their agents. Hundreds of them recruited from the former

International Brigades in Spain arrived from Russia in 1945–6 and many took posts in the Staatspolizei (Federal Police) or Austria's premier civilian intelligence agency, the *Generaldirektion für die Öffentliche Sicherheit* (General Directorate for Public Safety). The Interior Ministry itself was placed under Franz Horner, a leading Communist official who had fought in Spain, lived in Moscow during the war, and been parachuted into Yugoslavia by the GRU to help to organise an 'Austrian Liberation Army'.

One Anton Dobritzhofer, the chief of the police in Vienna's proletarian district of Floridsdorf, was instrumental in providing documentation for Soviet illegals. Dobritzhofer was a Schutzbund commander in Floridsdorf and after the defeat in 1934 of the Socialist revolt immigrated to the Soviet Union. In 1936 he, like Kleinjung and many others, was sent to Spain and returned to Moscow in 1939. Like almost every other former soldier of the international brigades who had retreated to the Soviet Union, he was recruited by the NKVD under the codename DUB ('Oak'). Together with Kleinjung, Dobritzhofer took part in a major Soviet military deception operation called BEREZINA at the end of the war. Then he surfaced in Vienna and after a brief spell as the district police chief he rose in the ranks to end his career in the Vienna City Police Directorate.

In September 1950 Khokhlov was commissioned as an active duty officer of the Ministry for State Security (MGB). As he continued to be an illegal, he was allowed and even encouraged to live under cover as a student of Moscow University. Sudoplatov claimed in his memoirs that he even helped Nikolai to be admitted as a full time student without bothering to take any entrance exams.

In February 1951 Khokhlov was invited to a Moscow safe house where he met the deputy chief of the Austrian desk – the same female operative who had taught him German in 1943 – and given a new assignment. The deputy chief of the Operational Group Austria (OGA) in Baden near Vienna, who was also present at the meeting, placed on the table four cards with Austrian names for Nikolai to choose as his future alias. Quite at random he selected that of 'Josef Hofbauer'.

Until I told him years later, Khokhlov had not realised how ill chosen was his cover. For another Josef Hofbauer, born in 1908 in Edelsberg, was a Gestapo officer in Upper Austria who had been accused of extreme brutality and sadism. His targets and victims were citizens of his own province, especially in Linz and Freistadt. His personal file in the Austrian archives contains fourteen thick folders. While Khokhlov was preparing for his first practice run under that name, the court in the American occupation zone in Salzburg was sentencing the other Hofbauer and his gang to various terms of imprisonment. By the time Khokhlov received his new Austrian passport with his own photo on the left side and the name 'Josef Hofbauer' on the opposite page, the former Nazi murderer was on probation.

Khokhlov was lucky that he was brought to Austria by a military aircraft that landed in Bad Voslau, near his department's operational base, because such Soviet facilities were well guarded and no Austrian passport or customs officer was admitted. He was chauffeured to Wiener Neustadt and quartered in a safe house. In July he was cleared to proceed further.

This 1951 test run turned out to be harmless. From April until August 'Josef Hofbauer' travelled around Switzerland, France, Denmark, Belgium and Holland, collecting visas and border stamps and opening bank accounts. He became over-confident, though, and apparently forgot that he was on a serious mission of establishing cover as an innocent traveller. Nikolai bought a high-quality accordion and tried to smuggle it into Austria – a risky operation even today. The customs seized both the instrument and his bags and fined him heavily.

By early next year more serious work loomed – for a moment. Deadly secret at the time, it hit the public press a half century later. In May 2004, the Russian weekly *Ogonyok* published a photo of Alexander Fyodorovich Kerensky, the moderate Socialist revolutionary who had served as head of the Russian provisional government from July to October 1917. It was accompanied by the text, 'Khokhlov helped him and managed to save his life'. At a very late date Khokhlov seems to have given himself some credit he did not really deserve.

It began in early 1952 when Georgy Malenkov, a Secretary of the CPSU Central Committee who would briefly become leader of the Soviet Union after Stalin's death, informed Sudoplatov that the party had a special task for him. The leadership was concerned about the imminent rise of Kerensky to head the Anti-Bolshevik Bloc of Nations, and had decided the old foe must be 'liquidated'.

In March Khokhlov was summoned to Sudoplatov's office and informed that he was to go to Paris where a veteran agent, Prince Gagarin, would lead him to the target. Khokhlov, according to his own words, was then to murder his victim with a Parker fountain pen adapted as a small pistol. Gagarin was then also to be eliminated, Khokhlov wrote in his memoirs, because he knew too much and had outlived his usefulness.

However, about ten days after Sudoplatov received this order, he read a TASS report about fractional infighting in the organisation that had effectively blocked Kerensky's election, and therefore he no longer presented any danger to the Soviet state. The next morning the operation was called off.

Instead of Paris, Khokhlov was sent to Karlshorst in East Berlin, then the largest operational base of the MGB in Europe, controlling KGB installations throughout East Germany – like Dresden where Putin was later stationed in 1985–90 – and operating into the West. In Karlshorst at that time Sudoplatov had thirteen officers from a so-called special illegal reserve, one of the most secret of the Soviet secret organisations. Heading the nearby Stasi directorate of East Berlin was Khokhlov's one-time partner Karl Kleinjung, as deputy to the Stasi chief Wilhelm Zaisser, soon to be replaced by Ernst Wollweber, who in the early 1930s was called 'the best saboteur in the world.' In December of that year 1952, the young Markus Wolf was made chief of the foreign intelligence service of the German Democratic Republic.

Now the team that Khokhlov would command on his next murder operation began to assemble. One of its members had been recruited in France.

Before the war France had been a major base for Soviet foreign operations. The new chief there in 1938, Lev Vasilevsky, had recruited a man named Kurt Weber in Paris, and codenamed him FRANZ. Weber moved to the south of France, married and lived well on Moscow subsidies. When Hitler's army occupied France, he joined the French resistance, and on one occasion, demonstrating great bravery and resourcefulness, Weber managed to get fellow *maquisard* Hans Kukowitsch out of a Nazi prison hours before the latter was doomed to die. They then became friends and after the war returned together to Germany and settled first in the American zone of occupation, and then in the Soviet zone. Weber found a job at a police station in Berlin-Köpenick. There this long-time agent was located and reactivated as agent FRANZ, under the special illegals unit, to be assigned to West Germany. He suggested finding his wartime friend, and soon Kukowitsch became agent FELIX.

Apart from Stalin's death in March 1953 and the arrest of Lavrenty Beria and his family the following summer, nothing extraordinary happened in the life of Nikolai Khokhlov until one September evening when a friend, also an officer and an illegal, appeared in the Khokhlovs' big Moscow flat. He was evidently drunk and announced that their chief Sudoplatov had just been arrested in his own office. That looked like the end of the legendary Bureau No. 1 of the MVD (successor of the MGB).

Perhaps the end of one designated unit, but not the end of the Soviet regime's need to eliminate its opponents abroad. (And beyond the Soviet regime: Lenin and Dzierżyński's legacy has survived to this day, almost twenty years after the collapse of the Soviet Union.)

Despite officers' worries, nothing changed. At the end of September, the new chief told Khokhlov that he had been selected for an important mission in West Germany – the murder of one of the NTS leaders in Frankfurt. Soon this 'Operation RHEIN' was approved by the Presidium of the Central Committee and the go-ahead signed personally by Khrushchev and Malenkov, the two most powerful men in the uneasy collective then ruling the country. The assassination project had thus become a top-level state priority.[9] For this mission, Khokhlov was personally 'handled' by Alexander Semyonovich Panyushkin, who in 1953, after his sojourn as Soviet ambassador in Washington had been appointed head of the KGB First (Foreign Intelligence) Chief Directorate.

During our long discussions Khokhlov always insisted that he was not to do the dirty work himself. The two German agents FRANZ (Weber) and FELIX (Kukowitsch) were to take care of that. They were brought to Moscow and given a five-week intensive course by the most experienced action officers the KGB could come up with. They were given driving and shooting lessons and taught how to spot and elude surveillance and avoid an ambush, how to 'dry-clean' and pull off brush contacts – in short, the tradecraft needed for a successful 'bang and burn' operation. Finally, they deposited their East German passports as 'Kurt Wetter' and 'Hans Schulze' and thanks to the help of agents in the Austrian police were given new bona fide Austrian documents in the names of 'Josef Leitner' and 'Hans Rotter'.

Vienna was to be the base. Khokhlov was there waiting for an order to move. Both agents arrived there by separate routes and were placed in a safe house in Baden. Later, a KGB arms expert delivered the specially designed weapons. The telegram came on 8 February 1954.

Khokhlov's itinerary was complicated, in an effort to smother any clear trace of his movements. He travelled so widely that he must actually have wondered sometimes which country he was in. His meanderings included a brief affair in Italy with a good-looking female courier who brought him his Austrian passport in the name of Josef Hofbauer before he was to cross into Switzerland. He arrived in Zurich just in time for a pre-arranged meeting with Weber. Kukowitsch joined them there. On 15 February Weber took the train directly to Frankfurt whereas Khokhlov ordered Kukowitsch to wait and follow four days later. He himself left Zurich on the same day as Weber, stopping over in Lausanne, where his briefcase with secret notes was left for safe-keeping at a bank, and in Geneva where he deposited most of his operational funds. Then he proceded to Frankfurt, where he arrived on the evening of the 17th and was met by Weber, now Leitner, at the Hauptbahnhof. Khokhlov checked into the Pension Zeppelin as 'Herr Hofbauer', an Austrian businessman.[10]

Like practically all Russian émigré organisations, *Narodno-Trudovoy Soyuz* (NTS), that Okolovich represented, had to be heavily penetrated by Soviet intelligence. A US Staff Intelligence Report concluded that the NTS was 'thoroughly penetrated by Russian agents, open to Soviet deception measures, unreliable and irresponsible'.[11] Khokhlov had studied four whole volumes of KGB files relating to the NTS. The KGB had collected so much inside information that no one should have any doubt or question about whom he was going to deal with in Frankfurt.

Noticeably, until only a few months before this, the files did not even show the target's address and telephone number. In 1948 agents had been sent to Limburg an der Lahn, where the NTS had been located at the time, trying to collect some basic information evidently not obtainable by the Soviets' penetrations of NTS headquarters. Those agents had failed to find Okolovich, but talked to his wife, who became very suspicious and told them that her husband rarely visited the place. The mission was abandoned.[12]

In 1951 the Soviets had tried to abduct Okolovich. A group of three German agents controlled by the Karlshorst base crossed the inter-sectional border and arrived in the small town of Runkel, less than four and a half miles away from Limburg. The group was equipped with ampoules of morphine, syringes and

15,000 German Marks in cash. Two of the agents immediately gave themselves up to the authorities. The leader managed to escape to the Soviet zone. All the spyware landed up with the police. A special bulletin of the NTS Executive Bureau, which reported about this failed operation and demanded vigilance from all members, was carefully filed among other documents in Moscow.

Khokhlov noticed that in those earlier years the files had only sparse information. After the NTS headquarters moved to Frankfurt all the KGB knew about Okolovich was that he often visited the Russian Information Agency, RIA, and that his wife worked at the Possev publishing house. It was not until mid-1953, after Moscow finally got a better source, that the necessary data had been acquired. Nikita Khorunzhy, ex-captain of the Red Army, who defected to the West in the spring of 1951, had been recruited to become agent WOLF. He lived in Germany under a cover identity as one 'Georg Müller' with a German woman. On 7 July 1953 WOLF reported that Okolovich lived at 3 Inheidener Strasse in Frankfurt-Bornheim, that he was officially employed by a news agency with an office at 42 Kronbergerstrasse, and that he was driving a black Mercedes with such and such licence plate. Also attached was a recent photo showing Okolovich and his wife at their flat in the company of Khorunzhy.

Now the KGB had enough information to launch Operation RHEIN.

It was very unprofessional for Okolovich to open the door to a total stranger that evening – surprisingly so, when one considers his past life and his current situation:

> For a moment, the two looked at one another. They made an odd contrast. The intended victim was a shamble, slightly dishevelled figure in his fifties, with spectacles perched on his high-bridged nose, looking far more like an unworldly professor than a man who had dedicated most of his adult life to a relentless underground battle against the Soviet regime. His would-be murderer was twenty years younger and his blond hair, blue eyes and neat appearance perfectly fitted (as they were intended to) his bogus identity as an Austrian businessman. But, for all the difference, it was one Russian looking searchingly at another. The older man acted, as he usually did, on impulse. Slav instincts told him now that he was faced with a compatriot who had, in truth, just joined him as a renegade. His reply, when it came, was disarmingly simple. 'Well, in that case,' he said, 'you had better come in and have a cup of tea.' And, as a gesture of trust, he turned and walked ahead of his visitor, presenting his back to him as a target.[13]

Such was the end of the operation codenamed RHEIN but real adventures began for Khokhlov some time later – when he became the murder target, not the murderer.

The exact topic of the discussions between Okolovich and Khokhlov during that Thursday evening of 18 February will probably never be known. As may be judged from the following events, it concentrated mainly on the future fate of Khokhlov himself, his plans for his family, and, most important for Okolovich, the Soviet agents in and around the NTS.

The alternatives were the following: to forget about the family and continue with his mission; to try to bring the family to the West using NTS channels; to compromise the whole operation and return to the USSR as a victim of somebody's negligence or failure, thus claiming innocence and maintaining the status quo. The life of Okolovich would be saved and hopefully nobody would be punished.

The experienced Okolovich quickly realised that the NTS had very limited ability for secretly exfiltrating Khokhlov's wife and his 2-year-old boy without risking their lives, and that his return to the Soviet Union would not be to the benefit of Khokhlov, his family and the NTS. So he said exactly what he should have said: let me contact the Western authorities on your behalf and see what they can do.[14]

Late in the evening, having met Okolovich's wife and telling her that he had come directly from Moscow to organise the murder of her husband, Khokhlov left the apartment and returned to his pension by tram. Soon he would dispatch his agents to Augsburg to collect the arms, which, according to the plan, were to be delivered to Germany by a courier. To be able to blow the operation, Khokhlov had first to mount one.

The next evening he was meeting FRANZ and FELIX in a restaurant on Friedrich-Ebert-Anlage, the site made famous by the international trade fairs that had been held here since 1240. They ordered a modest dinner.

During the meal, Khokhlov supplied the agents with cash and instructions to meet a courier in Augsburg on Tuesday, 23 February. Both Germans knew the courier's identity and Weber had even seen him once in Vienna. After collecting 'a parcel' – a suitcase and a car battery, which contained cigarette case weapons, miniature handguns with silencers, and a variety of ammunition including poisoned lead pellets, they were to bring it to Frankfurt and deposit it in the left-luggage office of the main railway station that was not far from where they were sitting. Khokhlov ordered Weber and Kukowitsch to wait for him on February 24, 25 and 26 on the opposite side of the same street. Should he not appear, one had to rush to Berlin, and the other immediately retreat to Austria.

While the agents were travelling, the Americans detained Khokhlov suspecting him to be an NTS fake. They had good reason to think so.

First, he came virtually from the skies. No one knew about him and no detailed information was available to Western sources about the 9th Department (the former Bureau No. 1, Sudoplatov service) or the special tasks force. Second, the émigrés sometimes went to bizarre lengths to prove their worth to the West. One organisation, for example, went so far as to secretly blow up its own headquarters in order to justify its claim that it posed a real threat to the KGB.[15]

So it was quite logic that Khokhlov was considered to be an NTS plant especially devised to attract attention to the NTS and its leaders.

Khokhlov described to me one of his American interrogators, whom he called 'Leonard' in his book, as an evil, blunt and narrow-minded person, sent to destroy him and ruin his intricate plan. I believe 'Leonard' to be Nicholas Andrew Natsios, a distinguished US intelligence officer[16] who, together with Robert N. Crowell, acting head of the Frankfurt counter-intelligence (CI) section, introduced to Khokhlov as 'Paul', had in front of them an absolutely genuine Austrian passport with Khokhlov's photo, $20,000 in different European currencies, and a poor-sounding legend that seemed too far fetched to be true. Even with Khokhlov's excellent command of Russian and his detailed knowledge of current events and life in the USSR, it was hard to believe he came straight from Moscow.

There was a chain of coincidences interwoven with bad luck which later made one of the participants in this operation say with bitterness, 'We all had egg on our face.'

> It was the car battery that settled the issue. At Thursday noon, on 25 February, Khokhlov persuaded a sceptical American officer to observe the meeting he had arranged with his agents. As he missed his first date, the meeting was at an alternative address, this time near the Old Opera. Both Germans were seized on the spot and taken to an American safe house, where they were searched and, in the words of one of the participants, 'stubs from the baggage check facility' found. Khokhlov joined them after some time, explained the position and urged that they too, being now hopelessly compromised, should elect to stay in the West. Both men agreed without much argument. Then the battery was dragged in and Khokhlov started chipping away, first at the ebonite cover and then at the lead plates. Glued to the wall inside were two plastic packages that were revealed once the sulphuric acid had been emptied out. The weapons they contained corresponded exactly with Khokhlov's earlier description. The Americans were astounded, delighted and apologetic in equal proportions.[17]

Their apathy was now converted into an all-out effort to smash or, better still, to rope in the entire KGB operational network in Austria, so far as Khokhlov's story had exposed it.[18] Next thing David Murphy, who would later become chief of the CIA's Soviet Russia Division, came storming to Frankfurt and said a *mea culpa*. By that time Deriabin's information from Vienna had already reached the headquarters and that not only helped to establish Khokhlov's bona fides but also added an entirely new dimension to the understanding of Soviet demolition and sabotage operations.

The start was promising. With FRANZ and FELIX already whisked off to an interrogation centre, Khokhlov was instructed to go on sending messages to his controller in Vienna explaining why the mission was being delayed. He received back replies that indicated that the Russians had no inkling that the whole assassination party had been in American hands[19] and singing.

At the end of February, over a weekend, the Americans moved Khokhlov to a hunting lodge in Königstein not far away from Oberursel, where he spent an unpleasant night at the 7707th European Command Intelligence Centre, better known as Camp King. The British SIS took over, and Nick, as they started to call him, was very pleased with the way an officer who arrived from London handled things. At least he was very different from 'Leonard', who disappeared. (Natsios returned to Greece where he served as political adviser in the military secretariat of the US Military Mission in Athens.) French intelligence was also given a piece of the pie – they were busy checking the records of Weber and Kukowitsch. Khokhlov was taken to Lausanne where he retrieved his secret notes. Back in Frankfurt, he decoded them in the presence of Okolovich. That was a valuable take for both British and American counter-intelligence as well as for NTS internal security.

22 April was a Thursday, just a week after Easter. In Bonn it was sunny and very warm. Everybody was nervous. The High Commissioner began to speak. Within half an hour Khokhlov was called into the conference room. Flash of bulbs, click of cameras. He was placed in the middle between Charles Malamut of the European staff of the Voice of America (VOA) and a German interpreter. Nobody asked questions. At the same time, the VOA started broadcasting his appeal to the world's public opinion. After some time, audience members were invited to submit questions. There were not many. Apparently, in 1954 it was not easy for the Western press to grasp the significance of the operation that had just rolled up. After the press conference was over, he was surrounded by guards and led through the back door to the waiting car.

What was the spark that set the forest on fire? What did he say? What secured Khokhlov a prominent place in the intelligence history? It was not what he actually pronounced, it was the fact of his physical existence. Since its first days the Cheka had been sending assassins abroad to murder enemies of the Kremlin. From Georges Agabekov in 1930 to Alexander Litvinenko seventy years later the Chekists who defected to the West told the world about those crimes. But before Khokhlov, there was not a single person who ever came to his victim with the words, 'I have been sent to kill you, but I refuse to do it and I leave myself at your mercy.' Khokhlov's statement had an enormous impact on Western governments and people.

After the press conference, Khokhlov was invited to London for a lecture tour, and gave an interview to the BBC. His story received the full blare of publicity. On 6 May 1954 he was flown to Washington DC on board an aircraft of the US Air Force.

After his arrival in the United States, Khokhlov became a persistent critic of Communist Russia, lecturing widely through Europe and the USA. After the four articles he published in the *Saturday Evening Post* under the guidance of Milton Lehman entitled 'I Would Not Murder for the Soviets', interviews with him appeared in major American newspapers and magazines. To enhance the effect of the *Post* articles, the evening before the first of them appeared Khokhlov was invited to CBS studios as a guest on 'Meet the Press'.

In September 1957 he returned to Europe to take part in an important conference that had been planned long before and announced in advance.

The Botanical Garden of Frankfurt was the scene in the middle of that month of an assembly of several hundred anti-Communist activists from various lands. The place was the hall of the Palmengarten, set amidst palms and greenhouses, where conventions and concerts were held.[20]

According to Khokhlov, with whom I discussed the episode in every detail, on Sunday, 15 September, the closing day of the conference, he addressed the audience briefly and then stepped out on the terrace and ordered a cup of coffee of which he drank less than a half. He went out to see off some delegates from London and then came back to attend the entertainment programme. From behind the closed doors leading to the concert hall he could hear the performers carrying on and the sounds of laughter and applause from the audience.

Nikolai suddenly felt very fatigued and thought that it was due to the three days of nervous tension, speeches and discussions. He ordered a glass of juice but immediately realised that he could not drink it as he suddenly felt a severe, persistent abdominal pain. When he heard the voice of Irene Salena of the Frankfurt Opera, he decided that in spite of the feeling of nausea, he should go and listen. Tomorrow he would sleep late, he thought.

Khokhlov returned to the concert hall and found a seat, feeling no better. He felt the need to go out, and the fresh, cool air slightly revived him. He got into the car and in a few minutes was at his bed-and-breakfast guest house. Then he fainted away.

When Khokhlov came round he felt feverish, his heart was beating rapidly and he was shivering. Picking up the keys, he dragged himself to the entrance feeling worse every minute. Somebody called a doctor and he himself managed to call Okolovich, though suffering from vomiting and diarrhoea. The paramedics transferred him to hospital.

By 00:30 a.m. that night a bed was found for him. The physicians diagnosed his sickness as acute gastritis. Nobody suspected poisoning and Khokhlov was pleased with the diagnosis of gastritis, as it meant that he would be leaving shortly.

For five days he was treated for acute gastritis and kept feeling worse. His fingernails showed strange horizontal lines as if colour was disappearing and he started feeling pain in his feet and hands.

Then there was hypovalemia or loss of fluids. Khokhlov's hair suddenly started to fall out and his skin yellowed. The doctors ran a series of tests. The head physician brought in consultants. A skin specialist suspected thallium.

Khokhlov had no doubt as to the identity of those who planned and carried out the operation.

Subsequent developments proved that the biochemists in the secret laboratory in Moscow knew their profession. While the German specialists were pouring all kind of antidotes into him, Khokhlov's system continued to disintegrate at a galloping rate.

As a professional from the department that was the customer of the Naumov's lab product, Khokhlov knew better than anyone else that everything had been figured out in advance: the inexperience of Western physicians, the inertia of authorities, the scepticism of the public, as well as symptoms of gastritis to disguise the action of an obsolete poison transformed by modern science into a powerful radiological weapon.[21]

On Sunday afternoon, 22 September, nearly a week to the hour after his collapse, the doctors discovered that an incredibly rapid process of destruction was going on in Khokhlov's bloodstream. The number of the white corpuscles was falling dangerously, and at one time a count showed a drop from the normal 6,000–7,000 to 700. A puncture into his chest bone produced a sample of the marrow, and a microscopic examination of it established that the blood-building cells in the bone marrow were dying off. The blood in his veins was gradually turning into useless plasma. The saliva glands in his mouth, throat and alimentary canal were drying up. It became difficult to eat, drink, and even speak. Khokhlov sank into apathy and was growing feeble. That Sunday evening, his friends later told him, he looked very much like a dying man.

They were waiting in the corridor. Professor Schrade, the head physician, told them: 'It's very bad. To be honest, it's hopeless. It is hard for me to say it: we simply do not understand what is happening to him. His blood is turning into water. And we cannot do anything about it. Of course, we must resort to transfusions. We are looking for the right type of donor, and by morning we will locate one. But then what? None of us really knows. It looks as if your friend will soon be dead.'

'But from what?' Okolovich broke in. 'What is the cause of this? Is it possible that medical science is unable to determine what is killing him, and attempt to fight it?'

'Ah, medical science! All that we know is based on experience. How can one fight unknown poison?'[22]

But the doctors of the Barnet Hospital in London, not to mention the UCLH that claims to 'employ leading health care professionals in an extensive range of clinical services', *had* this experience. It is always a matter of time. Practising physicians don't have time to read books.

On Monday morning, 23 September, NTS held a press conference. Vladimir Poretsky, the chairman, recited Khokhlov's history and stated that he was suffering from poisoning by a combination of drugs. Okolovich also spoke and explained the reason why the Soviet government wanted to get rid of the defector.

In the meantime, the patient, unable to take food, was being fed intravenously.

But unlike Sasha Litvinenko, Khokhlov was extremely lucky. On 27 September, the twelfth day of his illness, the Americans intervened. A group of American healthcare professionals arrived at the hospital and went into conference with the German colleagues in Khokhlov's ward. On the same day he was moved from the Frankfurt University Hospital to the US Army facility where the doctors started to administer specialised treatment.

By the middle of October, Khokhlov was discharged from hospital fully recovered. That was quite a miracle.

The official Memorandum written by Colonel F.Y. Leaver, MC, Commanding Officer of the United States Army Hospital, Frankfurt, APO 757, US Army, stated:

Subject: Hospitalization of Mr. Khokhlov.

Mr. Khokhlov was admitted to the United States Army Hospital, Frankfurt, on September 27, 1957, as a transfer from a local German hospital.

He had been hospitalised there on the 16th of September with what appeared to be an acute gastroenteritis, however, several days after admission he developed a severe hemorrhagic skin eruption, ulceration of the mouth, some mental confusion, loss of body hair, and severe depression of the bone marrow with a total white blood count of 750 and virtual disappearance of granulocytes. It was the impression of the staff of the German hospital that this probably was caused by poisoning, very likely thallium.

On admission to this hospital on 27 September (11 days following the onset of his illness) he was acutely and critically ill with marked bone-marrow depression, high fever, and he was unable to eat because of the hemorrhagic skin eruption which involved not only the body surface but included the mouth, throat, and mucous membranes. There was marked epilation and loss of hair on all body surfaces including the scalp. He was emotionally disturbed and sometimes confused.

As his condition was critical, he was immediately placed on the seriously ill list. He received special nursing care in a private room. His treatment consisted of antibiotics, ACTH, steroids, as well as local treatment for his skin and mouth lesions. His condition gradually improved. He has been able to be up and about his room during the past few days. Temperature was normal, and skin lesions cleared. The blood picture returned to approximately normal. He lost most of his body hair. At the time of discharge from the hospital on Tuesday afternoon, October 8, 1957, he was weak, but was able to eat without difficulty and was gradually regaining his strength. He was considered essentially recovered.

Symptoms and clinical findings are believed to have been due to poisoning, probably by thallium and/or other chemical agents. Toxicological studies were performed on his hair, skin, and urine, which were negative, however, no specimens from the early period of his illness were available for study.

Back in America specialists explained to Khokhlov that he had been poisoned with radioactive thallium.

A week later he was invited to testify before the US Senate. It turned out to be a difficult session. Among other things, he said: 'I gave everything I had to the United States. All the secrets that could help the United States.'[23]

The US government helped him to settle in North Carolina. But before he changed professions, the Agency sent Khokhlov to Viet Nam. Here Nikolai met Nick Natsios again.[24]

After Viet Nam they were both posted to Seoul, South Korea, Natsios as a senior political officer at the US Embassy, Khokhlov working in the Russian service of the American radio, which broadcast daily in the Russian language. From here Khokhlov, as he told me, sent an application to Duke University in North Carolina for admission as a post-graduate student to the Faculty of Psychology.

He remarried in the USA in 1963. Her name was Tatiana and she was a German-born daughter of one of the NTS activists.

After five years at Duke University, in 1967, Nikolai Khokhlov wrote a thesis and a year later defended his PhD in psychology. Immediately after that he left Duke University and settled in California joining the Department of Psychology at California State University in San Bernardino (CSUSB).

In 1992 Dr Khokhlov celebrated his seventieth birthday. For many years he had been living and teaching in the sunny and wealthy state, a dream of millions of Americans. He decided to retire, taking advantage of a golden handshake retirement incentive programme offered by the CSUSB system. Both senior members of the faculty, Khokhlov and Herold, who retired at the same time, were awarded the title of Emeritus Professor of Psychology by the university. A retirement party was held at Bill Cowan's Ocean Grill Restaurant in Redlands to honour the two professors. According to the official report, both were presented with the traditional solid gold watch. 'In December I was given a gold-plated pocket watch,' Khokhov scornfully remarked in 2004 to a Moscow journalist. 'A useful gift to a retiring professor.'

That year was indeed a memorable one. By Special Decree No. 308 of 27 March Russian President Boris Yeltsin granted him pardon for high treason. Now that the sentence was withdrawn, Khokhlov could visit Moscow. Before he stepped onto Russian soil, there was a long exchange of correspondence between him and the then KGB chief Vadim Bakatin.

Nicholas Bethell took care of him during the visit. He was commissioned by the *Daily Telegraph* to write about this visit, so they met in Frankfurt and together flew on to the Russian capital. Lord Bethell was not a reporter or correspondent, but an influential member of the European Parliament, to which he was first nominated in 1975. Having acted as a Lord-in-Waiting to the Queen between 1970 and 1971, Lord Bethell, author of several books on the history of intelligence, also worked as a consultant to the Police Federation of England and Wales. Now he acted as a 'guardian angel' for Khokhlov, using his great authority to insure that nothing unexpected happened.

At the end of the visit Bethell reported that they had been met at Sheremetievo airport by some of Khokhlov's university buddies and his son Alexander. They visited a tiny one-room apartment that Yana had shared with her son and his baby child. There is every evidence that she refused to see Nikolai. 'Sadly,' as Lord Bethell wrote in his article, this was due to their 'main concern of how their own lives may be disturbed by the return of this "legendary traitor to the Motherland".'

At the KGB headquarters, the British lord and the Soviet defector were received by the 'new KGB'. 'But the people manning the new KGB, and most of the senior positions in the new Russia,' wrote Lord Bethell two years later, 'were the same one who had been there in the old Soviet Union . . . The doctor who had declared Vladimir Bukovsky insane on KGB orders carried on practising as a senior mental health specialist.'[25]

After seeing the Lubyanka and its representatives, Lord Bethell met Pavel Sudoplatov, Khokhlov's former chief, then 85. The old general who had served over fifteen years in Vladimir prison, didn't want to see his former protégé. After the diplomat told Khokhlov about their meeting, the latter spat, 'That nauseating mass-murderer!'

When my small monograph about Khokhlov was published in May 2005 as part of the *Personal Files* series, telephone calls from California stopped together with emails.

In late November 2006 we were having a drink with Ben Macintyre of *The Times* in the Connaught bar and I told him the thallium story. Ben promptly found Khokhlov and published a long article in his newspaper about the man whom KGB poisoned with radioactive substance but who lived to tell the tale. He even dug up a rare old photo of Khokhlov made in a London airport in 1954 from *The Times* archives.

Steve LeVine read the article and got his chance. In June 2007, after months of telephone and email exchanges, he went to San Bernardino to meet Khokhlov. A year later Steve published his book.

As expected, the KGB veteran turned professor of psychology told Steve a lot of tales that, alas, had nothing to do with what really happened. Old habits die hard.

But LeVine has a talent of understanding people, a rare gift. He quickly realised that the figure in front of him was extremely sensitive, complex, and difficult who felt misunderstood by almost everyone. Besides, LeVine found Khokhlov a deeply emotional and sometimes self-pitying man who didn't always own up to his embellishments.[26]

For the American, Khokhlov's relationship with Tatiana was a bit of a mystery. The two of them had separated two decades before but still had obvious affection for each other. After his physical condition worsened, they spoke almost every day. She screened calls for him, cooked for him, and let him entertain guests at her home. But they did not attempt to hide their disagreements. He was rude and condescending towards her, extremely chauvinistic. When she attempted to speak, he simply talked over her or said, 'May I have the floor?' and then took it.[27]

Steve, however, describes his new acquaintance as 'most often being extremely polite and possessed of a self-effacing sense of humour. He had a coughing fit at one point and Tatiana asked if he needed anything. "Yes, a new throat," he replied.' (When I read those lines I immediately thought of Gordievsky with whom I was spending a great deal of time.)

Discussing the Litvinenko case with his guest, Khokhlov was certain that the successor agencies to his former service had carried out the notorious murder in London. For Steve LeVine, Nikolai and Sasha thus shared an unusual distinction. They were the only known victims of radioactive poisoning in the entire history of assassinations worldwide. But Steve was wrong.

'He had the last laugh,' observed his widow, Tatiana, as their four grand-children scampered about and guests mingled in a tree-filled backyard on the day of Khokhlov's September 2007 funeral.[28] She was certainly right.

Bogdan Stashinsky, the assassin, Germany, 1957–9

When in March 1989 the General sent a message to Tom Mangold, the journalist was not surprised. During his long and brilliant career, Tom met and interviewed more spies than any seasoned MI5 investigator could ever dream of, so he expected that whenever it came to serious business he would probably be one of the first to be contacted.

The message from General Hendrik van den Bergh, the legendary chief of the South African Republican Intelligence/Bureau for State Security (RI-BOSS), transmitted through one of his ablest officers, Mike Geldenhuys, read: 'Tell anyone who asks that I can't remember about Loginov, and I don't want to remember. Tell them I do not suffer from verbal diarrhoea. We should stay out of this.'[1]

Yuri Nikolayevich Loginov was a Soviet illegal arrested in South Africa. On 12 July 1969, Geldenhuys and Loginov flew to Germany for the spy swap.

Loginov's most unusual story is covered in several books, some of them better or worse than the others, but none is correct, I am afraid, as each represents a version of an interested side. Therefore, the General was right – until the documents from the KGB archives are declassified, we should stay out of it.

On 12 August 1961 a telephone call reached an operator in the CIA Berlin Base. A Berlin police duty officer informed the Americans that a man accompanied by a woman had turned himself in and was requesting contact with the US representatives. That was the end of the career of Bogdan Nikolayevich Stashinsky, who was to become widely known as 'the Assassin'.

Stashinsky was a schoolteacher from Borshovitsy, Ukraine, just on the Polish border between Lviv and Kraków. One day, caught riding a train home from the school without a ticket, the police pitched him for service as an informant. Whether it was this unusual way or another, Stashinsky began to inform, and not long afterward, in the summer of 1951, he was assigned to a secret police task force that employed strong-arm and sometimes bizarre tactics to round up the Ukrainian nationalist underground.[2]

After a year, this handsome 20-year-old was invited by the Ukrainian MGB to start training for a clandestine work abroad and for the next two years went through the intensive course in tradecraft and foreign languages in Kiev. Then he was sent to Poland to study and adopt his new cover legend.

It was clear that initially the chiefs viewed Stashinsky as an errand boy who could serve as a courier or an occasional cutout for more important operators and indeed he was sent to East Germany where he was given menial work. But young Stashinsky was evidently talented, for while posing as an ethnic German of Polish origin (named 'Josef Lehmann') he rose to become an interpreter in the Ministry of Trade in Berlin. Of course, it was the KGB who placed him there.

In the Tanz Casino in East Berlin Lehmann met a 21-year-old hairdresser who introduced herself as Inge Pohl. She was of common, sometimes sloppy appearance but he was no James Bond and fell in love.[3] As a safety-measure, being aware of honey traps and other provocations, he duly reported the contact but was assured that the girl was all right.

In January 1956 Stashinsky was summoned to a nondescript two-storey villa at the corner of Rheingoldstrasse and Waldorfallee in Karlshorst where he reported to Lieutenant Colonel Kovalenko and met other officers of the KGB's 13th Department. Kovalenko's deputy, Major Sergey Meshcheryakov, would become his handler. The first assignment given to Stashinsky was to go to Munich and find Ivan Bissaga, a Ukrainian exile and a Soviet agent who had managed to penetrate the Ukrainian émigré community in Bavaria and found a job in the staff of the anti-Soviet newspaper *Ukrayinski Samostiynik*.[4]

Bissaga was a small fish but he regularly supplied his Moscow bosses with valuable insider information and Stashinsky's task was to collect this information and deliver cash to the agent. It was a typical cutout job.

However, his KGB mission changed. During one of the *Treffs*,[5] Stashinsky asked Bissaga whether he would be willing to take part in the abduction of Lev Rebet, the editor-in-chief of the *Ukrayinski Samostiynik*, in order to bring him to Russia to face court on charges of anti-Soviet extremism and propaganda. Bissaga blankly refused saying that he felt insecure and believed he was being watched. He was not, though in October 1956 he was questioned on suspicion of anti-Constitutional activities. Shortly afterwards Stashinsky brought him the papers that allowed the émigré Bissaga to return to the Soviet zone.[6]

On a spring day in 1957 Stashinsky was summoned to a safe house in Karlshorst where Sergey was waiting for him. The Ukrainian was informed that his new assignment would again be in Munich and the target would be Rebet – and the task at hand murder.

At that time the Berlin Cathedral and the Reichstag were still in ruins and the whole Communist system did not look any better. In June 1953 the country had erupted in a series of riots and demonstrations that threatened the very existence of the regime. The uprising soon spread from Berlin to more than 400 cities, towns and villages throughout East Germany and chants were heard calling for 'Death to Communism' and even 'Long Live Eisenhower'. As Christian

Ostermann noted in *Uprising in East Germany, 1953*, for the first time ever 'the 'proletariat' had risen against the 'dictatorship of the proletariat'. There were riots in Poland in 1956, and Khrushchev had to send in Russian troops to help the pro-Moscow Polish government put them down. Following the example of the Polish workers from Poznań, there were major riots in Hungary that started in October and were accumulating force until on 4 November a thousand Russian tanks rolled into Budapest killing several thousand people and restoring Soviet rule. Vladimir Kryuchkov, future chief of the foreign intelligence, was stationed in Hungary at the time assisting Ambassador Yuri Andropov, who would become the KGB chairman, in deceiving the Hungarian government until it was too late. According to Christopher Andrew, 'Andropov remained haunted for the rest of his life by the speed with which an apparently all-powerful Communist one-party state had begun to topple.'⁷ But as the Soviet leader, Khrushchev, was a Ukrainian to the tips of his shoes, he was most of all troubled by the Ukrainian opposition with its vigorous underground movement directed from West Germany.

After the Khokhlov operation rolled up, Kremlin murder plans were in the air with other performers. The KGB hired the services of a German contract killer, Wolfgang Wildprett, to assassinate Vladimir Poretsky, the chairman of the NTS. Like Khokhlov, however, Wildprett had second thoughts, decided not to go ahead with the murder and in December 1955 secretly tipped off the police.

For his mission in Munich Stashinsky was given a West German passport in the name of 'Siegfried Dräger', an appropriate amount of cash, addresses where to find Rebet and a photo. Bissaga, who pretended to be the editor's friend, had taken several photos. (When I learned about this, I immediately thought of Chekulin in the company of Berezovsky and Litvinenko. Chekulin also duly photographed everybody around while in London later to use those photos in his smear campaign.)

While Stashinsky flew to Munich to start a long surveillance routine establishing patterns of Rebet's movements and noting down his work schedule, special laboratories in Moscow were given orders to produce a new silenced weapon. As usual, the idea was that even after an autopsy the death should be attributed to natural causes. Though only 45, Rebet could not boast of good health as during the war he had been interned by Nazis in Auschwitz for three years.

In 1956 Rebet published a fundamental work *The Theory of Nations* and by the time Shashinsky started to follow him in Munich was busy doing research in law, politics and sociology and contributing to the Ukrainian émigré newspapers that were smuggled to the Soviet Ukraine. The KGB considered Rebet an important theorist and ideologue of the Organization of Ukrainian Nationalists (OUN), a hated and feared opposition force.

By the autumn of 1957 Stashinsky knew all that he needed to know about his man. At the same time KGB scientists and engineers had developed a weapon – the special technology laboratory modified their earlier silenced tube gun into a poison gas gun while the chemical laboratory came up with the poison – hydrogen cyanide (HCN). When inhaled, it causes what is called 'chemical asphyxia' – immediate unconsciousness, convulsions and almost instantaneous death ideally imitating myocardial infarction, also known as a heart attack.

The gas-firing gun, like its predecessor, was to be hidden in a rolled-up newspaper, a favourite gadget of the Chekists. The firing lever activated a firing pin, which detonated a percussion cap, rupturing an ampoule of acid. The acid evaporated into HCN and was propelled out of a small hole in the muzzle. The gun was just 7 inches (18 cm) long.[8] The disadvantage was that it had to be fired directly into the victim's face.

In late September or early October a weapons expert arrived in Karlshorst with three guns and instructions to train the assassin. The next day Stashinsky drove with his handler, the Moscow armourer and a dog to the outskirts of East Berlin. The poor pet was tied to a tree and Stashinsky stuck the tube within eighteen inches of his snout and pressed the lever while his colleagues watched at a distance. The dog immediately collapsed without a sound but continued to writhe in agony for almost three minutes.[9]

Stashinsky later recalled the incident: 'I was sorry about the dog. I could hardly even bear to look at him. When I approached him, carrying the weapon, he tried to lick my hand. From then on the dog was ever-present in my mind. I had killed him.'[10]

In his short foreword to the book version of the *Life* article, Allen Dulles wrote:

The Soviets had obviously tried to drill any human sensibilities out of Stashinsky for years, using a kind of Pavlovian deconditioning and hardening scheme in order to turn him into a perfectly functioning robot-murderer. To equip the human monstrosity they hoped to create they also had invented new murder weapons whose use was clearly and solely for assassination purposes.

Stashinsky's instruction was that after the action he should clear the Munich area immediately. Stashinsky never told anybody about a support team and when he later confessed his action he presented the operation as an exclusively one-man show. In KGB practice, however, there would have been a courier who secretly brought the gun, somebody to watch the scene and another to evacuate the assassin quickly in case of an unexpected problem. It seems that in the circumstances Stashinsky decided not to betray his KGB colleagues. The human element, always the human element.

On 12 October Stashinsky had been waiting for his victim since 9:00 a.m. near the offices of the *Suchasna Ukraina* ('Modern Ukraine') at 8 Karlsplatz known as 'Stachus' among the locals. The assassin entered the building just ahead of Rebet and started climbing the staircase. When he heard someone opening the door and entering the small entrance hall, he turned and started to slowly descend holding the gun rolled in a newspaper, as instructed, in his right hand. He kept to the right of the staircase allowing the OUN man to pass on his left. When they were on the same level, the assassin shot ejecting the poison gas directly into the victim's face while continuing to go down and turning his head away. Before he left the building, he heard Rebet stumble but did not look back. Quite composed, he left the crime scene, drowned the gun in a nearby canal and returned to the hotel. In a few minutes he was at the Hauptbahnhof just opposite his hotel and the Karlsplatz where a police car and an ambulance were now present, and boarded the train for Frankfurt am Main. Here he spent the night in a hotel and the following morning took a flight to West Berlin.

In May 1938 Pavel Sudoplatov assassinated a Ukrainian nationalist leader, Yevhen Konovalets on Stalin's personal orders. For two years Sudoplatov had been masquerading as a courier from the Ukrainian underground and was well trusted by the émigrés. Konovalets met him alone at a restaurant in Rotterdam at about noon, presented him with a box of chocolates, and after a short discussion agreed to meet again at five. Shortly after he left the premises, the bomb exploded killing Konovalets. When Sudoplatov became the chief of Bureau No. 1 – the special tasks force – Khrushchev ordered the murder of Stepan Bandera, the closest associate of Konovalets and a prominent figure in the OUN movement.

That time it didn't work but twenty years later the mission was entrusted to Stashinsky.

In spite of many photos and descriptions in the KGB files, the assassin wanted to meet Bandera in person in order to be sure he would not miss his victim or confuse him with somebody else. Following an agent's report that Bandera was to deliver a graveside eulogy in Rotterdam on an anniversary of the death of Konovalets, Stashinsky flew to the Netherlands to attend the services. He saw Bandera and was now sure he would recognise the man.

Documented as 'Hans Joachim Budeit', Stashinsky made several trips to Munich only to discover that there was no secure way to approach the Ukrainian who was experienced and careful and rarely came out alone. Besides, the apartment building at 7 Kreittmayrstrasse, where he lived under the alias 'Stefan Popel', was always locked.

Moscow sent a lock-picker to sort out the problem and soon the assassin was able to go in and out of the building whenever he wished. He used to practise at times when the premises were vacated so as not to attract anybody's attention. In his later testimony Stashinsky described a problem with the key but said that he made a sketch from which an appropriate key was produced. This is hard to believe. Even an expert entry specialist can hardly produce a key without working on the lock itself.

On the second week of October 1959, Stashinsky made his last trip to Munich as part of the Bandera operation. He later told the investigators that he was alone and himself carried his new weapon – a modified model of the tube gas gun, this time with a double barrel. This was unlikely, as it grossly violates the established KGB practice but no one seems to have noticed the discrepancy.

On 15 October at about 12:45 p.m. the assassin was waiting for his victim near the house where Bandera resided. He knew the Ukrainian had gone out shopping and was due soon. At about one o'clock he spotted Bandera's dark blue Opel Kapitan with the Munich licence plate entering the garage and let himself through the doors. As with Rebet, he went upstairs to wait for his victim to get into the house. Finally he saw Bandera fiddling with his keys at the front door as he carried several bags of groceries in his right hand. Stashinsky went down to help him with the door, and let Bandera in while blocking the way out by holding the entrance door with his foot. Then he asked Bandera about the lock and when the latter turned to him to answer fired both barrels point-blank into the victim's face. He closed the door behind him and was off. Stashinsky left Munich at once and was soon reporting to his handler in a safe house near Karlshorst.[11]

Stepan Bandera was found at 1:05 p.m., bleeding and barely alive. A medical examination established that the cause of his death was cyanide gas. Evidently the KGB's weapon had left undesirable traces.

The assassin was summoned to Moscow where at a secret ceremony the chairman of the KGB pinned a highly valued combat medal of the Order of the Red Banner to his blazer. (He was not a commissioned officer and did not have a uniform.)

On Christmas Eve Stashinsky confessed to his girlfriend what he was allowed to say: that he was not 'Lehmann' and not German or Polish, but a Ukrainian working for the Russian secret police. Inge Pohl was obviously not overly surprised and soon agreed to go to Moscow with him. They were married in 1960. In September she informed her husband – and he duly reported to his boss – that she was expecting a child. In January 1961 Inge was permitted to return to East Germany for the birth. Afterwards she prepared to travel back to Moscow with their infant son. Stashinsky had not seen him yet. A day before her scheduled departure the baby choked to death while feeding. It must have looked to Stashinsky like God's retribution.

Stashinsky was allowed to attend the baby's funeral accompanied by his KGB minder, Colonel Georgy Sannikov. On 12 August, one day before the wall dividing East and West blocked any chance of escape, he and Inge boarded the elevated S-Bahn train to West Berlin. When they entered the shelter of a police station, darkness was covering the city as it prepared to be split into two worlds for twenty-eight years and one day.

It was not easy for Herr Lehmann, who spoke excellent German, was properly documented and married to a real German girl, to prove to Western authorities that he was who he had said he was. The authorities took their time to investigate thoroughly and Soviet-ops specialists had long debriefing sessions with the defector before deciding that he was bona fide. When he was finally cleared their problem was what to do: without doubt the assassin could not be accepted by the

USA or West Germany. It was agreed that he would have to face trial for his crimes. After a time in prison he could be dispatched to a third country.

His trial began on 8 October 1962 and lasted a week. The verdict was announced on 19 October and Stashinsky was sentenced to eight years. The High Court judge ruled that the Soviet government in Moscow was guilty of political assassinations.

After Stashinsky had served six years of his prison sentence in West Germany, the BND (the Federal Intelligence Service) contacted South African Republican Intelligence (RI) because, as Mike Geldenhuys, the retiring police commissioner told the *Cape Times* in March 1984, 'they were convinced [that South Africa] was the only country where he would be comparatively safe from KGB agents'. Stashinsky underwent intensive cosmetic surgery and was given a new family background legend and identity.[12]

In July 1969 after a dramatic spy swap on a border post between West and East Germany that had been delayed for three hours because Yuri Loginov, a Soviet illegal, did not want to return to the USSR, Geldenhuys prepared to take a flight from Germany to Cape Town in the company of a blond tanned man who looked nothing like a Ukrainian. Perhaps the eyes, those deep-set and expressionless eyes of an assassin that stared back with frank candour remained unchanged, but they were now covered by glasses.

'*Naand, meneer.*'

Geldenhuys did not hear the blond man approaching him and even less expected to be greeted in his own language. He smiled.

'*Naand. Praat jy Afrikaans?*'

'*Nee.*' Then he paused. '*'n Bietjie. A little.*'

Geldenhuys decided that he rather liked the former KGB assassin he was now going to take to the country where eleven official and eight non-official languages are spoken.

He later was best man at Stashinsky's second marriage to 'a girl from Durban' (no records exist of what happened to Inge Pohl). Apparently, only the Minister of Justice, van den Bergh and Geldenhuys knew of the arrangement. Geldenhuys told the *Cape Times*: 'As a KGB agent who had been awarded the Order of the Red Banner for carrying out . . . political assassinations for the Soviet government, he had been initiated into the closely guarded secrets of the Soviet intelligence service. He was able to supply our intelligence service with a vast amount of invaluable information.'[13]

Two years after Victor Yushchenko became the President of Ukraine, the Lviv town administration announced they wanted to transfer the tombs of Yevhen Konovalets, Stepan Bandera and other key anti-Soviet opposition leaders to a new area of Lychakivsky cemetery dedicated to Ukrainian national liberation movement. In October 2007 a statue of Bandera was unveiled in Lviv.

Stashinsky is alive. Nobody knows where he lives or what he does.

Operation VLADIMIR, Part III

Some words came into his mind, words from long ago, in a language that he could speak only a little, but this English ballad about bravery he understood and liked. 'To every man upon this earth death cometh soon or late . . .' Has Marina ever seen a volume by Thomas Macaulay bound in dark green roan leather with two figures of warriors embossed in gold on his shelf? She could not recall. The house was sealed on that horrendous night when police came after two o'clock to tell her and Tolik that they had to leave their home in Muswell Hill at once, maybe never to come back again. And Sasha was not there to protect them.

Next day, after the fatal meeting at the Millennium Hotel, Litvinenko called Andrei Lugovoy at 7:30 a.m. to say that he was not feeling well and would probably not be able to make their morning meeting with Erinys. He had complained of stomach-ache and promised to call again in the evening. He did, only to say it was not getting any better. Next day Lugovoy departed to Moscow leaving radioactive traces all around him, including members of his family.

At 2:00 a.m. on 2 November Litvinenko asked, 'Please call the ambulance, I can't hold on any more.' Marina called. Two girls came, looked at him and said that he should drink more water. They checked his blood pressure, took his blood sample to test for the glucose level and said that at any hospital they would do the same, so there would be no sense going there.

On the next day he suffered severe diarrhoea with mucus and blood in addition to the previous two days' constant vomiting. That looked much like dysentery so Marina called a friend, a Russian physician living in London. He checked Sasha and said they should call for an ambulance immediately. At that stage, Sasha was feeling so bad he couldn't even walk. Litvinenko told his wife, 'Marina, when I was at a military school, we learned about such cases. It looks like a chemical weapon.' She said, 'Saaasha, what chemical weapon, please, you must be joking!'

At 10:30 a.m. Scaramella called from the IMO conference lobby. Marina took the receiver and said that Sasha was very ill and that the ambulance was there. She also told him that half London was in bed with stomach flu with symptoms like vomiting and diarrhoea – a doctor would call it 'gastric flu' though it is not really the flu but an infection in the intestines.

The second ambulance took Litvinenko to the local hospital on Wellhouse Lane in Barnet. The *NHS Choices* website modestly describes its cleanliness and comfort as average. The paramedics transported the new patient to A&E.

According to the official record, Litvinenko was admitted to hospital that day, 3 November, with what doctors at first believed was a simple case of gastro-enteritis – inflammation of the stomach and intestines. But tests revealed that the initial diagnosis was wrong. Dr Andres Virchis, the consultant haematologist and cancer specialist who treated Sasha said: 'He was actually about to be discharged on November 7 because he was suffering from just diarrhoea and vomiting. Then we got the result of a test, which revealed a bug that needed treatment. That was the first time he said who he was and wondered if he could have been infected with this on purpose.'[1] The doctor mentioned that Litvinenko was registered at hospital under his English name: Edwin R. Carter.

On 6 November Litvinenko phoned Oleg Gordievsky at his house in Surrey. Sasha complained that he was suffering from something weird and said he was suspicious that it might be deliberate poisoning. He told Oleg Antonovich that the only man who could have poisoned him was Mario Scaramella. Gordievsky, who disliked the Italian, agreed. He then called Marina at home and said that it could indeed be poisoning. Marina grew very worried.

Dr Virchis recalled: 'He mentioned that he heard of the bug before and of potential other cases of people being purposely infected and wondered if that had happened to him. Knowing who he was, there was some concern, but it was just a concern.'[2]

On the day that Litvinenko was about to be discharged, 7 November, Lugovoy called his mobile and Marina took the phone. When she recognised who was calling, she passed it over to her husband. Sasha said he had been unconscious for two days and that he suspected he had been poisoned. He added that now he was feeling better and would probably be back at home soon. They agreed to call each other in a week.

In the meantime, Sasha and Marina became increasingly concerned that there was something seriously amiss.

'We told the doctors,' Marina recalled, ' "Please check him for possible poison-ing, it is not a typical case . . ." They only listened. I now blame myself, why didn't I start screaming, why didn't I insist . . . They told me that on Tuesday they would let him go home.'

Tuesday, 7 November, was to be a long day.

'At 7:00 p.m. a group of doctors came. They said they had two pieces of news – one good and one bad. Bad news was that they would not let him go home. Good news, according to them, was that they knew for sure what was wrong with him. They said it was a virulent bacterium in his intestines,' Marina said. 'Back home I checked via the internet and learned that only antibiotics could cause this bacterium's toxic activity. But Sasha didn't take any antibiotics before he was accepted to the hospital.'

Nobody in the City of London and its thirty-two boroughs, not a single one of its proud 7.5 million citizens paid any attention to a sick young man in a three-storey building in the north of the great metropolis. However, in the Kremlin, Lubyanka and Yasenevo three senior officers in civil suits impatiently looked at their calendars. They did not need to phone one another to know exactly what each of them thought.

Berezovsky had not heard the news before he returned to London from an overseas trip and visited his friend at the Barnet hospital. Knowing well enough – at least from his years at the top in Russia – whom they were dealing with, Boris still did not believe in poisoning until it was too late. They may paint him as a devil but Boris Berezovsky is a very peaceful man who hates all forms of violence. His tour de force is always in self-defence.

On 11 November Akhmed Zakayev's website, Chechenpress.info, published the news that Litvinenko had been poisoned. The BBC Russian Service quickly got the tip and phoned Litvinenko at his hospital bed:

Q: Hello, how are you?

A: I am listening.

Q: Russian press is reporting that there has been an attempt to poison you. Is this information correct?

A: Look, now after a serious poisoning I am still in very bad shape, I feel badly and I am staying at one of London's clinics.

Q: Do you think what happened is connected to any event? There are reports that there was a plan to give you some documents about the murder of Russian journalist Anna Politkovskaya and after that you felt sick?

A: I was contacted by a person, he suggested a meeting, the meeting happened on the 1st of November at one of London restaurants. He passed me some papers, where the person was named, who apparently might be connected to the murder of Anna Politkovskaya. That's it. After several hours I felt sick with symptoms of poisoning.

Q: Could you tell us where this happened? In what area of London?

A: In the centre, in central London.

Q: Whereabouts?

A: I don't want to name the restaurant. Police are investigating this right now – let them work, let them work without distraction

Q: Was it Westminster or Chelsea?

A: I told you, police are investigating, let them work quietly.

Q: I understand.

A: When I feel better, when I am back home, I will pass these papers to *Novaya Gazeta* [the newspaper where Politkovskaya worked]. To police and to *Novaya Gazeta* – that's all.

Q: But to your mind these two events are connected?

A: I don't know whether they are connected. I guess you can make your own conclusion on this.

Q: But the name which is quoted in Russian press, does it make sense?

A: It does.

Q: And the documents – are they solid, can you trust them?

A: The documents are in English. I did not even manage to study them properly because when I was home I felt sick in just a few hours.

Q: Many thanks. Take care. Get well soon.[3]

The police were not investigating anything at the time but Litvinenko expected that after their telephone conversation almost a week ago Gordievsky could have at least informed the security service, MI5. It was a vain hope.

Radio *Ekho Moskvy* ('The Echo of Moscow') listened to their British colleagues and correctly decided to ask a person who should be best of all informed of what had been going on in the Berezovsky circle. Alex Goldfarb said he got their call in Paris.

But his recollections of the events are almost certainly not accurate.

In his book Alex writes that the Moscow radio station called him on Saturday, 11 November 2006, while he was en route to London. Alex also says that he didn't know anything about his friend's condition so he went on to the internet to check.[4]

I have every reason to believe that the call was made on Friday and that Goldfarb was in London on the same day to communicate with Berezovsky, Zakayev and Marina. She almost certainly informed Gordievsky and he promptly sent me an email before leaving for Cambridge were he was expected to lecture at the intelligence seminar chaired by Professor Christopher Andrew on Friday evening.

The day to 'Meet the Press' was set up for Saturday. On 11 November, after the news appeared on the Chechenpress site, the BBC Russian Service called and then the RFE/RL to whom Sasha repeated the story in a shorter version. In the evening I saw Goldfarb in the news relating the poisoning theory to the mainstream media. Those who followed the events also read the information published by the KavkazCenter.com site on the same morning pointing a finger at Mario Scaramella and claiming that the Italian was 'a close associate of the FSB deputy chief Victor Kolmogorov and visited the FSB headquarters in Moscow several times'. This was wrong: Mario never met Kolmogorov and had never been at the Lubyanka.

The problem in mid-November was that Berezovsky, Sasha and Marina trusted Lugovoy completely. According to Akhmed Zakayev, Lugovoy was their closest friend. On 1 November Lugovoy and Sasha had discussed some promising business plans that would improve Sasha's financial situation. He was earning money only from occasional consulting jobs for a security company, and that, together with Marina's dancing lessons, usually brought in less than £1,500 a month. That was a miserable sum compared to what he had been earning from Berezovsky's office. Such a helpful and trusted friend as Lugovoy, who called several times after Sasha got into hospital, simply could *not* be a poisoner. So a scapegoat had to be found.

'It wasn't until about 10 or 11 November that it became clear this was not just gastroenteritis: he was becoming more and more ill, his hair began to fall out and his blood counts were beginning to drop,' Dr Virchis said. 'That was when it became very clear there was more to this than meets the eye.' Like many people, the doctor was not too careful about the dates, but it is strange that he was equally inattentive to symptoms.

'Some time later, he started feeling better,' recalled Marina. 'The doctors even allowed him to use a communal toilet instead of an individual [one] . . . Then on Saturday, 11 November, he complained that he had a sore throat and it was painful to swallow. They said it was also because of antibiotics.'

'When I came to visit him on Monday, 13 November, I experienced a real shock,' she said. 'He could not open his mouth, couldn't speak or call a nurse. The whole of his mucous membrane was inflamed. I started to shout, the doctors came and explained that it could also be a reaction to the antibiotics.'

'On the same day [13 November] he started to lose hair. I asked the doctors and they told me that his tests showed that his immune system was failing. His skin became yellow. So the doctors started to check him for AIDS, suspecting that he got infected with HIV . . .'

On Monday, 13 November, the Russian media reported that Scotland Yard had been contacted but had refused to confirm that they were starting an investigation of Litvinenko's poisoning. The police acted correctly. There was no information from the hospital about poisoning therefore no reason to open a case.

'Sasha used to joke,' said Marina, 'This bacterium that got inside me has Russian [KGB uniform] shoulder-straps. Strange that the British doctors do not understand it . . .'

With his hair falling out, he was moved to the department of oncology. There they made tests for toxins. Marina suggested that it would perhaps be better to move him to a specialised hospital. The doctors responded that if and when they consider it necessary to do so, they would.

There must have been a storm of anger and frustration in the Yasenevo Russian foreign intelligence headquarters among the handful of informed senior officers when the news reached them that on the evening of 14 November a Russian illegal posing as a Canadian citizen 'Paul William Hampel' had been arrested at the Pierre Elliott Trudeau International airport in Montreal just prior to boarding an outbound flight. When searched, the counter-intelligence officers found in his possession a fraudulent Ontario birth certificate, a large sum of US dollars in five currencies, a short-wave radio, two digital cameras, three mobile phones and five SIM cards that are used to store information in mobile phones, according to the Associated Press report.

After three weeks in detention and vehemently denying any wrongdoings, the man, speaking to the authorities through a solicitor, finally admitted, according to the Agence France-Press, that 'he is not Paul William Hampel, that he is a Russian citizen, born on October 21, 1961, and that he has no legal status in Canada. He is ready to leave Canada, but he does not admit being a spy,' his lawyer added. The Russian ambassador also denied that Hampel was a spy, saying that type of Cold War espionage was over.[5]

Hampel had a consultancy in Dublin, Ireland being a traditional training ground for Soviet illegals. He was finally deported to Moscow and the scandal was hushed up. As part of the deal, the Federal Court Justice decided to 'seal' the man's real name. There should have been tremendous pressure on the Canadian authorities, as the illegal was arrested when Sasha was in hospital struggling for his life. But neither the police, nor the MI5 were informed about it.

On Wednesday, 15 November, Sasha was feeling lousy and Goldfarb began to be slightly worried. As he put it: two weeks was just a bit too long for food poisoning:

> What I saw when I arrived at Barnet Hospital did not make me feel better. They kept Sasha in an infection-safe environment. I had to put on plastic gloves and an apron before entering the ward, and refrain from touching him, to protect him from accidentally catching a bug from outside.
>
> 'He is neutropenic,' the doctor said, meaning that his white blood cells count was down. This happens when the bone marrow stops producing cells needed to fight off infection. No food poisoning would cause such a symptom.[6]

Goldfarb asked whether the hospital had notified the police.

'At this point the cause can be benign or sinister,' he was told. 'We can't contact them until we are sure. We're waiting for a toxicology report.'

Though there were a lot of people around, Litvinenko seemed to have been alone. No Chervonenko was nearby to pray for him and beg his angels for help. Or even better, to make a swift and sound decision.

The next morning Goldfarb went to the hospital with Berezovsky, who like himself had initially discounted Litvinenko's illness as a stomach bug. Sasha was visibly worse. He was suffering tremendously from an apparent inflammation of his gastrointestinal tract, all the way from his mouth, which was so painful he could barely talk or swallow, down to his bowels. It was as if his insides had been burned by an unknown irritant. The doctors had started him on painkillers. They still did not know the cause of it all.[7]

On the same day, 16 November, Goldfarb contacted Professor John Henry, a London toxicologist who had correctly diagnosed the cause of Victor Yushchenko's sufferings simply by studying his photographs and reading a short medical report. Based on Litvinenko's symptoms Henry speculated that he had been poisoned with thallium. The Barnet hospital specialists agreed. Tests sent to Guy's Hospital, in Central London, confirmed those fears, showing significantly excess levels of the heavy metal in Sasha's body. On the same day this information was officially sent to the police.

According to Marina Litvinenko, in the evening a nurse came and said that Sasha had tested positive for thallium and that he should take an antidote, which in the case of thallium poisoning was Prussian blue. They didn't have it in capsules, only in powder that looks like tiny needles and is very painful to swallow, especially with such an inflammation. The level of thallium was three times higher than the normal level, Marina said.

By the 13th, three Moscow papers had picked up the story – *Kommersant*, *Moscow Times* and the *Moscow News* – but no one from the mainstream British media, not to mention the American press, agreed to publish anything until the police got involved. The Chechen site, KavkazCenter.com, who did daily coverage as the poisoning story progressed, wrote bitterly that Scotland Yard proved 'unable to find any sign of a crime related to Litvinenko' quoting a Russian newspaper whose reporters rushed to London for the news after the BBC interview.[8]

In his book, Alex describes visiting Litvinenko at the Barnet hospital on 15 November, when they tried to reconstruct Sasha's movements in London on the tragic day of his poisoning. 'His last meeting with Lugovoy,' writes Goldfarb, 'was on November 1, in the Pine Bar of the Millennium Hotel on Piccadilly, two hours after he went out with Mario Scaramella. Lugovoy was with another Russian, Sasha said, whom Sasha had not met before. "He had the eyes of a killer," he said. He knew the type.'[9] Marina also recalled that Sasha did not like the man, whose name he could not remember and who was only interested in 'wedge' or 'dough' – money in normal language. He called them *babki* in Russian.

Books are often written in a hurry and human memory is not perfect. There are also psychological factors that sometimes prevent us from seeing the real picture. The Millennium Mayfair Hotel is on Grosvenor Square, not Piccadilly, and Litvinenko was in the Pine Bar less than thirty minutes after he left Mario. The 'other Russian' who was with Lugovoy in the bar was not someone Sasha had not met, but Dmitry Kovtun, with whom he had had a few meals and spent quite some time, calling him Dima – a diminutive form for Dmitry, but also for Vadim.

The problem with Goldfarb's account was that both Marina and Alex knew only about the afternoon meeting in the Pine Bar. When Litvinenko told them that Lugovoy brought along a man whom Sasha had never seen before and who had 'the eyes of a killer', he was thinking of the man he had met in Lugovoy's hotel room four hours *before* the second meeting. Neither Marina nor Alex could follow him, as they knew nothing about that early meeting. And neither of them had ever heard of Kovtun so for them he was a new man. But not for Sasha. Substitution, tricky substitution.

The two names – 'Vadim' and 'Vladimir' – later appeared in the media. I told Gordievsky the whole story but he forgetfully started to call the illegal, whom Sasha met early on that day in room 441 in the company of Lugovoy, 'Vladimir' or 'Vadim' in his interviews. This explains the confusion. Anyway, I like VLADIMIR as the codename for the Litvinenko operation – for this case, it makes a lot of sense.

According to Alex Goldfarb, the police never gave Marina any hint in support of the third-man theory, but they did not dispute it, either.

After talking to Professor Henry and getting a laboratory confirmation about thallium, Goldfarb managed to bring David Leppard, assistant editor (home affairs) of the *Sunday Times* – well known for his passion for explosive news – to the hospital to interview Sasha.

But before the reporter had a chance to see Litvinenko, others had gathered for a strategy meeting to discuss further actions: Berezovsky, Goldfarb and Lord Timothy ('Tim') John Leigh Bell, founder of Bell Pottinger Public Affairs and Boris's media adviser. Goldfarb recalls:

> Tim Bell was extremely concerned.
>
> 'Boris,' he said, 'you have cast yourself as the archenemy of Putin: politically, personally, and ideologically. Reasonable people believe that you are on the good side in this crusade, even though they may question your motives. For the people at large, this is all pretty irrelevant because it's all about politics in a faraway land. But this time, the situation is very different. A crime has been committed on British soil, an attempted murder. The story will reach many people, who will react intuitively. The problem is, most people will not *want* to believe it was Putin. People are instinctively averse to the idea of governments or presidents ordering murders. The more it seems obvious, the deeper they will go into denial. You will be going against the tide, and you are the anti-Putin. If people don't want to think it was Putin, then they'll think it must be you. The louder you say it was him, the more this will happen.'[10]

David Leppard finally got his story. 'Scotland Yard is investigating a suspected plot to assassinate a former Russian spy in Britain by poisoning him with thallium, the deadly metal,' he wrote in the Sunday paper. 'A toxicology test at Guy's hospital last Thursday confirmed the presence of the odourless, tasteless poison.' David got it wrong and caused speculation and confusion. The laboratory test had in fact revealed only that the amount of thallium in Sasha's body was considerably higher than the norm. That was all.

Professor Henry was later interviewed for *Vanity Fair* article by Bryan Burrough. 'That was my fault,' the expert said, sighing. 'I spent all day Saturday on-camera giving interviews. Thallium, thallium, thallium. Saturday evening I got to see the man. I told Goldfarb he should be transferred to a private hospital. Goldfarb said there was no need. The doctors were saying he'd have muscle pain for months, but that he'd live.' Later the doctors backtracked and transferred Litvinenko to University College Hospital, a facility better suited to treat him.'[11]

Again, people tend to confuse things. Goldfarb picked up Henry on Saturday morning to bring him to the University College London Hospital (UCLH). Thallium, he explained as they drove, 'is tasteless, colourless, odourless. It takes about a gram to kill you. For the first ten days or so it looks like a typical case of food poisoning. Hair begin to fall out only after two weeks, which gives the assailant ample time to get away. It's poisoner's ideal weapon,' he said.[12]

Marina Litvinenko told me that the police started to act only when they were informed by the hospital about the alleged thallium poisoning. The armed and uniformed police escort arrived at the Barnet Hospital on Friday, 17 November, and without any ceremony transported Litvinenko and his wife to UCLH in Euston. She was frightened.

On a beautiful spring afternoon a few months later, I was drinking coffee with Marina in the cosy Richoux on South Audley Street not far from the Millennium Mayfair Hotel where it all happened. She was still wearing dark glasses most of the time with tears dancing in her eyes.

'They put me in a police car and drove to Euston with sirens, beacons and very high speed as if in a police operation,' Marina said. 'Another group went to Muswell Hill and took Tolik from Akhmed's house. We were practically under arrest. They were the local Haringey police and they didn't know what was going on. [Procedures, damn procedures. But they were right.] Then Alik [Alex Goldfarb] came to the hospital and bumped into two antiterrorist unit officers from the Yard who had just arrived. Very soon they took over and all was cleared up.'

'Look, I'm sorry,' one of the officers said to Goldfarb. 'They've overdone it a bit. They were told to secure the witness.'

'Why are you holding the kid?'

'He was at a police station, and they are bringing him back to Mr. Zakayev's house right now. I apologise again.'[13]

I later found out that the detective's name was Holmes. Not Sherlock. Detective Superintendent Mark Holmes.

In the meantime Akhmed joined Goldfarb in the hospital. A moment later Marina appeared shaken, but trying to smile. 'Thank you for rescuing me, boys,' she said. It was past midnight.[14]

During one of our meetings in Oslo, Ivar Amundsen, a Norwegian businessman and the president of the Chechnya Peace Forum as well as Zakayev's Honorary Consul to his country, told me that the police were investigating the area around the Millennium Hotel already on the weekend of 18–19 November. The detectives soon learned that the CCTV footage of the early days of the month had been destroyed, as according to the instructions it must have only been kept for two weeks. Ivar didn't know the procedures inside the hotel.

Marina told me: 'When they finally decided to move Sasha to the new facility, the doctors kept on telling me that his condition was not deteriorating. I quickly understood that even in this new and modern hospital they had no idea what was going on with my husband.'

In UCLH, Litvinenko immediately recognised Henry's authority. 'I know you'll get me out of this, Professor,' he said.

'You are doing well,' responded Henry cheering him up. 'Let me see how strong you are. Squeeze my hand. Oh, you are strong!'

But out of the ward, Professor Henry looked perplexed.

'It looks very strange. They are treating him for thallium, but with thallium he should have lost his muscle strength, and he has not.'[15]

As soon as he was transferred to the new hospital, the Metropolitan Police started to interview Litvinenko at once. The officer in charge was Detective Inspector Brent Hyatt. Like every professional he knew only too well the chilling fact of secret operations: there may never be a 'next time'. The hunt for a perpetrator was codenamed Operation WHIMBREL.

DI Hyatt and a colleague set up temporary headquarters in a room next to Litvinenko's in order to stay close at all times. With the officers at his bedside, Sasha was in the unenviable and utterly improbable position of being the prime witness in his own murder investigation.[16]

On Monday, 20 November, Berezovsky visited Litvinenko at the hospital again. On the same day Sasha was photographed by Natasja Weitsz, a young graduate of the University of Johannesburg who worked up at Snappy Snaps round the corner of Tim Bell's office.

Yet by Monday, 20 November Litvinenko was finding it ever more difficult to speak. His mouth was flecked with foam. He had survived almost three days of intensive questioning, but now he was weakening. Long before Litvinenko asked his family and friends what his chances were, the police officers with him knew he was going to die. The case, meanwhile, had burgeoned into a major crime. Over the weekend, three or four officers had been involved. By Monday, sixty police officers were following leads from Litvinenko's testimony. Police also spoke separately and at length to Marina Litvinenko and perused her husband's diary, assembling a clear picture of Litvinenko crisscrossing London's West End with his contacts from Moscow in the two weeks before he became ill.[17]

On Tuesday, 21 November, however, Sasha was still talking to the detectives answering their questions for about three hours. According to Alan Cowell, months later Detective Inspector Hyatt told his friends he had never realised 'that a human being could be quite that brave and quite that dignified' while enduring such pain.

While Litvinenko was using the last chance to help the police, Dr Amit Nathwani, whose speciality is cancer and clinical haematology, one of the team of the physicians treating the former KGB officer, said on camera: 'The levels of thallium we are able to detect are not the levels we expect to see in toxicity.' In other words, not poisoned. I immediately recalled Dr Wicke from Vienna. He was also a radiologist but not an internist, like Dr Nathwani was not a specialist in clandestine poisonings by radiological weapons. (Unlike Wicke, however, Dr Nathwani was right that the levels of thallium found in Sasha's body proved that thallium was not the toxin used to attack Litvinenko.)

The day before Professor Henry had called Goldfarb: 'I checked my books,' he said. 'Thallium is a gamma-emitter. They would have detected it in the hospital. But they should keep looking for alpha-emitters. I will have to talk to Scotland Yard.' By that time Henry realised it could have been a radioactive poison.[18]

On the morning of Wednesday, 22 November, the *Wall Street Journal* came out with my article 'Russian Venom: Who wants to kill Alexander Litvinenko.' The article read:

> When I heard the other day that Alexander's condition was worsening, I thought that the doctors had perhaps made the same mistake as in the Khokhlov case. Thallium has never been known to attack the blood stream, but that's what's happening to Alexander Litvinenko. Specialists at the American military hospital in Frankfurt only later discovered that Mr. Khokhlov was exposed to radioactivated thallium, which initially only results in non-specific gastrointestinal symptoms. Only later did they observe a moderate elevation of blood lipids, leukocytosis and anaemia that occurs in most high-level intoxications. By the time the symptoms known to be after-effects of radiation began to appear, the radioactivated thallium had already disintegrated making it very hard for doctors to find and for investigators to confirm the poisoning. The same scenario may be playing out with Litvinenko.[19]

In the same article I also stated that it was likely to be the work of the Russian secret service that had been after Sasha for years and that this poisoning looked to be directed against Boris Berezovsky.

But even before the article appeared in print, I sent several messages to the BBC hotline that had been established after it was clear that Litvinenko had indeed been poisoned. All in vain. The messages were censored and I never got any comment from the editors.

They decided to comment only when the *Wall Street Journal* article was reprinted by two English-language newspapers in Russia – the *Moscow Times* and the *St Petersburg Times* on 23 November: 'Boris Volodarsky is alone in openly accusing the FSB of poisoning Mr Litvinenko . . . asking if the Russian leader is in control of his "squabbling entourage" '. The BBC didn't bother to mention my radioactive poison version.

On the same day Litvinenko's heart stopped. Marina was called to the hospital at 11:50 p.m. She telephoned Akhmed Zakayev and they went together. When they arrived, Litvinenko's heart stopped for the second time.

'When I was leaving the hospital on Thursday [23 November] at 2:00 a.m., Sasha was not able to speak. The doctors said, however, that his condition was normal and they were only concerned about his blood pressure,' Marina said later.

She recalled that though still remaining quite motionless, her husband looked much better. At 9:21 p.m. he died. His father was at his bedside.

'Three hours before he passed away the specialized laboratory [the Atomic Weapons Establishment (AWE), which is under the authority of the Procurement Executive of the MoD, located at Aldermaston, in Berkshire] managed to figure out polonium-210. But still the doctors didn't know anything. We were allowed to see and kiss him without any protection or anything,' Marina told me.

'After 2:00 a.m. on the same night the police came to me to announce I must collect some of my possessions and leave the house. I said, "Why, what's wrong, for three weeks no one took any care of us, what's going on?" And then they said, "We never came across such a thing, we do not know what it is and what can be the consequences." And then they named polonium.'[20]

***

Damn Monday! When those in Moscow who knew about the operation in the ISLAND got to their offices on 20 November, they did not like the morning reports from London at all. The article in the *Sunday Times* made it clear that Litvinenko was still – and quite miraculously – alive, the police and the services were at work and that in spite of all assurances that the new very special toxin would be impossible to identify, it might soon be found out. No one was able to imagine what would really follow, but each man had an unpleasant sensation in his chest – a kind of spontaneous panic. 'Firekin ell, as they say in that Goddamn country,' they thought. 'Why do the British always drive on the wrong side of the road?' They, three of the most powerful people of Russia could do nothing but sit and wait.

During the last decade of November several groups of men and women concerned with the Litvinenko case began to move, and move fast.

First and by far the most effective was the Metropolitan Police. 'Tomorrow's threat may include the use of chemicals, bacteriological agents, radioactive materials and even nuclear technology,' Dame Eliza Lydia Manningham-Buller, then director general of MI5, proclaimed in a speech in early November, and the police were on high alert. On 2 October the new Counter Terrorism Command was launched, taking over the roles and responsibilities of the Anti-Terrorist

Branch and Special Branch. It became known as SO15, an internal police service designation reflecting the fact that it was one of a number of Special Operations branches within the Met. The new unit – headed by deputy assistant commissioner Peter Clarke – employed 1,500 staff in London. They all received new badges and identity cards packed in imposing-looking black leather covers.

As the detectives were going about their business – some still in the hospital, others interviewing everybody who knew Litvinenko and was in recent contact with him – Clarke, a father of three, looking more like a school teacher than a policeman, created what was called a 'gold' group, drawing in representatives from the HPA, the Atomic Weapons Establishment, the NHS and the Foreign Office. To maintain coordination with the investigators, scientists moved into offices on the eleventh floor of New Scotland Yard. For the first time the police also set up a new kind of unit called a Knowledge Management Centre where one group of analysts would bring together and quickly process all incoming intelligence in one place. Clarke himself liaised directly with his opposite numbers at Thames House on Millbank, the London headquarters of the security service.²¹

Reporters were the second very active group. As soon as David Leppard published his article, all hell broke loose. The journalists readily dived into the murky waters of international espionage – a classically erotic topic in the UK – turning themselves into detectives and collecting every scrap of news. For months there were lines of waiting cars and vans at Gordievsky's house with reporting teams from all over the world including Japan, Australia and South Africa. Until the end of January I was banned by my contract with *Panorama* from meeting the press, so when not working in the studio's little villa on Woodstock Grove, I spent my time in the evenings helping Oleg cope with the media.

Gordievsky's position was always firm and unbending regarding the perpetrators. As the highest-ranking British defector from the KGB, Gordievsky could speak with authority and conviction about his former service. When he stated that it had been the work of his one-time colleagues, there was little room for doubt. Even without any specific knowledge of the operational details it was sufficient to persuade the public. Besides, he knew Sasha personally and that added extra value and weight to his words. But he had a tendency to improvise and in this case stated as fact what in reality were his suppositions, that the polonium used against Sasha 'cost millions of dollars,' that a man allegedly seen with Kovtun at Heathrow (Kovtun wasn't there at the time) was an illegal whom the police suspected of murdering Sasha, and that that illegal carried a Lithuanian passport. Many analysts, historians and press people followed these apparent leads but naturally came to nothing.

One day Steve LeVine, then a reporter for the *Wall Street Journal,* came to interview Oleg for his book on the Litvinenko case. Oleg was eager to see a new man from Washington. He met Steve wearing a dark blue double-breasted blazer, a peach shirt and a red silk hanky sprouting from his jacket pocket. Steve observed:

There was no visible security at his home, but I knew this man – the West's biggest Cold War catch ever – he was well protected by surveillance. Gordievsky was cordial, inclined towards coarse humour punctuated with heavy laughs. At dinner with his English girlfriend [his companion Maureen] along, he whispered conspiratorially alerting me that she shouldn't hear.

'Russians want to hear rough language. They think it brings life to the conversation,' he said, giving both sides of his face a light slap for emphasis. 'This is why Russian men can speak impolitely to their wives,' he said.[22]

Besides this valuable information Gordievsky revealed that 'he had two opposing theories: that Lugovoy was the team leader in "a typical KGB operation", or had been used as bait to befriend Litvinenko and finally lure him to the bar, where the actual assassins could do their work'. In support of the latter scenario – which in fact was mine — Gordievsky cited Lugovoy's 'slow approach, the cultivation of Litvinenko for ten months, enticing him, promising him deals'. Once Lugovoy had cemented his relationship with Litvinenko, the trap was sprung, he surmised.[23]

Oleg forgot that there were no 'actual assassins' in the Pine Bar and that at least two factors left little doubt of when and how Litvinenko was poisoned: the time when Sasha started leaving radioactive traces and *the witness*, interviewed by the police.

Nick Priest, a bespectacled and affable professor of environmental toxicology at London's Middlesex University, interviewed for the BBC *Panorama* programme, made a serious contribution to the understanding of the polonium issue. First of all, he explained that though polonium-210 is an alpha emitter, once in about 100,000 decays it lets out gamma ray. For me, this meant that those who had sent the deadly vial to London could not rely on its passing through the airport controls undetected – and must have opted for the only two other channels of transportation – the VOLNA ('Wave')[24] or a courier arriving by car or ferry. The diplomatic bag and the Eurostar may be left alone as both are surely controlled for radiation.

The second thing that Nick confirmed is that polonium, as used in the Litvinenko poisoning, was not expensive. 'It would have cost only a few thousand dollars,' he said.

Finally, Professor Priest made a curious supposition. He speculated that before it was taken to London, the poison would have been divided between four people. He never explained why four, and not two or five, but elaborated that the toxin had to be recombined in a hotel room. According to this expert, that's when the trouble would have begun: at the moment the seal was broken the spider of contamination started to spin its web of 'soiling'. The first release of minute traces of polonium would be dancing around central London and elsewhere thanks to Lugovoy and Kovtun – and then be possible to follow.

Whatever the method of delivery, Priest's supposition explained perfectly why and how the pair got contaminated on 16 November and why they hurriedly left the Shaftesbury Hotel in Soho hours after they arrived there, and why they moved to the much more expensive Parkes Hotel on the other side of the city, otherwise too luxurious and sophisticated for such travellers.

Steve LeVine also interviewed Nick Priest.

'It's entirely possible,' the scientist told him, 'that they didn't know what they were handling or [else] they would have taken precautions. It's possible they were only told it was poison. Otherwise they might have been frightened. Also, if you knew the properties of polonium, you would change your clothes [after lacing the tea], and then throw them away. You'd use gloves. You'd have to be an idiot to leave a contamination trail behind.'[25]

I doubt that they were ever told it was poison and certainly they had no idea it was a radiological weapon. Weeks after the events while undergoing tests in Moscow Hospital No. 6, Kovtun continued to call the substance 'poloniumum' in his interview to the Spiegel TV.

While I was working on the BBC *Panorama*, two curious episodes took place outside the 3BM studio.

The first happened one night as I came home from work and was met by Gordievsky announcing that a Spiegel TV team was waiting for me in an ambush with mikes and cameras ready. While Oleg was dealing with them Anna Sadovnikova, their Hamburg reporter, startled me in our unmarked car parked at a distance from the house, and tried to recruit me for her programme. Though I categorically refused, she later helped a lot by sending some very useful footage that she made with Lugovoy and Kovtun in the sauna telling her about their London experience.

During that interview Kovtun admitted that together with his friend they drank six glasses of gin in the Pine Bar. He suddenly said he had his own partner in London with whom he had been discussing oil and gas deals. (In the meantime, Spiegel TV had learned that Kovtun had worked as a waiter in Hamburg.) Completely out of the blue the German announcer suggested that the cost of polonium-210 in the Litvinenko case could be 30 million Euros. These were quite spontaneous improvisations.

My second strange episode was my clandestine meeting in Mayfair with a young editor from the *Mail on Sunday*. We met in a bar; he ordered whisky and soda for himself, tomato juice for me, after which he decided to pitch me on the spot. Without pause he suggested that I 'consult' him on a daily basis about the course of the investigation for which he promised to pay a very substantial fee. I agreed and gave him my article to publish in his newspaper. He took it and disappeared – and never came back.

Another of the groups that went into action was the Russians. But they were quite slow gathering speed, waiting for fresh instructions from Moscow's disinformation specialists. The whole Russian propaganda machine immersed in the task of covering up the Litvinenko murder. Overall command was placed in the hands of goggle-eyed Dmitry Peskov, first deputy press secretary of President Putin.

Peskov was not not only acting for Putin, the Russian president, but for Putin personally. Shortly before his boss moved to the PM's office, Peskov also moved there, where he would become the press attaché of the chairman of the Russian government, i.e. Putin again. Peskov has been Putin's personal press chief since April 2000.

Like Limarev and Margelov, Peskov graduated from the Institute of Asia and Africa at Moscow State University and then joined the foreign ministry in 1989. Born in 1967, he is generally considered a career diplomat but he had ample chance to graduate from the AVR (Foreign Intelligence Academy) when he spent two years in Moscow between 1994 and 1996, after his first posting in Turkey. When Litvinenko was talking to the Americans in Ankara on his way to Britain, Peskov was first secretary of the Russian Embassy there, traditionally an SVR slot. Since we first met in Vienna in 2005, Peskov's eye-popping progressed – and so did his career.

When news about Sasha's poisoning leaked into the media, the Kremlin decided to keep a low profile and tried to duplicate their success in the case of Anna Politkovskaya. Shortly after that extraordinary assassination most Russians were manipulated to believe that the courageous journalist was an American spy and a traitor to her country. Putin first refused to comment and when pressed muttered something like 'murder is a very grave crime before society and before God. The criminals should be found'. As observers quickly noted, the Russian president could have left it there but chose to add: 'Politkovskaya's political influence inside the country was of little significance. She was more known in human-rights circles and to the Western media. And I think that Politkovskaya's murder caused more harm to the Russian and Chechen authorities than her publications.'

The Kremlin chose the same tone to cover up the Litvinenko murder. Speaking at a press conference in Helsinki, Putin said: 'Alas, Mr. Litvinenko is not Lazarus. Unfortunately, tragic events are used for political provocations.' It is unclear which of the two men named Lazarus from the New Testament Putin had in mind and why he cited either of them. (Was the atheist former KGB spy comparing himself to Jesus Christ and Litvinenko to Lazarus of Bethany? It is not inconceivable, because only a few months later he claimed to be the world's only 'pure' democrat and compared himself to Mahatma Gandhi.) Putin also added that he had seen no evidence that it was a 'violent death'. In Moscow, they had evidently not expected the use of polonium to surface, so they were poorly prepared. The fact that the Russian secret services took the unprecedented step of publicly denying that they had anything to do with Litvinenko's murder, with

Peskov calling the very idea of Russia's involvement in this crime 'nonsense,' is highly unusual.

It didn't take too long for the Russian propaganda and disinformation specialists to realise that they had irrevocably lost the first half of the match played against the Western media.

With the so-called Russian 'political technologists' having shown themselves incapable of influencing the West, the Kremlin, in or about May 2006, commissioned Ketchum, the American PR company with truly global reach, to 'repackage an autocratic East European leader [Putin] with a new image that would make him palatable to a Western audience', as the *Guardian* put it. According to some sources, the contract was worth £4 million.

This had become necessary because the G8 was to meet in June 2006 in St Petersburg. Russia held the presidency but the contract with Ketchum, for whatever reason, was to run until December. Was it a sheer coincidence, considering the dates of the Litvinenko operation? A reporter from the *Guardian* found out that the campaign was being handled by Ketchum's Brussels-based sister company, GPlus, which was co-founded by Peter Guilford, a former civil servant at the European Commission. He in turn subcontracted the British part of the business to Portland PR, which was established by Tim Allan, Tony Blair's former deputy press secretary. Allan, a New Labour stalwart, became head of corporate communications at BSkyB after he left politics, and has impeccable contacts in the press, particularly among the lobby correspondents with whom he used to cross swords.[26]

Peskov was placed personally in charge of all the Western contractors. As the paper described the team:

Tim Allan: Founded Portland PR after a successful stint at BSkyB, where he was director of corporate communications. But his background is in politics. He was the Prime Minister's spokesman and spent a period as Alastair Campbell's deputy. He worked as Tony Blair's research assistant during the Labour leader's years in opposition.

Peter Guilford: A civil servant in Brussels for over a decade, Guilford is a former spokesman for the European Commission. He spoke on trade issues before being appointed deputy spokesman for the former Commission president Romano Prodi. Guilford resigned in 2000 to help set up the lobbying firm GPlus.

Angus Roxburgh: A journalist for 20 years, Roxburgh was a Brussels-based Europe correspondent for the BBC before joining GPlus earlier this year. He was the corporation's main Moscow correspondent for nearly six years. He is also the author of the books *Pravda: Inside the Soviet News Machine* (1987) and *The Second Russian Revolution* (1991).[27]

It was Tim Allan who advised the prime minister to appoint Benjamin Wegg-Prosser to the post of director of strategic communications at 10 Downing Street in the autumn of 2005. Wegg-Prosser is known as a Russia champion who is married to a Russian woman. Their wedding was in Moscow. Prior to Downing Street, Wegg-Prosser worked at the *Guardian* as publisher of its politics website. When this book was being sent to press, he was Director of Corporate Development for SUP Fabrik, a Moscow-based internet company founded in 2006.

Mary Dejevsky, a London-based journalist, admitted that she did not like spy stories and never liked covering them as a reporter. However, she made a solid contribution to the Litvinenko story, writing extensively on the topic. Her first article 'Caution . . . handle allegations of poisoning with care' appeared in *The Independent* on 20 November 2006 when Sasha was still alive. Dejevsky wrote:

> The new James Bond film is playing to rapturous audiences across the country and right on cue a real-life tale bursts on to the scene from the sleazier end of the 007 repertoire. Alexander Litvinenko, a former Russian secret agent granted asylum in this country, is in a London hospital after supping with a fellow spook at a sushi bar in Piccadilly.

She moved on from this to develop her thesis, overlooking facts, calling Litvinenko a 'spy' and ignoring the difference between political asylum and defection: 'Spies who have defected I find doubly sinister: once someone has betrayed one set of loyalties, how much easier it must be to betray another.'

Her article went on to deal with the Anna Politkovskaya murder. It was 'regrettable', she noted, 'but Politkovskaya had other powerful enemies, too. And the Kremlin's current efforts to improve its image would militate against Putin's involvement. The murder of an already sidelined journalist was arguably the last thing that Putin needed.' To make Dejevsky's literary passage complete, one final phrase is missing – that Politkovskaya's murder caused more harm to the Russian authorities than her publications.

In closing, the *Independent* reporter mentioned yet another story:

> I would also recall this. In February 2004, journalists were invited to a plush hotel (as it happens, also in Piccadilly), to be regaled with an extraordinary story from a bedraggled Russian MP, who was standing against Putin in imminent elections. The MP, Ivan Rybkin, gave a muddled account of being abducted, put on a train, drugged and filmed in compromising positions. It was all, we were told, the doing of Putin and his secret agents. The truth turned out to be rather different. Rybkin, not for the first time, had been on a bender. He and his supporters abroad had found an ingenious way of 'explaining' his absence to his wife and discrediting Putin at the same time. Alas, Rybkin could not keep up the pretence.

And how does she know that Rybkin was lying? Does the reporter have any sort of a document to prove that the respected politician and presidential candidate 'had been on a bender not for the first time'? What is the source of her 'truth'? Ironically, both former KGB officers, Litvinenko and Kalugin, wrote that they had no doubt that a psychotropic drug was given to Rybkin. And Vadim Birstein, author of *The Perversion of Knowledge*, agreed.

Dejevsky ended her article sowing doubt and stressing that 'a great many questions remain open.' Certainly, she had seen no evidence that it was a 'violent death.'

But the reporting on the Litvinenko murder was flawed in other ways, too, as noted by Dr Birstein who sharply criticised Dejevsky.[28] The scientist analysed another case when two London academics had put themselves squarely on the Kremlin side of the Litvinenko affair: Julia Svetlichnaya and James Heartfield, researchers at the Centre for the Study of Democracy, University of Westminster. Both made headlines in Europe and the USA with stories about Sasha and his supporters.

The first such story was published by *The Telegraph* the day after Litvinenko's tragic death was officially announced – perfect timing. The themes were that Litvinenko 'was caught up in events bigger than he understood . . . conspiracies that finally caught up with him', and that he was as criminal and ruthless as those whom he accused.

Heartfield wrote that 'One target [Litvinenko] was ordered to destroy was another security officer who had blown the whistle on some of the FSB's nefarious activities' and 'another he was told to kidnap to trade for FSB officers taken hostage by Chechens was a prominent Chechen businessman based in Moscow.' The author neglected to tell his readers that Sasha had not destroyed his friend Mikhail Trepashkin, nor had he kidnapped the businessman, Umar Dzhabrailov – and that Litvinenko's refusal to take part in this and other crimes was one of the reasons of his break with the *kontora* in 1998.

Shortly after this prelude, the *Observer*, the Sunday sister paper of the *Guardian*, published a much stronger attack on Litvinenko based on stories propagated by Svetlichnaya and Heartfield. Svetlichnaya was quoted as saying

> He told me he was going to blackmail or sell sensitive information about all kinds of powerful people including oligarchs, corrupt officials and sources in the Kremlin. He mentioned a figure of £10,000 they would pay each time to stop him broadcasting these FSB documents. Litvinenko was short of money and was adamant that he could obtain any files he wanted.[29]

The article further stated that 'Litvinenko proved he had sources in the heart of the Russian security services by producing what he said was a 100-page confidential FSB report from 2005 and forwarding it to Svetlichnaya.'[30] But the paper failed to reproduce even one page of this sensational secret report. It had never reached the police or security service and, as far as I know, had never been mentioned again.

However, the *Observer* reporters did not stop here:

Among the theories that remain open is that the poisonings were an accident that happened while Litvinenko tried to assemble a dirty bomb for Chechen rebels. Those who know him believe he was crazy enough to attempt such a thing and, in the past week, some have implicated him in the smuggling of nuclear materials from Russia.[31]

On 13 December an interview with Svetlichnaya was published by *Komsomolskaya Pravda*, whose title is unequivocally translated from Russian as 'The Truth of Young Communists'. It described her as a 33-year-old native of Cherepovets, a provincial Russian town on the bank of the Rybinsk Reservoir of the Volga. It also said that she studied at the Faculty of Journalism of St Petersburg State University and had lived in London for thirteen years.

Svetlichnaya told the paper that together with Heartfield she had been exploring a new scientific theory about the beginning of the war in Chechnya. In this pursuit she had called Berezovsky one day in 2006 and the tycoon had advised her to contact Litvinenko. This Russian student of the Centre for the Study of Democracy never heard about Litvinenko, she said – and repeated what she had said to the British papers, that she was sure Litvinenko had done it to himself (i.e. poisoned himself with polonium) to attract attention to his person.

Dr Birstein decided to check up on these writers and found, on the website of the University of Westminster, that Julia Svetlichnaya's thesis, entitled 'Art of Empire,' concerned the relationship between art and politics' and had nothing to do with Chechnya. According to the site, Svetlichnaya has published abstracts entitled 'Art of absence against valorisation of subjectivity' (2005), and 'Relational Paradise as a Delusional Democracy – a Critical Response to a Temporary Contemporary Relational Aesthetics' (2006) in the proceedings of two conferences.[32] An abstract:

Alix Lambert gets married to four different people in six months and subsequently divorces them all. In this way the artist undermines the institute of marriage. All these examples refer to rather weak modes of human inter-action such as loving, sharing, conviviality and friendliness, which [Nicholas] Bourriaud takes as a platform for social bond. There are, however, stronger ways of relating such as aggression, fear, hate or racism.

With this background, why was she talking to Litvinenko, reasonably asks Dr Birstein.

The website's description of Svetlichnaya's co-participant in the interviews on Litvinenko, James Heartfield (born James Hughes), reveals that he was studying European integration and economic regeneration. Another website sheds light on why he was involved in the Litvinenko case:

He is a Manchester branch organizer of the now defunct Revolutionary Communist Party; in the early nineties wrote for *Living Marxism* until it was closed by a libel action in 2000. He helped write the party's manifesto.[33]

Given the background of these two, writes Vadim Birstein, did anybody verify if Svetlichnaya, in fact, had hundred emails from Litvinenko? I did.

On 2 February 2007 a seminar furthered the smear campaign against Litvinenko and the world media who dared to speak up against the Kremlin. The floor was given exclusively to Heartfield and Svetlichnaya and among the public I noticed . . . Vladimir Teplyuk. During the whole event he never said a word, hardly understood much as the discussion was in English, but made notes. Shortly before the conference, in a private meeting with an English gentleman who often served as Litvinenko's interpreter, he had tried to spread the tale that Berezovsky offered him millions of pounds for giving false evidence at a London court. He was stirring up anew old allegations that had been discredited four years earlier. One could think that Teplyuk was acting on his own initiative but just two months later, on 7 April, he repeated them in a TV programme known as *Vesti Nedeli* ('News of the Week') on the Russian channel Planeta. When Berezovsky later sued the Russian Television and Broadcasting Company (VGTRK), responsible for the channel, VGTRK asked the judge to refuse jurisdiction over the claim, on the basis that 'Pyotr' – as Teplyuk was introduced during the interview – was a Russian state-protected witness.

At the end of the seminar I asked Svetlichnaya whether she had any documentary proof whatsoever – an email, a text message, any sort of a document or an audiotape to support her allegations. She said no. That was the end of the Svetlichnaya affair.

The first public event Moscow organised for Lugovoy, Kovtun and Sokolenko was an interview on 24 November 2006 – the day Sasha was announced dead – on the popular Moscow radio station Ekho Moskvy. The stage management was poor and it was later corrected and improved but the full record of the interview remains and makes enlightening reading.

At the beginning of the show the cast of characters was presented as: a successful Russian businessman and producer of wine and non-alcoholic drinks (Lugovoy); an expert in foreign investments into the Russian market (Kovtun); and a modest representative of the group of companies called Ninth Wave engaged in personal protection, in his free time a great football fan (Sokolenko). They all admitted that they graduated from the same Moscow military school but

Kovtun failed to mention that he was a former army officer and an FSB *seksot* (collaborator).[34] Sokolenko forgot to say that, like Lugovoy, he had served first in the KGB's 9th Directorate and then in the Federal Protection Service (FSO). The FSO is similar to the American Secret Service and was in charge of the personal protection of the president and other state figures.

Not once in their many public appearances did they ever mention former 9th Directorate Captain Alexander Talik, another important protagonist in this story. Not once did they let slip the name of Victor Zolotov, a 9th Directorate officer when they all served in the KGB and – at the time when the events unrolled – head of the Russia president's personal security service. The bodyguard of Putin.

The radio interview started on a jovial note, though the business at hand was, as usual, murder.

'In our studio here are all three persons whose names figure [in connection with the Litvinenko case],' a presenter said, upon which Lugovoy prompted, 'I would call to your attention that there is no man named Vladimir here. There were plenty of insinuations during last weeks about someone named Vladimir – a tall man with sharp facial features. They meant Dmitry, I suppose, who is far from this description.'

Lugovoy was really amusing himself during that first talk on the radio, showing that he was as ill mannered and poorly educated as Kovtun was, but both men were becoming more and more self-assured and aggressive in further meetings with the press.

***

At the end of November the atmosphere at the House of Commons was rather like an Agatha Christie novel, according to the *Daily Telegraph*. An atrocious crime had taken place and the bewildered guests and members of the House assembled in the great hall to ask who could have done such a ghastly thing. All expected the Home Secretary, John Reid, to cast some light on events.[35]

It looked like a repeating of the Yushchenko scenario when two Austrian Social-Democratic MPs questioned the credibility of Dr Korpan in the National Council.

> Two Tories with London seats embarked on dubious or at least premature lines of thought. Mark Field (Cities of London and Westminster) wanted to know 'on what basis a former senior KGB officer' like Mr. Litvinenko 'was given asylum in this country' and asked: 'Should we not now give serious consideration to ensuring that people who come to this country and intend to become political agitators against other sovereign states are not allowed to stay?'
>
> 'Mr. Reid limited himself to saying: 'I am not entirely sure that I agree with the honourable gentleman.'
>
> Greg Hands (Hammersmith and Fulham) observed that thousands of political dissidents and émigrés have taken refuge in this country because they believe they will be safe here, and went on: 'In my opinion, this incident has been severely negative to the reputation of this country and not just Russia's.'

Mr. Reid bridled at that suggestion: 'To cast aspersions as he has is to criticise, unduly and unfairly, our security services, police and all the many people who are trying to ensure that this remains a safe country where opinions can be stated without fear or favour.'[36]

Sasha Litvinenko had always been enormously proud that he could say *civis Britannicus sum* – I am a British citizen. But Alan Cowell was wrong to assert that Sasha 'brandished his pristine plum-coloured passport proclaiming that it was his protector'. Maybe it could be, indeed. But Sasha never saw his British passport. It arrived on 4 December.

In December 2006 the Kremlin's contract with Ketchum expired and was immediately extended until February next year. The subject matter of the contract was described as 'consultations in the sphere of public relations, lobbying, and assistance in media communications'.

***

An authoritative and popular Western television programme gave time and space to Peskov's propaganda escapades. It was the BBC's *Panorama* on which I had helped. As mentioned, we started at the end of November 2006 and worked non-stop except for a short break for Christmas. The working atmosphere was pleasant and Andrei Nekrasov, a film-maker and Sasha's friend, joined us sometimes at the Shepherd Bush offices. Finally, our programme was reduced to less than thirty minutes and Andrei's own film entitled 'My Friend Sasha: A Very Russian Murder' was shown as part of the *Storyville* – BBC Four's flagship international documentary strand – on the same evening.

Panorama's reputation helped to bring in well-qualified interviewees, albeit an entirely pro-Litvinenko group. Alex Goldfarb was the first and answered John O'Mahony's questions on camera for two hours. But not a second of it was included in the documentary. Then, two days after Litvinenko's funeral, came Akhmed Zakayev, Walter Litvinenko and Sasha's younger brother Maxim. Several hours of brilliant interviews moved everyone – but did not appear in the final version. Then Scaramella and I were filmed in a countryside inn. Some short time before we had visited Gordievsky in his house to interview him off camera. I also received written agreements from Oleg Kalugin and Pete Bagley but none of those three intelligence officers was ever called for.

Marina and Boris Berezovsky were among the last interviewees, Marina in a house that belonged to one of the Blakeway/3BM studio's executives, and Boris at a public place.

By mid-January everything was ready. I brought a witness to the studio who testified on camera that Litvinenko called him on 1 November 2006, almost certainly from a hotel, between 12:30 and 1:00 p.m. for a business consultation. He said he heard there were other people in the room and recognised Lugovoy's voice. My witness explained exactly what they discussed and how he shared that fact with the detectives who had been interviewing him for two days. John O'Mahony, the producer, decided in this sensitive case not to trust a cameraman and duly filmed the man himself. Again, nothing of this was shown and the episode had never been mentioned.

It had always bothered me that John was a Russian speaker married to a Russian girl and visited Moscow often. As I know from my experience, such people were frequently, sooner or later, approached by the KGB with an offer that was hard to refuse.

All the time we worked together, John was particularly interested in secret documents that regularly came my way, and in the interviews that Oleg Gordievsky and I had given to the Metropolitan Police. He was also eager to know questions and answers in the investigator–witness confidential interviews. John showed his true colours when he learned from the Italian senator Paolo Guzzanti about a secret video showing Alexander Litvinenko giving testimony to the Mitrokhin Commission of the Italian Parliament on 3 February 2006 in Rome. He was desperate when he learned that the film was hidden in Gordievsky's house. Probably already in Moscow, John sent me the last SMS offering any money for the DVD. (In February 2009 O'Mahony suddenly contacted me again. We met for a five o'clock tea at a usual place. John's main interest was this book and though I admitted that I had delivered the manuscript to the publisher I refused to disclose who the publisher was. In turn, I asked him whether the KGB approached him when he lived in Russia. John said no, they never did.)

During the last messy week before we would see a broadcast of the *Panorama* programme on Monday, 22 January, John O'Mahony and John Sweeney rushed to Moscow to grab Dmitry Peskov, the chief Kremlin spokesman. Reporting with a fur *shapka* on his head right from the Lubyanka Square, Sweeney informed the spectators that the police was investigating a series of attempts to kill Litvinenko. That claim supported the version of the Russian General Prosecutor's Office that there was an attempt to poison Litvinenko and his 'business associates, Lugovoy and Kovtun, in mid-October' and that was the ground for the Russians to start their own investigation 'of the attempt to poison Russian citizens'. It was also the only chance for Moscow to explain how two of its operatives got contaminated with polonium two weeks *before* Litvinenko was poisoned. Who was behind this attempt became clear when Peskov directly accused Boris Berezovsky of this crime.

Berezovsky was also given a short few seconds. He was not asked any important questions and made no revealing comments so bringing him into the programme seemed rather to support and illustrate the Kremlin's version.

Speaking into the camera, John Sweeney erroneously claimed that Kovtun was ex-KGB, that the polonium trail began at the Parkes Hotel and that Lugovoy and Kovtun were drinking with a third Russian when Litvinenko arrived at the bar. With John's voice-over, the camera mounted on a moving car showed a dirty building covered by snow with Sweeney calling it 'poison laboratory no. 12' whereas in reality the building, at 11 Varsanofyevsky Lane, could not be seen from the street as it was in the inner court. It is well known that the special laboratory there was closed in the 1970s. And in his Kremlin interview with Peskov, the *Panorama* reporter gave the liar a good chance to vindicate his boss, Putin.

'Russia has not done it,' Peskov claimed.

Marina said, 'Something happened. Can happen again. What is next? What are they going to use next to kill us? Atomic bomb?'

The title of the programme – 'How to Poison a Spy' – was out of place, because there was nothing at all in the BBC investigation that could throw any light on how indeed a professional security officer (not a spy) could have been poisoned in the middle of London. Instead it sowed confusion. At its end the dynamic show sloped down to a dialogue between Marina Litvinenko, fighting for her family and her husband's honour and accusing president Putin of being behind everything that is 'Made in Russia', and Peskov, who was publicly calling the widow 'a liar in these words' and denying any involvement of his country in this monster crime. The *Panorama* team gave Peskov ample time to deliver his message to the British public.

On the same day two smashing ITV pieces broadcast at prime time shortly before and after the *Panorama* programme showed footage of Litvinenko's last interview with Scaramella accusing Romano Prodi of being a KGB man. Bill Neeley, International Editor for ITV News, reporting first from the steps of Scaramella's prison in Rome and then in front of the Italian Embassy in London, challenged the prime minister of Italy to respond. As expected, nothing followed.

At the end of February I was in Rome discussing the developments with Guzzanti and visiting Scaramella in his jail, Carcere Guidiziano. The senator was received politely by the director himself, a pleasant Italian of medium height, and a group of senior officers accompanied us as we crossed the guarded space into a spacious corridor that looked more like a church than a detention facility. From there through an inner yard we went into another, more modern building and climbed to the third floor. While Paolo discussed the convicts and their problems with the prison governors, I was accompanied into a solitary cell where Mario was waiting. We had about forty-five minutes one to one with no one interfering.

Mario, whom I saw hours before he and his family left London on Christmas Eve flying home to Naples, told me about his arrest at the airport by the local police and security chiefs, a search of his house and the prosecutors' demand that he sign a statement accusing Senator Guzzanti of manipulating evidence in order to compromise Berlusconi's political rival, Prodi.

The police broke down the doors of all Scaramella's family houses and confiscated his computers and documents. After the arrest Mario was kept in a solitary cell though the police failed to produce any formal accusation.

He also told me about the arrest of six Ukrainians on 20 October 2005 who were charged with smuggling arms when two VOG 25P grenades were found in their cargo. These were no toys and VOG 25P, known as the 'Frog', is especially vicious. After being fired from a grenade launcher and before exploding, it springs about a metre into the air and then detonates, killing a lot of people. Amazingly, after they had been several months in custody, the case against the Ukrainians collapsed 'for lack of evidence'.

Leaving the facility, Paolo and I met Amedeo, Mario's father. 'It is purely political,' he said, 'my son is a political prisoner.'

'*Mi dispiace*,' I tried to calm the man. 'We shall do our best.'

Mario Scaramella was finally released after Prodi lost a vote of confidence in the Senate in January 2008 and had to step back from the Italian politics.

On May 22 Sir Ken Macdonald QC, Head of the Crown Prosecution Service and Director of Public Prosecutions, made a long-awaited statement. Here is the full text:

> On 23 November 2006 Mr Litvinenko died in a London hospital of acute radiation injury. He was found to have ingested a lethal dose of polonium-210, a highly radioactive material. During his difficult, fatal illness and following his death, the Metropolitan Police Service in London conducted a careful investigation into how this had happened.
>
> Among the people of interest to police in this inquiry was a Russian citizen named Andrey Lugovoy.
>
> In late January 2007 the police sent a file of evidence to the Crown Prosecution Service so that we could make a decision about whether criminal charges should be brought against anyone who might have been involved in these events.
>
> Prosecutors from CPS Counter Terrorism Division have carefully considered the material contained in that police file. They have also asked the police to carry out further inquiries, which are now complete. And, finally, they have consulted with me.
>
> I have today concluded that the evidence sent to us by the police is sufficient to charge Andrey Lugovoy with the murder of Mr Litvinenko by deliberate poisoning.
>
> I have further concluded that a prosecution of this case would clearly be in the public interest.
>
> In those circumstances, I have instructed CPS lawyers to take immediate steps to seek the early extradition of Andrey Lugovoy from Russia to the United Kingdom, so that he may be charged with murder – and be brought swiftly before a court in London to be prosecuted for this extraordinarily grave crime.[37]

Observers were surprised that the British authorities never mentioned Kovtun as a suspect though he was constantly present throughout the Pine Bar episode. For me, it was a confirmation that my version of events was more right than wrong.

Throughout 2007 a media war raged, with Litvinenko in the epicentre. On the one hand, there was the Kremlin black propaganda facility pulling its punches by making a disaster seem funny. On the other, a group of people in different countries did their best to learn and tell the world what really happened in London. The conclusion of the CPS based on a meticulous police investigation and undeniable evidence was unequivocal – it was a murder and Lugovoy was charged with this crime. It was clearly 'Made in Russia'.

After the announcement, Peskov stopped commenting on the case. There were now other mechanisms at work.

Before Sir Ken's statement, slews of whodunit theories were jostling for prominence and bringing delight to those who had planned the operation. Now they considered it was time to change their tactics and go from the defensive and on the offensive. The fact that the whole state machine now took an active part, including their controlled media, deputies, the Russian Prosecutor General's Office, and the president personally, speaks for itself.

While in the West professional PR companies did a good job for their Moscow paymasters, the Russian disinformation operations intended for the inner market looked amateurish. On 31 May Lugovoy and Kovtun held a press conference organised by the Interfax news agency. Lugovoy read a statement prepared for him, never looking away from his papers. He accused Berezovsky and Litvinenko of being SIS agents and claimed that unnamed representatives of the British secret service were trying to recruit him to collect information on President Putin. Though quite sensational for the Russian media (and the Russia Today television channel broadcasting its programmes in the English language did its best to spread news as widely as possible), these allegations were doomed to go nowhere in the West. Those who invented them could not produce a single proof. And no one could explain why Her Majesty's Secret Intelligence Service might need a former oligarch and an unemployed security consultant, not to mention a *kvass* (Russian soft drink) brewer, as he was wont to introduce himself to the listeners of the Ekho Moskvy station.

Certainly, in most lies there is an element of truth and it can be outstanding.

Lugovoy: 'Just think of it: they have found a Russian James Bond, who enters into nuclear centres and in cold blood poisons a friend of his and, at the same time, poisons himself, his friends, children and wife. And all that was done single-handedly by the terrorist Lugovoy. Who – as a result – loses his business and clients. And the main question: what for? Where is the motive for my crime?'

There is truth to the assertion that he had no idea about the poisoning agent and no visible motive. Indeed, it was not his crime. But that did not mean that he had not committed it. Lugovoy said in this statement:

For some reason, all British newspapers are saying that the poisoning took place on 1 November, but Litvinenko and I met twice in October. Moreover, we met in his home in summer, when his wife Marina was away. By the way, Berezovsky didn't know of that meeting. It was almost the ideal place for a poisoning. However, when conditions were ideal, it didn't happen. But in a bar with a lot of people, when he could have failed to turn up, in the presence of dozens of witnesses, it happened. This means that someone wanted us to be seen together in the Millennium Bar.

Certainly, the operation planners wanted them to be seen in a public place on that day. It was their alibi. And simple logic does suggest that the Pine Bar was the wrong place for committing such a sophisticated crime.

Those who know Sasha can confirm that he never drank or smoked. Neither I nor Dima [Dmitry Kovtun] can remember whether he ordered anything, tea or water, because we were preparing to go to a football game at the time and, since it was cold, had drunk a good amount of spirits. What kind of idiot poisoner would it take to act in such a primitive way? Again, somebody wanted to set us up.

Wrong. But the poison was indeed administered in another place and at another time of the day. At a moment when Lugovoy was perfectly sober.

Lugovoy also said: 'It's hard to get rid of the thought that Litvinenko was an agent who got out of the secret service's control and was eliminated.'

Though Sir Colin McColl, a former SIS Chief and the current President of the Special Forces Club in London, once said that 'Secrecy is our absolute stock in trade, it is our most precious asset', it had always been an undisputed fact that what principally differed the British secret service from the KGB is that SIS did not kill people. It was precisely because SIS had not indulged in such excesses that the organisation had avoided the kind of inhibiting Congressional oversight that had hamstrung the CIA.[38] Paradoxically, the KGB had been indulging in assassinations, murders and terrorism throughout its whole history but until this day have not only managed to avoid any public oversight but moved to run the country without any restrictions.

In early June Peskov announced that the contract between the Russian presidential administration and Ketchum had been prolonged again and that the PR company's responsibility would now include not only the USA but also other countries. In reality, the contract had worldwide application since the very beginning.

During the same month an influential Russian magazine *Kommersant Vlast* (nos 24–25) published a long interview with Evgeny Limarev – an SVR agent who had settled in France but managed to penetrate the Berezovsky circle masquerading as Sasha's friend.

Limarev was the one who sent three messages to Scaramella pushing him to the meeting with Litvinenko exactly when the Moscow planners wanted the Italian to be there. When Senator Paolo Guzzanti came to London in January 2007, we discussed Limarev's role in the operation and then Paolo went to meet the Russian personally in Cluses. Their interesting discussion was recorded and is now reproduced in the new book written by Guzzanti, with the audiofile available on Paolo's website.[39]

In his Moscow interview Limarev accused Litvinenko of shadowy dealings and partially supported Svetlichnaya's allegations that Sasha was planning to blackmail some Russian businessmen. As proof he could only give a dead man's words. Limarev pointed his finger at Lugovoy saying that he had been a Berezovsky man, implying that Berezovsky could have organised Sasha's murder. He also accused Litvinenko of overpricing open-source materials and selling them to the British security company with a huge mark up. Limarev named the sum of 10,000 as Litvinenko's fee for a 'dossier' – again confirming Svetlichnaya's allegations without offering any proof – and produced a copy of the report that Litvinenko allegedly sent to him as a product sample. Incidentally, it appeared to be the document that Lugovoy proudly sold to one of the London security companies that he visited together with Sasha. Certainly Limarev could only produce a DVD copy of the report as the FSB, who concocted it, could come up with as many copies as necessary. No wonder soon after the interview was published, Moscow Centre of the Political Information identified it as based on their own works in public domain. The magic trick was revealed. Amazingly, no one mentioned Lugovoy but in a RFE/RL programme 'The summer highlights of the Litvinenko case' on 3 July, based on the Limarev's material, all attention was on Sasha and his 'unsavoury behaviour'. It was one of the worst programmes covering the Litvinenko story that was ever made by this otherwise excellent station.

Limarev also accused Guzzanti, Gordievsky and myself of 'leaking' his name to the media and 'bringing him into this story'.

Quite surprisingly for me at that moment, Limarev named Sergey Ivanov, then a very powerful First Deputy Prime Minister, a promising presidential candidate, and a former KGB colleague of Putin's, as a possible organiser of Litvinenko's assassination. Only later, when Putin endorsed Medvedev, who was actually elected the President of Russia, did I learn that Ivanov had started secretly sending trusted couriers to places like London and Washington to arrange visits for him there, with meetings at a high level that could show that Western leaders' supported his candidacy. That was a faux pas that did not remain unnoticed by the man who slipped a word to the Russian leader's ear.

On 6 July the FSB Public Relations Centre announced that legal proceedings were opened on the charges relating to conspiracy to commit espionage. They claimed that Vycheslav Zharko gave himself up at the end of the previous month and confessed to having been recruited by Berezovsky and Litvinenko as a British agent. Mark Franchetti, correspondent of the *Sunday Times* in Moscow, who became a friend of Lugovoy and even made a documentary about him that the

BBC broadcast at the end of November, wrote:

> Zharko said he met his British handlers regularly in Turkey, Finland and Cyprus and supplied them with analytical reports on Russia's economy and politics. In return, he claims, he was paid about £60,000. He estimates that MI6 spent an additional £150,000 on expenses.'I needed money so when Litvinenko told me that I could earn easy cash by collaborating with British intelligence I agreed,' Zharko, 36, told *The Sunday Times* in his first interview with a Western newspaper. 'I saw myself as a consultant. I began to worry after Litvinenko's death because I feared I'd be sucked into something too dangerous. That's when I turned myself in.
>
> The FSB, which has investigated Zharko, backs his claims but will not prosecute him for espionage, saying that he did not reveal any state secrets and had come forward voluntarily.
>
> 'The Brits have been waging an information war against us and now we are responding in kind,' said an FSB spokesman. 'We have gone public with Zharko's story because it proves that Britain is actively spying against Russia and that Litvinenko was in cahoots with MI6.'
>
> Zharko said that at first his British handlers had been interested in information on several Russian companies. Then they asked him to compile a series of analytical reports on the political situation in Ukraine in the run-up to the country's Orange revolution and were also interested in information on any FSB operations against Western non-governmental organisations working in Russia.[40]

Fortunately, Franchetti was one of only a few Western journalists who reported this red herring.

The pretty kettle of fish so carefully cooked by the FSB had three distinctive aims: to show to the Russian public that Western intelligence services were behind NGOs working in Russia; to demonstrate that Britain was spying against Russia; and to accuse Litvinenko of dealing with terrorists and as a result of poisoning himself with polonium-210. The reporter Franchetti missed two of them.

The self-declared MI6 'spy' Zharko named several of his 'handlers' and among them Martin Flint, in reality one of four directors of the company Risk Analysis already mentioned by Chekulin in 2004. Among the others were 'John' and 'Ken', in reality Quentin, whom FSB knew as British diplomats working in Moscow in the 1990s and whose names any proficient internet surfer could quickly find along with the fact that Quentin was a British consul in Istanbul in 2004. Finally, 'Martin' and 'Lee,' who were only identified by these first names and whom Zharko allegedly met in Finland. The large SVR Helsinki station knows most of the intelligent officers under cover of other embassies, so had no difficulty selecting the two. It is notable that several Russian spy services had been supporting the Zharko operation and providing intelligence to the scriptwriters.

Zharko also named 'Paul' – a young man the FSB had grounds to dislike. However, it would be hard to prove that Zharko had ever met him.

Zharko added spice by 'recalling' an episode that allegedly took place in August 2005. He claimed that Litvinenko had a meeting with two 'Arab-looking terrorists' in his Istanbul Hilton hotel and that after the meeting he carried a container (in another interview – 'a small black tin') saying that 'now Putin is finished – a major terrorist attack that will shake Russia and the world' would take place soon.[41]

Here Zharko hit his lowest point. Sasha had never been in Turkey after he left it in 2000 with Marina and Tolik, and for most of his life he had been fighting terrorism and organised crime. But the hint about Putin was traceable.

***

An echo of the Soviet propaganda campaign to smear Litvinenko and clear Putin emerged when in March 2008 an elderly American investigative journalist, Edward J. Epstein, published a hair-raising article in the *New York Sun* questioning everything that had to date been established beyond reasonable doubt regarding the Litvinenko case. He had his new facts from Moscow. To investigate all circumstances behind the Litvinenko murder, as he put it, he had gone to Moscow to meet 'with the Russian prosecutors in charge of the case'. Moscow? When the crime scene was London? Epstein was evidently satisfied with what he was told there, for he informed his readers that the Russians in his case had demonstrated 'full cooperation'. They told him, 'The media often reproach the Russian side for its unwillingness to cooperate with the British side, when in reality the situation is the reverse.' Perhaps Epstein had swallowed the Kremlin's lies.

Theory was certainly not part of this book's plan. But as the world functions according to the laws of nature, behind every intelligence operation, whether it is an assassination or deception, there are also sets of strict rules, classic principles. From early days, Russian deceptions have sought on the one hand to hide the real and on the other hand to project the false picture. As time went on these principles were applied on a broader scale of multi-stage information wars using not only the media, politicians and diplomats but also *agents provocateurs*, doubles and dangles, agents of influence and so-called 'useful idiots' (whose numbers increased with the collapse of the Soviet Union).

The Litvinenko cover-up operation was in full swing long enough to offer a rich opportunity to observe Russian techniques. They include compromising and discrediting a target and his personal life, dissimulating (hiding the real), simulating (projecting a false picture), substituting (one notion, idea, concept, person or event for another) and disorientating by flooding the media with conflicting information. Two specialists in this field, Donald Daniel and Katherine Herbig, call the latter 'ambiguity-increasing' operations, cluttering the target's sensors with a mass of contradictory indicators ensuring that the level of ambiguity always remains high enough to protect the secret of the actual operation.

Deception theory states: 'The deceiver's job is to induce deception by projecting a false picture of reality.'[42]

Epstein, evidently drawing on his sources in Moscow, wrote:

> In London Mr. Berezovsky had an extraordinary agenda, which he himself described as overthrowing the regime of his arch-enemy, Mr. Putin. Litvinenko, whom Mr. Berezovsky now supported through his foundation, took a key role in this ambitious enterprise. He wrote books accusing Mr. Putin's FSB of everything from collaborating with the leadership of al-Qaeda to framing Chechen rebels for bloody acts of terrorism that FSB agents themselves committed, such as the bombing of six apartment houses in which over 300 people died. In addition, Litvinenko also had less visible employment as a consult [sic] for two closely connected security companies housed in Berezovsky's office building at 25 Grosvenor Square.

Facts: Sasha never played a key role in Berezovsky's plans; Boris certainly reserved this role for himself. And the security companies at 25 Grosvenor Square had nothing whatsoever to do with Berezovsky's office building at 7 Down Street. Epstein chose the wrong city for his detective exercises.

Epstein: '[Scaramella] had been involved with Litvinenko in, among other things, a Byzantine plot to penetrate the operations of a suspected trafficker in prostitutes, arms, and enriched uranium.'

Fact: There had never been such a plot.

Epstein: 'Andrei Lugovoi, who had also served in the FSB up until 1999.'

Fact: Lugovoy never served in the FSB and had only served in the KGB and then the FSO until 1996.

Epstein: 'Litvinenko was moved to University College Hospital and given massive doses of the cyanide-based antidote for thallium, which did not work.'

Fact: As an antidote for thallium Litvinenko was given Prussian blue, a non-toxic pigment.

Epstein: 'A few hours after Litvinenko died on 23 November 2006, Mr Goldfarb arranged a press conference and released the sensational deathbed statement accusing Mr Putin of the poisoning. Giving further weight to this theory, British authorities switched the alleged crime scene from the Itsu restaurant, where Litvinenko had met the Italian Mr Scaramella, to the Pine Bar, where he had met the Russian Mr Lugovoi.'

Fact: Not true. The British authorities could amply respond to this distortion.

Epstein: 'When polonium-210 was discovered in London in late November 2006 in Litvinenko's body, however, no [weapons of mass destruction] proliferation alarm bells went off. Instead, the police assumed that this component of early-stage nuclear bombs had been smuggled into London solely to commit a murder.'

Fact: The police knew from the experts that the dose used against Sasha would weigh only thirty-millionths of a gram. As Alan Cowell put it, Litvinenko had been killed by a toxin virtually without weight or mass.

Epstein: 'Russia's nuclear authority claims that the sole reactor that had been manufacturing its polonium-210 had been shut down in 2004, and the small quantity exported to America in 2005 and 2006 – approximately 3 ounces each year – came out of its stockpile.'

Fact: Polonium-210 has a half-life of 138 days plus a fraction. That means that after less than four months, half of it turns into one of the most stable isotopes, plumbum-206 or lead. What stockpiles?

Epstein: 'The polonium-210 found in London could also have come from stockpiles in many countries, including America. According to the IAEA's Illicit Trafficking Data Base, there had been fourteen incidents of missing industrial polonium-210 since 2004.'

Fact: Polonium-210 survives only 138 days.

Epstein: 'As if to demonstrate [their full cooperation] the Russian investigators provided me with access to the British files.' [Epstein is trying to persuade the reader that the British had not supplied enough, and important documents were missing.]

Fact: The reporter fails to say how many pages of the British extradition request there were and in what form he was shown it. As Epstein himself writes, 'in the file was an affidavit by Rosemary Fernandez, a Crown Prosecutor, stating that the extradition request is "in accordance with the criminal law of England and Wales, as well as with the European Convention on Extradition 1957".'

Epstein: 'When Mr. Lugovoi flew from Moscow to London on 15 October on Transaero Airlines, no radiation traces were found on his plane.'

Fact: Lugovoy did not fly to London on 15 October. He flew on the next day – and the aircraft that brought him to the British capital was never offered to the British experts for inspection.

Epstein: 'The most impressive piece of evidence involves the relatively high level of polonium-210 in Mr Lugovoi's room at the Millennium Hotel. Although the police report does not divulge the actual level itself (or any other radiation levels), Detective Inspector Lock states that an expert witness called 'Scientist A' found that these hotel traces "were at such a high level as to establish a link with the original polonium source material".'

No comment.

Epstein: 'The Russian investigation could also have veered into Litvinenko's activities in the shadowy world of security consultants, including his dealings with the two security companies in Mr. Berezovsky's building, Erinys International and Titon International, and his involvement with Mr. Scaramella in an attempt to plant incriminating evidence on a suspected nuclear-component smuggler – a plot for which Mr. Scaramella was jailed after his phone conversations with Litvinenko were intercepted by the Italian national police.'

Facts: First, neither Erinys International nor Titon International had ever been located in Berezovsky's building. Also, the legal foundation for Scaramella's arrest (as I learned from the official document of the Italian Prosecutor's Office, Procura della Repubblica, sent to me by Dr Sergio Rastrelli, Mario's solicitor), reads quite differently:

> In the presence of the police officials and under his own signature
> SCARAMELLA, being fully aware of his innocence, accused TALIK
> Alexander, former official of the Russian secret services, of offences to import,
> keep and carry ammunitions and firearms with the aim of committing a
> terrorist act in the view of preparing an attack to cause damages to him,
> Senator Paolo Guzzanti and [a Russian-Italian translator] for their work in the
> Parliamentary Enquiry Commission investigating the Mitrokhin dossier and
> particularly the activities of the Italian intelligence.

Epstein: 'The British extradition gambit ended the Russian investigation in Londongrad. It also discredited Mr Lugovoi's account by naming him as a murder suspect. In terms of a public relations tactic, it resulted in a brilliant success by putting the blame on Russian stonewalling for the failure to solve the mystery. What it obscured is the elephant-in-the-room that haunts the case: the fact that a crucial component for building an early-stage nuke was smuggled into London in 2006.'

Facts: A nuke without any weight or mass? Hardly an elephant in the room.

Epstein's conclusion: 'My hypothesis is that Litvinenko came in contact with a polonium-210 smuggling operation and was, either wittingly or unwittingly, exposed to it . . . His murky operations, whatever their purpose, involved his seeking contacts in one of the most lawless areas in the former Soviet Union, the Pankisi Gorge, which had become a centre for arms smuggling. He had also dealt with people accused of everything from money laundering to trafficking in nuclear components. These activities may have brought him, or his associates, in contact with a sample of polonium-210, which then, either by accident or by design, contaminated and killed him.'[43]

Facts: Litvinenko had never been in the Pankisi Gorge and had never been involved in the activities mentioned above.

Epstein's article, carrying on Moscow's disinformation campaign, would not merit comment had it not achieved wider dissemination – in no less official a publication than the Congressional Record. Congressman Ron Paul introduced Epstein's views as the US House of Representatives was voting on House Congressional Resolution 154 that would express the Congress's 'concern' over Russian involvement in Alexander Litvinenko's murder:

> Madam Speaker, I rise in strong opposition to this ill-conceived resolution. The

US House of Representatives has no business speculating on guilt or innocence in a crime that may have been committed thousands of miles outside US territory. It is arrogant, to say the least, that we presume to pass judgment on crimes committed overseas about which we have seen no evidence.

The resolution purports to express concern over the apparent murder in London of a shadowy former Russian intelligence agent, Alexander Litvinenko, but let us not kid ourselves. The real purpose is to attack the Russian government by suggesting that Russia is involved in the murder. There is little evidence of this beyond the feverish accusations of interested parties. In fact, we may ultimately discover that Litvinenko's death by radiation poisoning was the result of his involvement in an international nuclear smuggling operation, as some investigative reporters have claimed. The point is that we do not know. The House of Representatives has no business inserting itself in disputes about which we lack information and jurisdiction.

At a time when we should be seeking good relations and expanded trade with Russia, what is the benefit in passing such provocative resolutions? There is none.

Madam Speaker, I would like to enter into the Congressional Record a very thought-provoking article by Edward Jay Epstein published recently in the *New York Sun*, which convincingly calls into question many of the assumptions and accusations made in this legislation. I would encourage my colleagues to read this article and carefully consider the wisdom of what we are doing.[44]

On 2 May 2008, Mary Dejevsky gave a detailed summary of Epstein's article in her own piece under the title 'The Litvinenko files: Was he really murdered?' published in *The Independent* and in what seemed an impossible turn, Epstein repeated all his allegations again word for word in the article 'What does Britain really know?' in the *International Herald Tribune* on 29 August. There was no time to respond: Russian tanks were in Georgia.

Back in 1983 together with the Soviet Special Forces I was to be in Kabul on a mission. My angels guarded me and let me avoid the war. But Ahmad Shah Massoud, a Kabul University engineering student turned military leader, was there. Many Afghans called him Amer Sahib e Shahid, Our Martyred Commander, and he played a leading role in driving the Soviet army out of Afghanistan, earning him the nickname 'Lion of Panjshir'.

Frederic Forsyth's novel *The Afghan* was published in 2006 – the Litvinenko year. I read the book and thought about Sasha:

And he recalled Ahmad Shah Massoud, the Lion of Panjshir, talking by the camp fire. 'We are all sentenced to die, Angleez. But only a warrior blessed of Allah may be allowed to choose how!'

Colonel Alexander Litvinenko made his choice.

Dead Souls: From Stalin to Putin

Seated in seiza he repeated each line as it was spoken by a senior member of the dojo: 'Hitotsu-Warewarewa, We will observe the rules of courtesy, respect our superiors, and refrain from violence.' After the exercise Victor Zolotov, the personal bodyguard of Putin, went to his Kremlin office adjacent to that of the president himself to contemplate the operation that would take place in London on 1 November. His duty was to protect his boss. And to hell with courtesy.

> Today is 3 February 2006. I am in Rome. My name is Alexander Walterovich Litvinenko. I am a former officer of the KGB and FSB. I occupied the position of a department chief in its most secret department that was involved in political assassinations of undesired persons . . .[1]
> My name is Pavel Anatolyevich Sudoplatov, but I do not expect you to recognize it because for fifty-eight years it was one of the best-kept secrets in the Soviet Union. My Administration for Special Tasks was responsible for sabotage, kidnapping, and assassination of our enemies beyond the country's borders. It was a special department working in the Soviet security service. I was responsible for Trotsky's assassination . . .[2]

The old man spoke straight into the camera. 'It is strange to look back fifty years,' he said, 'and re-create the mentality that led us to take vengeance on our enemies with cold self-assurance. We did not believe there was any moral question involved in killing Trotsky or any other of our former comrades who had turned against us. We believed we were in a life-and-death struggle for the salvation of our grand experiment, the creation of a new social system that would protect and provide dignity for all workers and eliminate the greed and oppression of capitalist profit.'[3]

Three years after the death of Lenin, opposition to Stalin was still thinkable. Significant resistance to his growing personal power came from within the Bolshevik party in the form of the 'Left Opposition' led by Trotsky and Zinoviev. During 1927, the OGPU – later to be called KGB – was busy following the 'power game' at the top of the Bolshevik leadership. By autumn, it was over. In

November, Trotsky, Zinoviev and almost a hundred of their followers were expelled from the Party. Zinoviev agreed to recant, denounced 'Trotskyism', and was readmitted to the Party. Trotsky refused and in January 1928 was sentenced by the OGPU to internal exile in a remote corner of Kazakhstan on the Chinese border.[4]

From February 1929 onwards Stalin became increasingly preoccupied with the opposition to him within the Communist Party. After Trotsky was removed from the Soviet Union and deported to Turkey, Yakov Blyumkin, Trotsky's former bodyguard, sympathiser, and now a famous Chekist and chief illegal *rezident* in the Middle East, not only visited the former leader of the Bolshevik revolution in his exile but also helped the Trotskyist movement financially. Esther Rosenzweig, better known as Liza Gorskaya (*aka* Elsa Hutschneker, *aka* Elisabeth Zarubina *aka* Zubilina), Blyumkin's mistress and a Soviet illegal, betrayed him to the OGPU. Blyumkin was recalled to Moscow, arrested and shot. After that episode, Stalin began to fear that there were other, undiscovered Blyumkins within the Cheka foreign department. Soon the mass purges within the Soviet intelligence services began that continued on and off until Stalin's death in 1953.

Blyumkin was certainly not the first and far from the last victim of Stalin's hatred for his Enemy No. 1. Trotsky's assistants were brutally dealt with: S. Sermuks and I. Poznansky perished in the Gulag; M. Glazman, driven to despair, committed suicide; G. Butov died in prison in 1928. The last victim, albeit coincidental, was Jean van Heijenoort, Trotsky's secretary from 1932 to 1939, who was murdered in Mexico City in 1986 aged 73.

Among other tasks assigned to the Soviet advisers during the Spanish Civil War was annihilation of the Trotskyites in the Republican camp. What should be termed the secret war within the civil war began in the spring of 1937. It mirrored the events in Russia.

Like many similar enterprises of the NKVD, activities in Spain were divided into several parts. First, the POUM – the Workers' Party of Marxist Unification, the fusion of the Trotskyite Communist Left of Spain and the Workers and Peasants' Bloc – had to be rendered harmless together with its leaders – Andrés Nin, Julian Gorkin, Juan Andrade, Pedro Bonet, Gironella (Enrique Adroher), Jordi Arquer. It is now known that among this group Nin was on the Kremlin's hit list not only as Trotsky's former secretary but also as the one who offered to accept Trotsky in Catalonia as a political refugee, an intolerable provocation in Moscow's view. In addition to Nin, the hit list contained other *literniks,* the euphemism used by the Centre to mark those whom Stalin doomed to die. The names sent from Moscow included Marc Rein, Alfredo Martínez, Hans Freund (Moulin), Erwin Wolf, Kurt Landau, Rudolf Klement, and others less well known, who at one moment worked for or with Trotsky. They had all fallen victims of Stalin's sinister mind.[5]

Lev Nikolsky alias 'Alexander Orlov', Stalin's loyal henchman and the chief of the NKVD stations in Madrid and Valencia, was fully employed in eliminating the 'Trotskyite-Fascist element' from Spanish territory.

Stalin first assigned the murder of his archenemy to Nikolsky's boss, Sergey Spiegelglass, codenamed DUCE, in 1937. But as the Kremlin leader later told Sudoplatov, Spiegelglass 'had failed to fulfil this important government mission'. So he was shot.

As usual in any successful assassination operation the victim's entourage had to be infiltrated with Moscow's agents. Apart from Mark Zborowski (codenamed TYULPAN) in Paris, Maria de Hernández d'Harbat de las Heras (aliases Maria Luisa de Marchette, Maria de la Sierra, África de las Heras, codenamed PATRIA), recruited by Naum Eitingon ('Colonel Kotov'), Orlov's deputy in Spain, operated in Trotsky's secretariat from 1937 until 1939. In April 1940 a young American agent, Robert Sheldon Harte (codenamed AMUR), posing as a New York Trotskyite, was placed as a volunteer guard in Trotsky's villa in Cocayan.

In March 1939, Stalin summoned Sudoplatov to the Kremlin and verbally instructed him to assassinate Trotsky, simultaneously appointing him deputy head of foreign intelligence. The old spymaster later recalled that the Soviet leader preferred indirect words like 'action' to describe the murder, noting that if the operation were successful the party would forever remember those who were involved and would look after not only them, but every member of their family.[6] Sudoplatov moved to office no. 735 on the seventh floor of the Lubyanka building where the experienced illegal Eitingon, who just returned from Spain via France, joined him in supervising the plan to kill Trotsky. Eitingon suggested that it should be codenamed Operation UTKA ('Duck'). In Russian *utka* has the same meaning as 'canard' in English – 'to start a canard' is to disseminate disinformation, 'duck shooting' also universally means a good hunt full of fun. For them, enemies of the state were personal enemies and they enjoyed their work.

At least in one way the Trotsky operation was unusual: the cover-up preceded the hit. Starting from the late 1920s the Kremlin, actively using agents of influence recruited by its secret political police all over the world, started a fierce smear campaign against the Great Heretic who was painted as an enemy doing his best to discredit the Soviet state and its leadership. It was said that Trotsky aimed to blacken Russian achievements and opposed Stalin's aspirations to make the country a superpower. All Soviet newspapers were duly publishing materials supplied by the secret police and its collaborators. A special task force was established within the secret police to monitor all Trotsky's calls, visitors and correspondence, making monthly reports to the Big Boss. As Trotsky himself had announced his struggle against the 'Kremlin winner' and the need to use force, the Soviet propaganda accused the exile of plotting the violent overthrow of Soviet power.

In Stalin's logic, Trotsky was planning to accomplish his plans by bringing powerful politicians including some Politburo members to his side so that those secret followers would one day mount a palace coup. As Trotsky had enjoyed enormous political influence in Russia before being forced to exile, Stalin believed that Trotskyite opposition in the country was able to overthrow the regime. This led to infamous Moscow trials of 1936–8, the execution of most of the defendants, and the Great Purge better known as the Great Terror.

In his persecution of any form of dissidence, the Soviet leader presented his exiled opponent as a bloody terrorist, imperialist spy, ruthless killer and scum of international proportions, expecting that one day there would be no country willing to accept him.

In reality, Stalin cunningly used the name of Trotsky over a period of about ten years to accumulate absolute personal power in his hands. By 1938 the time had come to get rid of the nuisance.

The assassination plan as usual consisted of two parts and accordingly two groups were dispatched to carry out the operation.

The first was headed by a Spanish Communist Eustacia Maria Caridad del Rio Hernández, whom Eitingon had recruited in Barcelona and who was given a simple codename MOTHER, and her son Ramón Mercader, recruited by Nikolsky-Orlov, with an equally uncomplicated codename RAYMOND. Caridad came from a wealthy family, among her ancestors were governors of Cuba and her grandfather had been a Spanish ambassador to the Tsar. She had deserted her husband, a Spanish railroad magnate, and fled to Paris with their four children in the 1930s. When the Spanish Civil War broke out, she returned to Catalonia, joined the anarchists, and was wounded in an air raid. Her eldest son was killed in action. Her middle son Ramón served in a guerrilla detachment. The youngest son, Luis, and her daughter came to Moscow in 1939 with other children of Spanish Republicans who fled from Franco.[7]

Kyrill Khenkin, who served with him in Spain, recalled that Ramón Mercader was sent to Moscow in the summer of 1937 for formal recruitment and training.[8] Afterwards he arrived in Paris on a doctored Canadian passport in the name of Frank Jacson (with a mistake in the family name spelling, typical of the NKVD forgers). With the help of another NKVD agent, Mercader got acquainted with Sylvia Angeloff, an American Trotskyite, who played a key role in introducing him to the Trotsky's inner circle. They both attended the founding conference of the Fourth International in September 1938.

According to Sudoplatov, there was still another important agent in Paris, an Englishman named Morrison and codenamed HARRY, who was instrumental in stealing the operational records of the Trotsky organisation in Europe in December 1939. Allegedly the agent had good connections in the Directorate-General of the National Gendarmerie and was able to provide his Soviet handlers with real French police stamps for forged passports and permissions for agents to remain in France.

In August 1939 Caridad and Ramón sailed from Le Havre to New York. Eitington was supposed to follow them soon after but was detained by some problems with his forged documents. The head of station in Paris, Lev Vasilevsky, who served as Consul General under the alias 'Tarasov', was supporting the operation and was instructed to secure valid papers for the agents' overseas travel. The only problem was an American visa.[9]

The NKVD connection with the American consulate was through a respectable businessman from Switzerland, who was in fact another Soviet illegal named Maxim Steinberg.[10] Within a week Steinberg obtained the visa in Bern and a courier returned with it to Paris where Eitingon was waiting in hiding.

Eitingon arrived in New York in October 1939 and quickly registered an import-export company as a front for the operation. Mercader later travelled to New York to get instructions and money from his handler. Moscow also used it to communicate with their man. Due to the secrecy of the whole operation they had to dispatch a case officer from the headquarters whenever they needed to convey a message. Fortunately for them, there was no counter-intelligence in America at the time.

On 1 January 1940 Stalin – the instigator of this murder operation – was named Man of the Year by *Time* magazine.

According to the initial plan, the attack on Trotsky's family (to include him, his wife and a small grandchild) was to be led by a second group of agents drawn from veterans of the Spanish Civil War, headed by the celebrated Mexican painter and Stalinist David Alfaro Siqueiros. But before they were put into action, Beria decided to strengthen the force and assigned the young illegal named Iosif Grigulevich to the Sudoplatov group. Grigulevich, known as Grig among friends, was an assassin who spoke impeccable Spanish with Latin American accent and who operated in Spain documented as 'José Ocampo'. Grig arrived in Mexico in January 1940 and under Eitingon's instructions established a reserve illegal network in Mexico and California. He also cooperated with the Siqueiros group.[11]

In Mexico Grigulevich managed to recruit Antonio Pujol (codenamed JOSE), a former pupil of Siqueiros, whom he later described as 'very loyal, exceptionally reliable and quite bold'. Among his other recruits was his future wife and assistant, the Mexican Communist Laura Araujo Aguilar (codenamed LUISA). Though this group of former International Brigades fighters was formally headed by Siqueiros with Pujol acting as his second-in-command, KGB records seen and copied by Vasili Mitrokhin identify Grigulevich as the real leader of the assault.[12]

The attackers had in their disposal a floor plan of Trotsky's villa that had been drawn by agent PATRIA before she was recalled to Moscow. She also made an assessment of the bodyguards and gave the Moscow planners detailed character analyses of Trotsky's secretariat. This piece of intelligence was to be very useful at the final stage of the operation.

The first attack on the Trotsky's villa, in the small hours of 23 May 1940, failed. Their gunfire missed the targets. Siqueiros's gunmen dispersed and the alternative plan came into effect: Mercader was promoted from penetration agent to assassin. In the meantime, Moscow was actively spreading the story that Trotsky himself had organised the assault on his house to attract attention to his person.

Recalling the details, Sudoplatov said that 'it was important to suggest a motive for the act that would undermine Trotsky's image and discredit his movement.' If caught, as was likely, Mercader would explain his act as personal revenge for Trotsky allegedly having discouraged Sylvia Angeloff from marrying him. He was also to claim that the Trotskyites wanted to use his financial contribution for personal gain instead of political activities and that Trotsky had tried to convince him to join an international terrorist group planning to assassinate Stalin and other Soviet leaders.[13] If all this had not been written by the chief of the Soviet 'special tasks' years before the Litvinenko operation – for which it looks like a blueprint – I would think it had been invented. It is more likely that Moscow's assassins were using Sudoplatov's book as an instruction manual.

Mercader fulfilled Stalin's orders on 20 August 1940 using an ice-pick as the murder weapon. After his release from prison twenty years later, he was given the medal of the Hero of the Soviet Union in addition to the Order of Lenin. In 1966 Siqueiros was awarded the Lenin Peace Prize.

* * *

On the second floor of the Kremlin, down the long, wide, carpeted and empty corridor, one of the high doors opened to let visitors to the huge reception room with three writing tables. Behind them there were two people in tunics the same style as Stalin's and one in military uniform. It was Stalin's personal bodyguard, General Nikolai Vlasik.

Vlasik was born in a small and poor village in Western Byelorussia in 1896. His father was a peasant and the family could not afford more than three years in a local parish school that although retained its church connection essentially provided secular education in accordance with standards set by the government. At the age of 17, Vlasik was a menial labourer and navvy before he was drafted to the Tsarist army. When the Bolshevik revolt broke out in Petrograd, he was a militiaman in Moscow and soon joined the party of workers and peasants. In 1919 Vlasik was transferred to the Cheka.

Some of his biographers claim that he was together with Stalin from those early days as a young guard. According to the documents, Vlasik was promoted to a senior position in the Operational Department, responsible for the protection of the heads of the party and government, in November 1926. Five years later, in early 1931, he became chief of Stalin's personal protection service in the Kremlin.

Lana Peters, Stalin's daughter and an American citizen, remembered Vlasik as an 'illiterate, silly, rough and extremely impudent despot'. (In an almost impossible turn of fate, Lana, born Svetlana Alliluyeva, emigrated to the United States in 1967 and fifteen years later settled in Cambridge, England, becoming a neighbour of the famous Soviet dissident Vladimir Bukovsky.)

Vlasik was completely devoted to Stalin and served him well, taking care of his children and running all the necessary errands for the household apart from the bodyguard job – also acting as Stalin's barber and personal photographer. But one thing made him quite outstanding – he became so corrupted with authority that from the man behind Stalin's back he positioned himself as someone second only to the leader, accumulating an unlimited power.

There was a certain reason for that. Being as suspicious about his own secret police under Beria as about the army marshals, Stalin established a top secret 'inner cabinet' that included his personal secretary Alexander Poskrebyshev, whose wife, a very distant relative of Trotsky, was eventually arrested, charged with espionage and shot; Georgy Malenkov, described by one Western diplomat as 'the most sinister thing in the Soviet Union'; and Vlasik. It was a kind of private think-tank and Stalin's own intelligence service in one. As Vlasik was subordinate only to the Big Boss, he, with Poskrebyshev, was watching the secret police, the army and the Politburo for his master.

The system operated quite independently of the MGB and was completely under Stalin's personal control. According to Peter Deriabin, who was a member of the Kremlin guards, as they used to be known, the key elements of the dictator's personal protection force consisted of a vast and overlapping bodyguard system, numbering some 50,000 at the time when Deriabin was there, with independent capabilities for shadowing, spying, liaising with other agencies, and eliminating people. It also included the directorate's own investigative unit known as *operod* – the operational department. Besides, a special section within the MGB's Technical Operations Department was subordinated to the Vlasik's directorate. Finally, the Praetorian Guard, military units under the commandant of the Kremlin, though largely ceremonial, counted some 3,000 elite troops with powerful weapons, high discipline, and loyalty to Stalin.[14]

But even with the gift of the rank of lieutenant general and an impressive military force under his command, this poorly educated lout was ill fitted for his role. Vlasik had many mistresses (often seducing his friends' wives) and engaged in drinking bouts and orgies in government dachas. Moreover, he allowed his lovers and friends to attend official ceremonies in the Kremlin and Red Square, booked government theatre boxes for them and overlooked some serious embezzlement of funds from his department. Sudoplatov claimed that it took torture and beatings to make Vlasik confess all those crimes, but during the court hearing on 17 January 1955, two years after Stalin's death, the former bodyguard quite freely admitted his negligence of duty.[15]

As the head of the Chief Directorate of Protection of the Ministry for State Security from 1947 to 1952, he said, he indeed kept secret documents at home, appropriated valuables captured during the war – after his arrest virtually tons of hand-blown lead crystal and cut-glass accessories, tableware, vases and glasses, in addition to fine china and fourteen cameras with various lenses, were confiscated from his state apartment and dacha. Certainly a sex champion, Vlasik cohabited with more than fifteen women during a short period of time and, as he himself admitted, was on the lowest level of moral degradation. But he never was asked and never mentioned his role as a backstage mover in the Kremlin.

The 'inner cabinet' was a sophisticated setup. While Malenkov managed Stalin's personal secretariat, Poskrebyshev was in charge of the Special Sector of the Central Committee that was later transformed into a secret sub-department, the tyrant's political police inside the party that reported only to him. Parallel to that, Stalin's personal protection service under Vlasik watched everybody, including the chief of the MGB, in terms of their loyalty to the leader. Thus, Stalin was not only under a triple guard, but had all power structures of the state under his complete and complex control.

Stalin's daughter recalled in her memoirs that Vlasik 'began to dictate to art workers and arts tastes of comrade Stalin', and '. . . figures listened and followed his councils'. No important function at the Bolshoi Theatre or the Kremlin ornate white-marbled St George's Hall took place without his sanction. She added that Vlasik also damaged the lives and careers of many people.

Wittingly or unwittingly, but certainly because of the personality of the Soviet leader at the time, Vlasik established a new precedent when he moved up from private bodyguard to hidden Kremlin puppeteer. The Kremlin leader himself had elevated his position to that of a counsellor. Would he kill for Stalin? Only in one case – when there would be a direct attack or a threat. For the 'wet jobs' at large Stalin had Sudoplatov's service.

In May 1952, Beria managed to undo Vlasik's power and transfer him to Asbest, in Sverdlovsk region, 900 miles east of Moscow, as nothing more than deputy commandant of a correctional labour camp.[16] In November Beria succeeded in removing Poskrebyshev from the Kremlin and a few weeks later the arrest of Vlasik followed. Two Russian authors who recently published a book about Stalin uncovered an eyewitness account of Vlasik's saying: 'If I am arrested, Stalin doesn't have much time left.' Indeed, Stalin was gone in three months allegedly with a cerebral haemorrhage.

Thirty years later, Deriabin, a former subordinate of General Vlasik, wrote:

> The story of Stalin's downfall, as I know it, has an ironic twist. It required the dismantling of a protective system unequalled in history – and this before the eyes of a man who knew better than anyone alive how to defend himself against plotters. Stalin had built around himself a mysterious apparatus whose capabilities were not fully known to any but the top bodyguards themselves and to a few of Stalin's closest associates. It protected him not only against the people but also against his own courtiers – spying on other leaders, blackmailing them and striking from the dark to murder or discredit any who, to Stalin's increasingly suspicious eye, might oppose him.[17]

In 2003, a joint group of Russian and American historians announced their view that the Soviet leader had ingested warfarin, a powerful rat poison that inhibits coagulation of the blood and thus may lead to haemorrhagic stroke. As there was no forensic examination and Stalin was embalmed four days after his death, this could only be accepted as a theory. Vlasik and a few others accused Beria of being Stalin's poisoner.

* * *

Besides complete devotion and readiness to risk his life, a bodyguard of a Russian leader must have some other qualities making him appealing to his master. Lenin's bodyguard Peter Pakal whom Stalin subjected to repression in the 1930s, was a simple man who came from a worker-and-peasant family. Mikhail Soldatov, the bodyguard of Khrushchev, sang Ukrainian songs with the bold leader to help him to calm down and change his mood. Vladimir Medvedev, who served for fourteen years as the bodyguard of Brezhnev and then another six as the personal bodyguard of Gorbachev, was an intelligent and pleasant man, never engaged in palace intrigues.

However, on 19 August 1991, when Mikhail Gorbachev and his family were in the Crimean Black Sea resort of Foros accompanied, as usual, by their personal bodyguard, Yuri Plekhanov, head of the 9th Directorate of the KGB, summoned Mevdedev and ordered him to leave Foros at once. At that moment, the KGB chairman Kryuchkov with a couple of accomplices was attempting a coup d'état in Moscow. Without too much thought, General Medvedev obeyed the order. The Gorbachevs never forgave him.

While the General Secretary was frustrated and locked at his Foros dacha with all communications cut off and nobody to rely on, Boris Yeltsin, the President of Russia, arrived at Moscow's White House at nine o'clock in the morning and climbed the tank with Alexander Korzhakov, the man who would shortly after become the third most influential politician in the country. Thanks to CNN, the whole world saw Yeltsin's 42-year-old bodyguard, with the paunch acquired during two years out of service, wearing a grey baggy suit and a blue tie as he covered his boss while the President of the Russian Federation addressed the nation.

The August Putsch was over in a record time. Kryuchkov was arrested together with others and hours later, on the night of 23–24 August , the monument to Felix Dzierżyński, the founder of the Cheka, in front of the KGB Lubyanka building, was dismantled.

In those August days of 1991 very few people were actually aware of the person standing together with Yeltsin on the tank. In five years every Russian household would know his name.

Alexander Korzhakov was born in January 1950 to a factory workers' family in Moscow. After finishing school he laboured as a metal worker at the Moscow Electro Mechanical Plant. In the army Korzhakov was recruited to the KGB and in 1970 joined the government bodyguards.

At that time Sergei Antonov, an old KGB hand, was in charge of the 9th Directorate. When General Antonov learned that Kalugin just arrived from Washington to work at headquarters, he gave his old friend a call suggesting him to join the directorate as a section chief. The section had more than 1,500 officers whose job was to make sure no harm could be done to the Kremlin leaders. Besides, they were permanently recruiting the service staff – drivers, cooks, house-keepers, and other employees – as secret informers. 'You would have great power,' Antonov said, 'and great perks. You don't even have a decent place to live. With us you'll get everything – an apartment in the best building in Moscow, a car by your door every morning, and first-class food.'[18] Kalugin thought it over and refused.

For many years Korzhakov had served under Lieutenant General Yuri Storozhev and in 1983 was assigned to the bodyguard detail of Andropov, the Chief. In 1985 Korzhakov became one of three bodyguards of Yeltsin, then a candidate to the Politburo.

After Yeltsin was sacked from his high-ranking party positions in October 1987, Korzhakov did not last long and was retired from the service in 1989. In the same year he joined the secretariat of Yeltsin who had been moved to an obscure position as the chairman of the parliamentary committee supervising construction and architecture.

On 12 June 1991 Yeltsin won 57 per cent of the popular vote in the elections for the Russian presidency. In less than half a year the Russian Federation took the Soviet Union's seat in the United Nations. The next day, President Gorbachev resigned and the Soviet Union ceased to exist. In his fifth year in office, Russia's President Vladimir Putin described the collapse of the Soviet Union as 'the greatest geopolitical catastrophe' of the twentieth century.

After the August events Korzhakov was with Yeltsin all the time and in December 1991 became the chief of the newly established Presidential Protection Service and deputy head of Main Protection Directorate, formerly the 9th Directorate, known to its officers as 'the Ninth'. He was now a general commanding a considerable force that, apart from its numerous staff and support, included the Centre for Special Operations.

Yuri Felshtinsky, whose book, *The Age of Assassins: The Rise and Rise of Vladimir Putin* (2007), deals in great detail with the situation, notes that 'after successfully implementing the idea of creating an independent presidential security service and filling all key positions in other newly formed [power] agencies with people personally loyal to himself, Korzhakov effectively became – without this being noticed by anyone, least of all by his boss, Yeltsin – the second man in Russia.'[19]

'Yeltsin's main dilemma throughout his entire administration,' writes Alex Goldfarb, another well-informed insider, 'was just how far he was willing to violate democracy in order to save it. In fall 1993, the Supreme Soviet – the parliament, which was still full of ex-Soviet apparatchiks – had blocked his reforms and called on federal regions to rebel. Yeltsin disbanded the legislature and sent tanks to smoke out the deputies who barricaded themselves inside; 140 died in the melee. It was a tough choice, but the alternative had seemed worse: total economic collapse and political implosion.'[20]

It was clear that the battle for voters and subsequently for the course the country would take lay in the control of the media, and first of all, television. Ostankino TV was effectively influencing the opinions of some 200 million people who inhabited the territory of the now defunct Soviet Union. To bring them to the side of the president was the matter of primary importance.

Two people understood that better than anyone else. One was Boris Berezovsky, who had recently gained access to Yeltsin with the help of Valentin Yumashev, and Vladimir Gusinsky, nicknamed Goose, a former show-master and the owner of NTV – at that time, the only private television network in the country – and of Most-Bank, which served the Moscow's mayor's office. Yumashev was a successful journalist with the country's *perestroika*-era most popular magazine *Ogonyok* when I got to know him in 1987. Valentin, usually called by friends and colleagues by his diminutive, Valik or Valya, was then in charge of the readers' letters department. He later rose to become deputy editor and then editor-in-chief of the magazine and was chosen to ghostwrite the president's memoirs. There he met Yeltsin's good-looking daughter, Tatiana Dyachenko, who was married, in her second marriage, to a businessman, and would soon give birth to her second son. Valik and Tatiana got along well and arranged that Berezovsky be introduced to two important people of the Yeltsin's inner circle: Victor Ilyushin, the former chief of his secretariat at the Supreme Soviet, and in the Kremlin at the time first assistant to the President; and Alexander Korzhakov, Yeltsin's most powerful bodyguard.

Berezovsky's concern was Channel One, broadcasting news and programmes across ten time zones, because that would be instrumental in Yeltsin's presidential campaign of 1996. Boris suggested privatising it with 51 per cent belonging to the state and the rest to private investors and convinced Yeltsin's closest assistants that 'he was the man who could control the airwaves for the benefit of the reforms and the president'. Soon the ORT was born that stood for Russian Public Television, a.k.a. Berezovsky's channel, as Goldfarb put it.

In this attempt to control the airwaves, Gusinsky with his NTV turned to be Boris's natural rival.

On that memorable day in December 1994, Goose's motorcade left his country's dacha as usual. In the lead was a fast car with watchers scanning both sides of the road. Then came Goose's armoured Mercedes, followed by an SUV swaying from side to side to make sure that no one attempted to pass, and finally a windowless van carrying a team of former paratroopers led by a fierce, egg-headed gorilla nicknamed Cyclops.

Suddenly word came through the guards' earphones: 'We have company.'

Someone was tailing the convoy. Gusinsky's driver floored the gas pedal and they screeched up to the Most-Bank headquarters, located in one of the city's tallest buildings, which also housed City Hall. It was formerly the headquarters of Comecon, the economic command centre of the Soviet bloc. Shielded by bodyguards, Goose disappeared inside and rushed straight into the safety of the mayor's office.

Moments later his pursuers arrived, about thirty strong, in flak jackets and balaclavas, armed with automatic weapons and grenade launchers. For the next two hours, in horrified disbelief, Goose watched from the mayor's window. The attackers, who evidently belonged to a branch of the secret service, disarmed his men and put them facedown in the snow, where they remained for nearly two hours, in full view of a crowd of spectators and TV cameras. The city police, called to the scene, exchanged a few words with the attackers and then quietly drove away. So did an FSB squad, alerted by Most-Bank staff, who thought a robbery was in progress.

Eventually the assailants left, as mysteriously as they appeared, without identifying themselves or explaining the reasons for the raid. The next morning Goose took his family to London and the safety of the Park Lane Hotel, where he remained for several months. The managers of his vast business empire shuttled back and forth from Moscow to London.'[21]

'Hunting geese is among my favourite hobbies,' Korzhakov told a Russian weekly on 18 January 1995. Indeed, duck-hunting and goose-shooting have always been the Kremlin hard men's most favourite pastime. For Yeltsin's bodyguard it was revenge for humiliation. But demonstrating power was not Korzhakov's only aim. As one of the officers of his Special Operations Centre later recalled, 'Our task was to provoke Gusinsky into action and to find out whose support he had secured in the government.'

They quickly found out that Gusinsky had called Eugeny Savostyanov, the chief of the FSK (the successor of the KGB, later to be renamed the FSB) Directorate for Moscow and Moscow region. On the same day as his men raided the tycoon's domain, Korzhakov insisted that General Savostyanov should be replaced. Anatoly Trofimov, an experienced investigator close to Korzhakov, was installed instead.

On 30 August 1995 Yeltsin's second grandson, Gleb Dyachenko, was born and in March 1996 Tatiana joined her father's presidential election committee as its leading member. By that time many changes had taken place in Moscow.

Better than anyone else, Korzhakov was aware of his boss's ailing health. Shortly before the elections, Yeltsin was recuperating from a series of heart attacks. Puffing and bloated with medication, he was watching his popularity closing to zero. Domestic and international observers also noted his occasionally erratic behaviour. Under the circumstances, Korzhakov wanted to surround himself with people who would secure his prominent behind-the-scenes role in the Russian state affairs. But being a simple and dull-witted person, he based his choice on primitive considerations. He chose Mikhail Barsukov, the newly appointed FSB director who had previously been the head of the Main Protection Directorate, Korzhakov's own service, and First Deputy Prime Minister Oleg Soskovets, whom he hoped one day to install in the president's office and who was under an ongoing investigation in Kazakhstan for financial abuses and corruption (he was never prosecuted). As an extra advantage, neither of the two could boast an intellectual superiority to Korzhakov. So he concentrated on removing Anatoly Chubais, First Deputy Chairman of the Russian government now in charge of economy and finance, as his main adversary.

Chubais, a young 'dissident economist' from Leningrad, worked as deputy to the law professor named Anatoly Sobchak, a prominent democrat elected the Chairman of the Leningrad Council in 1990. He became Sobchak's economic adviser when the university professor was elected mayor. In May 1990, Sobchak appointed Vladimir Putin as his adviser on international affairs. Korzhakov sent one of his officers, Victor Zolotov, as an official government bodyguard to the Leningrad mayor during whose time in the office the city restored its original name, St Petersburg. Having settled in the northern capital, Zolotov established a private security firm named Baltic Escort, one of the first in the city, and installed Roman Tsepov, a former captain of the internal militia troops, as its head. Tsepov's people started to protect Putin and his family and soon Baltic Escort became the biggest and the most important security company of St Petersburg. Tsepov was not only in charge of the security matters, but showed himself as a talented organiser and an indispensable liaison with the criminal underworld of the most corrupt city of Russia.

In November 1991 Chubais became a minister in the Yeltsin's Cabinet in charge of the State Property Committee. He would soon be scornfully called 'the Privatiser' for his role in Russian privatisation.

The programme was launched by the decree signed by President Yeltsin on 19 August 1991. As deputy chairman of the government, Chubais organised the 'loans-for-shares' privatisations that quickly made two dozen Kremlin-connected businessmen, who became known as 'oligarchs', enormously wealthy. Initially, the Privatiser wanted to sell state companies to highest bidders. But the Russian parliament approved a voucher privatisation scheme similar to the one adopted in the Czech Republic where each citizen was given a voucher allowing him or her to acquire a share of state property at auction. The scheme had led to a fiasco in the Czech Republic and in 1997–99 was sharply echoed in Azerbaijan. Amazingly, in both Prague and Baku, one and the same international fraudster, named Viktor Kozeny, was the main perpetrator of the elaborated financial fraud that rid the investors of hundreds of millions of dollars. In Moscow, a handful of men and a woman managed to make a fortune. Chubais headed the State Property Committee until November 1994.

His apparent favour with the West, 'from the Clinton administration, to the World Bank and International Monetary Fund, to the flock of Harvard University advisers who were helping him build such capitalist institutions as a stock market and a tax service,'[22] certainly made Chubais a liability in the Korzhakov's mind.

In January 1995 Korzhakov managed to install Nikolai Yegorov, a hard-liner, as Yeltsin's chief of staff. As in June Barsukov was elevated to become the director of the security service and Yuri Krapivin was appointed head of the Main Protection Directorate, Korzhakov arranged that it was placed under the command of the Presidential protection service (SBP), that is, himself. A year later, in early January 1996, the pro-Western Foreign Minister Andrei Kozyrev was replaced by an arch-hawk, Evgeny Primakov, the former chief of the Russian foreign intelligence. Without doubt acting on the tip of his personal bodyguard, Yeltsin opened his presidential election year by sacking Chubais from the government and appointing Soskovets to chair his re-election staff assisted by two generals: the FSO's Korzhakov and the FSB's Barsukov, at one fell swoop.

While all those battles were fought in Moscow, Frederick Forsyth was working on his novel, which would soon come out as *Icon*, in the comfort of his English countryside. The writer predicted a neo-fascist coup with the Russian democracy only saved at the last moment by a small group of Western intelligence wizards. In reality, it was saved, albeit not for long, by Boris Berezovsky and a few people whom he could persuade that his course was just. Not that they had much doubt that if Yeltsin lost, the Communists would hang them from the lamp-posts.

It was a difficult victory, but they had won. In June Korzhakov, who by that time had become First Assistant to the President in addition to his post of the chief of SBP, was dismissed. Yeltsin's daughter, Tatiana, became her father's loyal and capable assistant. In July Anatoly Chubais was appointed Yeltsin's chief of staff to be succeeded eight months later by Valentin Yumashev. Together with Korzhakov, the president in a nationally televised address also fired two of his buddies, Barsukov and Soskovets.

Next morning, when Litvinenko arrived at the Lubyanka headquarters, a Barsukov assistant summoned him to his office. 'Tell Boris that if Korzhakov or Barsukov are arrested, he is dead,' the man said. Sasha dutifully delivered the message.[23]

They were never arrested. In the run-off on 3 July Yeltsin won 53.8 per cent of the vote in a decisive victory against the Communists. After one year of virtual unemployment in the active reserve, Barsukov was appointed to oversee the presidential dachas and later downgraded to chair the commission in charge of subterranean facilities. Korzhakov attempted to sue the president but the court rejected the suit. In February 1997 he was elected member of parliament and soon joined the Defence Committee. Korzhakov's revenge was an anti-Yeltsin book *From Dawn to Dusk* that he published in Moscow in the same year.

Contrary to some expectations, Yumashev married not Tatiana Dyachenko but the sister of Oleg Deripaska, who ten years later would become the richest man of Russia. Yumashev's daughter, Polina Deripaska, was born in London.

On Christmas Eve, *Time* magazine announced their Person of the Year 2007: Vladimir Putin. The article that followed the picture of the man with cool eyes devoid of any emotion was entitled 'A Tsar is Born'.

It is a peculiar quality of Russian politics that the principal of the Kremlin, be it a tsar, a general secretary or a president, is endowed with a mystical quality of *vlast*, or 'right of power,' which instils in the populace a measure of instinctive humility and respect. This regal ingredient of supreme authority links all historical rulers in Russia into a single virtual dynasty from the House of Romanovs through Lenin and Stalin down to Gorbachev and Yeltsin.[24]

Eight months before the election, Boris Berezovsky met Putin in the old KGB building.

'Volodya, what about you?' he asked.

'What about me?' Putin did not understand.

'Could you be president?'

'Me? No, I am not the type. This is not what I want in life.'

'Well, then, what? Do you want to stay here forever?'

'I want . . .', he hesitated. 'I want to be Berezovsky.'

'No, you don't really,' Boris laughed.[25]

I dare say that *Time* was wrong, as it was twice wrong with Stalin. After his two terms in office a tsar was not born in Putin. But he almost managed to become Boris Berezovsky. Now he needed to eliminate the prototype.

In the autumn of 2008 I had been tempted for quite some time to call Masha Gessen in Paris warning her that her life was in danger. Finally, I decided not to frighten the brave lady who probably fully realised it herself, as she was the author of a brilliant article about Putin published in the October issue of *Vanity Fair*, a very popular magazine. The banner read:

Few saw what he really was, or the way he brutally erased his footprints on the climb to power. Fewer still survived to decode him. As Russian forces bend Georgia to their will, Masha Gessen tells how one small, faceless man backed by the vast secret-police machine that formed him – took control of the world's largest country.

Masha almost managed to decode the man. Her story is very compelling, but not complete.

After returning from his tour of duty in East Germany, where his spy work neither brought any results nor gave any push to his KGB career, Putin joined the mayor's staff that Sobchak hurriedly formed from those he knew at the university, and in June 1991 was promoted to head the Committee for External Relations. At that time he never planned to make a prominent career not to mention a top post in Moscow so he did what all bureaucrats do best of all: took bribes. But being a cautious former intelligence officer, Putin knew the basic laws of tradecraft. One of them dictates that someone else must always do the dirty work, and another that the situation when one could be caught must by all means be avoided. There's still the third rule that says there must be no witnesses. And, of course, yet another important principle is to deny any involvement. Putin played by the rules.

Obviously an observant journalist, Masha has noticed a thread that runs all through the Putin story: everyone who knows anything about him is leaving in exile or dead or working in the Russian government very close to the man himself.

One of those exiles, she reports, Marina Salye, now lives in a village in Russia more than 100 miles from St Petersburg. Throughout the 1990s, Salye was a leading liberal politician in St Petersburg, deputy of the legislative assembly of the city, one of only two women prominent on the national liberal political scene since *perestroika*. (The other, Galina Starovoitova, was shot dead in her apartment building in St Petersburg in 1998.) In 1992 Salye headed a committee of the city council formed to investigate the activity of the deputy mayor, Vladimir Putin. After she and another deputy, Yuri Gladkov, presented the results of the investigation, the city council passed a resolution calling for the mayor to fire Putin and to have the prosecutor's office investigate apparent corruption and misappropriation of funds. The mayor ignored the recommendation. In early 2000, in the run-up to the presidential elections, Salye campaigned against Putin, attempting to draw attention to the conclusions of the committee's investigation.[26]

Then, abruptly, she left St Petersburg and disappeared. Masha learned why. Around New Year's Day 2001, her sources told her, Salye received a holiday telegram from President Putin. 'Here is wishing you good health,' the telegram said, 'and the opportunity to use it.' The next day, she packed up and moved to the most obscure place she could find. Salye today won't speak publicly about this or anything else. The fact that this account of her disappearance is believed by many Russians active in liberal politics, including some who know Putin, speaks volumes about the way the former (and, quite possibly, the future) president is perceived not only as small-minded and vengeful but also as vulgar and unsubtle.[27]

And what happened to Yuri Gladkov? The deputy chairman of the Legislative Assembly of St Petersburg died on 6 October 2007 from amyotrophic lateral sclerosis (ALS). Experts know that ALS can be simulated by mercury intoxication or exposure to other heavy metals. And the date, as in the case of Anna Politkovskaya, is remarkable – Putin's birthday. (Had Gladkov survived just a couple of hours longer, he would still have been well in time; certainly no autopsy had ever been performed.)

Putin's Committee for External Relations was also used to register business ventures in the city. With the help of Tsepov, Putin was attempting to gain control over the emerging gambling industry of St Petersburg. In the end, he succeeded in securing for the city 51 percent share of all casinos – but this, he later claimed, did nothing for the city's coffers, because casino managers ran with the cash. Something similar, Putin explained, also happened with federal credits the city was supposed to use to stimulate food imports: he claimed that the private companies contracted by the city vanished with the money. The 1992 investigation by Salye and Gladkov drew a different conclusion: partnerships with private companies were structured in such a way as to siphon money with impunity. This was not the only allegation of misconduct levelled against Putin: in 1999 the St Petersburg prosecutor's office launched an investigation into the alleged misappropriation of some $4.5 million earmarked for reconstruction projects; the investigation was closed in August 2000, after Putin became president. One of the investigators on the case has since joined a monastery while the other has retired. Everyone named by the investigation now has a top government position – including Russia's president at the time of writing, Dmitry Medvedev, who, if the prosecutors are to be believed, was the man who actually engineered the transfers of earmarked funds.[28] The investigation commission also concluded that Putin understated prices and issued licenses permitting the export of non-ferrous metals valued at a total of $93 million in exchange for food supplies from abroad that never came to the city, wrote the *St Petersburg Times* when Putin entered his second term as president.

In 1992 while the commission was investigating, Putin travelled to Frankfurt am Main in Germany as part of the city delegation to attract investments. Vladimir Smirnov, a budding St Petersburg businessman, was another member of the delegation. Smirnov explained to those who were eager to listen that the best return on their capital would be by investing money in real estate of their choice in the second most important city of the country whose economy would soon be booming. As it was fashionable at the time, he suggested setting up a Russo-German property-development joint-venture company. The St Petersburg city government was giving its wholehearted support to the project, he said. Soon Putin's Committee for External Relations duly registered the St Petersburg Real Estate Holding Company (known by its German acronym, SPAG) with Smirnov managing its Russian operations. As usual, staying in the shadow (another professional trait), Putin was among the officials registered as 'advisory board' separate from the board of directors.

The company operated in obscurity until Putin became the prime minister of Russia, when SPAG caught the eye of US and European intelligence agencies. Its name turned up in a probe by Germany's BND of alleged money laundering that was operated through Liechtenstein, a notorious tax haven. The BND accused the company's cofounder, Rudolf Ritter, who contributed much of SPAG's seed capital, of laundering funds for both Russian organised crime and Colombian drug traffickers. A German intelligence report also suggested that Russian criminals were using SPAG to buy property inside Russia.[29]

In 2000 Putin's newly appointed spokesman, Dmitry Peskov, denied the president had ever 'worked for it as an adviser'. Ritter was later investigated on money-laundering charges and this was widely reported by the world's media.

The *Newsweek* investigation, however, revealed that Putin was at least in regular, and sometimes close, contact with some of the company's key Russian and foreign directors over a period of years, and even signed important St Petersburg city documents for the company's benefit. Klaus-Peter Sauer, a German account-ant who helped found SPAG and at the time of investigation was still a company director, said he met Putin about six times both in Russia and Frankfurt. Sauer said SPAG founder Ritter travelled to St Petersburg and met Putin at least once.[30]

He remained on the advisory board of SPAG from the day of its inception in 1992 until March 2002. The SPAG records obtained by *Newsweek* from a German commercial registry showed that in December 1994, Putin signed an affidavit on St Petersburg's behalf giving Smirnov voting power over the city government's 200 shares in the company.

In 1994, as deputy mayor, Putin granted the Petersburg Fuel Company (PTK) a virtual monopoly over petrol sales in the city and all municipal buses, taxis, ambulances and police vehicles were obliged to fill up their cars at the PTK petrol stations. The president of the PTK was Vladimir Smirnov and the vice-president Vladimir Kumarin, the leader of the powerful Tambov gang in St Petersburg. Kumarin was also listed as a director of one of SPAG's most important subsidiaries.

But Putin's contact to Kumarin was not so much through Smirnov as via Tsepov, who was his liaison with the city's underground. It is documented that Alexander Tkachenko, nicknamed Tkach, the leader of the Perm organised crime group, was a one time employee of Baltic Escort; Ruslan Kolyak, another criminal authority, worked in one of the companies controlled by Tsepov; Alexander Malyshev, organiser of the Malyshev gang (at the time of writing under arrest in Spain), was Tsepov's 'business associate'; and there were other criminals, most of them later murdered, engaged in racket, extortion, corruption including bribes to local government, and violent clashes with each other.

Two years after the PTK deal, Putin together with Smirnov co-founded the Ozero ('Lake') cooperative, an exclusive country cottage settlement on the Komsomol Lake near St Petersburg. By that time Smirnov had already been placed in charge of investments and the real estate belonging to the city as the general manager of the public joint stock company especially established for this matter.

According to Masha Gessen, it was as deputy mayor that Putin finally got to play the roles he had yearned for as a child: he was both a shadow ruler and a thug. But if some or even all the claims of wrongdoing are true, she notes, by the standards of 1990s Russia, Putin was no more than small-time crook in a large city. He just happened to be the only small-time crook to become the president of Russia.

In 1996 Putin was in charge of his former teacher's re-election and Sobchak lost. Almost immediately, the city prosecutor's office, fortified by forty investigators from Moscow, launched a probe into corruption. A year later, the former mayor and an acknowledged democrat fled to France with Putin's help while at least one member of his administration was arrested and another killed, shot to death in broad daylight in the centre of St Petersburg. But, as the *Vanity Fair* reporter observed, Putin made an uneventful transition to Moscow, as though airlifted by an invisible KGB hand.[31]

In reality, all was much simpler. The former deputy mayor called his friend Chubais, who was heading the 'analytical group' created by Berezovsky to get Yeltsin re-elected, and begged his former colleague to take him to Moscow. Chubais saw no objections. Perhaps he exchanged words with Boris who recalled how Putin had helped him to set up shop in the city when Berezovsky owned a car dealership and that the deputy mayor neither demanded nor accepted a bribe. In June 1996 Putin was appointed Deputy Chief of the Presidential Property Management Department.

The year was the turning point for many events that were to follow. In 1996 Zolotov and Lugovoy, and then Sokolenko and Talik left the FSO, formerly the 9th Directorate of the KGB, to start their careers as officers of the active reserve elsewhere. Zolotov remained in St Petersburg in control of the growing business formally under Tsepov. Lugovoy was employed by Berezovsky as chief of the security service of his ORT. Sokolenko started a private security business and Talik went to try his luck in Ukraine, as, according to him, he couldn't find any job in Russia. During the same year, Limarev became a 'public adviser' to Gennady Seleznev, the Communist speaker of the Russian parliament. In December 1999, Talik arrived in Italy where he settled illegally.

It is hard to say how Valentin Velichko, a low-profile counter-intelligence officer of the foreign intelligence directorate, who had been expelled from Holland as a spy in the late 1980s, came across Limarev's radar. He was just one of the KGB vets chairing a veteran organisation called 'Honour and Dignity'. A much better candidate to come into the limelight would be Valery Velichko, likewise a KGB vet and chairman of the veterans' club Vega, who had supported Kryuchkov's putsch in 1991. Before retirement, this Velichko had served as the chief of staff of the 9th Directorate and was one of the co-founders of the Russian National Economic Security Service and Centre for Bodyguards and Protection Personnel Training. My guess is that owing to the too obvious ties of Valery Velichko with the all-important players of the Litvinenko operation, he was substituted – a standard trick – by another man with a very similar name. This said, it seems quite obvious that neither Valentin nor Valery Velichko had anything to do with the Litvinenko operation. Many journalists spent time and energy researching the substitute and his career until finally he became quite well known.

In the Kremlin Putin was moving up rapidly enough. On 11 March 1997 Yumashev succeeded Chubais as Yeltsin's chief of staff and two weeks later named Putin his deputy. In June Putin finally defended his master's thesis in economics at the St Petersburg Mining Institute. Corruption was at play even there. According to Clifford G. Gaddy, a senior fellow at Brookings Institution, a Washington think-tank, sixteen of the twenty pages that open a key section of Putin's work were copied either word for word or with minute alterations from a management study, *Strategic Planning and Policy*, written in 1978 by US professors William King and David Cleland. The study was translated into Russian by a KGB-related institute in the early 1990s.[32]

In November 1997 Putin went to St Petersburg to organise 'the rescue of Sobchak'. The corruption case against the mayor's office finally reached the mayor himself and criminal proceedings were launched against him. They say he suffered a heart attack while under interrogation, on the same day as the Attorney General signed his arrest warrant. From the police cell Sobchak was taken to a hospital where Yuri Shevchenko, a military physician and Putin's friend, diagnosed a serious heart disease. For a while, Sobchak was hospitalised in Military Hospital No. 122 and then was transferred to the Military Medical Academy headed by Shevchenko. On 7 November Putin allegedly used his contacts to smuggle his ailing teacher and former boss to Paris by a private jet.

I have some doubt about the altruism of such a move. Putin has not been noted as a kind, honest or helpful person either before or since. And the St Petersburg FSB could not fail to notice a former mayor and very famous Russian politician leaving hospital or boarding a plane to Europe. They had informers enough to be forewarned of such activities anyway: Zolotov and Tsepov were there, Evgeny Murov, future director of the FSO, was at that time deputy chief of the FSB in St Petersburg from 1992 headed by Victor Cherkesov,[33] an appointment believed to have been engineered by Putin, who was his friend. According to Masha Gessen, to this day Cherkesov's name makes former dissidents from St Petersburg cringe, so he could hardly miss the opportunity to grab Sobchak, one of the leading liberals. For whatever reason, the security service decided to allow Sobchak to escape and Putin to help him. This certainly greatly enhanced his reputation and favourably impressed the president especially when the story of Putin's 'heroic behaviour' and devotion to the mayor reached the Kremlin. In reality, it was a criminal act as he was helping someone to escape justice. But no one seemed to care at the time.

In May 1998 Putin was appointed First Deputy Chief of Staff for regions with the job of preparing agreements granting more power to the local authorities in the former autonomous republics of the Russian Federation like Chechnya, Tatarstan or Bashkortostan. Before Putin, they were allowed to bite off as much sovereignty as they could chew, but with him chairing the commission no more agreements were signed. Putin's wish to preserve the Soviet Union as it had been under Stalin would later be reflected in his aggressive policy towards Estonia, Ukraine, Georgia, Moldova and Chechnya.

One summer day Yumashev, who often discussed major government appointments with Berezovsky, asked for his opinion about Putin.

'Why?'

'We are considering him for the FSB directorship.'

Yumashev explained that the principal quality the president was seeking in a new security chief was loyalty, but he didn't trust any of the FSB generals. If Putin had one defining feature, he said, it was staunch loyalty.

Boris liked the idea of putting a lieutenant colonel over generals; the newcomer would not be a part of the old-boy network and would almost certainly be snubbed by the top brass, which would only strengthen his loyalty to the Kremlin.

'I support him 100 per cent,' Boris said.[34]

As usual, he was wrong about people.

When the new director took office on 25 July, Boris said to Sasha Litvinenko: 'Go see Putin. Make yourself known. See what a great guy we've installed, with your help.'[35]

In fact Litvinenko had not helped at all to instal Putin at the Lubyanka; he had never heard of the man until Boris mentioned him. But Sasha was happy to comply and took time to prepare for the meeting.

They did not hit it off at once. Putin was cold and formal. He listened in silence to Sasha's passionate depiction of corruption in the service, and refused to accept hand-drawn diagrams that Litvinenko had prepared to show relations between the FSB officers and the criminals. Putin said he would call if he needed the, hmm, lieutenant colonel further.

'I know a man by his handshake,' Sasha told Marina after that meeting. 'His was cold and spongy. I could see it in his eyes that he hated me.'[36]

Certainly, no one cared about what Sasha Litvinenko thought when in 1999 the Family, which by that time included Putin and Roman Abramovich, a future boyfriend of Daria Zhukova, decided to make the former petty spy first prime minister and then president. The image-makers presented a completely unknown 47-year-old as a loyal and honest young man who would shepherd Russia into a bright economic future and stable democracy. Folk will gulp down everything, a modern Russian proverb says. And the folk did.

For her *Vanity Fair* article Gessen managed to interview Marina Litvinovich who was a top manager at the think-tank that ran Putin's campaign. 'We said he was young, energetic and would institute much-needed reforms,' Marina explained. 'People were so tired of Yeltsin that this was easy to sell. Even more incredibly,' the reporter added, 'Western leaders and the Western media bought the story, too.'[37]

Well, there are no fools and many Western leaders just pretended to believe in the newly projected image of Putin, each pursuing his private priorities in the first place. It may have been establishing his public image, as in the case of Tony Blair, or economic considerations, as with Silvio Berlusconi, or some long-range personal objectives, as with Gerhard Schröder. However, unlike in Russia, there are no illusions in the West about how economy and democracy work. There are rules.

People who knew Putin even before he became a president came to understand that he was mean, small-minded, and vindictive. And very ill-mannered. In 1999, having only recently been appointed prime minister, he promised: 'We'll follow terrorists everywhere. Should we catch them in a shithouse, we'll waste them there.' In September 2000, when Larry King asked Putin what had happened to the *Kursk* nuclear submarine, whose crew perished when Russian officials refused to allow Norwegian rescue teams near the site of the accident, Putin smiled like a mischievous schoolboy and said, 'It drowned.' In November 2002, during a EU-Russia summit, a French journalist asked a question about bombings affecting the civilian population of Chechnya. Putin responded by suggesting that the questioner was an 'Islamic radical' who would do well to come to Russia to procure a circumcision, 'and I'd recommend that the operation be performed in such a way that nothing will grow there again'. In September 2004, after the tragedy of Beslan, Putin explained the failure of Russia's security services with the sentence, 'We were weak. And the weak are being beaten.' In October 2006, during a meeting with Israeli Prime Minister Ehud Olmert, Putin commented on the sexual harassment scandal that had brought down Israeli president Moshe Katsav. 'Your president is a mighty man,' he said. 'He managed to rape 10 women! We are all envious of him.'[38] With Russian tanks only 40 miles from Tbilisi, Georgia, in the August of 2008, French President Nicolas Sarkozy told Putin that the world would not accept the overthrow of Georgia's president. Putin seemed unconcerned. 'I am going to hang Saakashvili by the balls,' he declared. A lavatorial sense of humour.

It may be a coincidence, but in 2006 Litvinovich, who had contributed remarks about Putin to the *Vanity Fair* article, was attacked in the centre of Moscow and beaten senseless. Masha Gessen mentioned in her article that the attackers did not take any of her possessions.

In June 1999 the prosecutors dropped their charges against Anatoly Sobchak and he was able to return to Russia. It had nothing to do with Putin as he was still a rather small Kremlin cog. Only several weeks later Yeltsin appointed him director of the FSB and in August acting prime minister. By the time of Sobchak's return from his self-imposed exile in France, Yuri Shevchenko, a friend of the Putin's family, had already become federal health minister.

As soon as Putin became the prime minister, he immediately recalled Zolotov from St Petersburg and put him in charge of his personal protection service thus returning him to active duty in the FSO.

Sobchak became an enthusiastic supporter of his former student's quest for presidency. He probably hoped to get an important government post after Putin was elected. This might explain his exuberance when on 16 February 2000 Putin, already the acting president of Russia, asked him to fly to Kaliningrad urgently to campaign for him. As a matter of fact, no such campaigning was necessary as the media and advertising did the job smartly and Putin was the officially announced heir apparent anyway. But for whatever reason, he asked him. And he went.

Sobchak died suddenly three days later in his hotel room in the spa town of Svetlogorsk on the Baltic Sea. During the autopsy in Kaliningrad it was established that the initial diagnosis was falsified, that he never had a heart attack (Shevchenko claimed that he had three and the fourth finished him), and that the former mayor and popular politician died of acute myocardial infarction caused by a blood clot that stopped blood flow in his heart.

Sobchak's funeral in St Petersburg turned into a big public show for Putin, who was accompanied by Berezovsky, with major newspapers and television channels concentrating not on the gone professor, but on the alleged threat to the acting president. From that moment on, Zolotov was always behind his back.

***

Vladimir Vladimirovich Putin was inaugurated president on 7 May 2000. But even before that, in April, Dmitry Peskov was appointed first deputy press attaché for the president. On 18 May, following the advice of his personal bodyguard, Putin appointed General Evgeny Murov chief of the Federal Protection Service (FSO). Murov, a former foreign intelligence officer, was a contact person for Zolotov in St Petersburg and last served as deputy chief of the Economic Department at the headquarters where he was guarding and multiplying the cash flow of his superiors. In May, Putin also installed Sergey Lebedev as chief of foreign intelligence, the SVR.

Thus Putin 'inner cabinet' was formed. It included Dmitry Medvedev, who worked with him and Sobchak in St Petersburg, following Putin to Moscow as deputy chief of presidential staff in December 1999. Subsequently, Medvedev was put in charge of Putin's presidential election campaign. Two other of the most important and closest assistants who physically guarded the president were Murov and Zolotov. They were also in charge of 'special tasks' and formed both Putin's secret police and his private intelligence service. Another very important figure was Igor Sechin, traditionally the deputy chief of Putin's administration (all key figures of his shadow inner cabinet are characteristically given formal second roles). In the 1980s Sechin worked in Mozambique and Angola as an interpreter, which was usually a cover for intelligence or a special reserve officer but Stratfor was certainly wrong claiming that he was the KGB *rezident* in those countries.[39] Another allegation that Sechin was 'the USSR's point man for weapons smuggling to much of Latin America and the Middle East' could be true – a source of mine, himself a retired dealer living in hiding in Paris, confirmed this information.

Finally, Peskov became a trusted member of the Russian president's closely knit team. With this inner group of cronies in place, Putin started to drive the country his way.

In September 2000 the world leaders planned to hold the United Nations Millennium Summit in New York and the newly elected Russian president was going to attend. In summer, Murov sent his deputy, Alexander Lunkin, to Manhattan to take care of the security arrangements for the visit. Upon arriving, Lunkin first of all called his old acquaintance whom he knew from their Komsomol years in the KGB. Sergey Tretyakov was now the deputy SVR station chief in New York based at the UN headquarters. He managed the impressive group of sixty intelligence officers working under different guises in the Big Apple and over 150 foreign sources – contacts with a different degree of trust, from recruited agents to useful informers – who provided the Russian foreign intelligence with much needed information.[40] And not only information.

One of Tretyakov's operatives under diplomatic cover became a pivotal player in the UN humanitarian aid programme using his position to help Russia steal hundreds of millions of dollars that were supposed to be spent helping the civil population of Iraq. Another important source, a Russian immigrant living in the United States, delivered millions of dollars' worth of stolen medical research that landed on the table of Putin's friend, doctor Yuri Shevchenko. Still another under-cover SVR officer, a permanent representative to the UN from Azerbaijan, was delivering top-grade intelligence about the Clinton administration's plans and strategy in oil-rich Baku. This intelligence could have helped the SVR to make a valuable input into Victor Kozeny's famous fraud scheme in the republic, his two closest assistants being an American, Thomas Farrell, and a Swiss, Hans Bodmer, who both pleaded guilty in the Baku affair, admitting wrongdoings. It is inter-esting that before and after the Kozeny operation in Azerbaijan that went on from 1997 to 1999, Farrell lived in St Petersburg and worked in local security firms while Tsepov, Kumarin and Zolotov were fully in control of the protection busi-ness there. At the time of writing, Farrell was still in St Petersburg, permitted to return there after he struck a deal with the American prosecutors. He now owns the famous Shamrock Irish Bar near the Opera. The Swiss lawyer, Bodmer, was also allowed to return to Zurich where he continued wheeling and dealing for his Moscow masters, most recently being a defendant in another case of massive money-laundering and fraud involving structures close to the Kremlin. The Kozeny scam stripped American investors of $200 million. Kozeny, who was indicted in October 2005 by a federal grand jury in Manhattan, escaped to the Bahamas where he now lives in Lyford Cay. After a local court ruled against his extradition to the United States, he is as free a man as Lugovoy – not being able to travel anywhere.

Sitting round a dinner table with an old chum in Tretyakov's New York apart-ment, Lunkin reported news from Moscow. He said that two guards, Murov and

Zolotov, were especially close to the president. But the Russian spymaster didn't get it exactly right when four years later he told Pete Earley that Zolotov 'had been a steelworker before he was hired as a bodyguard by the St Petersburg mayor'.

Victor Zolotov was born in January 1954 and after finishing secondary school indeed worked for a while as a steelworker at the Moscow car factory, widely known in the Soviet Union by its acronym AZLK that produced the infamous Moskvich car. After the army, where he almost certainly served with the Kremlin regiment (the young lieutenant Andrei Lugovoy would later serve there as a drill instructor), Zolotov was recruited to the 9th Directorate of the KGB where he spent almost twenty years honing his skills to become a real professional. He also acquired a taste for marshal arts becoming a master of Oyama Kyokushinkai karate-do and a follower of Mas Oyama's teaching: 'Keep your head low, eyes high, mouth shut; base yourself on filial piety and benefit others.'

When Korzhakov sent him to Leningrad as the personal bodyguard of the mayor, Zolotov was a hard man but felt filial piety to his masters and kept his mouth shut. Putin, who knew him well, greatly appreciated those traits and summoned Zolotov to Moscow as soon as he was able to, placing him in charge of the newly reshuffled Presidential Protection Service. In 2000 Zolotov was a colonel. By the end of Putin's second term – colonel general.

Zolotov is known for his penchant for black sunglasses and – when not in his cornflower blue general's uniform – black suits. His people are called 'Men in Black' in the FSO. They are always armed and very dangerous.

During their friendly dinner in New York in the summer of 2000, Lunkin, who evidently knew his colleagues well, told Tretyakov that Murov and Zolotov were 'common thugs' and warned his friend to be wary of them. The FSO man recalled how Putin felt jealous of his own chief of staff, Alexander Voloshin whom he had inherited from Yeltsin. For years since then he had been deputy to Yumashev and until he left Putin's presidential administration at the end of October 2003, Voloshin was the grey cardinal of the Kremlin. In Lunkin's presence Murov and Zolotov were discussing plans to get rid of Voloshin. Based on his discussions with his old mate, Tretyakov later informed the American authorities that one plan was to murder him and blame Chechen terrorists, while another was to make the Mafia shoulder the blame. Murov and Zolotov knew no one would ever investigate. Or, if they do, any investigation will soon hit a dead end as in the case of Politkovskaya.

'So what happened?' the SVR man asked.

Lunkin said they finally agreed that murdering Voloshin would not end Putin's problems. According to Murov's deputy, two officers closest to Putin also discussed a possibility of assassinating some Russian oligarchs and members of the press corps. He said they finally decided to make a hit list of people they would have to 'liquidate' to give their boss unchecked power. After the list was compiled, Zolotov is said to have announced, 'There are too many. It's too many to kill – even for us.'[41]

Lunkin admitted he was quite embarrassed because Murov and Zolotov commanded a formidable force of some 20,000 troops that included, apart from the leadership, the Special Communication and Information Service, the Special garage, the Kremlin Commandant service and the presidential regiment and orchestra, in addition to underground command bunkers and a wide and well-hidden network of subterranean transportation systems that connected key government facilities.

In August, Murov and Zolotov arrived in New York for a final inspection before the visit.

As Pete Earley puts it:

Sergey [Tretyakov] met frequently with both, and one afternoon they asked him to take them to Brighton Beach to eat at the Tatiana Café, which was where he had taken General Trubnikov [a former KGB chief] and other important visitors. Murov, Zolotov and Sergey were sipping beer and waiting for their meals when Sergey asked Zolotov about the specialised training that his 'Men in Black' received. Zolotov boasted that his bodyguards were much better trained than their US Secret Service counterparts. President John F. Kennedy had been assassinated while riding in an open car, he declared. Whenever Putin travelled, his motorcade consisted of seven specially constructed automobiles, none of which was a convertible, making it impossible for a sniper to know in which car the president was riding. Indian Prime Minister Indira Gandhi was murdered by her own security service in 1984, Zolotov continued. This was why Putin had only his closest friends, such as the two of them, in charge of his security. Gandhi's son was killed when a woman suicide bomber threw herself at him while setting off explosives hidden in a bouquet of flowers. Putin was always ringed by at least twelve of Zolotov's bodyguards whenever he was in public to prevent any such attack. 'No one can get through my men and me and attack him,' Zolotov proudly declared.

Clearly enjoying himself, Zolotov told Sergey that Putin's 'personals' [*lichniki* in Russian] – as his most trusted 'Men in Black' were called – carried 9mm *Gyurza* ('Blunt-nosed viper') pistols that held eighteen bullets and were powerful enough to penetrate bulletproof vests up to fifty-four yards away. They rode in armour-plated jeeps equipped with AK-74 assault rifles, AKS-74U machine guns, Dragunov sniper rifles, RPK machine guns, grenade cup discharges, portable *Osa* ('wasp') rocket launchers, and other powerful armaments that, Zolotov insisted, would enable them to destroy an 'entire battalion' if necessary. In addition to having that weaponry, each 'personal' was a martial arts expert, capable of killing an attacker with a single blow.

Without any warning, Zolotov suddenly swung his hand in the air and struck Sergey in his temple. The blow knocked him off his chair and unconscious on the café floor. Moments later, Sergey awoke with Murov and

Zolotov standing over him. Murov was furious.

'You could have killed him!' he yelled.

Zolotov began apologizing as he helped Sergey into a chair.

'Lunkin was correct,' Sergey said later after meeting Murov and Zolotov. 'They were dangerous.'[42]

At the time of writing, they still are.

On 6 September 2000, Putin spoke at the opening session of the United Nations Millennium Summit of World Leaders. VOA correspondent Breck Ardery reported: 'Mr Putin told the gathering of world leaders that the control of nuclear weapons and the elements used to make them should be a major priority for the world.'

Back in May, Vladimir Smirnov, Putin's business partner in SPAG, Foreign Currency Stock Exchange and the Lake dacha cooperative, was summoned to Moscow and appointed general manager of the mysteriously named Enterprise for the Supply of Goods, a state company working directly with and for the presidential administration.

Two years later Smirnov became the director general of Techsnabexport, one of the four Russian companies licensed to deal in polonium-210 and the only one authorised to export it.

On 3 July 2003 Yuri Shchekochikhin, an investigative journalist, writer and liberal lawmaker who investigated the Russian secret services and the corruption scandal known as 'Three Whales', suddenly died in Moscow aged 53, a few days before his scheduled departure to the United States where he planned to meet FBI agents. Although the Putin government has sealed all the documents pertinent to the case, the broad understanding in Russia is that Shchekochikhin was poisoned.

On 29 June 2004 a St Petersburg journalist, Maxim Maximov, disappeared during a meeting with three police officers. He was never found and is presumed dead. The investigation was swift and led nowhere. Maxim was known to have been investigating some most serious cases implicating Zolotov and Tsepov and their contacts with the city's underworld as well as their shadow business deals. His assassins in uniform were allegedly reporting to Andrei Novikov, a St Petersburg militia man recommended by Tsepov as First Deputy Minister of Interior in charge of criminal police and economic security. The Russian sources report that Novikov was a protégé of Zolotov and the oligarch Oleg Deripaska. In November 2006, Novikov was suddenly dismissed from his high post and placed in charge of the Anti-Terrorist Centre of the Commonwealth of Independent States (CIS), an insignificant position.

Several months after Maximov vanished, Roman Tsepov was poisoned in St Petersburg when he was drinking tea at the local FSB directorate. It was a signature murder – he was poisoned on 9/11 by a radioactive isotope, similar to polonium-210, but not an alpha emitter (perhaps americium-241). His symptoms were very similar to those of Khokhlov and Litvinenko. Tsepov died thirteen days later.

Tsepov was such a popular and powerful figure in the northern capital that one day Deripaska flew in on his private jet just to give him a birthday present of expensive watches.

During 2004 Tsepov was actively seeking direct contacts with Putin whom he knew well personally from the time when he provided bodyguards for him and his family in St Petersburg. He even went to Sochi, Putin's summer residence, to meet him. However, Zolotov was straightforward and told his former associate that such a contact with the president would be undesirable.

Zolotov attended Tsepov's funeral together with Colonel General Novikov and Vladimir Kumarin, who changed his name to Barsukov. The cathedral where the service was arranged had been guarded by special forces and there were more generals than the place could accommodate. Dmitry Mikhalchenko, who was also present in the room when Tsepov was poisoned, was also there. After the funeral he quietly took over Tsepov's businesses.

The next signature murder was on 7 October 2006 when Anna Politkovskaya was shot on Putin's birthday. They certainly couldn't afford another method – the whole effect would be lost should she die in a car accident or of a heart attack. It was all self-protection, of course, as the lady had slapped Putin in the face by publishing her book *Putin's Russia* in the West.

Those who do not know Nikolai Gogol's *Greatcoat* (sometimes erroneously translated as 'Overcoat') would not understand the title of Anna's strongest chapter about Putin, whom she called 'Akaky Akakievich Putin II'. Doesn't matter. Politkovskaya, recognised as the conscience of the Russian post-Soviet journalism, wrote:

> I have wondered a great deal about why I have so got it in for Putin. What is it that makes me dislike him so much as to feel moved to write a book about him? I am not one of his political opponents or rivals, just a woman living in Russia. Quite simply, I am a 45-year-old Moscovite who observed the Soviet Union at its most disgraceful in the 1970s and '80s. I really don't want to find myself back there again.[43]

Three weeks after Politkovskaya's murder Sasha Litvinenko was poisoned. He was a personal enemy of Putin and abused him publicly not only by calling the president a paedophile, but by collaborating with the Chechens, by writing books about the Lubyanka criminal gang, by standing on the side of Berezovsky, by investigating Putin's fledglings in Spain, Austria, Italy and elsewhere, and by calling Romano Prodi 'a man of the KGB'. Prodi might have thought of playing a role similar to that of Schröder when he got an offer, but did not dare.

After the Litvinenko crime was committed and the dust settled, Lugovoy, a nonentity, was rewarded by election to the Duma, the Russian parliament, joining his senior comrades there: spies, recruiters, gangsters, neo-fascists and other Russian politicians.

The head of foreign intelligence, the SVR, General Sergey Lebedev (who had been a senior intelligence officer in Karlshorst where Putin reported from Dresden, and had been a friend of Putin's) was soon dismissed and sent to a minor post at the CIS headquarters. The Litvinenko poisoning had been done professionally, but the polonium trail had been overlooked.

General Nikolai Patrushev, the director of the FSB, was also dismissed and placed in command of a largely symbolic National Security Council. He was in charge of the Russian side of the Litvinenko operation. Litvinenko died, but the consequences for the president were devastating.

In August 2007, a special squad that arrived from Moscow in two SUVs arrested Vladimir Kumarin-Barsukov in St Petersburg. He was then transferred to Moscow's Lefortovo prison where he is still being held. An official representative of the Investigative Committee of the General Prosecutor's Office announced a continuing investigation into Kumarin's possible involvement in a series of crimes, including forming a criminal gang, misappropriation of several enterprises, murder, and attempted execution-style contract killing.

After she was blacklisted by Putin's press service, Masha Gessen moved to France. From time to time she meets Alex Goldfarb in Paris.

Alex tried to explain why it was not just the Kremlin but Putin himself who was behind Litvinenko's murder. 'To set something like this in motion, you need a top-level decision,' he said. 'Even back in the USSR, it was the Central Committee that approved plans to kill someone outside the country. So who can give permission at the top level? Someone who wields power over both the FSB and the nuclear agency. Bear in mind that polonium has a half-life of four months, so this thing had to be well planned and coordinated. And yet it was a crime of passion.'[44]

Surely it was a crime of passion. But the only service that could overrule both the SVR and FSB and had unlimited access to the best weapons including poisons was the Presidential Protection Service. There is no doubt in my mind that Zolotov masterminded the whole operation. And Putin knew, for sure. He was covering it up himself.

Every one from the Putin's 'inner cabinet' remained with him still fiercely fighting for their master when this book was being sent to presses. While others are technicians, Zolotov is his executioner and Peskov his public face and voice. When Putin speaks himself, it comes out clumsily.

***

London, November 2006. Sasha's statement is released to reporters outside University College Hospital:

I would like to thank many people. My doctors, nurses and hospital staff for doing all they can for me. The British police who are pursuing my case with vigour and professionalism and are watching over me and my family.

I would like to thank the British government for taking me under their care. I am honoured to be a British citizen. I would like to thank the British public for their messages of support and for the interest they have shown in my plight.

I thank my wife, Marina, who has stood by me. My love for her and for our son knows no bounds.

But as I lie here, I can distinctly hear the beatings of wings of the angel of death. I may be able to give him the slip, but I have to say my legs do not run as fast as I would like.

I think, therefore, that this may be the time to say one or two things to the person responsible for my present illness.

You may succeed in silencing me, but that silence comes at a price. You have shown yourself to be as barbaric and ruthless as your most hostile critics have claimed. You have shown yourself to have no respect for life, liberty or any civilised value. You have shown yourself to be unworthy of your office, to be unworthy of the trust of civilised men and women.

You may succeed in silencing one man. But a howl of protest from around the world will reverberate, Mr Putin, in your ears for the rest of your life.

May God forgive you for what you have done, not only to me, but to beloved Russia and its people.

***

I am Boris Borisovich Volodarsky. I promised myself to finish this book on 23 November, Litvinenko Day. Today is 23 November. Not too much sun, to which we are used in London, but an extremely quiet Sunday, a good day to remember Sasha kindly.

Epilogue

In October 2000, when Litvinenko and Goldfarb were leaving no stone unturned trying to get Sasha and his family accepted by the Americans, Sergey Tretyakov defected to the CIA. He was not only an SVR colonel and the deputy station chief in New York, but for the past three years he had served as an agent-in-place delivering top-grade intelligence to the FBI and CIA. It was the most prized catch since the collapse of the Soviet Union. Quite a few people received well-deserved promotions but for Sasha and Marina it was bad luck.

Since both the Clinton and the Bush administrations stopped considering Russia as an adversary, the White House had become reluctant to get involved in matters that could seriously irritate the Kremlin. The CIA was (and still is) very selective about accepting defectors partly because of the expense and responsibility involved in relocating, protecting and financially supporting them. The fact that Tretyakov received an impressive resettlement package and that he, his wife and their daughter had breezed through the process was a demonstration that he was extremely valuable. That also suggests that he must be a hunted man. Especially because he exposed Zolotov.

When Putin took her father's office, Tatiana Dyachenko continued to work in his administration but soon tendered her resignation. In winter 2001 she moved to London with Valentin Yumashev where their daughter, Masha, was born. On 23 April 2007 her father Boris Yeltsin, 'a giant of history', as the BBC called him, died in Moscow. All his democratic achievements had been swept away by the Putin regime.

Anatoly Chubais survived an assassination attempt in Moscow in March 2005. When Putin came to power, Chubais was moved away from the Kremlin though he continued to occupy high positions in the government. For ten years from 1998, he had been head of United Energy Systems of Russia, a symbiosis of a holding and a utilities supply company. In 2008 Putin appointed him director general of the Russian Nanotechnologies Corporation.

My Surrey neighbour, Badri Patarkatsyshvili, was found dead on 13 February 2008 in his mansion known as Downside Manor near Leatherhead. We were of the same age but he looked like my grandfather. It was hard to make billions from the scratch and his life was never easy.

In August his Georgian wife won a court battle in Moscow to have Badri's marriage to Olga Safonova annulled.

Asked just days before if he planned to return to his home country, Badri said: 'I intend to stay in London. I haven't decided to die yet so I'm not going to go to Georgia for the moment.' With all his fortune he did not know that it was not he who would make such a decision.

Back to business. As Keith Dovkantz correctly noticed in the *Evening Standard*, even if a post mortem revealed Patarkatsyshvili had died from a heart attack, should there be no evidence of a long-term heart disease police inquiries must continue. This is because the KGB's poison factory has never been shut down and a number of substances can induce heart failure and leave no trace. One is sodium fluoroacetate, a potent metabolic poison that occurs naturally in various plants.

Ahead of the second anniversary of Sasha's tragic death, Lugovoy and Kovtun decided to meet a British journalist in Moscow. They summoned *The Times* to make an offer for Kovtun to travel to London to try to clear their names. He was not made a suspect when the Crown Prosecution Service charged Andrei Lugovoy with murder, but remains under investigation by German police. Tony Halpin, who represented his newspaper, called Kovtun 'the main witness in the case'.

I have my own version. Kovtun is not a witness in this case and there is nothing new that he can reveal to the prosecution. But since 2006 Kovtun has aged considerably, a man with the stamp of death on his lined and drawn face, with cropped hair now grey. The Russians know that the first thing Scotland Yard will do is to submit the man to a medical check. They probably did their best in Moscow but Kovtun is suffering from a radiation disease and the only way to save his life would be to try the latest Western medical achievements: the United States and Japan are very far advanced in their treatment methods, so Britain must be on that level.

As always with the KGB, their aim is twofold. If Kovtun survives, he will claim that Sasha contaminated him in October. If they lose a pawn, the British authorities will be accused of murdering him. It's the classic checkmate game. But the world chess champion is not a Russian any more.

The Litvinenko case over, I was planning to fly to Washington, DC. Oleg Kalugin had agreed to share a drink while talking about things and John 'Jack' Dziak, an adjunct professor at George Washington University and a Soviet specialist, invited me for lunch in Sette Bello, Arlington, directly across from the Clarendon Metro Station. And, of course, there was that big story in Baku that had been investigated for almost ten years. What a fascinating topic for the next book: crooks, crime, corruption, and an American billionaire facing thirty years in jail and a gigantic forfeiture for doing absolutely nothing wrong. A little bit greedy, perhaps, but otherwise absolutely innocent. (The man was convicted on two counts out of three as this is written.)

Before a wonderful family Christmas in Vienna, I still planned a meeting in Europe with two former officers of the former 9th Directorate who had promised to bring along a Very Important Person to discuss the Baku affair. They never showed up.

In the meantime, I met Pete Bagley in Brussels. We discussed a recent attempt to abduct a former chief of the Kazakh intelligence who lived in Austria as a political refugee. In January 2009 the 'gas war' between Russia and Ukraine was still at its peak and many countries were virtually freezing because Russia stopped all supplies of its gas to Europe. When I finally returned to London, the newspapers were writing about the attack on a former bodyguard of the Chechen president Ramzan Kadyrov – the young man who changed sides and was accusing his onetime boss of tortures and other crimes was shot dead in the Austrian capital.

In February 2009 the *New York Times* reported:

On January 9, after consulting with one of Umar Israilov's legal advocates, *The Times* notified Mr. Putin's office that it sought interviews with Russian officials about these allegations. Mr. Israilov was prepared to publicize his story.

Dmitri Peskov, Mr. Putin's spokesman, declined to comment in detail, saying, "It's not wise to comment on any rumors."

On Jan. 13, Mr. Israilov left his apartment, where he had been watching his three young children while his pregnant wife was away, to buy yogurt at a nearby market. Outside, he was confronted by at least two men.

They argued, and one of the men tried to pistol-whip Mr. Israilov, according to Gerhard Jarosch, a spokesman for Austria's prosecutor. Mr. Israilov bolted. He still had received no protection [from the Austrian authorities, though he asked for it]. In broad daylight on a Vienna street, he ran for his life alone.

One of his pursuers opened fire. Mr. Israilov fell, shot in an arm, a leg and the abdomen, according to Mr. Jarosch. A short while later, he was dead.

In March, another Chechen, a former GRU Spetsnaz commander and a fierce opponent of President Kadyrov, was shot in Dubai.

On 7 May Vice-premier Sergey Ivanov reported to Premier Putin: 'What concerns special services – FSO, FSB, SVR – they are technically equipped 100 per cent'. Characteristically, the Federal Protection Service (FSO) was put on the first place.

Three weeks later, on 28 May 2009, Russian President Medvedev received Lugovoy in the Kremlin. By this time, the suspected assassin had been promoted to the rank of colonel and become a prominent Russian politician.

In July 2009, Natalia Estemirova, a human rights activist and a close friend of Anna Politkovskaya, was abducted in the Chechen capital of Grozny, then shot and murdered in the nearby republic of Ingushetia.

Many people prefer not to get involved. For those who are rather bored and want to entertain themselves in a safe way one evening, here's something new to do with pineapple chunks: try putting the pieces together again (KENNETH WILLIAMS). Nifty.

Notes

Funeral

1 Alex Goldfarb with Marina Litvinenko, *Death of a Dissident: The Poisoning of Alexander Litvinenko and the Return of the KGB* (London and New York: Simon & Schuster, 2007)

2 Christopher Andrew and Oleg Gordievsky, *Instructions from the Centre: Top Secret Files on KGB Foreign Operations, 1975–1985* (London: Hodder & Stoughton, 1991).

3 This document has never been made public. Personal archive of the author.

Georgi Markov, London, September 1978

1 Until 2006 orders came from the Kremlin, and before the collapse of the Soviet Union from the Politburo, but after Vladimir Putin became the Russian prime minister the centre of Russia's decision-making moved to the White House in Moscow, seat of the Russian government.

2 The 'illegals' or officers operating 'in black', always under an assumed name and nationality and without the benefit of diplomatic immunity. After a restructuring of the service some time ago, it is one of the operational departments under the DDO.

3 Oleg Kalugin with Fen Montaigne, *SpyMaster: My 32 Years in Intelligence and Espionage Against the West* (London: Smith Gryphon Publishers, 1994).

4 See Vladimir Bereanu and Kalin Todorov, *The Umbrella Murder* (Bury St Edmunds: TEL, 1994).

5 See Kalugin, *SpyMaster*.

6 See 'Revealed: The Umbrella Assassin,' Windfall Films, 2006.

7 See Bereanu and Todorov, *The Umbrella Murder*.

The KGB's Poison Factory

1 Boris Petrovsky, 'Ranenie i bolezn Lenina' [Lenin's wounding and illness], *Pravda*, 25 November 1990.

2 For example, see reports by Nikita Petrov, a researcher and intelligence historian at the Moscow's 'Memorial' historical and civil rights society (in Russian); Vladimir Bobrenyov, a former investigator at the Russian general prosecutor's office and his co-author, Valery Ryazantsev, a military journalist (in Russian and German); Vadim J. Birstein, a Russian-American geneticist and historian (in English); and Pavel A. Sudoplatov, a former high-ranking NKVD (predecessor of the KGB) official (in Russian and English).

3 NKVD Order no. 00362 of 9 June 1938.

4 See Vadim J. Birstein, *The Perversion of Knowledge: The True Story of Soviet Science*,

paperback (Boulder, CO: Westview Press, 2001)

5   Ibid.

6   Deriabin later published this information in a book, written with Frank Gibney, *The Secret World* (London: Arthur Barker Ltd, 1960).

7   Quoted from Birstein, *The Perversion of Knowledge*.

8   Ignatyev's report to the Politburo, No. 951/I of 8 March 1953.

9   Boris Volodarsky, 'KGB's Poison Factory', *The Wall Street Journal*, 7 April 2005. My original source of information was Natalia Gevorkian and Nikita Petrov, *Terakty* ('Acts of Terror'), an account based on the authors' archival research and published in the *Moscow News* 31, 1992.

10 On Felfe, see Tennent H. Bagley, *Spy Wars: Moles, Mysteries and Deadly Games* (New Haven and London: Yale University Press, 2007).

11 Yevgenia Albats, *The State Within a State: The KGB and Its Hold on Russia – Past, Present and Future* (New York, NY: Farrar, Straus and Giroux, 1994).

12 See Pavel Sudoplatov and Anatoly Sudoplatov with Jerrold L. and Leona Schecter, *Special Tasks: The Memoirs of an Unwanted Witness – A Soviet Spy Master* (London: Little, Brown and Company, 1994).

13 See Ken Alibek with Stephen Handelman, *Biohazard: The Chilling True Story of the Largest Covert Biological Weapons Program in the World – Told from the Inside by the Man Who Ran it* (London: Arrow, 2000).

14 Ibid.

15 Ibid.

16 Markus Wolf with Anne McElvoy, *Man Without a Face: The Memoirs of a Spymaster* (London: Jonathan Cape, 1997).

17 See Alexander Kouzminov, *Biological Espionage: Special Operations of the Soviet and Russian Foreign Intelligence Services in the West*, paperback (London: Greenhill Books, 2005)

18 Ibid.

19 See Carey Scott, 'Poisons Tested on Stalin's Prisoners', *Sunday Times*, 15 October 1995.

20 Anna Politkovskaya, 'Poisoned by Putin', *Guardian*, Thursday, 9 September, 2004.

21 Another honest journalist, Andrei Babitsky, was detained on a specious pretext. As a result, wrote Anna, another journalist known for seeing his investigations through to the end and being outspoken in the foreign press was prevented from going to northern Ossetia.

22 Here and further in this chapter the technical information about poisons, if not referenced separately, is taken from Serita Stevens and Anne Bannon, *Book of Poisons*, paperback (Cincinnati, Ohio: Writer's Digest Books, 2007).

23 Anna Politkovskaya, *Putin's Russia*, paperback (London: The Harvill Press, 2004).

Those were the days

1   Andrew Cook worked for many years as a foreign affairs and defence specialist, and was aide to George Robertson (former Secretary of State for Defence) and John Speller (former Minister of State for the Armed Forces). According to Cook's publishers, the contacts he made enabled him to navigate and gain access via the Cabinet Office to classified intelligence services archives.

2   The letter was published in Yuri Felshtinsky, *VChK-OGPU* (Benson, VT: Chalidze Publications, 1989).

3   Nigel West and Oleg Tsarev, *The Crown Jewels: The British Secrets at the Heart of the KGB Archives* (New Haven and London: Yale University Press, 1999).

4   See Christopher Andrew and Oleg Gordievsky, *KGB: The Inside Story of its Foreign*

Operations from Lenin to Gorbachev (New York: HarperCollins Publishers, 1990).

5 Alexander Kolpakidi and Dmitry Prokhorov, *KGB: Spetsoperatsii sovetskoi razvedki* ['KGB: Special Operations of Soviet Intelligence'] (Moscow: AST, 2000).

6 Anonymous, 'How the Bolsheviks Took the Winter Palace,' *Guardian*, Thursday, 27 December, 1917.

7 Lenin, *Collected Works*, vol. 26 (London: Lawrence and Wishart, 1964)

8 See West and Tsarev, *The Crown Jewels*.

9 Pyotr Wrangel, *Memoirs of General Wrangel, the Last Commander-In-Chief of the Russian National Army* (London: Williams and Norgate, 1929).

10 Editorial, 'White Eagle', *Time*, Monday, 7 May, 1928.

11 See Christopher Andrew and Vasili Mitrokhin, *The Mitrokhin Archive: The KGB in Europe and the West* (London: Allen Lane, 1999).

12 Yelena Solntseva, 'Gallipoliiskoe sidenie' ['The Gallipoli Sitting'], RFE/RL, 19 May 2008.

13 See Kolpakidi and Prokhorov, *KGB: Spetsoperatsii sovetskoi razvedki*.

Operation VLADIMIR, Part I

1 The truck-mounted *Kolchuga* (or Hauberk) is sometimes described as radar, which is not correct. The Kolchuga, developed in Ukraine, is an electronic support system that helps to detect and track aircraft by triangulation and multilateration of their radio frequency emissions.

2 The letter was sent in May shortly after his meeting with Petro Shatkovsky, the SBU deputy chief. For more details, see Boris Volodarsky, 'The Ukraine's Tapegate Dilemma', *The Salisbury Review*, vol. 24 no. 2, Winter 2005.

3 See Semyon Shevchuk, '*Bolshie torgi*' ('Big Dealings'), *Ukrayinska Pravda*, 5 July 2005.

4 Vladimir Vodo, Alexander Vinogradov and Mikhaail Zygar, 'Boris Berezovsky gets closer to Russia,' *Kommersant*, February 28, 2005.

5 See, for example, Boris Volodarsky, 'License to Kill,' *The Wall Street Journal*, 20 December 2006, and 'Terror's KGB Roots,' *The Wall Street Journal*, 23–25 November 2007.

6 When it became clear the old Soviet system was about to end, the leaders of the Communist party decided to protect the party's vast wealth by transferring billions of dollars out of the country. However, due to the restrictive Soviet financial system that they themselves created, there was no way to send money easily to foreign banks. They turned to the KGB for help. Vladimir Kryuchkov, the then chairman and one of the orchestrators of the failed coup against Soviet leader Mikhail Gorbachev in August 1991, signed a secret decree earlier the same year authorising the KGB to create private businesses as fronts in Moscow for the 'purpose of protecting state security'. Money from the Communist party coffers was moved into these companies and secreted through them out of the Soviet Union. See Pete Earley, *Comrade J: The Untold Secrets of Russia's Master Spy in America After the End of the Cold War* (New York, NY: G. P. Putnam's Sons, 2007). Until his death in November 2007, Kryuchkov was often invited to the Kremlin advising Putin on security matters.

7 The English version was Alexander Litvinenko and Yuri Felshtinsky, *Blowing Up Russia* (London: Gibson Square, 2007)

8 David Satter, *Darkness at Dawn: The Rise of the Russian Criminal State* (New Haven and London: Yale University Press, 2003).

9 Ibid.

10 Simultaneously, in spring 1999 Zharko contacted Berezovsky concerning another case that he investigated and in the outcome of which the tycoon was greatly interested.

11 About Oleg Soskovets, see Peter Reddaway and Dmitri Glinski, *The Tragedy of Russia's*

Reforms: Market Bolshevism Against Democracy. (Washington, DC: US Institute of Peace Press, 2001). The authors present a fascinating account of multiple press and TV exposés linking Soskovets to various Russian crime groups. It goes without saying that Putin's mate had never been charged or prosecuted.

12 Shchekochikhin's letter to Putin (in Russian) was published on his political party's website.

13 IPOC International Growth Fund, Ltd, alleges in a federal racketeering lawsuit, filed on 8 June 2006. See 'Russian Oligarch Fridman, Corporation Sued for Racketeering, Fraud That Used U.S. Banks and Exchanges,' PRNewswire, 9 June 2006.

14 For more details, see Nikita Varenov, 'Conspiratology of Collapse' (in Russian), www.grani.ru/Politics/Russia/m.141544.html, 17 September 2008.

15 The man, Alexander Hinstein, was identified in one of the Litvinenko's books, published a year before the events, as an FSB agent.

16 British Parliament, Publications and Records, Hansard written answers for 13 January 2004: Column 654W.

17 As reported by the *Ukrayinska Pravda* on 11 December 2005.

Victor Yushchenko, the Ukrainian Patient, Kiev, September, 2004

1 See Askold Krushelnycky, *An Orange Revolution: A Personal Journey Through Ukrainian History*, paperback (London: Harville Secker, 2006).

2 See Jeremy Page, 'Could I have stopped this?' *The Times*, 1 April, 2005.

3 In several interviews given to the Ukrainian investigative reporter Olexiy Stepura and published by the *Ukrayinska Pravda*, I raised the question of waiters and the cook: strangely, to the day of this book going to press, they have never been officially mentioned or identified. To the best of my knowledge all three escaped to Russia.

4 See Boris Volodarsky, 'Getting the Reds Out of the Orange Revolution,' *The Wall Street Journal*, 14–16 October, 2005.

5 Translated from Ukrainian by Peter Byrne, an American expatriate living in Kiev.

6 See Statement by Alexander Zinchenko of 4 October 2004.

7 Hamilton Nolan, 'Euro RSCG clarifies role in Ukraine clinic's PR efforts', *PR Week* magazine, London, January 2, 2005.

8 See Tom Warner in Kiev and AP, 'Yushchenko links poison to meal with secret police,' *Financial Times*, Friday, December 17, 2004.

9 See Rudolfinerhaus Pressmitteilung, Wien, 2004-10-03.

10 Emil Bobi, 'Wahlkampf mit Bauchweh,' *Profil*, 11 October 2004.

11 See Chervonenko, interviewed by *Ukrayinska Pravda* in August 2008.

12 See Sudoplatov, *Special Tasks*.

13 Krushelnycky, *An Orange Revolution*.

14 Anonymous, 'Putin enters Ukrainian election row by attending army parade,' *The Independent*, 29 October, 2004.

15 Ibid.

16 See C. J. Chivers, 'Back Channels: A Crackdown Averted; How Top Spies in Ukraine Changed the Nation's Path,' *The New York Times*, 17 January, 2005.

17 See Krushelnycky, *An Orange Revolution*.

18 Ibid.

19 Bram Brouwer to the author, 10 February 2005.

20 Jeremy Page, 'Who poisoned Yushchenko?' *The Times*, 8 December 2004.

21 Glenn Kessler and Rob Stein, 'U.S. Doctors Treated Yushchenko: Secret Team Helped Find Dioxin Poisoning,' *Washington Post*, Friday, 11 March 2005.

22 Ibid.

23 Chrystia Freeland, 'Up from under,' *Financial Times*, 8–9 January 2005.

24 Ibid.

25 The Agency Press News (now RIA Novosti), the successor of the Sovinformburo, was not only a notorious part of Soviet disinformation operations but also, alongside the TASS Agency (now ITAR-TASS), housed Soviet and Russian spies abroad. Both RIA Novosti and ITAR-TASS continue to play the same role now.

26 See Bojan Pancevski, 'I received death threats, says doctor who denied that Ukrainian leader was poisoned,' *Sunday Telegraph*, 27 March 2005.

27 See Igor Naidenov, 'Orange Agent Yushchenko,' *Moscow News*, no. 48 (1266), 17–23 December 2004.

28 See Boris Volodarsky, 'The KGB's Poison Factory,' *The Wall Street Journal*, Thursday, 7 April 2005.

29 No. 2951/J XXII. GP

30 No. 2952/J XXII. GP of 27 April 2005.

31 R. Schmitt, 'Fall Juschtschenko: Nachspiel bei Wiener Staatsanwaltschaft!', *Heute*, 28 June 2005.

32 See Olexiy Stepura, 'Boris Volodarsky: Yushchenko was deemed to die. This is the golden rule of special services,' *Ukrayinska Pradva*, 2 September 2005.

33 No. 3525/J XXII. GP of 19 October 2005.

Béla Lapusnyik, the victim, Vienna, May 1962

1 *The Third Man* (1949) is an award-winning British film noir directed by Carol Reed and starring Josef Cotten, Valli Trevor Howard and Orson Welles. All the action of this thriller takes place in Vienna. The screenplay was written by Graham Greene, a war-time SIS officer who is rumoured to have done most of the writing in the Café Mozart just behind the back of the renowned *Staatsoper* where one of the scenes was shot.

2 AVH (*Allamvedelmi Hatosag*), was the much feared and hated secret police.

3 See Tennent H. Bagley, *Spy Wars: Moles, Mysteries and Deadly Games* (New Haven and London: Yale University Press, 2007).

4 See Andrew and Mitrokhin, *The Mitrokhin Archive*.

5 'Has the US Secret Service Murdered Lapusnyik?' *Volksstimme*, 6 June 1962.

6 Statement of Laszlo Szabo in *Hearings Before the CIA Subcommittee of the Committee on Armed Services of the House of Representative*, Eighty-Ninth Congress, Second Session, 17 March 1966.

7 Memorandum of Conversation, 'Meeting of A and B with Mr. Dulles 30 January 1967', 3 February 1967, declassified.

8 See Siegfried Beer and Igor Lukes, 'Spy, Scholar, Artist,' interview with Ladislav Bittman, August 2007, *Journal for Intelligence, Propaganda and Security Studies*, Vol. 2, No. 1, 2008.

9 Ibid.

10 Ibid.

11 See Frederick Forsyth, *The Deceiver*.

Nikolai Artamonov, the triple agent, Vienna, December 1975

1 Kalugin, *Spymaster*.

2 Quoted from Henry Hurt, *Shadrin: The Spy Who Never Came Back* (New York, NY: McGraw-Hill Book Company, 1981).

3 Indeed, in November 1962 the then KGB chairman Vladimir Semichasny approved a plan

for 'special actions' against a group of 'particularly dangerous traitors': 'As these traitors, who have given important state secrets to the opponent and *caused great political damage* to the USSR, have been sentenced to death in their absence, this sentence will be carried out abroad.' Those in the list were Igor Gouzenko, Anatoly Golitsyn, Peter Deriabin, Yuri Rastvorov, Vladimir and Evdokiya Petrov, Reino Häyhänen, Nikolai Khokhlov and Bogdan Stashinsky. See Andrew and Mitrokhin, *The Mitrokhin Archive*.

4 Kalugin, *Spymaster*.
5 Hurt, *Shadrin*.
6 Ibid.
7 Reg Whitaker, 'Spies who might have been: Canada and the myth of cold war counterintelligence,' *Intelligence and National Security*, vol. 12, no. 4, 1997.
8 Hurt, *Shadrin*.
9 Bagley, *Spy Wars*.
10 Hurt, *Shadrin*.
11 Ibid.
12 Kalugin, *Spymaster*.
13 See Hurt, *Shadrin*.
14 Ibid.
15 See, for example, Kid Möchel, *Der Geheime Krieg der Agenten: Spionagedrehscheibe Wien* (Hamburg: Rasch und Röhring Verlag, 1997).
16 Kalugin, *Spymaster*.
17 Ibid.
18 See Hurt, *Shadrin*.
19 Ibid.
20 Kalugin, *Spymaster*.
21 See Hurt, *Shadrin*.
22 Ibid.
23 BPD Wien, Staatpolizeiliches Büro, Aktenvermerk vom 23. Dezember 1977.
24 Greg Walter and Jack Crossley, 'Conman's Tale "Beats Le Carré" ', *Observer*, Sunday, 1 April 1979.
25 Edward Jay Epstein, as usual, made a mess commenting on his website that Shadrin was transported to Hungary. Epstein will later play a role in the Litvinenko case.
26 Oleg Kalugin recalled this conversation in his book.

Operation VLADIMIR, Part II
1 See Goldfarb and Marina Litvinenko, *Death of a Dissident*.
2 Alexander Litvinenko, *Lubyanskaya prestupnaya gruppirovka: ofitser FSB dayot pokazaniya* ('Organized Crime Group from the Lubyanka: The FSB Officer Testifies'), paperback (New York: Grani, 2002). Above extracts translated into English by Alex Goldfarb.
3 Goldfarb and Marina Litvinenko, *Death of a Dissident*.
4 Ibid.
5 Many of Litvinenko's articles and interviews were later published by Vladimir Bukovsky in a book entitled *Allegations: Selected Works by Alexander Litvinenko* (Slough, Berkshire: Aquilion Ltd, 2007).
6 See Goldfarb and Marina Litvinenko, *Death of a Dissident*.
7 Ibid.
8 See Oliver McIntyre, 'Major "Russian Mafia" Ring Busted', *Costa del Sol News*, week June 23–29, 2005.

9 See Yuri Felshtinsky and Vladimir Pribylovsky, *The Age of Assassins: The Rise and Rise of Vladimir Putin* (London: Gibson Square, 2007).

10 Russian television channel that belonged to Berezovsky.

11 See Daniel McGrory and Tony Halpin, 'Spies sent "to seize cash from Yukos exiles" ', *The Times*, 9 December 2006.

12 Anonymous, 'Poisoned Spy Accused Putin of being a Paedophile,' *Mail Online*, 20 November 2006.

13 According to my sources, Litvinenko gave Nevzlin several documents pertaining to the murder of Vladimir Petukhov, the mayor of Yugansk, shot to death on 27 June 1988. The crime is attributed to Yukos while in reality Petukhov's murky business dealings could have been the reason for the shootout.

14 Natalia Morar, 'Delo o Doskonte' ('The Diskont File'), *The New Times*, no. 15, 21 May; no. 16, 28 May; and no. 28, 20 August 2007.

15 See Alan Cowell, *The Terminal Spy: The Life and Death of Alexander Litvinenko* (London: Doubleday, 2008).

16 Mark Franchetti et al, 'Focus: Cracking the code of the nuclear assassin,' *The Sunday Times*, 3 December, 2006.

17 When measuring radioactivity with a detector, a unit of 'counts per second' (cps) is normally used. It can then be converted to measure the activity of the sample in becquerel. The Itsu restaurant remained closed by the Health Protection Agency from 24 November 2006 to 22 February 2007.

18 See Goldfarb with Marina Litvinenko, *Death of a Dissident*.

19 Leonid Shebarshin is a former chief of the Russian foreign intelligence (February 1989– September 1991). Together with two other former KGB generals Shebarshin founded the joint stock company Russian National Service of Economic Security (RNSES).

20 SISMI – *Servizio per le Informazioni e la Sicurezza Militare* (Military Intelligence and Security Service) was the military intelligence agency of Italy. When Prodi came to power, he replaced it by AISE on 1 August 2007.

21 *Médecins Sans Frontières* (MsF) – Doctors Without Borders – is a secular humanitarian non-governmental organisation best known for its projects in war-torn regions.

22 See Document 4. Courtesy of Mario Scaramella.

23 Cowell, *The Terminal Spy*.

24 Ibid.

25 Ben Felton et al, 'Net tightens on the amateur assassins,' *The Daily Telegraph*, 2 December 2006.

26 See Cowell, *The Terminal Spy*.

27 Ibid.

Nikolai Khokhlov, the illegal, Germany, 1954–57

1 Gordon Brook-Shepherd, *The Storm Birds: Soviet Post-War Defectors* (London: Weidenfeld & Nicholson, 1988).

2 TNA HS4/334, Circular from Gibbons, 22 August 1944.

3 See Boris Volodarsky, *Nikolai Khokhlov: Self-Esteem with a Halo*, paperback (Vienna: Borwall Verlag, 2005).

4 Ibid.

5 See Nikolai Khokhlov, *In the Name of Conscience: The Testament of a Soviet Secret Agent* (New York: David McKay Company, Inc., 1959)

6 Brook-Shepherd, *The Storm Birds*.

7 Ibid.

8 Andrew and Mitrokhin, *The Mitrokhin Archive*.

9 See Brook-Shepherd, *The Storm Birds*.

10 See Volodarsky, *Nikolai Khokhlov*; and Brook-Shepherd, *The Storm Birds*.

11 Stephen Dorril, *MI6: Fifty Years of Special Operations* (London: Fourth Estate, 2000).

12 Volodarsky, *Khokhlov*. The information came in the form of his unpublished manuscript that Khokhlov was kind enough to send.

13 Brook-Shepherd, *The Storm Birds*.

14 Ibid.

15 See Dorril, *MI6*. The case was not forgotten by Russian intelligence, which used it to accuse Litvinenko of making up a story when somebody threw a Molotov cocktail at his house in Muswell Hill in October 2004, shortly after he started collaborating with the Mitrokhin Commission.

16 See Volodarsky, *Khokhlov*, footnote 191.

17 See Brook-Shepherd, *The Storm Birds*.

18 Ibid.

19 Ibid.

20 See Khokhlov, *In the Name of Conscience*.

21 Ibid.

22 Ibid.

23 'Testimony of Nikolai Khokhlov, Care of International Research, Inc., New York, N.Y.', *Committee on the Judiciary*, United States Senate, 16 October, 1957.

24 Correspondence with Khokhlov, October 2003. Khokhlov arrived in Saigon in January 1959. Natsios served in Viet Nam as political officer, first secretary of the US Embassy, in 1956–60.

25 Bethell, *Spies and Other Secrets*.

26 See Steve LeVine, *Putin's Labyrinth; Spies, Murder, and the Dark Heart of the New Russia* (New York, NY: Random House, 2008).

27 Ibid.

28 Ibid.

Bogdan Stashinsky, the assassin, Germany, 1957-1959

1 Tom Mangold, *Cold Warrior. James Jesus Angleton: The CIA's Master Spy Hunter* (London: Simon & Schuster, 1991).

2 See John L. Steele, 'Assassin Disarmed by Love', *Life*, September 7, 1962, reprinted in Allen Dulles (ed.), *Great True Spy Stories* (London: Book Club Associates, 1984).

3 Ibid.

4 See Karl Anders, *Murder to Order*, paperback (London: Ampersand Ltd, 1965).

5 As Germany and Austria were main operational grounds of the Soviet intelligence before and sometime after the war, many professional terms were in German. *Treff* means a brief encounter, normally with the risk of surveillance.

6 Anders, *Murder to Order*.

7 Andrew and Mitrokhin, *The Mitrokhin Archive*.

8 See H. Keith Melton, *Ultimate Spy* (New York: DR Publishing, Inc., 2002).

9 See Steel, *Assassin Disarmed by Love*.

10 Karl Anders, *Murder to Order*.

11 See ibid. For a somewhat different description, see Steele, *Assassin Disarmed by Love*.

12 See James Sanders, *Apartheid's Friends: The Rise and Fall of South Africa's Secret Service*,

paperback (London: John Murray, 2006).

13 Ibid.

Litvinenko: Operation VLADIMIR, Part III

1 Peter Strebbings, 'A spy in our midst,' *Haringey Independent*, 29 November 2006.
2 Ibid.
3 The BBC Russian Service, 11 November 2006.
4 See Goldfarb with Marina Litvinenko, *Death of a Dissident*.
5 AP, 'Man accused of being Russian spy acknowledges he is Russian, will not fight deportation,' *International Herald Tribune*, 4 December, 2006.
6 Goldfarb with Marina Litvinenko, *Death of a Dissident*.
7 Ibid.
8 In March 2007, in English alone, searches on 'Litvinenko' and 'Murder' brought 585,000 entries on Google and almost 700,000 in Russian on Rambler, according to William Dunkerley, an independent media analyst.
9 Goldfarb with Marina Litvinenko, *Death of a Dissident*.
10 Ibid.
11 Bryan Burrough, 'The Kremlin's Long Shadow,' *Vanity Fair*, April 2007.
12 Goldfarb with Marina Litvinenko, *Death of a Dissident*.
13 Ibid.
14 Ibid.
15 Ibid.
16 See Cowell, *The Terminal Spy*.
17 Ibid.
18 Professor John Henry, 'toxicologist who did crucial work on poisoning and drug overdose and was always ready to explain it to the media,' as *The Times* obituary put it, suddenly died of heart failure while undergoing surgery on 8 May 2007.
19 Boris Volodarsky, 'Russian Venom,' *The Wall Street Journal*, Wednesday, November 22, 2006.
20 I spoke to Marina many times reconstructing the details of those difficult days of her life. Nevertheless, just for cross-checking, apart from her book with Alex Goldfarb, I used several published sources, among them Marina's interview to Natalia Gevorkyan ('Khronika obyavlennoi smerti', *Kommersant*, 21 December 2006) and 'Conversation with Marina Litvinenko' by Natalya Mozgovaya, first published in Russian in *Yedioth Ahronoth* (Israel) and then in English in *Shiva Yamim*, weekend edition, 13–14 January 2007.
21 See Cowell, *The Terminal Spy*.
22 LeVine, *Putin's Labyrinth*.
23 Ibid.
24 VOLNA is the KGB name of the secret channel of delivery of hazardous materials to and from the USSR. Usually, the Aeroflot flights are used for the purpose and the container is placed in the pilots' cabin where one of the pilots is an intelligence officer or a co-optee. According to Alexander Kouzminov, who served in the KGB's Directorate S (Illegals) before and after the collapse of the Soviet Union, after 1991 the use of this channel of transportation increased (see Kouzminov, *Biological Espionage*, p. 135).
25 LeVine, *Putin's Labyrinth*.
26 James Robinson, 'Smile when you do that, Mr. President,' *Guardian*, 17 July 2006.
27 Ibid.
28 Vadim Birstein, 'One more time on the Alexander Litvinenko case,' Johnsons's Russia List

(JRL) 2007–34, 11 February 2007.

29 Mark Townsend et al, 'I can blackmail them. We can make money,' *The Observer*, 3 December, 2006.

30 Ibid.

31 Ibid.

32 Birstein, 'One more time on the Alexander Litvinenko case.'

33 Ibid.

34 In his book with Marina Litvinenko, Alex Goldfarb erroneously called Kovtun 'a veteran of GRU army intelligence' (p. 340).

35 See Andrew Gimson, 'Hercule Reid keeps the House in suspense over unsolved riddle,' *The Daily Telegraph*, 1 December, 2006.

36 Ibid.

37 The Crown Prosecution Service, 22 May 2007.

38 Nigel West attributes these words to Dick White during a lunch with Graham Greene.

39 See Guzzanti, *Il mio agente Sasha*, p. 281. The interview with Limarev can be accessed on the website www.paologuzzanti.it.

40 Mark Franchetti, 'Moscow says it has MI6 spy "recruited by Litvinenko" ', *The Sunday Times*, 8 July, 2007.

41 Alexander Hinstein, 'A spy who left without saying goodbye,' *Moskovsky Komsomolets*, 30 June–2 July 2007. It is an open secret in Russia that Hinstein actively collaborates with the FSB.

42 David A. Charters and Maurice A.J. Tugwell, (eds.), *Deception Operations: Studies in the East-West Context* (London: Brassey's, 1990).

43 All above quoted from Edward Jay Epstein, 'The Specter that Haunts the Death of Litvinenko,' *The New York Sun*, March 19, 2008.

44 Congressional Record: April 1, 2008 (House), page H1841.

Dead Souls: from Stalin to Putin

1   From the interview to Mario Scaramella, broadcast by the ITV News, London, 22 January 2007.

2   Sudoplatov, *Special Tasks*.

3   Ibid.

4   Andrew and Gordievsky, *KGB: The Inside Story*.

5   See Boris Volodarsky, *The Orlov KGB File: The Most Successful Espionage Deception of All Time*, paperback (New York: Enigma Books, 2009).

6   Sudoplatov, *Special Tasks*.

7   Ibid.

8   Kirill Khenkin, *Okhotnik vverkh nogami* ['Hunter Upside Down: The Case of Rudolf Abel'] (Frankfurt am Main: Posev Publishing House, 1981).

9   Sudoplatov, *Special Tasks*.

10 Ibid.

11 Volodarsky, *The Orlov KGB File*.

12 Andrew and Mitrokhin, *The Mitrokhin Archive*. For the full story of Grigulevich, see Volodarsky, *The Orlov KGB File*.

13 Sudoplatov, *Special Tasks*.

14 Peter Deriabin, 'The elimination of Josef Stalin: a view from inside his guard,' 1985 (unpublished), courtesy of Tennent H. Bagley.

15 In December 1952 Vlasik was arrested and sentenced to ten years but in 1956 he was

pardoned and died in Moscow in 1967.

16 Before 1924 Sverdlovsk was known as Yekaterinburg. In July 1918 the family of the Russian Emperor, the Romanovs, together with their doctor and maid, were brutally murdered by the Bolsheviks. One of Lenin's bodyguards, Alexei Akhimov, recounted how he personally delivered Lenin's instructions to the telegraph, bringing back the tape to preserve the secret. Yakov M. Sverdlov, the head of state, for whom this city was later renamed, also signed the telegram. The city would later become a 'biological Chernobyl' when anthrax fumes leaked and killed many people.

17 Peter Deriabin, 'The elimination of Josef Stalin: a view from inside his guard.'

18 Kalugin, *Spymaster*.

19 Felshtinsky, *The Age of Assassins*.

20 Goldfarb with Marina Litvinenko, *Death of a Dissident*.

21 Ibid.

22 Ibid.

23 Ibid.

24 Ibid.

25 Ibid.

26 See Masha Gessen, 'Dead Soul,' *Vanity Fair*, October 2008.

27 Ibid.

28 Ibid.

29 See Mark Hosenbal and Christian Caryl, 'A Stain on Mr. Clean,' *Newsweek*, 3 September, 2001.

30 Ibid.

31 See Gessen, 'Dead Soul.'

32 See Tony Allen-Mills, 'Putin accused of plagiarising his PhD thesis,' *The Sunday Times*, 26 March 2006.

33 From 1992 until August 1998 Cherkesov was the chief of the Leningrad KGB, then he moved to Moscow to become Putin's deputy at the FSB headquarters. From May 2000 to March 2003 he was President Putin's plenipotentiary envoy to the North-western Federal District before Putin appointed him head of the Russian version of the Drug Enforcement Administration. At the time of writing Cherkesov was head of the federal agency for the procurement of military and special equipment in the Premier Putin's government.

34 Goldfarb with Marina Litvinenko, *Death of a Dissident*.

35 Ibid.

36 Ibid.

37 See Gessen, 'Dead Soul.'

38 Ibid.

39 See 'The Russian Resurgence and the New-Old Front,' *Stratfor*, 15 September 2008.

40 See Pete Earley, *Comrade J: The Untold Secrets of Russia's Master Spy in America After the End of the Cold War* (New York, NY: G. P. Putnam's Sons, 2007).

41 Ibid.

42 Ibid.

43 Politkovskaya, *Putin's Russia*.

44 Gessen, 'Dead Soul.'

Appendix
Selected Soviet and Russian operations abroad: from Lenin to Litvinenko and beyond

- Assassination of White Guard Lieutenant General Alexander I. Dutov, Suidun (now Shuiding), China, 6 February 1921
- Poisoning of Vladimir Nesterovich (Yaroslavsky), former GRU station chief in Vienna who defected to Germany, Mainz, Germany, 6 August 1925
- Poisoning of OMS/Comintern defector, Ignati Dzewalkowski, Poland, November 1925
- Shooting and murder of Ukrainian nationalist leader Symon Petlyura, Paris, 25 May 1926
- Poisoning of White Guard General Baron Peter Wrangel, Brussels, 25 April 1928
- Abduction and death of White Guard General Alexander Kutepov, Paris, 26 January 1930
- Shooting and murder of OGPU defector, former agent Georgi Zemmelmann, Vienna, 27 July 1931
- Abduction attempt (failed) at OGPU defector Grigory Agabekov, Constanza, Rumania, 11 January 1932
- Poisoning of Finnish ballistic expert Colonel Volter Asplund, manager of Lapua Cartridge Factory, who died in Lapua on 20 April 1932
- Assassination of Comintern courier Hans Wissinger, Hamburg, 22 May 1932
- Liquidation of GRU illegal Wilold Sturm de Strem, Vienna, December 1933
- Murder of the NKVD resident in the USA Valentin Markin: circumstances and perpetrators unknown, 1934
- Stabbing and murder of Soviet defector Dmitry Navashin, Paris, 25 January 1937
- Abduction and murder of Mark Rein, Barcelona, 9 April 1937
- Arrest and shooting of Italian anarchists Berneri and Barbieri, Barcelona, 6 May 1937
- Liquidation of Catalan Anarchist Youth leader Antonio Martinez, Barcelona, May 1937
- Abduction and killing of Juliet Poyntz, New York, 3 June 1937
- Arrest and further shooting of Andrés Nin, POUM leader, Alcalá de Henares near Madrid, 20 June 1937
- Abduction and murder of Georgy Agabekov, important OGPU defector and author, Paris-Barcelona, June 1937
- Abduction and murder of Hans Freund (Moulin), former secretary of Trotsky, Barcelona, 2 August 1937
- Shooting and murder of important NKVD defector Ignatz Reiss, Lausanne, Switzerland, 4 September 1937
- Abduction and murder of Erwin Wolf, a former secretary of Trotsky, Barcelona, 13 September 1937
- Abduction and then shooting in Moscow of White Guard General Evgeny Miller, Paris, 22 September 1937

Appendix

- Abduction and murder of former POUM secretary Karl Landau, Barcelona, 23 September 1937
- Successful exfiltration from Paris and later shooting of former NKVD agent General Nikolai Skoblin, Barcelona, October 1937
- Assassination attempt (failed) at the life of Ivan Solonevich, editor-in-chief of *The Voice of Russia*, Sofia, Bulgaria, 3 February 1938
- Blowing up of Ukrainian nationalist leader Yevhen Konovalets, Rotterdam, Holland, 23 May 1938
- Murder of the secretary of the Movement for the IV International, Rudolf Klement, Paris, 13 July 1938
- Attack on Trotsky's house in Mexico, 24 May 1940
- Killing of Lev Trotsky, Mexico, 20 August 1940
- Strange and under-investigated 'suicide' of defector Walter Krivitsky, Washington, 10 February 1941
- Abduction of the Swedish diplomat Raul Wallenberg, Budapest, 13 January 1945; he was subsequently poisoned in prison in 1947
- Murder of Czech Foreign Minister Jan Masaryk, Prague, 10 March 1948
- Abduction of the Chief Inspector of the Vienna police, 1948
- Abduction of the Chief of the East Berlin police, 1949
- Arrest of three Soviet agents of German origin who were preparing to abduct Georgy Okolovich, an NTS leader, Runkel an der Lahn, Germany, June 1951
- Assassination attempt against Marshal Josip Bros Tito of Yugoslavia, Belgrade, 1952–3
- Poisoning of Wolfgang Salus, one of Trotsky's secretaries, Munich, 13 February 1953
- Attempt to kill Georgi Okolovich, NTS leader and anti-Soviet émigré, Frankfurt am Main, 18 February 1954
- Abduction and killing of Alexander Trushnovich, an anti-Soviet émigré leader, West Berlin, British Sector, 13 April 1954
- Abduction of Valery Tremmel of the NTS, Linz, Austria, June 1954
- Abduction of Georgy Khrulev of the NTS, West Berlin, autumn 1954
- Abduction of Sergey Popov of the NTS, Germany, 1954
- Abduction of Robert Bialek, former General Inspector of the East German Interior Ministry, who defected to West Germany; Bialek was transported to East Berlin and executed in prison, 4 February 1956
- Radiological poisoning of Soviet KGB defector Nikolai Khokhlov, 15 September 1957
- Poisoning and murder of Ukrainian émigré leader Lev Rebet, Munich, 15 October 1957
- Poisoning and murder of Ukrainian émigré leader Stepan Bandera, Munich, 12 October 1959
- Blowing up an apartment house where NTS families, including children, lived – miraculously, no victims, Sprendlingen, Germany, July 1958
- Poisoning of the Hungarian AVH defector Béla Lapusnyik, Vienna, 2 June 1962
- Illegal arrest and transportation to the Soviet Union of the Czechoslovak leader Alexander Dubček, Prague, 20 August 1968
- Abduction and murder of the Soviet Navy defector and FBI/CIA agent Nikolai Artamonov, Vienna, 21 December 1975
- Attempt to poison and kill Bulgarian dissident Vladimir Kostov, Paris, August 1978
- Poisoning of famous Bulgarian dissident Georgi Markov, London, 11 September 1978
- Poisoning of famous Soviet dissident writer Vladimir Voinovich, Moscow, summer 1979
- Poisoning and then shooting of the Afghan leader Hafizzulah Amin, Kabul, 27 December

1979

- The Politburo and the Council of Ministers' decision to set up a special unit (called *Vympel*, 'Pendant') within the 8th Department of the KGB's Directorate S (Illegals) for clandestine operations outside the USSR; first commander – Captain 1st Rank Evald G. Kozlov, deputy – Colonel Yevgeny A. Savintsev, chief of staff – Lt. Colonel Felix A. Makievsky; the official name was Separate Training Centre of the KGB, military unit no. 35690, 19 August 1981
- Officers of Vympel sent to Cuba for training with Cuban Special Forces, 1985
- Assassination attempt (failed) to murder KGB defector Vladimir Kuzichkin, South East England, 1986
- Officers of Vympel take part in special operations in Angola, 1986–8
- Officers of Vympel, together with the Cubans, take part in special operations in Nicaragua assisting Daniel Ortega, 1990
- Protection Service (formerly 9th Directorate) and 15th Department are taken out of the KGB later to become the Presidential Security Service (SOP) and the Federal Protection Service (FSO) accordingly; besides, a new super-secret Chief Directorate of Presidential Special Programs is formed, 3 December 1991
- Vympel (278 officers) becomes part of the Presidential Security Service, 1993
- Assassination of Dzokhar Dudayev, first President of the Chechen Republic of Ichkeria, by two laser-guided missiles in a covert operation by the Russian special forces, Chechnya, 21 April 1996
- A Special Unit for clandestine operations Zaslon ('Covering force'), consisting of three departments, is formed within the Foreign intelligence service (SVR); it is manned by 300 operatives with previous experience in clandestine operations outside Russia, March 1998
- FSB director Vladimir Putin forms Special Purpose Centre within the FSB with covert operations groups Alfa and Vympel put under one roof; the Centre (military unit No. 35690) is based in Balashikha-2 near Moscow; first chief – General Valery G. Andreyev, succeeded in two weeks by General Alexander Ye. Tikhonov, 8 October 1998
- Poisoning and death of Samir Ibn-Salib Ibn-Abdallah al-Suwaylim, better known as Amir Khattab, a Chechen commander, Chechnya, 19 March 2002
- In spite of the official statement of the SVR director Sergey Lebedev that his service does not have personnel and facilities for clandestine operations abroad, two Zaslon units were in Iraq having arrived there before the Allied US-British forces entered the country and remained there after the invasion and defeat of the Iraqi military; yet another group took position in Iran on the Iraqi border, March 2003
- Blowing up of Zelimkhan Yandarbiyev, the acting president of Chechnya, Doha, Qatar, 13 February 2004
- Poisoning of the Ukrainian presidential candidate Victor Yushchenko, Kiev, 4–5 September 2004
- Assassination of the Chechen President Aslan Maskhadov by the Russian occupiers in Chechnya, Tolstoy-Yurt, 8 March 2005
- Assassination of the Chechen President Abdul-Halim Sadulayev by FSB special forces in Argun, Chechnya, 17 June 2006
- Shooting and murder of famous journalist Anna Politkovskaya, Moscow, 7 October 2006
- Poisoning of Alexander Litvinenko, London, 1 November 2006
- Attempt to kidnap Alnur Musayev, Kazakhstan's former intelligence chief, by four Russian-speaking gunmen, Vienna, 22 September 2008
- Assassination of Umar Israilov, former bodyguard of the Chechen president, who

abandoned the pro-Russian Chechen camp and became an outspoken critic of Chechen President Ramsan Kadyrov and Russian Prime Minister Vladimir Putin, Vienna, 13 January 2009

- Shooting of the former GRU Spetsnaz commander Sulim Yamadayev (alias Suleiman Madov) by the Russian agents in Dubai, 28 March 2009

Select Bibliography

Albats, Yavgenia, *The State Within a State: The KGB and its Hold on Russia – Past, Present, and Future* (New York: Farrar, Straus and Giroux, 1994)

Alibek, Ken, with Handelman, Stephen, *Biohazard: The Chilling True Story of the Largest Covert Biological Weapons Program in the World – Told from the Inside by the Man Who Ran It* (London: Arrow, 2000)

Anders, Karl, *Murder To Order*, paperback (London: An Ampersand Book, 1965)

Andrew, Christopher, and Dilks, David, *The Missing Dimension: Governments and Intelligence Communities in the Twentieth Century* (London: Macmillan, 1984)

Andrew, Christopher, and Gordievsky, Oleg, *Instructions from the Centre: Top Secret Files on KGB Foreign Operations, 1975–1985* (London: Hodder & Stoughton, 1991)

Andrew, Christopher, and Mitrokhin, Vasili, *The Mitrokhin Archive: The KGB in Europe and the West* (London: Allen Lane, The Penguin Press, 1999)

Antonov-Ovseyenko, Anton V., *The Time of Stalin: Portrait of a Tyranny* (New York: Harper & Row, 1981).

Bagley, Tennent H., *Spy Wars: Moles, Mysteries and Deadly Games* (New Haven & London: Yale University Press, 2007)

Bajanov, Boris (Bazhanov), *Avec Stalin dans le Kremline* (Paris: Les Editions de France, 1930)

Beaune, Daniéle, *L'enlèvement du Général Koutiepoff* (Aix-en-Provence: Publications de l'Université de Provence, 1998)

Bereanu, Vladimir, and Todorov, Kalin, *The Umbrella Murder* (Bury St Edmunds, Suffolk: TEL, 1994)

Bethell, Nicholas, *Spies and Other Secrets: Memoirs From the Second Cold War* (London: Viking, 1994)

Birstein, Vadim J., *The Perversion of Knowledge: The True Story of Soviet Science*, paperback (Cambridge, MA: Westview Press, 2001)

Bittman, Ladislav, *The KGB and Soviet Disinformation* (McLean, VA: Pergamon-Brassey's International Defense Publishers, 1985)

Bortnevsky, V. G., *Zagadka smerti generala Wrangelya: Neizvestnye materially po istorii Russkoi emigratsii* (St Petersburg: St Petersburg University Publishing, 1996)

Brook-Shepherd, Gordon, *The Storm Birds: Soviet Post-War Defectors* (London: Weidenfeld and Nicolson, 1988)

Brook-Shepherd, Gordon, *The Storm Petrels: The First Soviet Defectors, 1928–1938* (London: Collins, 1977)

Brook-Shepherd, *Iron Maze: The Western Secret Services and the Bolsheviks* (London: Macmillan, 1998)

Select Bibliography

Charters David A., and Tugwell, Maurice A. J. (eds), *Deception Operations: Studies in the East-West Context* (London: Brassey's, 1990)

Cook, Andrew, *On His Majesty's Secret Service: Sidney Reilly, Code-name ST1*, paperback (Stroud, Gloucestershire: Tempus Publishing Ltd, 2002)

Cowell, Alan, *The Terminal Spy: The Life and Death of Alexander Litvinenko* (London: Doubleday, 2008)

Deriabin, Peter, and Bagley, T. H., *The KGB: Masters of the Soviet Union* (London: Robson Books, 1990)

Deriabin, Peter, and Gibney, Frank, *The Secret World* (London: Arthur Barker Ltd, 1960)

Deriabin, Peter, with Evans, Joseph C., *Inside Stalin's Kremlin: An Eyewitness Account of Brutality, Duplicity, and Intrigue* (Washington-London: Brassey's, 1998)

Dewar, Hugo, *Assassins at Large: Being a Fully Documented and hitherto Unpublished Account of the Executions outside Russia Ordered by the GPU* (Westport, CT: Hyperion Press, Inc., 1981, reprint of the 1952 edition published by Beacon Press, Boston)

Dokuchayev, Mikhail S., *Moskva. Kreml. Okhrana* (Moskva: Business Press, 1995)

Dorril, Stephen, *MI6: Fifty Years of Special Operations*, paperback (London: Fourth Estate, 2001)

Dulles, Allen (ed.), *Great True Spy Stories* (London: Book Club Associates, 1968)

Earley, Pete, *Comrade J: The Untold Secrets of Russia's Master Spy in America After the End of the Cold War* (New York, NY: G. P. Putnam's Sons, 2007)

Felshtinsky, Yuri, and Pribylovsky, Vladimir, *The Age of Assassins: The Rise and Rise of Vladimir Putin* (London: Gibson Square, 2007)

Forsyth, Frederick, *Icon* (London: Bantam Press, 1996)

Goldfarb, Alex, with Litvinenko, Marina, *Death of a Dissident: The Poisoning of Alexander Litvinenko and the Return of the KGB* (London and New York: Simon & Schuster, 2007)

Guzzanti, Paolo, *Il mio agente Sasha – La Russia di Putin e l'Italia di Berlusconi ai tempi della seconda guerra fredda* (Roma: Aliberti editore, 2009)

Hinchley, Vernon Colonel, *The Defectors* (London: George G. Harrap & Co. Ltd, 1967)

Höhne, Heinz, *Der Krieg im Dunkeln: die Geschichte der deutsch-russischen Spionage* (München: C. Bertelsmann Verlag, 1985)

Huber, Peter, 'Die Ermordung des Ignaz Reiss in der Schweiz (1937) und die Verhastung dissidenter Schweizer Spanienkämpfer durch den Geheimapparat der Komintern,' in *Kommunisten verfolgen Kommunisten: Stalinischer Terror und 'Säuberungen' in den Kommunistischen Parteien Europas seit des dreissiger Jahren* (Berlin: Akademie Verlag, 1993)

Hurt, Henry, *Shadrin: The Spy Who Never Came Back* (New York, NY: Reader's Digest Press McDraw-Hill Book Company, 1981)

Jansen, Marc, and De Long, Ben, 'Stalin's Hand in Rotterdam: The Murder of the Ukrainian Nationalist Yevhen Konovalets in May 1938', *Intelligence and National Security*, vol. 9, no. 4, October 1994

Kalugin, Oleg, with Montaigne, Fen, *Spymaster: My 32 Years in Intelligence and Espionage Against the West* (London: Smith Gryphon Publishers, 1994)

Kern, Gary, *A Death in Washington: Walter G. Krivitsky and the Stalin Terror* (New York, NY: Enigma Books, 2003)

Kern, Gary, *The Kravchenko Case: One Man's War on Stalin*, paperback (New York, NY: Enigma Books, 2007)

Khlevnyuk, Oleg, *Politburo: Mekhanizmy politicheskoi vlasti v 30-e gody* (Moskva: Rosspen, 1996)

Klebnikov, Paul, *Godfather of the Kremlin: Boris Berezovsky and the Looting of Russia* (New York and London: Harcourt, Inc., 2000)

Kokurin, Alexander, and Petrov, Nikita (eds.), *Lubyanka: organy VChK-OGPU-NKVD-NKGB-MGB-MVD-KGB, 1917–1991. A Reference Book* (Moskva: Materik, 2003)

Kouzminov, Alexander, *Biological Espionage: Special Operations of the Soviet and Russian Foreign Intelligence Services in the West*, paperback (London: Greenhill Books, 2005)

Krasnov, Vladislav, *Soviet Defectors: The KGB Wanted List* (Stanford, CA: Hoover Institution Press Stanford University, 1986)

Kuzichkin, Vladimir, *Inside the KGB: Myth and Reality* (London: Andre Deutsch Limited, 1990)

LeVine, Steve, *Putin's Labyrinth: Spies, Murder, and the Dark Heart of the New Russia* (New York, NY: Random House, 2008)

Litvinenko, Alexander, *Allegations*, paperback (Slough, Berkshire: Aquilion, 2007)

Litvinenko, Alexander, and Felshtinsky, Yuri, *Blowing Up Russia: Terror from Within*, paperback (London: Gibson Square, 2007)

Litvinenko, Alexander, *Lubyanskaya Prestupnaya Gruppirovka: Ofitser FSB dayot pokazaniya*, paperback (New York, NY: Grani, 2002)

Lunev, Stanislav, with Winkler, Ira, *Through the Eyes of the Enemy: Russia's Highest Ranking Military Defector Reveals Why Russia is More Dangerous than Ever* (Washington, DC: Regnery Publishing, Inc., 1998)

Mangold, Tom, *Cold Warrior. James Jesus Angleton: The CIA's Master Spy Hunter* (London and New York: Simon and Schuster, 1991)

Marenches, Count de, and Christine Ockrent, *The Evil Empire: The Third World War Now* (London: Sidgwick & Jackson, 1986)

Medvedev, Vladimir T., *Chelovek za Spinoi* (Moskva: Russlit, 1994)

Melton, H. Keith, *Ultimate Spy* (London: Dorling Kindersley Ltd, 2002)

Politkovskaya, Anna, *Putin's Russia*, paperback (London: The Harvill Press, 2004)

Poretsky, Elisabeth K., *Our Own People: A Memoir of 'Ignace Reiss' and His Friends* (Ann Arbor: The University of Michigan Press, 1969)

Preston, Paul, *We Saw Spain Die: Foreign Correspondents in the Spanish Civil War* (London: Constable, 2008)

Rosenfeld, Niels Erik, *Stalin's Secret Chancellery and the Comintern Evidence about the Organizational Patterns* (Copenhagen: C.A. Reitzels Forlag, 1991)

Schafranek, Hans, 'Kurt Landau', *Revolutionary History*, vol. 4, nos 1–2, Winter-Spring 1992

Schafranek, Hans, *Das kurze Leben des Kurt Landau. Ein österreichischer Kommunst als Opfer der stalinistischen Geheimpolizei* (Wien: Verlag für Gesellschaftskritik, 1988)

Sheymov, Victor, *Tower of Secrets* (Annapolis, Maryland: Naval Institute Press, 1993)

Shvets, Yuri B., *Washington Station: My Life as a KGB Spy in America* (New York, NY: Simon & Schuster, 1994)

Sixsmith, Martin, *The Litvinenko File: The True Story of a Death Foretold* (London: Macmillan, 2007)

Snegiryov, Vladimir, 'Ubiistva zakazyvalis v Kremle', *Trud*, 24–25 July 1992

Starinov, I. G. Col., *Over the Abyss: My Life in Soviet Special Operations*, paperback (New York, NY: Ballantine Books, 1995)

Starinov, Ilya Grigoryevich, *Miny zamedlennogo deystviya: razmyshleniya partisana-diversanta*, Kniga 2 (Moskva: Al'manakh Vympel, 1999)

Starinov, Ilya Grigoryevich, *Zapiski diversanta*, Kniga 1 (Moskva: Al'manakh Vympel, 1997)

Sudoplatov, Pavel, and Sudoplatov, Anatoli, with Jerrold L. and Leona P. Schecter, *Special Tasks: The Memoirs of san Unwanted Witness – A Soviet Spymaster* (London: Little, Brown and Company, 1994)

Select Bibliography

Sudoplatov, Pavel, *Spetsoperatsyi Lubyanka i Kreml, 1930–1950 gody* (Moksva: Olma Press, 2003)

Tsarev, Oleg, and West, Nigel, *KGB v Anglii* (Moskva: Zentrpoligraf, 1999)

Vakhaniya, Vladimir, *Lichnaya sekretnaya sluzhba I. V. Stalina.* Sbornik dokumentov (Moskva: Svarog, 2004)

Viñas, Angel, *El Escudo de la República: El oro de España, la apuesta soviética y los hechos de mayo de 1937* (Barcelona: Crítica, 2007)

Viñas, Angel, *El Honor de la República: Entre elacoso fascista, la hostilidad británica y la política de Stalin* (Barcelona: Crítica, 2009)

Viñas, Angel, *La Soledad de la República: El abandono de las democracies y el viraje hacia la Unión Soviética* (Barcelona: Crítica, 2006)

Volodarsky, Boris, *Nikolai Khokhlov: Self-Esteem with a Halo*, paperback (Vienna: Borwall Verlag, 2005)

Volodarsky, Boris, *The Orlov KGB File: The Most Successful Espionage Deception of All Time*, paperback (New York, NY: Enigma Books, 2009)

Wark, Wesley K., *Twenty-first Century Intelligence* (London: Routledge, 2004)

West, Nigel, and Tsarev, Oleg, *The Crown Jewels: The British Secrets at the Heart of the KGB Archives* (New Haven and London: Yale University Press, 1999)

West, Nigel, *At Her Majesty's Secret Service: The Chiefs of Britain's Intelligence Agency, MI6* (London: Greenhill Books, 2006)

West, Nigel, *Mortal Crimes. The Greatest Theft in History: Soviet Penetration of the Manhattan Project* (New York, NY: Enigma Books, 2004)

West, Nigel, *The Illegals: The Double Lives of the Cold War's Most Secret Agents* (London: Hodder & Sloughton, 1993)

Wolf, Markus, with McElvoy, Anne, *Man Without a Face: The Autobiography of Communism's Greatest Spymaster* (London: Jonathan Cape, 1997)

Zakharov, Nikolai S., *Skvoz Gody* (Tula: Grif & Co., 2003)

Index

Index

Index

Index